Justice and mercy

artes liberales

Series Editors

Carrie E. Beneš, T. J. H. McCarthy, Stephen Mossman and Jochen Schenk

Artes Liberales aims to promote the study of the Middle Ages – broadly defined in geography and chronology – from a perspective that transcends modern disciplinary divisions. It seeks to publish scholarship of the highest quality that is interdisciplinary in topic or approach, integrating elements such as history, art history, musicology, literature, religion, political thought, philosophy and science. The series particularly seeks to support research based on the study of original manuscripts and archival sources, and to provide a recognised venue for increased exposure for scholars at all career stages around the world.

Previously published
Writing the Welsh borderlands in Anglo-Saxon England
Lindy Brady

Justice and mercy
Moral theology and the exercise of law
in twelfth-century England

Philippa Byrne

Manchester University Press

Copyright © Philippa Byrne 2019

The right of Philippa Byrne to be identified as the author of this work has been asserted by her in accordance with the Copyright, Designs and Patents Act 1988.

Published by Manchester University Press
Altrincham Street, Manchester M1 7JA
www.manchesteruniversitypress.co.uk

British Library Cataloguing-in-Publication Data
A catalogue record for this book is available from the British Library

ISBN 978 1 5261 2534 7 hardback
ISBN 978 1 5261 5590 0 paperback

First published 2019

The publisher has no responsibility for the persistence or accuracy of URLs for any external or third-party internet websites referred to in this book, and does not guarantee that any content on such websites is, or will remain, accurate or appropriate.

Typeset by Out of House Publishing

For Edward Grey, a great historian

Contents

List of figures	*page* viii
List of tables	ix
Acknowledgements	x
List of abbreviations	xii
Prologue: the vanishing adulteress	xv

1	Introduction	1
2	The problem with mercy: the schools	16
3	The problem with mercy: the courts	38
4	Twelfth-century models of justice and mercy	62
5	Who should be merciful?	87
6	Judgment in practice: the Church	122
7	Histories of justice: the crown, persuasion and lordship	162
8	Love your enemies? Popular mercy in a vengeance culture	207
9	Conclusion	222

Bibliography	234
Index	279

Figures

1 Diagram explaining the many parts and degrees of 'iustum'. Raoul Ardens, *Speculum universale*, I.15. Quid sit iustum, BnF, Ms. latin 3229, fo. 4v. *page* 175
2 Diagram depicting the different parts and degrees of 'honestum'. Raoul Ardens, *Speculum universale*, I.16. Quid sit honestum, BnF, Ms. latin 3229, fo. 5r. 176
3 Diagram depicting the different types and levels of the term 'expediens'. Raoul Ardens, *Speculum universale*, I.17. Quid sit expediens, BnF, Ms. latin 3229, fo. 5r. 177

Tables

1 Anselm of Laon's scheme of the relationship between the petitions of the Lord's Prayer, the beatitudes and the gifts of the Holy Spirit described in Isaiah. Originally identified by Lottin, 'La doctrine d'Anselme de Laon'. *page* 99
2 Hugh of St Victor's fivefold model for the relationship between the petitions, gifts and beatitudes, along with the vices and virtues, from *De quinque septenis*. 100
3 Thomas of Chobham's construction of the relationship between the petitions of the Lord's Prayer and the gifts of Isaiah. As found in *Summa confessorum*, 3.1. 100
4 A second table from Thomas of Chobham's *Summa confessorum*, connecting the seven beatitudes to their corresponding rewards. 101

Acknowledgements

> Forgive us our debts. Debts: and what debts are these? ... It would take a long time to set forth our debts, which it was easier to incur than it is to discharge, and so we are going to postpone this task to another day.
>
> Gervase of Tilbury, *Commentary on the Lord's Prayer*, ed. and trans. S. E. Banks and J. W. Binns, in *Otia imperialia. Recreation for an Emperor* (Oxford, 2002), appendix 3, 922–3

This book is about debts and the paying back of dues. When it comes to the repayment of debts incurred in the writing of this book, I suspect the following may prove inadequate.

I must first thank Matthew Kempshall, who has guided this project with unstinting generosity, patience, sound counsel (and other assorted classical virtues). It was his enthusiasm which persuaded me that medieval justice was an idea worth investigating. More fundamentally, he has shown me why intellectual history is worth doing and how it should be done. Without the support and advice of Jane Garnett and George Southcombe, this would be a much weaker book (and I a much worse historian). Between them, they made the process of learning the historical discipline not just easier, but genuinely thrilling.

This book was begun at Wadham College, an institution which has been unfailingly generous with its resources – intellectually, administratively and financially. It was a privilege to work in such a supportive environment, and a place which encouraged its historians to take ideas seriously. The college's librarians (Francesca Heaney, Sandra Bailey and Tim Kirtley) were ever-cheerful in responding to my requests, and I thank them for their forbearance. The final parts were put together as a postdoctoral fellow

Acknowledgements

at Somerville College – a convivial and friendly place to undertake such labours.

The Arts and Humanities Research Council funded the research behind this book, and Oxford's Faculty of History provided funding for research in the Bibliothèque nationale. A visiting fellowship at the Institute for St Anselm Studies in New Hampshire provided the space and time to refine some of the fuzzier parts of my theological thinking.

Colleagues and friends provided much feedback, and, like the mystical miller, helped grind coarse wheat into finer flour. Foremost among them are David D'Avray and Benjamin Thompson, who gently pointed out the missing links in many arguments, and who have been characteristically generous and supportive throughout this process. The final product would hardly amount to a book at all without the ideas and questions they raised. Paul Hyams has offered many thoughtful suggestions and has always been willing to share his expertise on English law. Ingrid Rembold generously read various drafts of several meandering chapters and provided wise commentary. Corinna Matlis has trekked to many seminars and conferences, critiqued many papers and endured many complaints.

Most of all, debts are owed to my family. To Gina Byrne, for preventing me from lapsing into the pomposity that historians are prone to. To Sheila Grey, Edward Byrne and Paula Byrne, for their patience, understanding and unceasing support. A couple of sentences on an acknowledgments page is hardly sufficient repayment for their indulgence. This is a little for a lot. Like Gervase of Tilbury, I can only hope they will indulgently postpone the full reckoning of my accumulated debts until another day.

Abbreviations

Ad Herennium   (pseudo-)Cicero, *Ad C. Herennium: De ratione dicendi (Rhetorica ad Herennium)*, ed. and trans. H. Caplan (Cambridge, MA, 1954)
Adam Marsh, *Letters*   *The Letters of Adam Marsh*, ed. and trans. C. H. Lawrence (2 vols, Oxford, 2006–10)
Becket Correspondence   Thomas Becket, *The Correspondence of Thomas Becket, Archbishop of Canterbury, 1162–70*, ed. and trans. A. Duggan (2 vols, Oxford, 2000)
BL   British Library, London
BnF   Bibliothèque nationale de France, Paris
CCCM   Corpus Christianorum, Continuatio Mediaevalis
CCSL   Corpus Christianorum, Series Latina
CM   Matthew Paris, *Chronica maiora*, ed. H. R. Luard, RS 57 (7 vols, London, 1872–81)
Codex   *Codex Iustinianus*, in *Corpus iuris civilis*, vol. 2, ed. Paul Krueger *et al.* (Berlin, 1887)
CSEL   Corpus Scriptorum Ecclesiasticorum Latinorum
De inventione   Cicero, *De inventione*, ed. and trans. H. M. Hubbell (London, 1949)
Decretum   *Decretum Magistri Gratiani*, in *Corpus iuris canonici*, ed. E. Friedberg (2 vols, Leipzig, 1879–81)
Dicta/dictum   Robert Grosseteste, 'Dicta', from Oxford, Bodleian Library, MS Bodley 798
Digest   *Digesta Iustiniani* in *Corpus iuris civilis*, vol. 1, ed. Paul Krueger and Theodor Mommsen (Berlin, 1909)

List of abbreviations

DNC	Walter Map, *De nugis curialium*, trans. M. R. James, revised by C. N. L. Brooke and R. A. B. Mynors (Oxford, 1983)
EH	Orderic Vitalis, *The Ecclesiastical History*, ed. and trans. M. Chibnall (6 vols, Oxford, 1969–80)
GFL	Gilbert Foliot, *The Letters and Charters of Gilbert Foliot, Abbot of Gloucester (1139–48), Bishop of Hereford (1148–63), and London (1163–87)*, ed. Z. N. Brooke, A. Morey and C. N. L. Brooke (London, 1967)
GO	*Glossa ordinaria*, PL 113–14 (Paris, 1852)
Institutes	*Institutiones Iustiniani* in *Corpus iuris civilis*, vol. 1, ed. Theodor Mommsen (Berlin, 1872)
LHP	*Leges Henrici Primi*, ed. L. J. Downer (Oxford, 1972)
Luard	*Roberti Grosseteste episcopi quondam Lincolniensis epistolae*, ed. H. R. Luard, RS 25 (London, 1861)
Mantello	*The Letters of Robert Grosseteste, Bishop of Lincoln*, trans. F. A. C. Mantello and J. Goering (Toronto, 2010)
MGH	Monumenta Germaniae Historica
MTB	*Materials for the History of Thomas Becket*, ed. J. C. Robertson and J. B. Shepherd, RS 67 (7 vols, London, 1875–85)
PL	*Patrologiae Cursus Completus, series latina*, ed. J.-P. Migne (221 vols, Paris, 1841–62)
Policraticus	John of Salisbury, *Policraticus, sive de nugis curialivm et vestigiis philosophorum*, ed. C. C. J. Webb (2 vols, Oxford, 1909)
QDP	Robert of Melun, *Questiones de divina pagina* in *Oeuvres de Robert de Melun*, ed. R. M. Martin, vol. 1 (Louvain, 1932)
QEP	Robert of Melun, *Questiones de epistolis Pauli*, in *Ouevres de Robert de Melun*, ed. R. M. Martin, vol. 2 (Louvain, 1938)
RS	*The Chronicles and Memorials of Great Britain and Ireland during the Middle Ages* = 'Rolls Series'
RTAM	*Recherches de théologie ancienne et médiévale*
SAP	Thomas of Chobham, *Summa de arte praedicandi*, ed. F. Morenzoni, CCCM 82 (Turnhout, 1988)

List of abbreviations

SC	Thomas of Chobham, *Summa confessorum*, ed. F. Broomfield (Louvain, 1968)
SCV	Thomas of Chobham, *Summa de commendatione virtutum et extirpatione vitorum*, ed. F. Morenzoni, CCCM 82B (Turnhout, 1997)
Sentences	*Magistri Petri Lombardi Parisiensis episcopi Sententiae in IV libris distinctae*, ed. I. Brady (2 vols, Rome, 1971–81)
SS	Alexander Nequam, *Speculum speculationum*, ed. Rodney M. Thompson (Oxford, 1988)
ST	Thomas Aquinas, *Summa theologica*, in *Doctoris angelici divi Thomae Aquinatis Opera omnia*, ed. Stanislas Eduard Fretté and Paul Maré (34 vols, Paris, 1871–80)
VA	Peter the Chanter, *Verbum adbreviatum: textus conflatus*, ed. Monique Boutry (Turnhout, 2004)

Prologue: the vanishing adulteress

De principis instructione, a moral treatise on the cultivation of virtue, composed by the Angevin courtier, scholar and litterateur, Gerald of Wales (c.1146–c.1223), exists today in only a single copy, a mid-fourteenth-century manuscript of unknown provenance.[1] There are no indications that the text was widely circulated, much less that it ever reached the eyes of rulers. Written and revised at intervals between 1190 and 1217, *De principis instructione* consists of three books (*distinctiones*), intended to teach both princes and prelates.[2] The first *distinctio* looks very much like a traditional *speculum principis*, praising virtues such as modesty (*modestia*), chastity (*pudicitia*) and prudence (*prudentia*), and explaining the difference between a king and a tyrant. The two subsequent books provide a narrative of how those virtues had, or had not, been practised by princes, in the form of a contemporary history of the Angevin and Capetian dynasties. As Gerald himself explained, the first book instructs through the precepts of theology and ethics, the second and third teach rulership through *exempla*.[3]

Along with much of Gerald's voluminous and varied oeuvre, *De principis instructione* was edited and printed in the late nineteenth century as part of the Rolls Series, one of seven substantial volumes.[4] The Victorian editors, however, found very little worthy of remark in the first book of *De principis instructione*, and, when preparing the text for publication, they excised many of the quotations and *exempla* which Gerald had so carefully worked into a coherent whole. Most recent scholars have agreed with that nineteenth-century judgment, regarding the first book of *De principis instructione* as little more than a collection of trite commonplaces culled from *florilegia* collections, which reveals little about the political, intellectual, or cultural life of late twelfth- or early thirteenth-century England. Robert Bartlett, Gerald's modern biographer, who has led the way in

Prologue: the vanishing adulteress

recognising the distinctiveness of Gerald's other works, did not find the first book of *De principis instructione* particularly engaging. He characterised the book as 'neither original nor very illuminating', a compilation of quotations intended to reinforce 'moral platitudes', and quite separate from the more valuable historical information contained in the second and third *distinctiones*.[5] There the meat of Gerald's text is to be found, in a critical history of twelfth-century rulership, its personnel and its failings. Thus, since serious academic study of the middle ages began, *De principis instructione* has been available in truncated – one is tempted to say 'mutilated' – form. Only when consulted in manuscript form could Gerald's careful selection of scriptural and classical quotations – and his own commentary upon them – be read and appreciated in full.[6]

Contained within Gerald's forlorn, forgotten and seemingly formulaic first *distinctio* is a chapter on clemency (*de principis clementia*). The focus of the discussion is the judicial role of the prince, and Gerald urges those who have the power to punish to control their anger, to remit offences and to mitigate due punishment.[7] To this end he quotes from a variety of authorities: from classical poets, moralists and historians (including Lucan, Ovid, Sallust and Cicero); from scripture (the prophets, the psalms, the gospels); from the exemplary history of the 'proto-martyr' Stephen, who prayed for his persecutors even while they stoned him to death; and from Ambrose of Milan's treatise on Christian duties, *De officiis*. Among these, Gerald takes an episode from the Gospel of John, the story of the woman caught in adultery (John viii.1–11), as an example of clemency. The guilty woman had been presented to Jesus by the Pharisees, who demanded that he pass sentence upon her. The law required that she be stoned to death, but Christ refused, arguing that only a sinless man could justly execute the woman. This pericope – like much other material dealing with moral theology – has been cut out of the Rolls Series edition of Gerald's text. That removal, in many ways, typifies the more widespread neglect of the practical influence and significance of moral theology by medieval historians. For Gerald to cite the example of Christ forgiving a sinful woman may have seemed to Victorian editors simply to represent a repetitious, formulaic argument for clemency. In fact, this passage has hugely important ramifications for the way in which twelfth- and early thirteenth-century authors sought to bring to bear the moral guidance of scripture on their interpretation of the law.

The episode of the woman caught in adultery was interpreted by medieval readers according to two distinct strategies. It had a central place in legal discussions about interpretation of law and dispensation from written law. In canon and civil law, John viii formed the basis for a legal stipulation

Prologue: the vanishing adulteress

concerning the procedural requirement for witnesses. Canonists and civilians specified the legal implications of the gospel passage: Christ had refused to condemn the adulteress because no witness to her crime could be produced: without a witness or witnesses to attest to the proof of the charges, judgment was manifestly unsound. In that legal tradition, the pericope said nothing about morality, but a great deal about procedure. By contrast, the interpretation offered by Gerald in *De principis instructione* takes Christ's treatment of the adulteress as a plea for mercy in judicial sentencing. Gerald follows glosses, scriptural commentaries and sermons in which Christ's words ('let he who is without sin throw the first stone') were treated as an admonition to the judge. Those appointed to sentence must be ever mindful of divine judgment on their own sins, and their own desperate need for mercy from the divine judge, lest they act too hastily or too severely towards the earthly sinners brought before them. In *De principis instructione*, Gerald places the example of the adulteress next to the injunction 'love your enemies and pray for those who persecute you' (Matthew v.44), and the example of Christ's forgiveness for his persecutors at the moment of his crucifixion (Luke xxiii.34).[8] Deployed in this context, then, Gerald clearly intended the woman caught in adultery to stand as a demonstration of how the judge should temper the harshness of punishment. Far from adding to a list of moral platitudes, Gerald was weighing in on a debate concerning how love for one's fellow man or woman might override the strict punishment pronounced by law.

The *exemplum* of the woman caught in adultery has obvious intellectual and cultural significance, and Gerald's choice here connects him to a long-running tradition of moral debate. The implications of the 'legal' interpretation of John viii – the doctrine of witnesses – has been discussed extensively, and the importance of this scriptural story in the development of *ius commune* legislation has been examined at length in modern historiography. Yet the interpretation of John viii according to moral theology – reading Christ's refusal to judge a sinner as an exhortation to clemency, the interpretation here provided by Gerald – has received almost no attention whatsoever from medieval historians. The argument of this book is that the role of moral theology in the understanding and application of law – exemplified here in the ramifications of the story of the adulteress – repays careful historical attention. Readings of moral theology and theological traditions shaped medieval responses to law, and, more particularly, considerations of how law should be implemented. Medieval theologians used scripture to argue that the demands of moral justice, not the dictates of written law, should claim primacy in sentencing. Theologians engaged with practice and, just as importantly, lawyers took notice. Most significantly of all, passages such as John viii were deployed to suggest that sometimes true justice lay in the mitigation of punishment and in the exercise of mercy. The definition of justice was, in short, just as much a matter for the schools of theology as it was for the schools of law. Examining medieval readings of John viii, as well as other scriptural, patristic and classical *exempla*, illuminates what may conveniently be termed the 'moral tradition' of justice. This tradition should not be dismissed as platitudinous, trivial or trite – theologians wielded real influence in shaping the ways in which the relationship between judgment, justice and the law was understood by contemporaries, and their discussions informed contemporary legal practice. That, in essence, is the underlying rationale for this book: we grasp only half of what it was to be a medieval judge if we do not grapple with the moral theology of judgment. Simply put, the adulteress, in her dual symbolism – bestriding the domains of theology and law – must be restored to the argument.

Notes

1 Gerald of Wales, 'De principis instructione', BL, MS Cotton Julius B XIII, fos 48r–173r.
2 Gerald of Wales, *De principis instructione*, in *Opera omnia*, ed. J. S. Brewer, J. F. Dimock and G. F. Warner, RS 21 (8 vols, London, 1861–91), 8, praefatio prima, 5–6.
3 Ibid., 6.
4 For the history of the series see David Knowles, *Great Historical Enterprises; Problems in Monastic History* (London, 1963), 99–134.
5 R. Bartlett, *Gerald of Wales: A Voice of the Middle Ages* (2nd edn, Stroud, 2006), 63. One significant exception to this modern neglect of the text is I. Bejczy, 'Gerald of Wales on the cardinal virtues: a reappraisal of *De principis instructione*', *Medium Aevum* 75:2 (2006), 191–201.
6 A situation which will be remedied with the expected publication of Robert Bartlett's edition of *De principis* in 2018.
7 *De principis*, 1.7, 21–7.
8 BL, 'De principis instructione', 1.7, fo. 55r.

1

Introduction

Renaissance and crisis

This book is concerned with justice and mercy, with how twelfth- and early-thirteenth century English judges wrestled with the requirement to be both just and merciful in their judgments. It that sense, it represents a study of one particular aspect of the medieval judicial office – the point at which impersonal law and personal virtue met, collided and conversed. But justice and mercy are vast ideas, and such a broad theme must reasonably invite the questions – why England; why this period? One could, after all, quite easily make the case that heated intellectual argument about the nature of justice is – if not a perennial problem – hardly a phenomenon discovered in, or exclusive to, twelfth-century England.[1]

The choice of twelfth- and early thirteenth-century England as the subject for this study is justified on two grounds. The period c.1100–c.1250 (the 'long twelfth century') in England saw two key and coinciding changes.[2] The first was the rise of scholasticism across Northern Europe, and the set of intellectual and cultural changes accompanying the proliferation of schools and the beginnings of the scholastic technique, often fitted under the umbrella term of the 'Twelfth-Century Renaissance'. The profound changes in the way in which learning was approached and texts were read placed tremendous conceptual pressure on the term 'justice' (*iustitia*), and its relative 'mercy' (*misericordia*). It generated a level of debate which – arguably – had not been seen for eight centuries. Those discussions primarily concerned how a judge should set punishment, and how, where and why mercy fitted into the judicial office.

The second development, equal in importance to the trans-national phenomenon of scholasticism, was the 'English' change: the emergence of

Justice and mercy

systematic law, or law with systematic aspirations, associated with Henry II's legal reforms. Although similar legal transformations were set in motion across Europe in the latter part of this period, English common law can still fairly be thought of as distinct and 'early' in its development, relative to its European counterparts.[3] This reorganisation of law is also packaged up with many other developments under the term 'Renaissance'.[4] But whether one describes it as a legal renaissance, or as a process of the professionalisation and systematisation of law, the law changed. In England, legal changes created the conditions and space for a 'crisis' of a conceptual and ethical kind: uncertainty regarding the moral duties associated with the office of the judge, and, most particularly, how a judge ought to exercise mercy in his judgments. That question became a matter of particular political and 'public' concern for English authors throughout the twelfth century. In the context of a judicial system aspiring to some level of uniformity and 'national' coherence, seemingly abstract questions about what justice should look like, and how mercy was to be defined, took on urgent practical relevance.

This book is, in part, an attempt to explain why defining justice, and its relative, mercy, presented such a complex problem for English moralists and judges in the period between 1100 and 1250, and how the struggle over those two terms was fundamental to the way in which the role of the judge was constructed. Of course, that problem was not static and unchanging, and over the course of a century and a half, its dimensions changed. It took on new shapes and was encountered in different settings. Criticisms of King Stephen's excessive use of mercy, for example, functioned in quite a different political context from later denunciations of the ways in which King John punished malefactors without mercy or abused the system of royal pardons. There is, however, a constant theme which draws these complaints and commentary together: an awareness that mercy and justice do not fit easily together, and a judge is obliged to think carefully about their relationship before giving judgment.

Determining how a judge should behave, and how he[5] should exercise his judgment, was not a question confined to England in this period. But the English dimensions to this problem are distinct. This is first due to the peculiar lineage, form and content of the common law itself, which emerged in a way markedly different from its Roman-law-derived European contemporaries. Secondly, the historian's discussion of how 'English' judges engaged with moral theology *must*, by necessity, follow different lines from those discussing continental judges. The thicket of historiographical assumptions and myths which have grown up around the common law, emphasising its

Introduction

isolation, particularism and even 'native purity', demand a treatment of their own.

Thus, before one can even approach the medieval law itself, one must consider exactly what historians mean when they talk about medieval justice and medieval mercy. To offer a history of medieval justice can mean to examine the arguments forged in the medieval schools – discussions of soteriology, sin, virtue and the just life, finding its apotheosis in Aquinas's pronouncements. Alternatively, it can take on a resolutely practical cast, with historians following trails of administrative documents, court records and procedural manuals. In short, a history of medieval justice can trace a history of competing concepts and definitions, primarily moral and biblical; or of actions encompassing the devising of laws and their application. How one defines and approaches justice, therefore, conditions what we look for as evidence of medieval mercy: it is either an ethical and personal choice relating to medieval ambitions to live the virtuous life; or it is a question of searching for pardon rolls that will show how much it cost to purchase forgiveness for a crime from the crown.

Because mercy springs from justice, this book begins from justice. Both intellectual history and (English) legal history have written their own histories of justice, and both disciplines have broadly differing views about the most significant moments of change in the way that medieval people thought about and used justice. There are few, if any, points of contact between the two chronologies. The intellectual history of justice charts shifts in thought and interpretation which have never been mapped onto a legal history of justice. That strict division between theory and practice has led to the assumption – usually implicit – that scholastic discussions about moral virtue had no connection to English legal practice. But, as this book argues, twelfth- and thirteenth-century judges thought very hard, very long and very carefully about both the operation of justice as a virtue and the realisation of that virtue of justice in legal practice. The place where concerns about virtue and the practical giving of judgments most intersected was when those men of the law were required to deal with the issue – or, perhaps more accurately, the problem – of mercy. To put it simply, this book argues that, first, when it came to determining the judicial punishment of offenders in twelfth- and thirteenth-century England, theological thought informed legal practice; and, secondly, that theological modes of thinking drove a sophisticated and long-running debate about judicial ethics. These, in themselves, may not appear to be particularly challenging or surprising statements: that it may prove so is testimony to the very sharp separation of the modern disciplines of intellectual and English legal history. I have tried to strike a balance: the first half of this book draws on the work of theologians and moralists – primarily those working in England but including those active across western Europe – in order to illustrate the depth and complexity of the discussions of justice, mercy and law taking place in the schools. The second half focuses on examples of judgment and judicial dilemmas within the English polity.

Justice and scholastic thought

The contemporary intellectual history of the medieval concept of justice was shaped by explanatory frameworks devised in the first half of the twentieth century. Modern studies take their cue from the work of Odon Lottin's magisterial *Psychologie et morale aux XIIe et XIIIe siècles*, an exhaustive exploration of scholastic moral philosophy, published in six volumes between 1942 and 1960.[6] Lottin's account of the development of scholastic moral thought was characterised by a clear teleology, where twelfth-century thought served to lay the foundations for the achievements of truly *systematic* thirteenth-century scholasticism.[7] Lottin's discussion of 'justice' in *Psychologie et morale* is in fact a slightly modified version of an article from the 1930s.[8] That article offers a similar narrative: twelfth-century analyses of the virtue of justice proceeded only in fits and starts. 'Justice' was only subject to a fully penetrating analysis with the thirteenth-century schools' re-engagement with Aristotle. This theme is evident even in the proleptic title of the original article – 'justice ... avant l'introduction d'Aristote'. It was only when scholastic thinkers had access to the Aristotelian categories of 'general' and 'particular' justice that they were able to give a full account of justice, and fully explain the relationship between a just (virtuous) life and specific (judicial) acts of justice. By contrast, discussions of justice before the mid-thirteenth century were to be characterised as, at best, idiosyncratic, and, at worst, chaotic and disorganised, a mishmash of borrowings from classical texts, lacking any compelling structural principle.[9] Subsequent historians have reiterated this idea: while there were flashes of brilliance in twelfth-century thought about justice – perhaps, most obviously, Abelard's ethics of intention – these ideas never entered the main corpus of scholastic thought, and left little legacy.[10] Much of the twelfth- and early-thirteenth century is characterised as frenzied discussion without lasting influence.

More recent scholarship has followed the lines laid down by Lottin, enquiring into the classification of *iustitia* in scholastic *summae*, *quaestiones* and works 'de virtutibus et de vitiis'. The focus has often been to place justice in relation to its fellow cardinal virtues, *prudentia*, *temperantia* and *fortitudo*.[11] Lottin's argument for a fundamental thirteenth-century shift has been upheld by, among others, István Bejczy, who has argued that the thirteenth century saw a changed conceptualisation of the cardinal virtues, with the view that virtue was a mental habit supplanting the opinion that virtue resided in the will.[12] Whereas twelfth-century authors argued that justice served an important role because it regulated the will, thirteenth-century thought argued that justice did not control its own mental power.[13] The thirteenth century conceived of only three faculties of the mind: reason, controlled by prudence; the irascible appetite, under the power of fortitude; and the concupiscent appetite, moderated by temperance. Like Lottin's, this narrative of a thirteenth-century shift in understanding and theorisation, too, condemns twelfth-century thought on justice to near-irrelevance.

This model of the apparent 'chaos' (or, at least, disorder) in scholastic thought on justice before the introduction of Aristotle is in keeping with modern narratives of the development of scholasticism itself. In purely formal terms, for example, the twelfth and early thirteenth centuries mark a period in which scholasticism was in something of a state of flux and experimentation.[14] The variety of organising principles on offer led to still greater variety in the expression of arguments about justice. Modern perspectives on justice have accordingly remained a depiction of intellectual disorder, and, as a result, the focus of historians has tended to be limited to salvaging the reputation and thought of individual authors.[15] Yet such studies can only be of limited assistance when attempting to establish what justice 'meant' in this period. The most interesting elements in any author's discussion of justice will be revealed only when their definitions are set alongside those of their contemporaries, and the broader contours of scholastic thought. Indeed, attempting to understand justice though the thought of one individual alone can be fundamentally misleading – because such an approach fails to reveal just how fissiparous and contentious the act of defining justice could be. Disagreement was the order of the day. Contributions to an often fractious debate on the meaning of *iustitia* might, for example, be hidden among otherwise more uncontroversial assertions in *speculum principis* literature or sermons. As a result, before the intricacies of that twelfth- and thirteenth-century debate about justice can be appreciated, the broader shape of medieval thought on *iustitia* must be fleshed out. That includes providing a chronology more sophisticated that Lottin's original schema of diversity of outlook in the twelfth century, followed by Aristotelian systematisation in the thirteenth. This means identifying, in detail, the arguments which made up that diversity of outlook, and examining exactly how they were deployed in defining *iustitia*.

The aim of this book is not to deny that twelfth-century debates on justice can be characterised by intellectual disagreement (although disagreement should be detached from the term 'disorder', which carries more unhelpful connotations), but to suggest that such disagreement is exactly what makes the period worthy of study. Justice was difficult to categorise not simply because Aristotelian answers still awaited rediscovery: justice was difficult to categorise – and many 'answers' were proffered – because scholastic authors recognised the complexity of its nature. Indeed, part of that complexity lay in sketching out the relationship between the concept of justice and its realisation in practice.

Justice and the common law

The historiography of twelfth-century scholasticism treats its subject as an international discipline, defined by personnel and debates that transcended national boundaries – as Richard Southern would have it, a truly 'European' phenomenon.[16] The same cannot be said of English legal history: going back to Maitland, and even beyond him, to Selden and sixteenth-century antiquarians, it has proudly proclaimed its insularity and particularity.[17] The common law has 'a life and logic of its own', and that life and logic are peculiar to England.[18] This historiographical tradition would appear to impede any attempt to draw meaningful connections between arguments in the medieval schools of northern Europe and contemporaneous developments in the English legal system. This may, in part, account for why the interpretation of the term 'justice' across the two disciplines (intellectual history and legal history) appears so starkly opposed in modern scholarship.

Indeed, 'justice' as an abstract idea is rarely invoked in this history. English legal historians have focused on the explicitly practical and procedural nature of common law, and the pragmatic approaches of its earliest practitioners. What is striking, however, is that, much like the history of scholastic thought in the twelfth century, twelfth-century English legal history is also framed as movement from disorder towards order, structure and systematisation. That 'structure' derives from a narrative of professionalisation – law becoming a full-time job, set against the background of the development of a national court system.[19]

The focus of English legal history – at least for the first century of common law, and before the emergence of the Inns of Court – has been the persons of its practitioners.[20] Much data has been accumulated on the social background of the earliest judges and advocates. English lawyers and administrators of the law have been characterised as largely self-interested landholders; men concerned with securing or maintaining titles and position. To do justice, therefore, was to carry out the wishes of the crown, and 'a great gap separated the ideal expressed in the decrees of councils, complaints or moralists, and commentaries of canonists and theologians from the practice of the Angevin kings'.[21] What drove the development of justice was the need to work around practical problems in administering the law – whether that was the requirement to uphold order, or to generate revenue for the crown.[22] This was the case, from the perspective of legal history, even when ecclesiastical officers served as royal justices. On this account, even in those circumstances, even when royal officers had profound knowledge of scripture, of theology or of the practices of canon law, this had no impact on their attitude to administering common law.[23]

Such assumptions should not be accepted uncritically, and it is worth considering – in some detail – the biographies of a number of those administrators. Richard FitzNigel, for example, the son of Henry I's treasurer, Nigel, Bishop of Ely, was promoted through both royal administrative and ecclesiastical hierarchies; serving both as a royal justice and Bishop of London. His *Dialogue of the Exchequer* (c.1180), explains the performance and routine of royal justice at the exchequer with explicit reference to the scriptural foundations of that justice.[24] It is not only Richard FitzNigel whose biography suggests at least a familiarity with moral arguments about justice. Eustace de Fauconberg (1170–1228), educated in either Paris or Bologna, served as a judge both at Westminster and on eyre, and followed a similar path to FitzNigel, as both treasurer of the exchequer and Bishop of London.[25] Godfrey de Lucy (d.1204), Bishop of Winchester and Chief Justiciar, was a *magister* who had studied both in London and abroad, and is a plausible candidate for the authorship of the legal treatise *Glanvill*.[26] Richard Barre, who studied in Bologna with the celebrated canonist Stephen of Tournai, subsequently worked as a preacher, served Henry II as a justice in 1172 and later acted as chancellor for the Young King Henry.[27] Barre had also made a study of the Bible, dedicating a compendium of biblical excerpts to William Longchamp, Chancellor of England.[28]

The reason for reciting these four brief biographies is not to claim that these men rewrote English law to serve 'theological' ends, but to show that all four had the education and experience which would have forced them to at least *consider* the ethical implications of their judicial office. There is no reason to assume that such individuals neglected their moral responsibilities as churchmen, or deliberately divorced their ecclesiastical and temporal identities, or conceived of their judicial roles as requiring them to play yes-men. The argument of this book is that theological precepts did impinge upon the behaviour of such men as judges. This is in no way to claim that they imported canonists' doctrines into English law – it is only to state that such figures understood that the act of judgment had ethical implications.

This book seeks to make that connection between English law and theology at a fundamental level. It is not to invoke the long-running, often fractious, and now rather tired debate about the relationship between English common law and the 'learned law' of the European *ius commune*.[29] Suffice it to say that the greater part of English legal history resists the claims that European law had a meaningful impact on English practices. That is an argument which stretches back to Selden's *Ad Fletam Dissertatio* of 1647. Selden believed that not only had medieval lawyers resisted the siren song of Justinian, but their Druidic predecessors had similarly scorned the Roman law impressed on them by Julius Caesar.[30] While the modern debate over the extent of *ius commune* influence on the common law is not directly relevant to this book, the lines of that argument do run parallel to some the questions considered here. There is an obvious analogy between the case made here for the importance of scholastic and explicitly theological ideas in shaping judgment in common law courts, and the argument of certain historians of canon law that there was a connection between the 'learned law' of the continental schools and some of the specific laws deployed in the English common law courts. The subject matter of this book, however, is broader than particular laws. It looks more generally at how we construct the wider categories of 'theology' and 'law'. More specifically, it considers the relationship between theological arguments from the schools and the application of the law in England by English judges at the moment of judgment. Its focus is not laws but individuals. Those with a formation in theology did not lose the habit of thinking in a theological mould if they subsequently departed the schools (whether of Paris or Oxford) to take up places in Angevin administration. Nor did they lose their theologically shaped convictions about the nature of judgment when they conversed with royal judges.

A second challenge to any analysis of the place of mercy within the early common law is the traditional historiographical focus on the development of procedural forms and procedural innovations. The history of English law has been written as the history of writs, not as a history of ethical dilemmas – not least because the material for a history of writs is plain, evident and the subject of scholarly discussion since the time of Maitland.[31] Ethical dilemmas – by their nature – leave much fainter marks in the historical record. But the unintended consequence of this approach has been,

Introduction

at times, to reduce the application of the law to a matter of instructions and formulae, by definition rendering the moral aspects of judicial office unimportant.[32] Focusing on procedure has allowed historians of the common law to bypass questions of moral theology and ethics. A rare exception to this concentration is Paul Brand's examination of the ethical responsibilities of the judge under medieval common law. Brand's conclusion is that the issue of judicial morals was, for this period, moot. On this account, until the final decade of the thirteenth century, when the impetus of scandal made it a pressing consideration, English legal practitioners largely ignored the issue of judicial morality. Although there was concern surrounding the selection of jurors (and the removal of unsuitable jurors), Brand contends there was no similar concern for enforcing judicial ethics. There was, he writes, simply no concern to develop a code that would control the behaviour of justices or to ensure 'unbiased treatment by a neutral judge'.[33]

There was no explicit written code of conduct regulating the behaviour of English judges in this period, but to state this is only to note the absence of such a document. It does not necessarily demonstrate a wider lack of engagement with judicial ethics. In fact, ethical principles were debated at length in moral literature and didactic texts. Judges may not have been measured against an explicit, externally audited code of ethics, but that still left room for an ethical code which judges were encouraged to apply by themselves and to themselves. As John Sabapathy has recently and persuasively argued, when discussing the rules governing the conduct of medieval office-holders, historians should be wary of discounting officials' self-consciousness 'as a real motor of official accountability'.[34] Though not codified in a single document, moral guidance for judges was available in abundance. The historian is not required to read between the lines in order to find explicit and complex discussions about judicial morality.

Theory and praxis: theology as social commentary

This book, therefore, aims to show how moral teachings (primarily distilled from the study of scripture) could be and, indeed, were applied, practically, to the task of judgment; how theology was married to law. It might, of course, be argued, that this flies in the face of the reality of medieval hierarchies of learning. G. R. Evans has expertly sketched out how *theologia* represented the highest form of *sapientia*, separate in aim from the 'lower wisdom' of the secular studies, an endeavour to be served by those lesser disciplines.[35] That apparent demarcation between the disciplines of theology and law is plain to see in the laments of medieval students, who drew

Justice and mercy

a sharp contrast between the worldly and avaricious individuals who chose to study law, aiming at wealth and success, and the impoverished students of theology who studied the 'Queen of the Sciences' with slim hopes of preferment or advancement.[36] A neat example of this disciplinary separation is furnished in Herbert of Bosham's *Vita Sancti Thomae*.[37] Herbert, who had been a distinguished master of theology in Paris, describes the dining arrangements in the household of Thomas Becket. Lawyers, he explains, were made to sit at a lower table than the theologians, a lesser place, suitable for those who concerned themselves only with worldly matters.[38] Herbert suggests a *cordon sanitaire* between the disciplines of law and theology.

Herbert of Bosham's line of demarcation between the world of theological abstraction and the pragmatic domain of law also reflects modern concerns about the apparent contrast between the abstracted world of the schools (and their conceptually complex discussions of justice) with the rough and tumble of twelfth-century politics. There is, admittedly, a considerable scholarly challenge in connecting *iustitia* as a virtue to justice in practice, moving from speculative commentaries to concrete legal change, as well as in the methodology employed in trying to detect practical judicial thought in speculative texts.[39] Cultural historians have often argued strongly against assuming that the settled and clear presentations of politics and lordly relations presented in the texts of highly educated authors reflect medieval *realpolitik*.[40] Indeed, so the argument goes, the words of an author such as (for example) John of Salisbury are not to be trusted, because John described the world as he wished it to be, rather than as it was – such texts are all persuasion, no description. By that same token, moralists who talk of 'justice' are engaging in wishful thinking, attempting to exert some edifying influence on the really rather unjust reality of everyday life. On this basis, over the past half-century, the perspective of revisionist cultural history has supported a strict separation between *iustitia* as an idea – intricately constructed, but entirely abstract – and the earthy, unlovely 'justice' of medieval political action. To accept that proposition would be to relegate the influence of scholastic ideas about justice – beyond the schoolroom – to near irrelevance. 'Justice' in political terms, it is argued, was a matter of might, not right: any action performed by the powerful or victorious could be retrospectively valorised as an act of 'justice'.[41] Such an approach assumes that the term held no particular meaning, and simply describes politically expedient practice, rather than politically charged theory.

This is the point made, recently and emphatically, in T. N. Bisson's *Crisis of the Twelfth Century*. The central argument of Bisson's *Crisis* is that kings and lords exercised a power which was essentially untrammelled and

Introduction

unchecked for much of the twelfth century.⁴² Moral discourses drawn from the Bible and classical philosophy on public power and lawful rule were simply 'platitudinous allusions', bearing no relation to the way in which twelfth-century society operated.

Bisson is primarily interested in recognising and rescuing the experiences of those who suffered under the infliction of lordly *potestas* in the twelfth century, rather than describing the origins of government. Moreover, though he deals with England, he aims at describing a common set of structures found across western Europe.⁴³ But in the course of capturing the experience of power, Bisson notes that the change which does occur in the late twelfth century is more closely related to growth in procedures for holding officers accountable, rather than the invention of a system of government. Power, unchecked and untrammelled for much of the century, was brought under control not by idealists, but by pragmatists, by kings interested in controlling their officers, rather than living up to moral expectations.⁴⁴

It cannot be denied that *Crisis* makes an important point about the dangers of anachronism when discussing medieval governance. It warns against viewing the past through a teleological lens which warps our reception of terms such as *administrare*, *gubernare*, *regere* or *res publica*, as they feature in medieval texts.⁴⁵ Bisson's critique has two aspects to it: first that we should not fill up medieval terms with modern meanings – that cannot be argued with. A twelfth-century 'jury' is not the same thing (in its make-up, its purpose, its place in the legal system) as a twenty-first-century jury. There is a danger in assuming that the modern term 'mercy' maps directly onto the twelfth-century *misericordia* – which is why this book works hard to explain and unpack its dimensions and associations. But Bisson's second point about the relationship between moralists, theorists, texts and power is more contestable: he argues for a wide gulf between the authors of texts about governance and those who really wielded power. Theoretical language belonged to the schools, where justice was analysed but not exercised. 'Power was felt more than it was analysed.'⁴⁶ The people who experienced power, the people who theorised power and the people who commanded power were distinct groups.

What follows here challenges that assumption. The employment of terms used to analyse the ethical nature of justice was not limited to abstract discussions. Those who 'theorised' about power also attempted to influence power. Moral arguments could be abstract and lengthy, but they could also be practical and conveyed with brevity, through the use of typologies and *exempla*. At one end of the scale, John of Salisbury's *Policraticus* was densely packed, full of classical learning and certainly 'abstract' (in some ways, though not in others). But *Policraticus* was not the only place that a discussion of justice and judges could be found – those arguments ranged more widely and could be fitted for less educated audiences. An examination of mercy's place within justice was not limited to dense theological tracts and philosophical treatises: it permeated the culture; was nearly inescapable; and it must be reckoned to have had some considerable impact on modes of thought and patterns of behaviour. The number and diversity of texts examined here speak to a society genuinely concerned to find a just course of action – and to 'do justice'.

The intellectual foundations, and precedent, for a fruitful study of the interplay between theology and law do exist. Southern, for one, argued that the very definition of the scholastic method that characterised theological learning was a practical one, seeking a 'unity of life and ideals' as its aim.[47] By clarifying and systematising the knowledge they had inherited from the ancient world, scholastic authors sought to impose order (*ordo*) on both knowledge and action, 'to give the truths thus clarified practical application by deducing from the them appropriate rules of conduct'.[48] Education in the schools prepared men for future careers in royal and ecclesiastical administration; scholasticism furnished the conceptual tools and systematic approach which produced a new type of European governance. John Baldwin's *Masters, Princes and Merchants* developed this line of argument, studying the work of the late twelfth-century masters in the circle of Peter the Chanter who addressed the most pressing practical questions of the age, ranging from economics to politics and ethics; taking in the problem of usury, standards of conduct for administrators and officials, and the behaviour of advocates and judges.[49] Baldwin's theologians were social commentators.[50] That argument is embraced, and developed, here. Moral arguments – drawn primarily from the Bible, but supplemented by classical texts – directly engaged with the practical matter of judgment and judicial ethics. But, beyond simply commenting on judicial behaviour, men with scholastic training used that learning to offer solutions to judicial dilemmas: the central and thorniest dilemma being how a judge was to reconcile the conflicting requirements of justice and mercy.

Notes

1 See, for example, Melissa Barden Dowling, *Clemency and Cruelty in the Roman World* (Ann Arbor, MI, 2005).
2 For the sake of simplicity and brevity, this book employs the term 'twelfth century' in an inclusive and 'long' sense, encompassing the period c.1100–c.1250.

Introduction

3 P. Brand, 'The English difference: the application of bureaucratic norms within a legal system', *Law and History Review* 21 (2003), 383–7.
4 The classic formulation of this is S. Kuttner, 'The revival of jurisprudence', in R. L. Benson and G. Constable (eds), *Renaissance and Renewal in the Twelfth Century* (Toronto, 1991), 299–323.
5 The use of the pronoun is deliberate. The judges considered here are all – to a man – men.
6 O. Lottin, *Psychologie et morale aux XIIe et XIIIe siècles* (6 vols, Louvain, 1942–60).
7 For the repetition of a similar teleology in recent work see C. Nederman, 'Aristotelianism and the origins of "political science" in the twelfth century', *Journal of the History of Ideas* 52 (1991), 179–94.
8 O. Lottin, 'Le concept de justice chez les théologiens du moyen âge avant l'introduction d'Aristote', *Revue thomiste* 44 (1938), 511–21; reproduced, with minor modifications, in *Psychologie et morale*, 3:283–99.
9 For example, M. Lutz-Bachmann, 'The discovery of a normative theory of justice in medieval philosophy', *Medieval Philosophy and Theology* 9 (2001), 1–14; I. P. Bejczy, 'The cardinal virtues in medieval commentaries on the *Nicomachean Ethics*, 1250–1350', in I. P. Bejczy (ed.), *Virtue Ethics in the Middle Ages: Commentaries on Aristotle's Nicomachean Ethics, 1200–1500* (Leiden, 2008), 199–221.
10 I. Bejczy, *The Cardinal Virtues in the Middle Ages: A Study in Moral Thought from the Fourth to the Fourteenth Century* (Leiden, 2011), 87–8.
11 For example, Bejczy, 'Gerald of Wales on the cardinal virtues'; Riccardo Quinto, 'The *Conflictus vitiorum et virtutum* attributed to Stephen Langton', in István P. Bejczy and Richard Newhauser (eds), *Virtue and Ethics in the Twelfth Century* (Leiden, 2005), 197–267.
12 Bejczy, *Cardinal Virtues*, 159.
13 Ibid., 73–133; cf. William of Auxerre, *Summa aurea*, ed. Jean Ribaillier (5 vols, Paris, 1980–87), 11.3.3, 4:190–1.
14 Marcia L. Colish, 'From the sentence collection to the sentence commentary and the *summa*: Parisian scholastic theology, 1130–1215', in Marcia L. Colish, *Studies in Scholasticism* (Aldershot, 2006), XII, 9–29.
15 For example, R. H. Rouse and M. A. Rouse, 'John of Salisbury's doctrine of tyrannicide', *Speculum* 42 (1967), 697–709; P. Delahaye, 'La vertu et les vertus dans les oeuvres d'Alain de Lille', *Cahiers de civilisation médiévale* 6 (1963), 13–25.
16 Cf. R. W. Southern, *Scholastic Humanism and the Unification of Europe* (2 vols, Oxford, 1995).
17 Sir Frederick Pollock and Frederic William Maitland, *The History of English Law before the Time of Edward I* (2 vols, Cambridge, 1895), 1:135; on the early modern connection between the distinctiveness of common law and English character, Brian Lockley, *Law and Empire in English Renaissance Literature* (Cambridge, 2006), esp. 113–41.
18 David J. Seipp, '*Bracton*, the Year Books, and the "transformation of elementary legal ideas" in the early common law', *Law and History Review* 7 (1989), 175–217, esp. 175.

19 See Susan Reynolds, 'The emergence of professional law in the long twelfth century', and the response of Paul Brand , 'The English difference', both in *Law and History Review* 21 (2003), 347–66 and 383–7.
20 Cf. Donald W. Sutherland, 'Legal reasoning in the fourteenth century: the invention of "color" in pleading', in Morris S. Arnold, Sally A. Scully and Stephen S. White (eds), *On the Laws and Customs of England: Essays in Honor of Samuel E. Thorne* (Chapel Hill, NC, 1981), 182.
21 R. Turner, 'Clerical judges in English secular courts: the ideal versus the reality', in R. Turner, *Judges, Administrators and the Common Law in Angevin England* (London, 1994), 178.
22 R. Turner, 'The reputation of royal judges under the Angevin kings', in *Judges, Administrators and the Common Law*, 112–15.
23 Cf. J. Hudson, 'Magna Carta, the *Ius Commune* and English common law', in J. S. Loengard (ed.), *Magna Carta and the England of King John* (Woodbridge, 2010), 116–17.
24 See J. Hudson, 'Administration, family and perceptions of the past in late twelfth-century England: Richard FitzNigel and the "Dialogue of the Exchequer"', in P. Magdalino (ed.), *Perceptions of the Past in Twelfth-Century Europe* (London, 1992), 75–98.
25 N. Vincent, 'Master Eustace de Fauconberg', in N. Vincent (ed.), *English Episcopal Acta IX: Winchester, 1205–1238* (Oxford, 1994), appendix 4, no. 30, 193–5.
26 R. Turner, 'Who was the author of *Glanvill*?', in *Judges, Administrators and the Common Law*, 71–102.
27 R. Sharpe, 'Richard Barre's *Compendium Veteris et Novi Testamenti*', *Journal of Medieval Latin* 14 (2004), 128; see also R. Turner, 'Richard Barre and Michael Belet: two Angevin civil servants', in *Judges, Administrators and the Common Law*, 181–98.
28 Sharpe, 'Richard Barre's *Compendium*', 135.
29 An outline of this argument can be found in R. M. Helmholz, *The Ius Commune in England: Four Studies* (Oxford, 2001), 3–15. See further P. Brand, 'Legal education in England before the Inns of Court', in Jonathan A. Bush and Alain Wijffels (eds), *Learning the Law: Teaching and the Transmission of Law in England, 1150–1900* (London, 1999), 51–84; T. F. T. Plucknett, *Early English Legal Literature* (Cambridge, 1958), esp. 85, 96.
30 John Selden, *Ad Fletam Dissertatio*, ed. David Ogg (Cambridge, 1925). For the context of Selden's work, see Reid Barbour, *John Selden: Measures of the Holy Commonwealth in Seventeenth-Century England* (Toronto, 2003), 151–4.
31 Cf. R. Turner, 'Henry II's aims in reforming England's land law: feudal or royalist?', in *Judges, Administrators and the Common Law*, 1–16. Patrick Wormald made a similar point when describing the difference between studying 'law as System' and 'law as experienced': *Lawyers and the State: The Varieties of Legal History* (London, 2006), 19.

Introduction

32 Plucknett, *Early English Legal Literature*, 102–3; see also H. D. Hazeltine, preface to *Radulphi de Hengham Summae*, ed. William Huse Dunham, Jr. (Cambridge, 1932).
33 P. Brand, 'Ethical standards for royal justices in England c.1175–1307', *University of Chicago Law School Roundtable* 239 (2001), 278.
34 J. Sabapathy, *Officers and Accountability in Medieval England 1170–1300* (Oxford, 2014), esp. 237.
35 G. R. Evans, *Old Arts and New Theology: The Beginnings of Theology as an Academic Discipline* (Oxford, 1980), 34.
36 S. C. Ferruolo, '"Quid dant artes nisi luctum?" Learning, ambition, and careers in the medieval university', *History of Education Quarterly* 28 (1988), 2.
37 For Herbert see D. L. Goodwin, 'Herbert of Bosham and the horizons of twelfth-century exegesis', *Traditio* 58 (2003), 133–73, and more recently Eva de Visscher, *Reading the Rabbis: Christian Hebraism in the Works of Herbert of Bosham* (Leiden, 2014), 1–22.
38 Herbert of Bosham, *Vita Sancti Thomae*, 3.12, *MTB*, 3:207.
39 See Alan Harding, 'The reflection of thirteenth-century legal growth in Saint Thomas's writings', in G. Verbeke and D. Verhelst (eds), *Aquinas and Problems of His Time* (Louvain, 1976), 18–37.
40 Cf. W. Davies, 'Judges and judging: truth and justice in Northern Iberia on the eve of the millennium', *Journal of Medieval History* 36 (2010), 193–203.
41 Frederick L. Cheyette, 'Custom, case law and medieval "constitutionalism": a re-examination', *Political Science Quarterly* 78:3 (1963), 366–7.
42 Thomas N. Bisson, *The Crisis of the Twelfth Century: Power, Lordship, and the Origins of European Government* (Princeton, NJ, 2009).
43 *Ibid.*, 19–21; for England see 168–81; 380–97.
44 For the development of accountability, and where it fits into the argument made here, see Conclusion, below.
45 Bisson, *Crisis*, 12–13; 16: 'classicising verbiage (not to mention a long lapse of time) may have distorted the reality'.
46 *Ibid.*, 3.
47 Southern, *Scholastic Humanism*, 1:3.
48 *Ibid.*, 1:5.
49 John W. Baldwin, *Masters, Princes and Merchants: The Social Views of Peter the Chanter and his Circle* (2 vols, Princeton, NJ, 1970).
50 See too, the work of Philippe Buc on the explicitly political and practical applications of biblical exegesis: *L'Ambiguïté du livre: prince, pouvoir, et peuple dans les commentaires de la Bible au moyen âge* (Paris, 1994).

2

The problem with mercy: the schools

The problem with mercy (*misericordia*), as has already been outlined, was twofold. In the schools, it lay in determining how to fit mercy within justice; in the courts, in fitting mercy within the law. This chapter examines the difficulties encountered by theologians who sought to give an account of both mercy and justice; the next chapter, the awkward place of mercy within law. While the ultimate aim of this book is to examine the substance of the connection between theology and law, for reasons of clarity in comprehending the intellectual background to the problem, the two are here (and here alone) treated separately. This chapter elucidates exactly how theology dealt with mercy – where it was placed in schemes of the virtues, how it related to justice; the following chapter considers how the common law treated mercy – in the sense of where and when legal texts recognised mercy, and the role it was acknowledged to play within law.

It is, perhaps, no surprise that scholastic argument acknowledged the importance of the virtue of mercy within a grander scheme of justice, even if there was considerable disagreement over its exact place and significance. What may be less obvious, however, given the traditional focus of histories of the common law, is that English law similarly acknowledged that mercy had a role to play in giving judgment. More important still, English legal treatises plot a crucial connection between the exercise of judicial discretion and the granting of mercy. The exercise of mercy – judicial mitigation of punishment – depended on the judge's choice, but that, in turn, meant that mercy might either be praised as the exercise of personal virtue, or attacked as the expression of partiality. In that sense, theologians and lawyers arrived at similar conclusions about the problems for merciful judges. In the schools, the danger was that too great an emphasis on mercy would undermine the way in which the virtue of justice was structured and conceived; in the courts, the danger was that the space that allowed for the expression of mercy could also permit corruption.

What are we thirsty for? A note on terminology

There are two considerable problems of translation evident in dealing with this topic, both of which derive from the gap between medieval and modern forms of expression and categorisation. The first concerns what this book (and, indeed, its subtitle) refers to as 'moral theology', a synthetic category. This is a useful shorthand, but not a term which the authors discussed here would have recognised.[1] Much of this chapter draws on the works of *magistri in sacra pagina*, and those ideas which I bring under the heading of 'moral theology' are drawn from the parts of their writings which most closely engage with the relationship between human society and divine example; there is necessarily selection at work here. The umbrella term 'moral theology' is used here for convenience, and because it usefully encapsulates the substance of discussions which were concerned both with judicial behaviour and with the principles and virtuous models for the judicial behaviour. It is used in preference to a term such as 'pastoral theology' (a more recognisably medieval category) because a discussion of judges – secular and ecclesiastical – extends beyond those whom we might typically think of as the audience for pastoral theology, i.e. priests and those engaged in preaching.

The second – and much greater – problem of translation lies in how we approach *iustitia*. 'Beati qui esuriunt et sitiunt justitiam', notes the Vulgate. Blessed are those who hunger and thirst for – for what, exactly? Any discussion of medieval *iustitia* raises the question of precisely how that term should be translated into English. In modern vernacular Bible translations, for example, the 'iustitia' of the Vulgate often becomes 'righteousness' in translation.[2] Similarly, there is a degree of overlap – and perhaps a certain conceptual fuzziness – when modern English is invited to distinguish between the idea of a 'just' individual and a 'righteous' one. In everyday language, the former term might be thought to denote a specific virtue, the latter a more general attitude of moral goodness. One might expect the 'righteous' individual to be just, but not necessarily vice versa. This lack of precision introduces complications, for example, when considering whether to translate Matthew v.6 as a blessing on those hungering and thirsting for righteousness or on those hungering and thirsting for justice. In the context of twelfth-century theology, this problem of translation may prove even more difficult. *Iustitia* might have a distinct meaning as part of a discussion of the process by which humankind is redeemed, a discussion which focused on Paul's Letter to the Romans. Paul engaged with *iustitia* in order to make an argument about justification and redemption, and the central role of Christ in this process. It was in this sense that commentaries on Romans – including those of Lanfranc and Abelard – treated Pauline *iustitia*.[3]

Necessarily, it is vital to consider context when translating such passages. The majority of writers addressed in this book deal specifically with dilemmas involving judges, and so there is a persuasive case in most instances for translating *iustitia* in straightforward terms as justice. Furthermore, that term 'iustitia' may sometimes denote the idea of 'virtuous judgment', whereas on other occasions it may be used to imply 'punitive justice', i.e. the opposite of merciful justice. I have attempted to note the instances where the meaning of the term is ambivalent, or the points at which an author exploits the potential of 'justice' to encompass both a specifically judicial and a more general sense of virtue. Particularly in this chapter, however, which addresses 'definitions' of justice, the distinction between justice and righteousness is a little less clear.

Explaining justice

Multiple ways of expounding the meaning of *iustitia* were available to the twelfth-century schools, a reflection of the earlier medieval tradition.[4] Calling these multiple *definitions* of justice is perhaps too hard and fast a term. One line of thinking which continued through this period was to describe justice as 'the constant and perpetual desire to give to each person their due' (*iustitia est constans et perpetua voluntas ius suum cuique tribuens*). This could be found in a number of texts, and was ultimately traceable to Cicero's *De inventione*.[5] It was, in turn, repeated influentially in Alcuin's *De rhetorica* and his *De vitiis et virtutibus* – which includes a description of justice as 'due' alongside an explanation that *iustitia* can be equated with *caritas*.[6] The same explanation was put forward by Roman law, found at the beginning of both the *Digest* and the *Institutes*, the work of the jurist Ulpian (c.170–233).[7]

It is hard to overemphasise the significance – or the ubiquity – of the description of justice as a due in texts written in the schools of northern Europe between 1100 and 1250. It is repeated in biblical glosses, in theological *summae* and *sententiae*, in monastic writings and works of pastoral instruction. It is evident in the gospel commentary *Enarrationes in Matthaeum*,[8] and the treatise *Ysagoge in theologiam*.[9] It is repeated by Peter the Chanter,[10] Thomas of Chobham,[11] Stephen Langton[12] and Robert Grosseteste,[13] to name only a few. An attractive element of this definition of justice was its flexibility: it allowed almost all earthly relationships to be fitted within a model of justice; it did not polarise 'political' and 'religious' duties. Thus, it is 'justice' to give to God the praise and worship which is his due; it is 'justice' when an individual in society acts rightly by giving 'due' to their neighbours; when an individual condemns wickedness, they give due hatred to sin, and this too is justice; finally, in resisting evil, 'justice' lies in paying an appropriate due (of contempt) to the devil.[14] Under this wide-ranging definition, then, giving to each their due is the duty of all in society – including both the secular judge and the priest.[15]

Such an account of justice also fitted neatly alongside another important aspect of the scholastic theological vocabulary: debt. For instance, the imposition of appropriate punishment could be described by the term 'debitum', a debt (or due) to be repaid. 'Debitum' itself, of course, was a multivalent term. In a secular judicial context, one could speak of 'pena debita'. The term 'debitum' to describe something needing repayment could equally be deployed in the context of penitential or Church judgment, echoing the words of the Lord's Prayer, 'dimitte nobis debita nostra'.

Within this model of justice-as-due, theological commentaries also throw up some minor points of distinction. Most texts omit the word 'ius' and begin with a brief description of justice as *suum cuique tribuens*. From this starting point, there was often some discussion of whether justice was better described as the will (*voluntas*) or intent (*intentio*) to give to each their due, rather than the virtue (*virtus*[16]) which actually does so, for although an individual may have the desire to act justly, the action of giving to each their due may not always be in his or her power.[17] Theologians also unpicked the significance of the term 'suum' in the phrase 'suum cuique tribuere' – was it to be understood as the 'due' owed by the giver, or the 'due' earned by s/he who would receive it? The problem was typically dealt with in short order: Alan of Lille's *De virtutibus et de vitiis et de donis spiritus sancti* and Alexander Nequam's *Speculum speculationum*, among others, determine that the 'due' refers to the recipient of an act of justice.[18]

Justice-as-due was an important idea, and a conceptually rich one: it could be developed into a discussion of the operation of justice in multiple ways. It was, however, not the only means of describing or explaining the nature of justice. Indeed, in many ways it was lacking, because – as Christian theologians had long recognised – referring to justice as a matter of strictly calculated due failed to capture one of the ideas frequently emphasised and endorsed by scripture: that justice and mercy were tied together, and that *misericordia* either represented an important constitutive part of justice, or was in some way a principle capable of overriding justice.[19]

Scripture argued for an understanding of justice which stood further from clear calculation of debt, due and reward, and moved closer towards *misericordia*: setting out a different conception of virtue and one accompanied by a different vision of earthly relationships. We find this view, emphasising the 'merciful' nature of justice, for example, in the *Sentences* of Peter Lombard (c.1150). The *Sentences* deal only briefly with justice – in fact, they afford all the cardinal virtues only limited attention. The Lombard does not provide any 'classical' (that is, pre-Christian or 'philosophical') definitions of any of the cardinal virtues.[20] Instead, he defines justice as 'in subveniendo miseris', the relief of the wretched or the suffering, a description taken directly from Augustine's *De trinitate*.[21] Such an approach omitted any notion of due and, in its stead, placed the concept of *misericordia* (the act of showing mercy to the wretched) at the very heart of justice.[22] It was influential, given the status which Peter Lombard's *Sentences* rapidly attained as a foundational textbook in the curriculum of the schools in the second half of the twelfth century.[23]

In one sense, an attempt to bring *misericordia* into justice was a reflection of both scripture and an ambivalent patristic heritage. It was not, of course, only in *De trinitate* that Augustine had offered a view on justice: in the *Enarrationes in Psalmos*, he had recognised that defining justice was complex precisely because of the sinful nature of humankind; that humans might not be able to be just, and might therefore only have mercy to hope for.[24] This kind of ambivalence – scriptural and patristic – blurred the distinction between *iustitia* and *misericordia* as discrete concepts.[25] It suggested the two were connected, though the precise nature of that connection remained undefined. Moreover, such a connection seemed undeniable from conventional assumptions about the nature of virtue – a just, virtuous person was surely also a charitable (and therefore merciful) person. In that sense, some part of justice had to be concerned with *misericordia*.[26]

Little of this was new: the earlier middle ages had access to these many and varied understandings of justice. The particular difference in the twelfth century lay in the scholastic method, which demanded more than the mere assembling of different descriptions of justice – it worked to understand how one might examine and test these quite different accounts of what justice was in order to work out what earthly justice should look like. And, at least when considered in the abstract, these two approaches threatened to diverge quite considerably, particularly when it came to the question of punishment: one strictly calculating the due to be paid back, the other emphasising the centrality of mercy and merciful treatment for offenders. We can see the problem being articulated from c.1100 onwards in glosses and early scholastic works, although arguably it is not until the second half of the century that the ramifications and implications of a 'choice' between justice and mercy are starkly expressed in theological writings.

Justice as due pays back precisely and exactly: it weighs the measure of a crime and repays it with an appropriate measure of punishment. The premise of *misericordia* flatly contradicted that principle, for it suggested that justice lies in going beyond due. It is on this problem – the conceptual and practical difficulties of reconciling merciful justice with due justice – that the first half of this book is founded. The judge who shows *misericordia* in mitigating the punishment of a criminal, or perhaps even in pardoning him for his crime, adheres to the definition of justice as mercy, but totally discards the idea of justice as due. Stephen Langton, in his *Summa*, crystallises the essence of this problem when considering how justice and mercy can be related at all, given that they seem to have such opposite effects: the purpose of justice being to inflict punishment, that of mercy to relax punishment. The relationship between the two, Langton notes, appears inversely proportional: as the justice of a sentence grows, the amount of mercy in that sentence decreases.[27]

What, then, did it mean to 'do' justice? And how did justice relate to mercy? The *Glossa ordinaria*, the great commentary on scripture compiled at the school of Laon in the early twelfth century, strongly implied that the two virtues were complementary, averring that 'mercy is the light of justice, and justice is the strength of mercy'.[28] In this sense, the ideal judgment seemed to be one which combined both justice and mercy. However, another early twelfth-century gloss on the Gospel of Matthew, explains that these are two separate principles: some judgments show justice, while others show mercy.[29] The challenge for scholastic authors was to reconcile these two definitions, or at least to demonstrate that one had priority over the other, and explain by which standard the virtue of justice ought to be measured.

It would have been relatively simple for theologians to resolve the dilemma of whether justice should be understood as 'due' or 'compassion' by distinguishing two distinct types of justice, one earthly, one heavenly. They might have argued that the justice defined as 'due' applied to judicial justice, the justice of the law courts, while the scriptural view of justice as 'mercy' expressed justice in the sense of charitable acts or alms-giving.[30] Yet, however neat and satisfactory this resolution may have seemed, it did not reflect the response of twelfth-century writers. Mercy was explicitly regarded by scriptural and patristic authorities as a judicial duty. This principle was stated on several occasions in the Bible, but most notably at James ii.13, 'judgment without mercy will be shown to anyone who has not been merciful', and Matthew vi.14, 'if you forgive others their sins, so will your heavenly father forgive you'. These passages were interpreted by twelfth-century commentators to mean that the human judge who fails to show mercy to an offender will not receive merciful treatment from the Lord on the Day of Judgment.[31] This principle (henceforth referred to as 'reciprocal mercy') was not brushed aside as an empty threat, but instead understood by twelfth- and thirteenth-century authors as integral to their conception of judicial duty. The unmerciful judge endangers his own soul. This understanding was reinforced by glosses on the Solomonic injunction of Ecclesiastes vii.17, 'noli esse iustus multum', an admonition typically taken to warn 'be not too just', a check on excessive severity in passing judicial sentence.[32]

A secondary point of reference in such discussions was the biblical pericope known as the parable of the unforgiving servant (Matthew xviii.23–34). The parable describes a servant brought before his master, to whom he owed a debt of 10,000 talents. The master, on the pleading of the servant, exhibited compassion and forgave the huge debt. The servant, on departing from his master, then encountered a second servant, who owed the first servant a much smaller amount. The first servant had the second cast into prison for his failure to repay the sum. When their master heard of this, he condemned the first servant's unmerciful actions and sent him to be tortured. Christ had concluded the parable with the words: 'this is how my heavenly Father will treat each of you unless you forgive your brother or sister from your heart' (*sic et Pater meus caelestis faciet vobis si non remiseritis unusquisque fratri suo de cordibus vestris*). For medieval commentators, this parable confirmed the vital importance of judicial mercy: as all humans seek mercy from God, so all have a duty to show mercy towards those over whom they are placed to judge. The parable was interpreted in both a literal way, as referring to simple debts, but also, as Peter the Chanter explained, in a spiritual sense, referring to sins or crimes.[33] A further problem which medieval authors recognised was that this principle of reciprocal mercy had the potential to place the personal justice of the judge in conflict with public requirements of justice. If it was deleterious to one's own soul to condemn a man to death without mercy, but beneficial for the public peace – which course was a judge to follow?

The most complicating factor in any discussion of justice and mercy, however, was the structural relationship of the virtues themselves, and, in particular, the role of *caritas*. As a theological virtue, *caritas* could naturally claim priority over the cardinal virtue of justice. Indeed, it has been argued that the importance of *caritas* as the principal virtue in Christian theological schema was growing during the twelfth century (overtaking a 'monastic' framework, in which *humilitas* was considered the root of the virtues).³⁴ One significant line of thought argued that the measure of the 'righteousness' of any action lay in its agreement with *caritas*. This was embodied in an oft-quoted Augustinian principle, 'habe caritatem et fac quidquid vis' (love and do what you will).³⁵ The fundamental intellectual problem here, however, was that such a principle could be used to dispense with the law altogether.³⁶ The Cistercian Aelred of Rievaulx noted that *caritas* could even permit divergence from the path of reason, for an act such as loving one's enemies was not reasonable, prima facie.³⁷ So long as a Christian acted in accordance with the dictates of *caritas*, they no longer needed to observe a strict definition of justice as the 'paying back' of dues. The specifically judicial dilemmas caused by giving *caritas* power over *iustitia* are apparent from a number of twelfth- and thirteenth-century treatises on the virtues which argue that *misericordia* is not a part of the cardinal virtue of justice, but instead belongs to the theological virtue of love. As a constituent part of *caritas*, *misericordia* can actually claim priority over justice. This is the case, for example, in *De fructibus carnis et spiritus*, composed in the second quarter of the twelfth century by the Benedictine Conrad of Hirsau.³⁸

Conrad's work places mercy as one of the *comites* (companions or associates) of *caritas*, alongside the virtues of *gratia, pax, pietas, mansuetudo, liberalitas, indulgentia, compassio, benignitas* and *concordia*.³⁹ *Misericordia* is defined as showing kindness and equal treatment towards all ranks, and inclining towards co-suffering (i.e. compassion) with the afflicted. The relationship between *misericordia* and *iustitia* is not explicitly spelled out by Conrad, but it seems that, in his opinion at least, *misericordia*, as a part of *caritas*, possesses the power to override or abrogate, and not simply to moderate, justice. For the moderation of justice, *De fructibus* offers another principle, *aequitas*, which it numbers among the *comites* of *iustitia*. *Aequitas*, the treatise explains, functions as the scales of justice, weighing the appropriate return of merits.⁴⁰ It is vital to note, however, that the principle of *caritas* alone does not necessarily condone unusually lenient judicial behaviour (although this is most typically the case). The invocation of *caritas* as a judicial principle could equally license more severe treatment of an offender, if a judge was motivated by love to impose severe discipline on an offender who is in dire need of correction. *Caritas* thus had a more austere side: it was accordingly sometimes understood as being divided into *caritas aspera* and *caritas suavia*: both of these are to be identified with mercy, but only the second is to be identified with the mercy which remits punishment.[41] Scholastic authors observe that sometimes it is more 'merciful' to discipline a sinner than to let him continue in his offence and endanger his immortal soul.

Alternative approaches

This book places the interaction – or tug-of-war – between justice and mercy as the centre point in twelfth-century discussions about judgment and judicial responsibilities. We can, crudely, define this problem as a question of how the moral injunctions of scripture were to be interpreted in the schools, how systematic theology encountered and worked through the Bible and how *caritas* and *misericordia* – flexible, elusive ideas – could be fitted into a model of judgment. It would, however, misrepresent the diversity of twelfth-century thought on this point to suggest that there were no other ways of approaching justice.

Augustine's contribution (and his emphasis on *caritas* and *misericordia* as pre-eminent) was vital – but one might wonder what place there was for Ambrose's examination of justice, not least because of the recognised significance of Ambrose's role in repackaging and repurposing the cardinal virtues for Christian consumption in his *De officiis*.[42] In general, however, Ambrose's influence on these particular sets of debates about judicial behaviour was less explicit and less directly felt. *De officiis* sets out a 'classical' understanding of justice – *quae suum cuique tribuit* – reinforced with the message that justice places protection of the community above desires of self (*utilitatem propriam negligit ut communem aequitatem custodiat*).[43] Ambrose ultimately divides justice into two parts: *iustitia* and *beneficientia*,[44] explaining that the first deals with 'sober judgment', the other with matters of kindness or goodness. *Beneficientia* itself divides into *benivolentia* and *liberalitas*. It was in this capacity that Ambrose, as Newhauser observes, had much to contribute to a discussion of economic justice and the proper use of wealth to treat the poor 'justly'.[45] Yet, in terms of judicial duties within a legal system, *De officiis* does not offer an 'alternative' solution that reconciles the tensions between justice and mercy. Ambrose's Christian recognition that goodness and care of others must be part of justice allows mercy back into the discussion – *iustitia* and *benificentia* did not, in conceptual terms, do much to untie that Gordian knot.

Where Ambrose's enduring legacy for twelfth-century discussions of justice must be appreciated, however, is in his emphasis on the role of the patriarchs as exemplars of justice. *De officiis* emphasises that Abraham, David and Solomon did justice by caring for their fellow humans.[46] Ambrose may begin from a classical philosophical structure, but this is quickly subsumed underneath biblical *exempla*. As will be seen in Chapter 4, the enduring impact of Ambrose was not the definitions he provided so much the precedent he set in considering 'justice' to be best explained by particular instances or events in the lives of the patriarchs or other scriptural figures.

Alternatively, another line of thought took justice as an expression of the will. This was the reading taken up by Anselm of Canterbury, considering justice in a more general and more spiritual sense, who had explained *iustitia* in his *De veritate* as 'rightness of the will preserved for its own sake' (*iustitia est rectitudo voluntatis servata propter se*).[47] The orientation of the will is the centre of this proposition. This, however, was not a definition much involved in questions of mercy, although it was clearly recognised in the twelfth-century schools – repeated, for example, by Bernard of Clairvaux and Robert Grosseteste.[48] The influence of an Anselmian line of thinking on conceptualisations of mercy is discussed in Chapter 8; but as we will see, there was relatively little discussion of rectitude of the will when it came to explaining the judge's task in determining how to punish offenders.

There was, finally, one further alternative way of conceptualising justice which was available to twelfth- and thirteenth-century theologians. This was a definition which set virtue – all virtue – as the midpoint between two vices, as a medium point between excess and deficiency. This is (at least in modern thought) a view most associated with Aristotle. Indeed, it could be found in the twelfth century in Aristotle's *Topics*, which had been circulating in Latin in the translation of Boethius since the early middle ages, but was given a new lease of life in the early twelfth century as part of the fresh translation of the *logica nova* undertaken by James of Venice.[49] The same idea, however, was more easily accessible through the discussion in Cicero's *De inventione* – explaining that virtue is bordered on both sides by vice.[50]

In general, the idea of a midpoint, mean or *medium* did not form the basis for any substantive definition of justice in twelfth- and thirteenth-century theology. Here, the reasons why some definitions were *not* taken up by medieval theologians prove just as revealing as understanding why others were. Certainly, there was a general appreciation of the idea of prudential moderation in all behaviours.[51] Peter the Chanter, for example, recognised the importance of *moderatio* in influencing the exercise of justice, and recognised that it is always better – whether as preacher, judge or confessor – to hold the middle way (*medium tenuere*). This, however, was generalised praise of the avoidance of excess, citing warnings from Cicero and scripture against the excesses of justice.[52] As we have already seen, the *Glossa ordinaria* endorsed the same point.[53] In the more sophisticated and lengthy discussions of *iustitia* found in scholastic *summae*, however, theologians reject the premise that justice can be described as a mean. On close inspection, justice did not seem to be an action with a single, virtuous, middle point.

The most instructive and detailed discussion of the problems with modelling justice as a midpoint between two vices is found in Stephen Langton's *Summa* (probably dating to the first years of the thirteenth century).[54] Langton begins his discussion by emphasising that justice is the act of giving to each their due (*reddit alicui quod suum est*). If due justice is the virtuous midpoint, then, Langton explains, it is possible to conceive of two vices opposed to it. The vice of giving more than is due, i.e. excess of justice, is called prodigality (*prodigalitas*), and the vice of giving to no one their due, i.e. deficiency of justice, is avarice (*avaritia*). However, Langton explains, the problem is that, rather than there being a single virtue of justice located at a midpoint between prodigality and avarice, there are in fact two virtues: largesse (*largitas*) and frugality (*parcitas*). Largesse is the action of giving to another slightly more than they deserve, but it is still a virtue, because it retains what is necessary for the support of the individual giver. Frugality, by contrast, is the action of retaining things for one's own use, yet it is still a virtue because this does not prevent it from giving to others what they deserve. In sum, then, both *largitas* and *parcitas* are virtues of justice because they both give to each their due. On this basis, Langton asserts, justice cannot be accurately described as a single virtue located between two vices. If this were to be the case, largesse and frugality would have to be considered the same action, an action which goes by different names on different occasions. But, as Langton has just established, they operate quite differently in relation to due. Conceiving of justice as a mean, therefore, does not fully capture the complexity of its effects.

The theologian William of Auvergne, teaching in the schools of Paris approximately two decades after Langton, considered the same set of arguments concerning justice-as-mean.[55] Justice, he concludes, is too complex a concept to be understood as a midpoint between excess and deficiency. William cites the same case of *largitas* and *parcitas* – both just, both virtues – to demonstrate the point and further discusses the idea with relationship to *misericordia*. The problem with conceiving of justice as a midpoint between giving too little and giving too much, he explains, is how such a position is to be reconciled with the knowledge that *misericordia* is

The problem with mercy: the schools

both a part of justice and a virtue which always advises a Christian to give to another *more* than is their due. Mercy and justice are both opposed to the vice of *iniustitia*, William concludes, and they are both, clearly, virtues. But – like *largitas* and *parcitas* – *misericordia* and *iustitia* cannot easily be fitted into a model of virtue as a mean. Twelfth- and thirteenth-century theological debate, in short, was driven by attempts to address the apparent incompatibility of *iustitia* and *misericordia*. That debate ruled out the relevance of the Aristotelian idea of the mean to resolving this pastoral problem. Aristotelian definitions *would* become relevant to discussions of justice, but not until the translation of the *Ethics* into Latin later in the thirteenth century, with its explicit reflection on the relationship between justice, law and the community.

More principles, more problems

Ambiguities surrounding the meaning of justice were more than simple squabbles over semantics. The period c.1100 to c.1250 is characterised by neither disorder nor simple disregard for the structure of justice. Instead, it is marked by the serious and increasingly complex confrontation of an intellectual dilemma. The problem was not that scholastic theologians *lacked* an organising principle with which to frame their analysis of justice, but quite the converse: theologians had to cope with a surfeit of competing organising principles, each of which seemed to shed some light on the nature of justice. In this sense, justice might be thought of as undergoing a crisis of meaning during the twelfth and thirteenth centuries, where the central problem stemmed from how one defined the relationship between justice (*iustitia*) and mercy (*misericordia*), two concepts which could either be harmonised as complementary virtues or contrasted as opposites. It is the potential for conflict, and the practical implications of that conflict, which have not been sufficiently appreciated in modern scholarly analyses of medieval justice. Indeed, a closer analysis of the terms related to justice will reveal exactly how complex the relationship between *misericordia* and *iustitia* was considered to be.

Scholastic theologians were broadly agreed on the constituent parts of justice, which were drawn, in particular, from Cicero's *De inventione*. Cicero had listed *religio, pietas, gratia, vindicatio, observantia* and *veritas* as the 'parts' of justice,[36] explaining that each of them involved the returning of due to some party: *religio* was to offer appropriate and fitting worship to the divine; *vindicatio* was the return of injury to one who had injured you; *observantia* was to offer honour to one's ancestors. The only significant adaptation made to this list by medieval authors was the addition of *misericordia* – although this was not always placed as part of justice. For Cicero, *misericordia* was never a part of justice, and he refers to it in *De inventione* only as a strategy which the accused may employ in pleading.[57] *Severitas*, too, might be added to this list of the parts of justice, or substituted for *vindicatio*: it had the general sense of the part of justice which returns due punishment for injury.[58] The anonymous twelfth-century treatise *Moralium dogma philosophorum*, sometimes attributed to William of Conches and a work which drew heavily on the writings of Cicero and Seneca, defines *severitas* as the part of justice which returns due punishment for injury. The *Moralium* considered *severitas* to be one of the two major constituent parts of justice, alongside *liberalitas* (generosity in giving). An extremely popular text, the work served to mediate classical philosophical definitions of justice to other twelfth-century authors.[59] Thus, Alan of Lille's treatise *De virtutibus, de vitiis et de donis spiritus sancti* (c.1170–80) extends Cicero's original list of six to a total of nine, listing *religio, pietas, innocentia, severitas, vindicta* [sic], *gratia, reverentia, concordia* and *misericordia*.[60] The inclusion of *innocentia* in this list points to a secondary influence on Alan's scheme, namely the early fifth-century Christian author Macrobius, whose *Super somnium Scipionis* followed Plato and Plotinus in listing the constituent virtues of justice as *innocentia, amicitia, concordia, pietas, religio, affectus, humanitas*.[61] These two descriptions of the 'parts' of justice (that of Cicero and that of Macrobius) were not necessarily incompatible, particularly given the flexibility of individual terms used as synonyms for *iustitia*. Sometimes they were simply listed side by side.[62]

Much of the complexity in defining the relationship between justice and mercy was bound up in issues of language and terminology. The semantic implications of a single word could be considerable, and, as such, the language of the debate must be approached with sensitivity. While the component parts of justice were common to most authors, it is a far harder task to identify the synonyms of *misericordia*. There were a number of Latin cognates for the modern English term 'mercy', as well as for the opposing idea of 'severity' (that is, justice as the strict return of due). In addition to *caritas*, for example, mercy might be expressed as *compassio, clementia, humanitas, indulgentia, lenitas, mansuetudo, misericordia, moderatio, mollitia* or *pietas*.[63] The rationale for the inclusion of *humanitas* as a synonym for mercy derived from Isidore of Seville's *Etymologies*, which had defined *humanitas* as a feeling of love and pity towards one's fellows,[64] broadly equating it with the idea of *compassio*, or co-suffering. Sometimes these terms are clearly used interchangeably: for example, the terms *misericordia, mansuetudo* and *mollitia*

The problem with mercy: the schools

were all applied to the same intercessory action of Moses.[65] Occasionally, however, an author utilises these differences in terminology to make a particular point concerning the nature and meaning of justice. For example, in Peter Abelard's *Collationes* (probably composed between 1127 and 1132), a pagan philosopher, arguing against a representative of the Christian religion, complains that *misericordia* denotes indiscriminate and undeserved pity, and, as such, it is not an admirable quality. The philosopher instead praises *clementia* as a true virtue, because it is reasonable to pity only those who have been punished unjustly.[66] Abelard was probably here drawing on the Ciceronian idea that *clementia* regulated justice because it belonged to the prudential virtue of *temperantia* (under which heading *moderatio* was also classified).[67] Other authors, however, while arguing that *clementia* regulated the distribution of justice, performing a function similar to that of *prudentia*, still maintained that *clementia* was a part of *iustitia*.[68] For other theologians meanwhile, *clementia* and *misericordia* performed such similar roles that they could, for the most part, be considered to be synonymous.[69]

Unyielding, punitive justice also had a number of synonyms, in addition to *iustitia* itself, which, when paired with *misericordia*, typically indicates a strict return of due, a more stringent judicial sentence. These terms included *asperitas*, *austeritas*, *districtio*, *excessus*, *rigor* and *severitas*. Of these terms, only *excessus* had inevitably negative connotations – of exceeding the limits of righteous justice.[70] *Districtio* bore the meaning of applying the full force of the law, without mitigation.[71] Some terms were more contentious than others. For example, Alan of Lille noted that some people did not consider *severitas* or *vindicta* to be virtues, because the desire to repel enemies derived not from nature (*natura*) but from human weakness (*ex infirmitate*).[72] Yet, as Alan observed, it was possible to construct a case for *severitas* as a necessary political action, even a praiseworthy virtue.

Alongside the vocabulary which described judicial sentences, a variety of terms were used to refer to the judge's ability to permit exemptions from the written law. The most neutral of these is *discretio*, particularly important in a monastic context and the idea of dispensation from monastic rules.[73] *Discretio* is, however, a term which requires careful elucidation when it occurs, since, while it may certainly carry a modern meaning of 'dispensation', it can also denote the process of discerning guilt or innocence, as its etymological root (*discernere*) implied.[74] Linked to the exercise of judicial discretion was the *voluntas* or *arbitrium* of the judge. These last two terms might simply convey the meaning of a judicial decision or judicial choice; alternatively, they might carry the association of partiality in sentencing, a decision arrived at not through reason, but exercise of personal will.

Justice and mercy

Beyond elucidating the different terms for *misericordia*, it should be noted that different 'types' or species of mercy were developed by scholastic authors, in part as an attempt to comprehend the acknowledged complexities of the virtue. Peter the Chanter, for instance, in his *Verbum abbreviatum* (c.1187), intended as a 'practical', accessible and introductory work of theology, embodies this attempt to work through the complexities of justice by working out the roles assigned to each of its constituent parts.[75] Peter distinguishes five distinct varieties of mercy, each of which has its own particular function and inflections. This approach is representative of the precision and care which characterises scholastic discussions of justice in general. First, Peter lists *misericordia ignoscendi*, the mercy which forgives debts and injuries.[76] Second comes *misericordia iudicandi*, whose province is the 'sparing and relaxing' of punishments.[77] Third is *misericordia corripientis*, the mercy of censure and correction. It is under this heading that Peter discusses the relationship between mercy and discipline.[78] On this basis, any action which is intended to correct the soul – including physical punishment, if necessary – can be considered compassionate. This definition is followed by a fourth type, 'interceding mercy', and a discussion of intercession specifically directed towards one's enemies.[79] The most important scriptural demonstration of this form of mercy is the example of the crucified Christ praying for his executioners. This discussion of intercession is then followed by a fifth category, 'rescuing mercy' (*eripere*), which is closely aligned with the idea of charity.[80] Most significant of all for the discussion of the relationship between mercy and due justice is Peter's first category of 'pardoning mercy' – *misericordia ignoscendi*. Offering an *exemplum* of a rich man whose son was killed by a pauper, Peter describes how the murderer was brought before the father who, by law, had the right to execute his son's killer. The pauper begged for mercy, acknowledging that he might justly be killed (*iuste occides*) by the father, but pledging that if he was spared, he would spend the rest of his life as a pilgrim, praying for the soul of the son. The centre point of his plea for pardon is an appeal to Christ: just as Christ had allowed himself to be crucified for the sake of all men, he asked that the father show him mercy in Christ's name, mercy which would then be returned in kind to him on the Day of Judgment, where God would reward the father above what he deserved.[81]

The logic of this plea contains a number of parts: an appeal to the dominance of mercy over strict judgment, demonstrated by the example of Christ, as well as an element of calculation – the father will stand before God on the Day of Judgment with charges against him, in need of mercy, just as the killer now stands before him. The argument was successful, and the father

The problem with mercy: the schools

put away his sword; and Peter remarks that he recognised that greater is he who defeats anger in himself than who acts out of anger. This *exemplum* demonstrates one very influential way of conceiving of the relationship between mercy and law, and the potential for mercy to override the commands of written law. For the murderer who seeks forgiveness for his crime, mercy means a stay of execution. *Misericordia*, as the offender admits, consists of the remission of due punishment. Mercy does not legitimise the crime, but, through an appeal to the example of the crucified Christ, mercy remits the penalty of death which is due by law. It also replaces a negatively reciprocal relationship, that is, punishment returned for a crime committed, with a more positive one – forgiveness towards the offender is matched by the promised divine mercy towards the one who forgives.

Peter the Chanter, for one, clearly allows the possibility of mercy 'dispensing' from law, in much the same way as the idea that *caritas* allowed an individual to do what was right and even permitted that individual to disregard the written law. Peter's *Verbum abbreviatum* was an immensely popular text, read and utilised by medieval students and masters alike.[82] But it was not only when consulting *Verbum abbreviatum* that students might be struck by quite how difficult it could be to judge. As part and parcel of their education in the schools, students encountered texts which made them aware of the complexity of justice and mercy. Indeed, the potential for conflict between the two can be found discussed in all types of texts produced in the schools, from the least complex to the most systematic works of theology – in *florilegia* collections, glosses, *distinctiones*, *specula*, *summae* and *quaestiones*. It was understood that different definitions of justice could license vastly differing patterns of judicial behaviour. A definition concentrating on what is 'due' allowed very little space for the exercise of judicial discretion, and, by extension, of judicial mercy. A definition of justice which emphasised the place of forgiveness and *misericordia*, on the other hand, accorded much better with a legal system in which pardon was a common practice. In short, in twelfth-century scholastic thought about mercy, what was crucial was the construction of the argument. The most basic and fundamental lesson of the schools was that mercy in judgment was not to be praised or condemned out of hand; it was first to be analysed.

The preceding discussion has delved into what might be described as 'academic' theology – although given that all theology was ultimately ordered to matters of salvation, constructing a strict division between 'academic' and 'practical' writing may be somewhat misleading, and in this regard, it may be more useful to make a distinction between the audiences for different texts. What should be emphasised, however, is that difficulties in defining justice ran deep. Twelfth-century authors did not believe that the apparent tension between justice and mercy was purely a product of their own contemporary social or legal structures, but found the same dilemmas in the writing of the Church Fathers and in scripture itself. There was relatively little sense of 'historical' distinction in this sense: Augustine's view of judgment might have been forged within a different legal system, but his commentary on justice remained wholly pertinent for twelfth-century judges.

Where these problems in determining the relationship between mercy and justice were felt most sharply was in discussion of the office of the judge, and how judges 'did' justice. It was in discussing judges that the consequences of privileging mercy over justice, or justice over mercy, became apparent – because different principles of justice translated into quite differing forms of judicial action. As such, a seemingly 'academic' and rarefied discussion of what justice *meant* could become a 'practical' problem of how justice was *done*. It is in moral theology that we find these ramifications of these 'academic' questions most thoroughly explored. As will be evident from subsequent chapters, not every discussion of justice in the judicial office begins with an explicit examination of the merits of Ulpian's definition of justice *versus* that of Augustine – although such texts might very well be ordered with some conceptual scaffolding, with references to the mentions of justice in the Gospel of Matthew or the Lord's Prayer. Rather than talking about justice in the abstract, moral theology provides a discussion of judges, and, at times, even a comparison of different kinds of judges. As will be seen in Chapter 4, one way in which this was achieved was through an appeal to specific biblical incidents or characters. Nonetheless, a fundamental question of definition and meaning lay beneath these 'practical' debates.

Notes

1 This might be considered a matter of both *theologia* and *ethica* – i.e. an account of how virtue should be ordered and developed by humans. Cf. Hugh of St Victor, *Epitome Dindimi in philosophiam*, 2.19, in *Opera propaedeutica: Practica geometriae, De grammatica, Epitome Dindimi in philosophicum*, ed. R. Baron (Notre Dame, IN, 1966), 195.
2 A useful introduction to this problem is provided in N. Wolsterstorff, *Justice: Rights and Wrongs* (Princeton, NJ, 2008), 110–13.
3 A. Collins, *Teacher in Faith and Virtue: Lanfranc of Bec's Commentary on Saint Paul* (Leiden, 2007), 121–2, 133; H. Lawrence Bond, 'Another look at Abelard's

commentary on Romans 3.26', in W. S. Campbell, P. S. Hawkins and B. Deen Schildgen (eds), *Medieval Readings of Romans* (London, 2007), 11–32. More broadly, for the development of medieval views on justification, see Alister McGrath, *Iustitia Dei: A History of the Christian Doctrine of Justification* (Cambridge, 1986), 55–207.

4 A valuable guide to this earlier (pre-1100) tradition can be found in Bejczy, *Cardinal Virtues*, ch. 1.

5 Cicero, *De inventione*, ed. and trans. H. M. Hubbell (London, 1949), 2.53, 328 ('Iustitia est habitus animi communi utilitate conservati suam cuique tribuens dignitatem'). For medieval use of, and engagement with, Cicero, see Chapter 7, below, and John O. Ward, 'What the middle ages missed of Cicero, and why', in William H. F. Altman (ed.), *Brill's Companion to the Reception of Cicero* (Leiden, 2015), 307–26.

6 Alcuin, *Disputatio de rhetorica et de virtutibus*, ed. and trans. W. S. Howell, *The Rhetoric of Alcuin and Charlemagne* (Princeton, NJ, 1941): c.44, 146, 'iustitia est habitus animi unicuique rei propriam tribuens dignitatem'); c.46, 150, in which *iustitia* is also described as nothing other than the love of God and the keeping of his commandments ('iustitia videtur esse nisi caritas Dei eiusque mandatorum observatio'), for there is nothing more just than this. For a commentary and some discussion of its influence, see Bejczy, *Cardinal Virtues*, 35.

7 Ulpian, *Digest*, 1.1.1, 1:29; *Institutes*, 1.1.1, 1:1.

8 *Enarrationes in Matthaeum*, PL.162.1286D, 'iustitia est reddere unicuique quod suum est, id est, Deo, et sibi, et proximo'; a tract usually attributed to Geoffrey Babion, Archbishop of Bayeux.

9 *Ysagoge in theologiam*, ed. A. Landgraf, *Écrits théologiques de l'école d'Abelard* (Louvain, 1934), 75, 'virtus communi utilitate servata ius suum cuique conferens'.

10 Peter the Chanter, *VA*, 2.28, 707–10, 'que cuique reddit quod suum est'.

11 Thomas of Chobham, *SCV*, 4.2.2. 143, 'iustitia sit virtus unicuique reddens quod suum est'.

12 Stephen Langton, BnF, Ms. latin 16385, fo. 42v, 'iustitie est unicuique suum reddere et non solum homini, sed etiam unicuique rei'. Cf. Lottin, 'Le concept', 513.

13 Grosseteste, *Dictum 56*, fo. 45v, 'amat igitur reddere unicuique quod suum est, atque iste amor iusticia est', and *Dictum 70*, fo. 51v, 'iusticia reddit unicuique quod suum est'.

14 *SCV*, 4.2.2, 144–5.

15 For example, Gervase of Tilbury, *Otia imperialia. Recreation for an Emperor*, ed. and trans. S. E. Banks and J. W. Binns (Oxford, 2002), preface, 2.

16 The term 'virtus' has multiple interpretations, including power, strength and the ability to perform miracles: see J. F. Niermeyer and C. van de Kieft, rev. J. W. J. Burgers, *Mediae Latinitatis Lexicon Minus* (Leiden, 2002), 5358–61. However, in the texts examined here – and unless otherwise noted – it can be appropriately translated as 'virtue' in the sense of *vis ad bene vivendum necessaria*.

17 For example, Grosseteste, *Dictum* 3, fos 3v–4r, cf. *Dictum* 70, fo. 51v, *Dictum* 103, fo. 106v.
18 *SS*, 4.21, 450.
19 One can find the pairing of *iustitia–misericordia* (sometimes with *veritas* standing in place of *iustitia*) occurring in many places in scripture. The most frequently cited in twelfth-century texts is James ii.13, raising the status of mercy above all else in judgment: 'superexultat autem misericordia iudicio'. See also Psalms xxiv.10; 'omnes semitae Domini misericordia et veritas his qui custodiunt pactum eius et testificationem eius'; Psalms lxxxiv.11: 'misericordia et veritas occurrerunt iustitia et pax osculatae sunt'. Numerous other verses in praise of mercy alone might also be cited, e.g. Luke vi.37: 'estote ergo misericordes sicut et Pater vester misericors est'. The passages and parables of particular interest to twelfth-century authors are discussed further below.
20 M. L. Colish, *Peter Lombard* (2 vols, Leiden, 1994), 2:504–7.
21 Peter Lombard, *Sentences*, 3.33.1, 2:188. Augustine, *De trinitate*, 14.9, ed. W. J. Mountain and F. Glorie, CCSL 50 (2 vols, Turnhout, 1968), 2:439.
22 For example, Grosseteste defines mercy as 'amor sive voluntas relevandi miserum a sua miseria', *Dictum* 2, fo. 1v. For a discussion of the etymological connection see Edith Scholl, 'Mercy within mercy: *misericordia* and *miseria*', *Cistercian Studies Quarterly* 42 (2007), 63–82.
23 For example, William of Auxerre, *Summa aurea* (c.1215–20), 3.42.4: 'et dicit Augustinus quod: iusticia est subvenire miseris', 4:819.
24 Augustine, *Enarrationes in Psalmos*, ed. E. Dekkers and J. Fraipont, CCSL 38–40 (Turnhout, 1956), on Psalms xcviii.6–7, 1383–4. See also Kevin Uhalde, *Expectations of Justine in the Age of Augustine* (Philadelphia, 2007), esp. ch. 4.
25 Augustine, it should be noted, was familiar with a definition of justice as 'due', though he used the model to emphasise a Christian's duty to render their due to Christ, in *De civitate Dei* 19.4; cf. R. Dodaro, *Christ and the Just Society in the Thought of Augustine* (Cambridge, 2004).
26 See Miri Rubin, *Charity and Community in Medieval Cambridge* (Cambridge, 1987), 55–98.
27 Sten Ebbesen and Lars Boje Mortensen, 'A partial edition of Stephen Langton's *Summa* and *Quaestiones* with parallels from Andrew Sunesen's *Hexaemeron*', *Cahiers de l'Institut du moyen-âge grec et latin* 49 (1984), 146–7.
28 'iustitiae lumen est misericordia, misericordiae virtus iustitia'. GO, Matthew v.6, PL.114.90; for the authorship and origins see Lesley Smith, *The Glossa Ordinaria: The Making of a Medieval Bible Commentary* (Leiden, 2009), 1–33.
29 *Enarationes in Matthaeum*, PL.162.1287.
30 This interpretation is discussed by Rubin, *Charity and Community*, 54–73.
31 See, for example, the gloss on James ii.13 attributed to Stephen Langton in BnF, Ms. latin 338, fo. 7v.
32 See Alan of Lille, *Distictiones theologicae*, PL.210.825A; *Policraticus*, 4.9, 1:266–7; *Decretum*, D. XXIII.4.32, 1:914.

33 Peter the Chanter, *Summa de sacramentis et animae consiliis*, ed. Jean-Albert Dugauquier (Louvain, 1954), 12–15. The parable also provided the structure for an early twelfth-century treatise by Odo of Tournai, the *Liber de villico iniquitatis*, PL.160.1121–50, in which Christ is the master, and Christians represent the servant.
34 Bejczy, *Cardinal Virtues*, 100–1.
35 The original citation (Augustine, *Tractatus in Epistolam Iohannis ad Parthos*, 7.8, PL.35.2033) is 'dilige et quod vis fac', but 'habe caritatem et fac quicquid vis' is more commonly given by scholastic authors. See Giles Constable, *'Love and Do What You Will': The Medieval History of an Augustinian Precept* (Kalamazoo, MI, 1999).
36 Bruce C. Brasington, 'Lessons of love: Bishop Ivo of Chartres as teacher', in Sally N. Vaughn and Jay Rubenstein (eds), *Teaching and Learning in Northern Europe 1000–1200* (Turnhout, 2006), 129–47.
37 Aelred of Rievaulx, *Speculum caritatis*, 3.17, in A. Hoste and C. H. Talbot (eds), *Aelredi Rievallensis Opera omnia*, CCCM 53 (Turnhout, 1971), 124.
38 Conrad of Hirsau, *De fructibus carnis et spiritus*, 13, PL.176.997–1006; for the attribution see R. Bultot, 'L'auteur et la fonction littéraire du "De fructibus carnis et spiritus"', *RTAM* 30 (1963), 148–54.
39 Conrad of Hirsau, *De fructibus*, 18, PL.176.1004A–1005B.
40 *Ibid.*, 18, 1003A–B.
41 See *QEP*, 1 Corinthians iv.21, 187.
42 M. L. Colish, *The Stoic Tradition from Antiquity to the Early Middle Ages* (2 vols, Leiden, 1985), 1:64; Bejczy, *Cardinal Virtues*, 13–17.
43 Ambrose, *De officiis*, XXV.118, ed. and trans. Ivor J. Davidson (2 vols, Oxford, 2001), 1:185.
44 *Ibid.*, XXVIII.130, 1:193.
45 R. Newhauser, 'Justice and liberality: opposition to avarice in the twelfth century', in Bejczy and Newhauser, *Virtue and Ethics*, 299–300.
46 Ambrose, *De officiis*, XXV.188, 186.
47 Anselm, *De veritate*, 12, in *S. Anselmi Cantuarensis archiepiscopi Opera omnia*, ed. F. S. Schmitt (6 vols, Edinburgh, 1946–61), 1:191–6.
48 Bernard, *Sermo* 72.2, *Sermones de diversis*, in *S. Bernardi opera*, vol. 6.1, ed. J. Leclercq and H. Rochais (Rome, 1970), 308, 'iustitia est rectitudo voluntatis, quae nec amat peccare, nec peccato consentire'; Grosseteste, *Dictum* 3, fo. 4r, 'iustitia est rectitudo voluntatis privata'.
49 L. Minio-Paluello, 'Iacobus Veneticus Grecus: canonist and translator of Aristotle', *Traditio* 8 (1952), 265–304. Aristotle, *Topica*, 4.3, trans. W. A. Pickard-Cambridge (Oxford, 1928), 43–4.
50 Cicero, *De inventione*, 2.54, 332; cf. C. J. Nederman, 'The Aristotelian doctrine of the mean and John of Salisbury's concept of liberty', *Vivarium* 24 (1986), 130–3.
51 For example, *Policraticus*, 3.3, 1:480; 8 (prologue), 2:711.
52 *VA*, 1.66, 437–8, quoting Cicero, *De officiis*, ed. and trans. Walter Miller (London, 1956), 1.10.33, 34–5.

53 *GO*, Numbers xx.17, PL.113.450.
54 Ebbesen and Mortensen, 'A partial edition of Stephen Langton's *Summa*', 146–8.
55 William of Auvergne, *De virtutibus*, 18, in *Opera omnia* (2 vols, repr., Frankfurt, 1963), 1:178.
56 Cicero, *De inventione*, 2.161, 328.
57 *Ibid.*, 2.51, 212; 2.56, 218; 2.107–8, 275.
58 *Das Moralium dogma philosophorum des Guillaume de Conches, lateinisch, altfranzösisch und mittelniederfränkisch*, ed. John Holmberg (Uppsala, 1929), 12–3.
59 J. R. Williams, 'The authorship of the *Moralium dogma philosophorum*', *Speculum* 6 (1931), 392–3.
60 For a comparison with other works (the list is largely identical), see R. Baron, 'À propos des ramifications des vertus au XIIe siècle', *RTAM* 23 (1956), 25–6.
61 Macrobius, *Commentary on the Dream of Scipio*, ed. and trans. W. H. Stahl (New York, 1990), 1.8.7, 122.
62 For example, both Cicero's and Macrobius's lists of the parts of justice are given in a late twelfth-century *florilegium* from Worcester: C. H. Talbot and P. Delhaye, *Florilegium morale oxoniense: MS. Bodl. 633* (2 vols, Namur, 1955–56), 1:85, 88.
63 The term *indulgentia* had not yet acquired the meaning of a remission for the punishment of sin. See R. W. Shaffern, 'Learned discussions of indulgences for the dead in the middle ages', *Church History* 61 (1992), 367–81.
64 Isidore of Seville, *Etymologies*, 10.116, trans. Stephen A. Barney et al., *The Etymologies of Isidore of Seville* (Cambridge, 2006), 220.
65 See Chapter 4.
66 Abelard, *Collationes*, 128, ed. J. Marenbon and G. Orlandi (Oxford, 2001), 140–3.
67 Cicero, *De inventione*, 2.163, 330: 'per quam animi temere in odium alicuius inferioris concitati comitate retinentur'.
68 Raoul Ardens, 'Speculum universale', BnF, Ms. latin 3240, x.64, fo. 49r.
69 For example, William of Auvergne, *De rhetorica divina*, 7, *Opera*, 1:343–4.
70 For example, Gerald of Wales, *Vita Sancti Remigii*, ed. J. F. Dimock, RS 21 (London, 1877), c.29, 68.
71 Cf. Innocent III's *Vergentis in senium* (1199), which calls for the use of *districtio* against heretics, X.5.7.10 (*Corpus iuris canonici*, 2:782–3).
72 Alan of Lille, *De virtutibus, de vitiis et de donis spiritus sancti*, ed. Odon Lottin, *Mediaeval Studies* 12 (1950), 1.2, 31.
73 For example, Aelred of Rievaulx, *Speculum caritatis*, 3.32, 141–3; *Benedicti regula*, ed. Rudolph Hanslik, CSEL 75 (Vienna, 1960), 70, 160–1.
74 See Edith Scholl, 'The mother of all virtues: *Discretio*', *Cistercian Studies Quarterly* 36 (2001) 389–401.
75 As noted by Bejczy, *Cardinal Virtues*, 129–30, Peter's discussion of all the cardinal virtues is heavily reliant on a letter of Hildbert of Lavardin to a nun; accordingly his treatment of justice emphasises its connection with humility.
76 *VA*, 2.8, 644–8.
77 *Ibid.*, 2.9, 648–50.

78 *Ibid.*, 2.10, 650–2.
79 *Ibid.*, 2.11, 652.
80 *Ibid.*, 2.12, 653–4.
81 *Ibid.*, 2.8, 646–7.
82 In addition to Baldwin's *Masters, Princes and Merchants*, see Eva Matthews Sandford, 'The *Verbum Abbreviatum* of Petrus Cantor', *Transactions and Proceedings of the American Philological Association* 74 (1943), 33–7.

3

The problem with mercy: the courts

A canon law parallel/parable

This chapter begins with a plea for the indulgence of canon lawyers, for whom the central argument of this chapter – that the law had significant difficulties in coping with the status of mercy – may seem, prima facie, unsurprising. That is because the history of canon law has long accepted that in the eleventh and twelfth centuries, there were both theoretical and practical anxieties about how judges should reconcile the conflicting demands of mercy and justice. Part of the work of 'harmonising' the canons was establishing how to respond to authorities which set out quite divergent positions in relation to the use of punishment.

The reason for beginning a chapter on English common law with an excursion into the canons is twofold. More than an interesting digression, canon law provides a necessary context for appreciating what was happening in England (as we will see in later chapters, when churchmen wrote to secular judges, they had canon law ideas, training and traditions to fall back on). We should listen out for the arguments being had in twelfth-century Paris, Rome, Cologne and Bologna. This is not to argue for canon law, or indeed Roman law more generally, as a direct 'source' for specific procedures and parts of English law; that would be to reopen a painful, fraught and tired debate about *ius commune* influence in England. Rather, it is a matter of recognising that conversations about the legal status and role of mercy were being conducted across Europe.

Second, and equally important, these debates can be used as a kind of historiographical tool: canon law can provide us with a parallel by which we might think through the status of mercy in English law in this period. Both canon law and common law were undergoing systematisation (albeit in quite different ways) in the twelfth century, and codification by which individuals attempted to put in writing the most important aspects of those laws. Though canon law and common law ended up as two quite different 'systems', it would be imprudent to overlook what canon law might tell us about one way of navigating this process in the twelfth century.

The potential for conflict between justice and mercy in the developing canon law was first addressed by Stephan Kuttner in his seminal essay, 'Urban II and the doctrine of interpretation: a turning point?'.[1] Kuttner argued that the conflict between *iustitia* and *misericordia* was a millennium-old theme in canonistic literature. The idea of tempering the canons, of mitigating the rigour of inviolable law with some concessions to human frailty, was a very conventional concept, expressed through a profoundly traditional vocabulary. Twelfth-century popes and canonists, speaking of mitigation of the canons for reasons of 'temporis necessitas', 'necessitate cogente' or 'pro consideratione temporum', invoked terms used by Leo I, Innocent I, Alexander I and Gregory the Great.[2] Kuttner's fundamental point bears repeating: the conflict between justice and mercy in the canons dated back to long before the advent of the twelfth, the 'legal', century: it was a constant in ecclesiastical law (and, indeed, in moral didactic literature) from almost the time of the early church. What was different in the twelfth century – and why the particular issue of *iustitia* and *misericordia* received such attention – was that increased scrutiny of the canons and the growing systematisation of church law forced canonists to confront the issue of exactly when and why a judge should be allowed to dispense from the law; in other words, how general rulings and principles should be applied in specific cases.[3]

The dilemma is clearly summarised by the preface to Alger of Liège's *De misericordia et iustitia*, a collection of canons composed at some point before 1121: 'for some canonical precepts address mercy, others address justice, indeed they are differentiated by various orders, persons, and times. Thus now mercy entirely relaxes justice, now justice entirely overrides mercy.'[4] Alger's preface emphasised the need to take account of the variety of circumstances and causes of offence, and to allow a flexible interpretation of the canons, so long as that interpretation was motivated by *intentio caritatis*, a righteous love which sought true justice.[5] Ivo of Chartres, writing in the final decade of the eleventh century, famously discussed the same question in the prologue to his *Decretum*: how ought two seemingly contradictory traditions within the canons to be reconciled?[6] Ivo, like Alger, believed that *caritas* ought to be the guiding principle for any judge attempting to interpret the canons, as *caritas* gave licence to temper the severity of the law.[7] Within a generation, the insights of both Alger and Ivo had been incorporated into the fundamental text of canon law, the *Decretum* (c.1140). This text included the crucial contention that application of the law ought to be determined by love, establishing the rule that 'ubi karitas non est, non potest esse iustitia' (where there is no love, there can be no justice).[8] According to all three of these texts, written law often had to be in some way adapted in order to fit the circumstances in which it was applied, both for the good of the Church and for the good of the individual who had transgressed. Only with consideration of the circumstances of each case could a judgment be given and a rule adapted, and in doing so, *caritas* provided the key to the legitimate modification of legal commands.

Throughout the twelfth century, canon law sought to find a way of translating this moral dilemma into judicial guidance: needing both to observe the justice which rendered what was 'due' to God, but also mercifully to seek the reconciliation and salvation of sinners. A revealing development in this regard was the decision by certain canonists to abandon the use of the blanket term *misericordia*, and replace it with a more precise, technical, vocabulary to describe the action of mitigating punishment.[9] The substitute that canonists generally settled on was the phrase *aequitas canonica*: this described the considerations and motivations which encouraged a judge to temper the severity of the written canons. *Aequitas* is a concept which canon law explicitly borrowed from civilians and Roman jurisprudence. Gratian's *Decretum* rarely uses the term *aequitas*, preferring to speak of *misericordia*,[10] yet by 1200, the latter term had almost been excised from the technical vocabulary of canonists.[11]

Canon law provides an instructive parallel for the study of English common law, for it demonstrates quite how much of a problem one law code could encounter when it tried to translate theological ideas into principles of legal guidance. This was a law code which was undergoing rapid change in the course of the twelfth century, which was struggling to deal with the role of the judge and judicial discretion and, which, as a result, developed a language and a terminology with which it could be understood. This is a model which needs to be kept in mind when considering the way in which judges who had been trained in this ecclesiastical law found themselves in England and being charged with the responsibility of applying common law. It should, however, be added that the act of reconciling justice with mercy was (in theory, at least) simpler for a judge in canon law than in common law. The way in which canon law was framed – as precisely the act of reconciling apparently contradictory rulings or arguments – brought the conflict between justice and mercy to the forefront of discussion, where it was explicitly recognised and discussed with reference to particular situations. Given the form which the common law adopted – the writ system – that same type of debate could not occur; and, given their format, even treatises on English law offered much less room for commentary and discussion.

What is mercy? The judge's problem

Where secular law is concerned, across Europe and prior to the twelfth century, any implicit intellectual contradiction between justice and mercy does not seem to have been considered as a particularly pressing political or legal problem. The term *misericordia* did not carry fixed legal implications, but fitted within a relatively informal and unwritten relationship between a vassal and his lord.[12] *Misericordia* was the process by which one made amends to a superior and sought forgiveness for wrongdoing: it depended upon the strength of personal and customary relationships; it was not subject to any exterior measure of rectitude, such as law, nor was it measurable against an abstract standard of 'justice'.[13] However, the status (and legitimacy) of this type of *misericordia* was fundamentally challenged in the period after 1100, as, across northern Europe, the idea of ordered legal systems became the norm rather than the exception. Royal power asserted itself through legal means and through claiming legal powers previously held by lesser authorities. This process of royal assertion was accompanied by legal systematisation, and a growing desire to make law 'orderly', by setting down the rules under which courts operated.[14] This narrative of the standardisation of justice applies particularly to England during the reign of Henry II, marking the expansion of royal administration and legal powers associated with the 'Angevin leap forward' and the transformation of English law 'beyond recognition'.[15] Baronial power over the laws was curbed; itinerant justices (an innovation first seen under Henry's grandfather, Henry I) were rolled out across the land from 1163 onwards. The crown consciously asserted its supreme judicial rights and deliberately shaped the law through the continued employment of its preferred justices.[16] Royal justice extended its reach, impinging on the lives of many more individuals than ever before. Alongside the expansion of royal judicial power came an emphasis on uniformity and regularity: royal justice was to be applied according to the same standards across the country.[17]

It seems beyond doubt that there was both a qualitative and quantitative difference in English justice under Henry II. Paul Brand has identified five key changes taking place under Henry II which fundamentally altered English law by 'professionalising' it.[18] Royal justices no longer merely presided over courts where local lords made decisions, but were empowered to give judgment themselves; sessions of the royal courts became continuous, rather than part-time commitments for local landowners; written records began to be kept, not only of final judgments, but of intermediate stages; royal courts were able to hear only such litigation as had been authorised by royal writ, pleas now having to be put in specific form; and, finally, truly national courts did emerge – where even the individual sessions of the General Eyre could be understood as 'individual local sessions of a national court'.[19] It is the first two of Brand's five changes which are directly relevant to the subject matter of this book. This national system of courts was run by men who – to all intents and purposes – can be considered professional, or at least semi-professional, judges and royal servants.[20] That aspiration to regularity and standardisation in judgment itself, and the way in which judgment was given, is novel and striking among the kingdoms of twelfth-century Europe.

The problem with routinisation, of course, is deviation from that routine. In the twelfth- and thirteenth-century common law, there remained one legal concept which resisted standardisation: mercy. This is seen most obviously in the granting of pardon: previously an informal agreement between a powerful superior and repentant inferior, pardon now had to be accommodated within a legal framework. Yet, by its nature, pardon envisaged an exceptional situation, which stood outside the normal judicial calculus. That point is expressed most clearly in what is, to date, the only dedicated study of the royal pardon in this period, Naomi Hurnard's 1956 work, *The King's Pardon for Homicide before 1307 AD*. Hurnard identifies the crux of the problem: pardon, the judicial exercise of mercy, could never be wholly regularised, as the reason for pardon always depended on special circumstances. The act of pardon was the act of 'substituting administrative discretion for judicial decision, uncertainty for predictability of punishment'.[21] Pardon, it must be noted, did not necessarily mean the abrogation of all punishment, but the substitution of capital punishment for a lesser one, typically a fine. In Hurnard's view, it was not until the reign of Edward III that the place of pardon within the English legal system could be described with any precision or clarity.[22] For Hurnard, the phenomenon of royal pardon in the twelfth century was a deliberate anomaly within common law. The possibility of pardon served to mitigate the (ever-increasing) severity of the law: 'the intensification of public prosecution and punishment could be pressed to its limits only so long as the prerogative of mercy provided a safeguard against undue severity in particular cases'.[23] Pardon was necessary not least because the common law made no differentiation, for example, between manslaughter and deliberate killing: any proven act of homicide was a capital offence.

This book is not a study of pardon as a process or practice, but a more general examination of the principles and problems of judicial mercy (of which pardon is just one, although perhaps the most dramatic, embodiment). What Hurnard's study does demonstrate, however, is that there was a continuing ambiguity in English law about the exercise of judicial discretion in mitigating punishment. Simply put, we encounter much praise of mercy, but very little specific direction about when and how it is to be used. Judges are exhorted to be merciful, without 'merciful' behaviour being defined.

This is a problem which can be glimpsed in English legal texts of the period (such as they are, and incomplete as the coverage they may offer is). *Misericordia* was a virtue, and, as such, it continued to be a virtue commended to judges and, most particularly, to kings when they acted as judges, even after a Henrician revolution in law.[24] The promise to do both 'justice and mercy' was a basic element in the pre-conquest English coronation oath,[25] and remained central to the conception of good lordship. The prologue to the treatise on English law known as *Glanvill* (c.1188) averred that the role of the king lay, on one hand, in asserting control over the ungovernable (*indomiti*), while on the other, it meant 'tempering justice for the humble and meek with the rod of equity' (*et humilium et mansuetorum equitatis virga moderando iustitiam*).[26] In demonstrating both of these qualities – and in balancing the calls for severity towards the wicked, equity for the weak – the king would 'show himself continually impartial in dealing with his subjects' (*in subditis tractandis equalis iugiter appareat*).[27] One might wish to comment here on the idea of 'continual' impartiality; implying that this balance is a project that runs throughout a king's reign; an animating and important principle contained within all royal action.

Glanvill's statement on the tempering of royal justice, may, on a first reading, appear as a throwaway line inserted into the in the prologue for the purpose of praising royal dignity. However, there is a strong case to be made that English legal texts (meaning those texts either setting out the law, or explaining its operation as a system) were intensely interested in the way in which mercy operated. This interest in mercy is evident before the structures of systematic common law were put in place and continued after Henrician legal reforms. In other words, though legal change had fundamentally altered the way in which courts operated, and the way in which the courts were constituted, giving adequate due to mercy still remained fundamental to the office of the judge.

The *Leges Henrici Primi*, written c.1116–18, collecting both old laws and laws current at the time of Henry I, also asserts that mercy is an important part of the king's discretion when applying the law. Pleas 'concerning more serious charges and meriting greater punishments shall be assigned to the justice and mercy of the sovereign alone, so that more abundant pardon may be had for those seeking it, and more abundant retribution for those transgressing'.[28] Much work remains to be done on the *Leges*, both in terms of its construction and its later uses.[29] But what the *Leges* has to say about the connection between judicial discretion and judicial mercy is worth dwelling on. The *Leges* offers some guidance to judges, which we might at least consider classifying as 'ethical'. In a chapter entitled 'on the giving of just judgment' (*de equo iudicio faciendo*),[30] the author quotes the principle that 'in all judicial proceedings the disposition of the judges must be irreproachable, not open to suspicion' (*affectus non suspectus*).[31] This principle ultimately derives from canon law maxims (it is, for example, found in the pseudo-Isidorian decretals,[32] and will later be repeated in the *Decretum*[33] and the letters of Innocent III[34]). But in canon law, 'affectus non suspectus' is applied to *accusatores* and *testes* – plaintiffs and witnesses – whereas in the *Leges*, it is applied to judges.

One might argue that this idea – effectively that the judge should be above suspicion – is a rather limited requirement and hardly counts as 'ethical'; it is perhaps a stretch to call it a rule of conduct. But the idea is then developed further in the chapter immediately following, for the text notes (seemingly justifying this principle it has just set down) that it is the poor (*pauperes*) who always suffer from corrupt judges. If we imagine the author of the *Leges* (whoever he was) as 'dismember[ing] the proclamations of earlier kings'[35] in order to create his text, and to show the workings of law at the most local level, attempting to clarify and systematise, then such comments – laced through the text – are surely important. The distinction between procedural safeguards and standards for conduct is not always clear-cut.

What is equally striking about the *Leges* is that certain 'procedural' points are tied to a discussion of permitting judges to show mercy. S.28 is the best example of this. Here the text specifies that parties in the court are frequently (*frequenter*) to be asked if they wish to add to what they have already said; that is, to clarify points which might be relevant to the adjudication of the dispute, but which might otherwise have been lost through 'trickery' (*surreptionem*).[36] In itself, this is unremarkable, but the reason for guarding against such deception is provided into the two following capitula, worth quoting in full. It is because of the problems that will be otherwise caused for the judge in coming to a decision:

28.5 The danger is so much greater to the judge than to the person who is being judged to the extent that we know, from the words of the Lord, that any judgment we pass on others is held in store for ourselves [Matthew vii.2].

28.6 Although the endless multitude of evil-doers may hinder a proper measure of mercy, one phrase serves to restrain us: 'Do not do to another what you do not wish to be done to yourself' [Luke vi.31].[37]

That is not to claim that mercy and justice are the sole animating principles of the *Leges*. But the need for judges to consider showing merciful compassion is not limited to a prologue; it runs though the text. Even if we were to consider these as mere passing mentions, it remains the case that the collector and editor of these laws has made the decision to include them.[38] Mercy is written into these laws, and this means more than those who are waiting for a pardon being classified as 'in misericordia regis'.[39] There is also some reflection on how mercy has changed and softened the law as it has evolved. For example, the *Leges* tells us, once, a woman who caused a foetus to be aborted would have been excommunicated, but 'now a milder provision has been introduced' (*nunc clementius diffinitum*).[40] Likewise, a woman who has married two brothers may be received back into the Church in her final hours 'as a measure of merciful humanity' (*propter humanitatem reconcilietur*).[41] The point here is not to consider every provision in the *Leges* which makes mention of *misericordia* or one of its cognates.[42] Rather, it is to indicate that the author understood concessions to mercy to be written into English law of long standing. The *Leges* also uses a variety of terms to describe mercy – *misericordia*, *clementia*, *humanitas* – though there does not appear to be an obvious rationale for the difference between these terms.

The *Leges* also provides a brief comment on the purpose of punishment. This is offered almost as an aside as part of a discussion of the 'characteristics' (*proprietates*) of legal causes. In the course of considering punishments, the text raises the question of when it might be appropriate to deny an individual communion with the Church.[43] The ensuing discussion includes a quotation from Augustine's *De civitate dei*, slightly modified: '[I]t is not only an angry God but also a merciful God who casts out sinners; they are cast out in two ways: like the Sodomites, so that the people themselves may be punished for their own sins, or like the Ninevites, so that the sins themselves of the people may be punished and destroyed.'[44] The thrust of the quotation is to suggest that punishment might function in multiple ways – as it is used by God, and, potentially, as it is used by those on earth. Nineveh was brought to repentance through punishment and the town was rebuilt. Punitive power might aim at striking out the offender, as Sodom was destroyed; it might alternatively aim at striking out the offence in order to preserve the offender.

Elsewhere, the *Leges* turns to Augustine and Jerome to explain how the courts ought to operate, and how just judgment is to be given.[45] Augustine's scriptural commentaries are also used to provide a definition of homicide, and to note the point that homicide can sometimes be carried out without committing sin – for example, if performed by a soldier, by a judge sentencing a criminal or by accident.[46] The recent work of Nicholas Karn has persuasively demonstrated that the *Leges Henrici Primi* should be understood as an assembly of contemporary laws and older practices, a carefully organised and ambitious description of the courts (intended to serve a practical function, rather than of merely antiquarian interest), constructed from the perspective of the hundred court. But recognising that, in the course of its collection and construction, it functions as a palimpsest of theological ideas, biblical quotations, and borrowings from canon law, is a point worth dwelling on when considering judicial mentalities.[47]

Although the *Leges* is often contrasted with later Angevin law books because of its antiquated appearance, content and organisation,[48] it explores themes in the discussion of mercy which will run and run throughout the common law. In the first instance, the doing of mercy is dependent on the virtue of the kingly judge rather than on the merits of the criminal who appears before him. In the second instance, the text utilises the words of the Sermon on the Mount as the basis for expounding a reciprocal concept of mercy, allowing the compassionate judge to store up mercy for himself (though whether in heaven or on earth is unclear in this context). Thirdly, mercy is given not because it is due to the criminal, but because of explicitly Christian ethical imperatives of restraint.

The same argument for mercy as a reciprocal good is subsequently found in an Angevin text, Richard FitzNigel's *Dialogue of the Exchequer* (c.1180). The treatise is a dialogue between FitzNigel and his student, in which the student, through questioning, elicits a detailed description of the Exchequer's operation, jurisdiction and officers. As a treatise on administration (broadly conceived), it is unsurprising that FitzNigel addresses the subject of pardon. What is striking, however, are the terms and basis of that discussion. FitzNigel, too, invokes the idea of reciprocal mercy. The first occasion for this is a discussion of pardon – specifically, pardon of danegeld or scutage, rather than a pardon for criminal acts. FitzNigel is concerned most particularly with the conduct of individuals who have been spared (*parcere*) payment by the king, advising them to be mindful of the reciprocal basis of those pardons:

> But the person who receives the prince's pardon or anything should be careful not to demand from those under him what was pardoned, but rather to remember the words 'forgive and you will be forgiven' [Luke vi.37]. For when such an act is discovered, the prince, following the teaching of the Gospel, will not forgive him and will not forgive his debt, but may punish him a hundredfold, because he clearly abuses the grace he was granted when he shamelessly demands from others what was freely given to him.[49]

In the final part of this exhortation, FitzNigel is unmistakably alluding to the parable of the unforgiving servant (Matthew xviii.23–34), in which the servant whose lord frees him of his debt then fails to show the same pity (*miserere*) to his fellow debtor. FitzNigel's focus here is the recipient of pardon, not the (royal) giver of it. However, in his account, there is still a conditional and reciprocal element to that pardon: mercy is abused when s/he with the power to show mercy does not consider their own need for merciful treatment.

A later passage in the *Dialogue* addresses royal pardon more directly, and this time in the context of excusing actions that would otherwise receive a capital sentence. This comes in a passage in which FitzNigel is offering an encomium of Henry II, discussing the king's actions after the rebellion of his own children, and praises Henry as a more gentle (*mitius*) ruler than King David. Even in the midst of a treatise focused on administrative practices, we see the assertion that legal process must make room for the exercise of royal virtue.

> Although the renowned King Henry had many examples and could have justly inflicted the most severe punishment on the rebels, he preferred to spare them, rather than to punish them, so that, though unwillingly, they would see his kingdom grow. ... May they [Henry's offspring] learn from both their father's example and their own how glorious it is to spare the conquered and beat back rebels.[50]

Thus, although victory over the rebellious is a sign of powerful kingship, it is the decision of the king to exercise his discretion and not to impose full and unfettered punishment that makes that kingship glorious.

This reading the *Dialogue* might, ostensibly, seem to disagree with John Sabapathy's recent interpretation of the text, which emphasises its purpose as a plain-speaking, practical piece, offering a 'pragmatic, instrumental picture of government'.[51] Sabapathy reads the text, and especially the dedication, as demonstrating that FitzNigel has minimal interest in royal virtue, and pays it only perfunctory attention.[52] Any accountability for royal action is deferred to God,[53] and FitzNigel is focused on describing how the king's will can be implemented, rather than improprieties or matters of right conduct. Fiscality, not goodness, is his concern.[54] I do not disagree that the central concern of the *Dialogus* is overwhelmingly fiscal, but that makes it these discussions of the rationale behind pardon all the more significant. This only goes to underscore the significance of mercy in twelfth-century society: a text aiming at the practical, at a description of Exchequer functions, cannot help but turn to biblical verses to explain how 'pardon' works. As for Sabapathy's point about royal accountability mattering only before God, the question is how we wish to read this. It can be taken lightly, as FitzNigel deferring questions about morality of action and conduct to the next life, but it might also be read more strongly: what greater, more threatening sanction can there be than the judgment of the Supreme Ruler? How else does one keep earthly rulers honest? Mercy and ethical conduct are not FitzNigel's priority, yet he is bound to discuss them, because they are fixedly (indeed, irremovably) attached to discussions of judgment.

The *Leges Henrici Primi* and FitzNigel's *Dialogus* both talk about mercy – as a virtue – by invoking the same, or similar, reference points that Peter the Chanter would do in the schools: namely, that mercy operates in a reciprocal way. That is one of its fundamental characteristics. Further, and in more general terms, even a text written at the heart of Henry II's court is happy to embrace the principle that virtue can – and should – divert the otherwise routine operations of the law. As will be seen, both these ideas remain, for this period, fixed points in English understandings of the relationship between law and mercy. This is not, in any meaningful way, to compare the texts of the *Leges* and *Dialogue* They operate in quite different contexts and serve quite different functions. But it is because the texts are so different that the commonalities are so striking – each feels the need to address the sensitive subject of mercy. The virtue of *misericordia* did have a place within the common law, even if that place was imprecise and explained only as an acknowledgement of judicial discretion. Moreover, again at the very least, both texts argue against the assumption that the creation of common law and the writing of legal textbooks constituted a purely 'secular' affair, and that self-denying compartmentalisation was ever practised by judges.

There is a third text which needs reviewing for what it says about law and mercy; however, its inclusion will not be uncontroversial, given its place and status in legal history. This is *De legibus et consuetudinibus Angliae*, commonly known as *Bracton* (c.1235, with further additions in the two

The problem with mercy: the courts

following decades).⁵⁵ *Bracton* contains an equally striking commentary on the importance of mercy to the judicial office. Justice, *Bracton* notes, is that which permits dispensation from the law in search of virtuous resolution; and the text emphasises the judge's role in weighing circumstances to determine the decision demanded by the case (*sed perpenso iudicio prout quaeque res expostulate statuendum*).⁵⁶ Thus, *Bracton* affirms, justice is a virtue (*virtus*). The text then goes on to offer general advice to the judge: that it is better to temper the law with benignity (*benignitas*), than impose it to the letter – 'punishments are rather to be mitigated than increased' (*et poenae potius molliendae sunt quam exasperandae*).⁵⁷ Judges are licensed to use mercy, although it should be the type of mercy which mitigates a punishment (*misericordia compassionis*), rather than the type of mercy which abrogates a penalty altogether (*misericordia remissionis*).

It might be possible here to claim some level of continuity: the need for mercy in the judge, a concern in the early twelfth century for the *Leges Henrici Primi*, remains a concern more than a century later. Crucially, however, the historiographical issue of the role of civilian and *ius commune* influence in the history of the English common law, as discussed above, is relevant here. *Bracton* may be a towering work in the history of the common law, a legal landmark by virtue of its aspirations to cover the entirety of the English legal system,⁵⁸ but it is a text which, in the view of English legal history, stands far outside the mainstream of the common law, due to its 'Roman' markings.⁵⁹ On this view, *Bracton* is in effect an outlier, a text written in the period (c.1230–50) at which the influence of Roman law reached its peak in England. *Bracton*'s structure, rhetorical flourishes and somewhat speculative and systematic approach to law are not reflective of the later developments – both immediate and long term – in the common law.⁶⁰

My aim here is not to attempt to bring *Bracton* back into the fold of medieval common law (such an endeavour would require a book in its own right). Yet regardless of where the ideas contained within the text are coming from – and even if they are to be classified as aberrant Romanisms – it can at least be said that someone in England, c.1235, was thinking about mercy in the judicial office. They may have been discussing it in Roman terms, but the conviction that mercy is a judicial duty was not alien to common law traditions. Of course, it might well be argued that the references to mercy above, and as found in other commentaries on English common law, are merely 'window dressing': they stand separate to the real meat of these texts, and the real meat of the common law – writ forms and detailed discussions of procedure. In that case, all talk of mercy is mere ornamentation, a flimsy appeal to ideals without foundation, and is to be taken with a pinch of salt, in the same way that one would treat the modesty *topos* found in the opening chapters of a medieval saint's life. The alternative reading, however, and the interpretation offered here, is that such texts cannot deal with mercy in any other way than in this rather imprecise manner. They must – and deliberately do – carve out space for the operation of mercy. Because of what mercy is – a virtue, which depends precisely on the set of circumstances of the judge, the court and the guilty party – these texts cannot go any further in describing it. To do so would be to circumscribe it. In other words, these texts create just enough space for mercy to ensure that legal practitioners know it is an option – without ever specifying how it is to be used, or laying down general conditions for merciful judicial action. In that sense, the continuing importance of mercy, even into the middle part of the thirteenth century, preserves something of the older relationship between judge and guilty party, even under a new 'regime' of standardised common law. Mercy is a question of virtue in two parts: primarily in the judge's right understanding of the need to 'balance' severity with leniency, but also in the special qualities of the individual 'criminal' in being deserving of mercy – according to some particular facet of their personal history or mitigation for their crime. In other words, mercy acts only where there is discretion; and, in order to leave space for virtuous mercy, these texts – and the common law more broadly – preserve significant space for judicial discretion.

While royal justices, charged with implementing royal writs, may not have had the power to pardon, they had considerable discretionary powers, as *Glanvill* recognises. A royal justice could recommend a defendant considered worthy of mercy for pardon by the crown; he could reduce sentences such as outlawry; where corporal punishment was specified, the judge had power to lessen it; he could decrease the sum to be paid as a fine. Such discretion – discretion which allowed the potential for mercy – was expected in every judge, whether that was the king sitting in *curia* or a provincial justice-in-eyre.[61] But discretion came with its own problems. So long as there was discretion in the system, there was scope for abuse. This, of course, was the fundamental paradox of any sort of mercy, not simply pardon: it depended on judicial *discretio* to mitigate a sentence and prevent injustice, but judicial partiality could equally be a source of injustice. The problem was recognised by civilian lawyers and the *ius commune* as well as by their English counterparts, who accordingly experimented with various legal means of restricting judicial discretion (and by extension judicial abuses).[62]

The problem with mercy: the courts

The structure of the English judicial system, however, made it almost impossible to grant 'impartial' justice. At every level, there was space for judicial discretion, and as a result the possibility of judicial abuse. The system rested on public service.[63] While judges received a stipend, their wealth was acquired through other means, partly from earnings as private pleaders, but also through extra-legal rewards for favourable judgment.[64] Judges may have been required to enforce the royal law, but the majority were also private landholders in their own right with private interests to protect.[65] Moreover, the greatest private landholder, the crown, was also expected to be the most impartial judge. To commence major litigation, to obtain certain writs 'de gratia' or even to speed along the process of justice, required a level of political influence, and, in some instances, royal blessing.[66] The role of royal favour should not be considered as part of a 'transitional' stage in the common law, moving from an entirely 'personal' kind of justice in 1100 to a wholly bureaucratic and impartial system by 1250.[67] It was not removed from the system; there was never any sustained attempt to remove it.

Periodically, however, the arbitrary and personal nature of royal justice was perceived to have become so extreme as to merit intervention. One such extreme occurred in 1209, when King John ordered all cases before the bench at Westminster and pleas from the eyres transferred to the court *coram rege*. Judgment was given only in the presence of the king. John's suspension of pleas at eyre meant that obtaining a favourable verdict was entirely dependent on gaining royal goodwill, and, indeed, access to the king.[68] Placing the crown as head of the judicial system meant, in theory, imposing a single arbitrating authority in disputes; in practice, it could mean that justice depended entirely on the royal will. Nor did the provisions of Magna Carta resolve the problem. Magna Carta may have curbed the worst excesses of arbitrary royal judgment, but it did not – it could not – remove the need to obtain royal goodwill in order to achieve anything at law.[69] Procedural innovations and the prescriptions of law books could never entirely exclude the role of personal judgment and private virtue in the operation of English justice. Nor, necessarily, did law books wish to circumscribe the scope for private virtue, given that judicial discretion was one very important means of mitigating the excesses of written law.

The elements of partiality and arbitrary decision-making in the common law, in fact, were a concern that was never adequately settled in the medieval period, as the historiography of the later thirteenth and fourteenth century well attests. Similar problems continued to be raised,

Justice and mercy

periodically – sometimes leading to moments of crisis – but were never resolved. The nature of justice was, for example, a major complaint during the Second Barons' War (1264–7). Christine Carpenter has convincingly identified a systematic flaw in the English legal system, under which the men who most criticised arbitrary royal intervention in the judicial system were those who benefited most from the system of judicial patronage. She describes a 'contradictory vision of the law, wanting it unbending but malleable'.[70] This was not a uniquely late medieval paradox: the same ambiguities are visible in the common law, and, from the twelfth century onwards, they crystallise in the form of a well-developed debate over the respective roles of justice and mercy. In other words, strengthening royal judicial power served only to strengthen the contradictions within it.

The trouble with documents

How and where should we look for evidence of mercy? We are faced with unequal kinds of evidence. Referring back to the canon law parallel at the start of this chapter, one fundamental problem is that Church judges (i.e. the administrators of canon law) are often more forthcoming than common law judges. As will be discussed in Chapter 7, while, for example, we may not know how Robert Grosseteste (or his deputised official) felt about every case in his own courts, we can trace out his feelings on mercy more generally, and identify a number of particular cases which troubled him.

What kind of evidence do we have for 'mercy' in the judgments of common law? The focus here is *criminal* (or quasi-criminal) cases; where, as the *Leges Henrici Primi* recognised, the issue of mercy or severity in treatment of the offender was most sensitive and most crucial. What did 'showing mercy' mean in such cases? Felonies – a category which include all homicides and thefts of significant value – attracted a capital sentence.[71] Once guilt had been established, execution (typically by hanging) was the only penalty available in strict legal terms. The written common law does not make a spectrum of punishments available to the judge. The only escape from a capital sentence (other than literal escape) was pardon, and pardon meant – often subject to a heavy financial penalty – that the offender was entirely excused. This, rather than substitution of a lesser physical punishment, was the way in which discretion could be exercised. In effect, pardon was an all-or-nothing proposition. One can speculate that in certain circumstances, pardon would also have been accompanied by some *de facto* form of 'community' punishment – the guilty individual, pardoned, but not necessarily forgiven, may endure some level of social stigma. Formerly rebellious barons or nobles who incurred royal displeasure for an 'offence' but were not formally accused of a particular crime, might prudently absent themselves from court for a period; such scenarios might end with a reconciliation where the ruler forgave the offence. In the common law system, the choice was stark. Capital crimes (felonies) were punishable by death, and only death; obtaining mercy meant, effectively, freeing the offender of everything but potential financial penalties (although these could be heavy indeed). There was, however, no 'middle option' in that sense: imprisonment was used only for hostages and those awaiting trial or sentence, not as a punishment in its own right. Alternative physical punishments for these offences were not generally discussed, although lesser crimes than capital offences, as *Glanvill* noted, could be dealt with merely by loss of limbs or some form of corporal punishment.[72] This distinction between capital and corporal punishment is somewhat less visible at the start of the period, where, following Anglo-Saxon legal traditions, the distinction between the punishments of mutilation and execution could be blurred: the *Leges Henrici Primi* states that either option could be the punishment for murder, treason, arson, robbery and false coining.[73] This type of mutilation was hardly a minor penalty: Henry I famously subjected moneyers who had counterfeited the royal coin to amputation of the right hand and castration.

Aside, however, from a few dramatic and well-attested moments of ruthless, public justice – such as Henry I's treatment of those who interfered with the integrity of his coinage – criminal proceedings were a relatively minor concern for the common law during this period. The primary concern of English law was civil pleas and, particularly, the ownership of land. The evidence for disputes concerning land litigation (cases of *novel dissesin*, *darein presentment*, *mort d'ancestor*, for example) is far more abundant – and abundantly commented upon – than that for the prosecution of felonies. This preference for civil pleas in the legal record may well reflect the attitude of common law judges themselves. John Bellamy went as far as to suggest that as it was litigation involving private actions which brought judges the greater part of their income (in the 'perks', or, more frankly, bribes, they could receive in return for favourable judgment), judges were much more inclined to hear civil pleas. Felonious offences were not money-spinners. There was never the same precision in the definition of criminal offences as there was for civil wrongs: plea rolls and Year Books demonstrate that, for example, the precise meaning of 'burglary' – a significant category – was never fixed.[74]

Justice and mercy

The great problem in discussing the early history of the criminal side of the common law is the sources. My approach here is to consider perceptions – not to take a statistical approach to a body of cases and decisions, or attempt to see if 'mercy' can be discerned in particular judicial outcomes – but, in any case, such a project would be near-impossible given the state of the evidence.[75] Because of losses of evidence, of gaps, partialities and variations in recording from county to county, records of gaol deliveries (for example) cannot provide a sound basis for evaluating crime in England during this period.[76] If looking for evidence of 'mercy' in the legal record, the historian is largely limited to searching for evidence for pardon. Pardon – whether financial or judicial – was obtained by writ;[77] but, even where such writs of pardon are extant, these are entirely formulaic documents which provide almost no insight into the varied and often protracted processes of suing for pardon. Here, too, there is also an issue of survival: writs of pardon had a specific purpose – to be presented as proof that the holder could not be taken to court (whether for the first time, or be brought back in) for the crime for which they had been pardoned. But given this, there was only value in preserving the writ of pardon for the lifetime of the named individual within it. Unlike records of civil disputes, records of pardon were not likely to be retained in familial or royal archives. Often we only encounter the trace of a pardon, by chance, when the writ has not been paid for in full and thus turns up on the rolls of debts stilled owed to the crown.

Because pardon was usually purchased, and mercy was bought from the crown, one means of proceeding, then, might be to build up a bigger picture of such purchases of royal mercy. Yet, even when trawling financial records, the results are extremely limited for most of the twelfth century, at least before the reign of John. Only those pardons which were not paid for immediately were enrolled on Pipe Rolls.[78] Even the term *amerciare* – with the etymological implication of being in receipt of mercy – was not used in a technical sense to denote the exchange of money in exchange for royal mercy before the 1190s at the earliest. Similarly, where the term *ammerciamentum* occurs in the records, it might describe one accused, tried, condemned or fined.[79] Even where, for later years, documentary evidence describing pardon is available, the discussions are frustratingly laconic, offering little to no insight into motivation or judgment. The limitations of pardon in the plea rolls are demonstrated if we take a rare example of such a case, heard in 1212 at York:

> Roger of Stainton was arrested because in throwing a stone he by misadventure killed a girl. And it is testified that this was not by felony. And this was

The problem with mercy: the courts

shown to the king and the king, moved by pity, pardoned him the death. So let him be set free.[80]

There are numerous questions raised by this (fairly typical) entry of a pardon. How long did this entire transaction take – from the moment of Roger's arrest to the recording of this pardon? How, and in what circumstances, was proof of Roger's case 'shown to the king'? This was not a routine process, and Roger of Stainton, or his relatives, would likely have gone to considerable lengths, possibly though the offices of patrons, in order to secure this document of pardon. They may well have been acting in order to obtain such a document long before the case was brought before the court.

The silence of the plea rolls on the extra-judicial activities involved in obtaining a pardon is almost deafening in a second case, heard at the Shropshire Eyre in 1221:

> Roger of Presthrope killed John of Patinton. And Roger came and proffered letters patent of King John, wherein is contained that he has pardoned the death of said John, whereof Juliana, John's wife, and Herbert his brother have appealed him, whereof he [the king] wills that he should have sure peace thereof, so that he may abide judgment if any shall wish to accuse him of it. ... And for that no one sues against him, let him go without day and quit so far as concerns the king. And be it known that he was not outlawed.[81]

Here it seems that Roger was being appealed, in 1221, that is, during the reign of Henry III, for a death which had occurred some years earlier – at least as early as 1216, the year of King John's death. The death, presumably, had not been prosecuted at the time, and, in the intervening period, Roger had thought to obtain a pre-emptive pardon from John. That document proved a wise investment, which he could now utilise, with judicial authority having passed to John's heir, Henry.[82] Yet how Roger came into that pardon, how he sued for it and what it cost him to obtain it cannot be understood from the skeletal level of detail provided by the plea roll. Simply put, looking only at the face of the legal record – even where it survives – is of little assistance in helping us understand what justice or mercy 'meant' in England between 1100 and 1250.

The relative taciturnity of legal records when it comes to explaining mercy is one reason why this book looks to other forms of evidence to provide a way of understanding judgments and justice and the judicial calculations being made. Part of this lies in reassessing our view of secular judges, how the model of a judge was shaped and what judges believed themselves to be doing when they set about giving judgment. As already discussed, the consensus view in the historiography is that common law

Justice and mercy

judges in this period saw themselves foremost as royal servants, dedicated first to fulfilling their duties to the crown – and any interest in virtue would have to come after this. This is not to say that royal judges are assumed to have been rapacious and immoral: Turner's view is that most royal judges took their oaths to render justice impartially to all seriously; and if judges saw the opportunity to profit from justice, they were no worse than many other royal servants.[83] This is not a shining recommendation, but nor is it particularly damning, either. But Turner, who has done so much to rescue the biography and careers of individual royal judges of this period from obscurity, piecing together fragmentary evidence, also came to the conclusion that twelfth-century English judges are fundamentally unknowable, lost to historians. As he wrote of two particular late twelfth-century judges:

> It is next to impossible to peer into the minds of royal servants such as Michael Belet or Richard Barre. We can assume that they, like other royal officials, held an exalted view of royal power and felt a responsibility to protect the king's interest and to increase his revenues. They doubtlessly shared the conventional view of society that their colleague Richard fitz Neal set forth in his *Dialogus de Scaccario*.[84]

This is too pessimistic a verdict. If it is not possible to peer into the minds of Belet and Barre, it might – with imagination and care – be possible to recreate ideas of what a judge should be like; his conduct and behaviour. That these two men had an exalted view of royal power is not in doubt; but they might also have been susceptible to other visions of their office; other job titles. They were royal servants, yes, but they were also judges who moved through a world full of praise for the exalted role of judgment and caution about the perils of improper application of that judgment. It may not have been their royal service alone that gave them an elevated sense of their status: their office encompassed not just royal duties, but the governance (and peace) of the realm and their own souls.

Much of this comes down to a question of emphasis, and how seriously we believe twelfth-century judges took the warning that merciless judges would meet a merciless fate after their deaths. When Turner notes that Michael Belet's devotions were 'conventionally pious',[85] the question then becomes how we construct 'conventional piety' for a twelfth-century man of his background. 'Conventional' piety by the standards of the mid-twelfth century would necessarily impinge on judicial responsibilities. It was 'conventional' to apprehend the importance of mercy; any exposure to conventional religion entailed being taught about the relationship between justice and mercy and the necessity for both. Conventional sermonising included within it a lofty place for the office of judge – and considerable warning for those who failed to live up to those judicial virtues. Conventional piety contained a great deal of moral theology. There is no reason that becoming a royal servant changed this: there remained two masters to satisfy, one earthly and one heavenly. As the king is answerable to God, and must do his best for justice, so too must his judges.

Notes

1 Stephan Kuttner, 'Urban II and the doctrine of interpretation: a turning point?', *Studia Gratiana* 15 (1972), 66–9.
2 *Ibid.*, 69.
3 Jane E. Sayers, *Papal Judges-Delegate in the Province of Canterbury, 1198–1254: A Study in Ecclesiastical Jurisdiction and Administration* (London, 1971), 100–1.
4 'Quia enim precepta canonica alia misericordia, alia sunt iustitie, adeo discrete variis ordinibus, personis et temporibus, ut nunc misericordia omnino remittat iustitiam, nunc iustitia omnino dissimulet misericordiam.' Alger of Liège, *Liber de misericordia et iustitia*, ed. N. Kretzschmar (Sigmaringen, 1985), 187.
5 *Ibid.*
6 For the date of Ivo's *Decretum* (the first stages date to the 1080s, the final form to c.1094, but with continuous revisions), C. Rolker, *Canon Law and the Letters of Ivo of Chartres* (Cambridge, 2010), 160–1.
7 Ivo of Chartres, *Prologue*, in Bruce C. Brasington, *Ways of Mercy: The Prologue of Ivo of Chartres* (Münster, 2004), 115–42.
8 *Decretum*, C.XXIV, q.1, c.29, 1:977; cf. Anders Winroth, *The Making of Gratian's Decretum* (Cambridge, 2000), 20, for the relationship of that text to Ivo's writings.
9 K. Pennington, 'The practical use of Roman law in the early twelfth century', in Matthias Lutz-Bachmann and Alexander Fidora (eds), *Handlung und Wissenschaft: die Epistemologie der Praktischen Wissenschaften im 12. und 13. Jahrhundert* (Berlin, 2008), 13.
10 For example, *Decretum*, C.II, q.7, c.36, 1:494; C.XII, q.2, c.39, 1:700; cf. D.XLV, c.10, 1:165.
11 G. Conklin, 'Stephen of Tournai and the development of *aequitas canonica*: the theory and practice of law after Gratian', in S. Chodorow (ed.), *Proceedings of the Eighth International Congress of Medieval Canon Law* (Rome, 1992), 369–86.
12 Hincmar of Rheims, *De regis persona et regio ministerio*, PL.125.846.
13 G. Koziol, *Begging Pardon and Favor: Ritual and Political Order in Early Medieval France* (London, 1992), 215–16; and John Hudson, 'Power, law and the administration of justice in England 900–1200', in P. Anderson, M. Münster-Swendsen and H. Vogt (eds), *Law and Power in the Middle Ages* (Copenhagen, 2008), 153–70.
14 Kenneth Pennington, *The Prince and the Law, 1200–1600: Sovereignty and Rights in the Western Legal Tradition* (Berkeley, CA, 1993), 142; G. I. Langmuir, 'Community and legal change in Capetian France', *French Historical Studies* 6 (1970), 276–82.

Justice and mercy

15 See G. J. White, *Restoration and Reform, 1153–1165* (Cambridge, 2000), esp. 211–12; for the quotation, R. C. van Caenegem, *Royal Writs in England from the Conquest to Glanvill* (London, 1959), 204.
16 Paul Brand, '*Multis vigiliis excogitatam et inventam*: Henry II and the creation of the English common law', in Paul Brand, *The Making of the Common Law* (London, 1992), 77–102. For 'centralisation' see Joseph Biancalana, 'For want of justice: the legal reforms of Henry II', *Columbia Law Review* 88 (1988), 534–6.
17 John Hudson, *Land, Law and Lordship in Anglo-Norman England* (Oxford, 1994), esp. 270–5.
18 For what follows, Paul Brand, *The Origins of the English Legal Profession* (Oxford, 1992), esp. 1–33, and here 15–16. 'Professionalisation' of the law, in the sense of the courts becoming the domain of experts, can be considered a broader twelfth-century phenomenon. See James Brundage, *The Medieval Origins of the Legal Profession: Canonists, Civilians and Courts* (Chicago, 2008).
19 Brand, *Origins*, 17.
20 *Ibid.*, 27: Brand considers Simon of Pattishall (d.1217) the first 'judicial specialist'.
21 Naomi D. Hurnard, *The King's Pardon for Homicide before 1307 A.D.* (Oxford, 1969), vii.
22 *Ibid.*, 223.
23 *Ibid.*, 21.
24 For example, *Curia Regis Rolls of the Reign of Richard I and John* (London, 1922), 1:382, 'et dominus rex [John] motus misericordia et per consilium recipit oblationem ipsius Hawisie'. See D. M. Stenton, *English Justice between the Norman Conquest and the Great Charter 1066–1215* (London, 1965), 93, 114, for a discussion of this record and John's acts of 'mercy'.
25 P. L. Ward, 'The coronation ceremony in Medieval England', *Speculum* 14 (1939), 160–78; H. G. Richardson, 'The coronation oath in medieval England', *Traditio* 16 (1960), 111–202.
26 *De legibus et consuetudinibus regni Angli* ('Glanvill'), ed. and trans. G. D. G. Hall and M. T. Clanchy (Oxford, 1993), prologue, 1.
27 *Ibid.*
28 *LHP*, 11.16a, 83.
29 See Nicholas Karn, 'Rethinking the *Leges Henrici Primi*', in Stefan Jurasinski, Lisi Oliver and Andrew Rabin (eds), *English Law before Magna Carta: Felix Liebermann and 'Die Gesetze der Angelsachsen'* (Leiden, 2010), 199–220.
30 *LHP*, 28.1, 128.
31 *Ibid.* See 31.6, 134 for a similar statement on judges suspected of partiality.
32 *Collectio decretalium*, PL.130.77D.
33 *Decretum*, C. III, q.5.
34 Innocent III, Ep. 139, PL.216.928C.
35 Karn, 'Rethinking', 219.
36 *LHP*, 28.4, 131.

The problem with mercy: the courts

37 '28.5 Tanto enim maius est periculum iudicantis quam eius qui iudicatur, quanto ex verbis Domini iudicium super alios habitum nobis scimus reservari.

28.6 Et licet infinita delinquentium multitudo modum miserationis incommodet, uno verbo concludimur: quod tibi non vis fieri, alii ne feceris.' *Ibid.*, 28.5–6, 131.

38 For example, *LHP*, 59.20, 188: 'it shall be fitting that individual persons above all observe true justice and exercise mercy in respect of evil-doers in such a way that they do not leave unpunished an outlaw or a thief caught in the act' (*per omnia iustitiam teneant et ... misericordiam sentient*).

39 This is discussed at *LHP*, 13, 117, where it is clearly employed as a set quasi-procedural phrase, rather than denoting an ethical choice by a judge; cf. 19, 123.

40 *Ibid.*, 70.16a, 222.

41 *Ibid.*, 70.17, 224.

42 These two examples are taken from s.70, collecting the customary laws of Wessex.

43 *LHP*, 5.18a.

44 'Peccatores non solum Deus iratus set etiam miseratus evertit; evertuntur autem duobus modis aut sicut Sodomite ut pro peccatis suis ipsi homines puniantur, aut sicut Ninivite ut ipsa hominum peccata puniantur et destruantur.' *Ibid.*, 5.20, 90–2.

45 *Ibid.*, 33.6–7, 136.

46 *Ibid.*, 72.1b–1c, 226–8. The citation in the text is to Augustine's commentary on the Sermon on the Mount, in fact the reference is to *De libero arbitrio*, 1.4.25. The same quotation is also found in Ivo of Chartres's *Panormia*, c.38, PL.161.1313B.

47 For example, the use of biblical quotations as legal commentary: 1 Kings xx.42 at 72.1e, 228; Proverbs xxvi.4 at 84.4, 260.

48 See P. Hyams, 'The common law and the French connection', *Anglo-Norman Studies* 4 (1982), 77–92.

49 'Caveat autem cui dimittitur aliquid a principe ne postea sibi dimissum requirat a subditis, set magis memor sit verbi illius "dimittite et dimittemini", quia cum hoc fuerit deprehensum princeps, evangelice emulator doctrine, nec dimittet eum, nec debitum dimittet ei, set forsitan in centuplum puniet, quia impensa sibi gratia videtur abuti cum ab aliis irreverenter exigit quod gratis sibi dimissum est.' *Dialogus de Scaccario*, ed. and trans. E. Amt (Oxford, 2007), 1.8, 74–5.

50 'Licet autem rex insignis pluribus habundaret exemplis et posset in eos iustissimam excercere vindictam, maluit tamen expugnatis parcere, quam eos punier, ut eius regnum crescere viderent vel inviti ... paterno simul et proprio discant exemplo quam gloriosum sit "parcere subiectis et debellare rebelles" [cf. *Aeneid*, vi.853]'. *Ibid.*, 2.1, 116–17.

51 Sabapathy, *Officers and Accountability*, 95–6. Sabapathy also makes the point – which I echo here – that the text is, in form, structure and purpose, exceptional, with few equivalents as a genre of writing.

52 *Ibid.*, 97.

53 *Ibid.*, 99.

54 *Ibid.*, 101.

55 For the problems of dating the text, P. Brand, 'The date and authorship of *Bracton*: a response', *Journal of Legal History* 31 (2010), 217–44.
56 *Bracton: On the Laws and Customs of England*, ed. and trans. G. E. Woodbine and Samuel Thorne (4 vols., Cambridge, MA, 1968–77), 2:25.
57 *Ibid.*, 2:299. Here *Bracton* is quoting from the *Digest*, 48.19.42.
58 See B. Tierney, '*Bracton* on government', *Speculum* 38 (1963), esp. 295–6.
59 See F. W. Maitland, *Bracton's Note Book: A Collection of Cases Decided in the King's Courts during the Reign of Henry the Third* (3 vols, London, 1887), 1:10.
60 See Seipp, '*Bracton*, the Year Books', 180.
61 *Glanvill*, 7.1, 74.
62 See R. M. Fraher, 'Conviction according to conscience: the medieval jurists' debate concerning judicial discretion and the law of proof', *Law and History Review* 7 (1989), 28.
63 S. L. Waugh, 'Reluctant knights and jurors: respites, exemptions and obligations in the reign of Henry III', *Speculum* 50 (1983), 937–86.
64 *Ibid.*, 981.
65 Cf. A. Spitzer, 'The legal careers of Thomas of Weyland and Gilbert of Thorton', *Journal of Legal History* 6 (1985), 62–83.
66 S. Mooers Christelow, 'The royal love in Anglo-Norman England: fiscal or courtly concept?', *Haskins Society Journal* 8 (1996), 31–2.
67 Cf. D. Carpenter, 'Justice and jurisdiction under King John and King Henry III', in D. Carpenter, *The Reign of Henry III* (London, 1996), 24–5.
68 M. T. Clanchy, 'Magna Carta and the common pleas', in Henry Mayr-Harting and R. I. Moore (eds), *Studies in Medieval History Presented to R. H. C. Davis* (London, 1985), 219–32.
69 Carpenter, 'Justice and jurisdiction', 43.
70 C. Carpenter, 'Law, justice and landowners in late medieval England', *Law and History Review* 1 (1983), 213.
71 There is no definitive list of these crimes, but see the comments in *LHP*, 13.1, 116; H. Summerson, 'Attitudes to capital punishment in England, 1200–1350', *Thirteenth Century England* 8 (2001), 123–33.
72 *Glanvill*, 176–7.
73 *LHP*, 116, 108. For a fuller discussion, see C. Warren Hollister, 'Royal acts of mutilation: the case against Henry I', *Albion* 10:4 (1978), 330–40.
74 J. G. Bellamy, *The Criminal Trial in Later Medieval England: Felony before the Courts from Edward I to the Sixteenth Century* (Toronto, 1998), 13.
75 For example, J. B. Post, 'Some limitations of the medieval peace rolls', *Journal of the Society of Archivists* 4:8 (1973), 633–9.
76 A. Musson, *Public Order and Law Enforcement: The Local Administration of Criminal Justice 1294–1350* (Woodbridge, 1996), 209.
77 Cf. A. H. Hershey, 'Justice and bureaucracy: the English royal writ', *English Historical Review* 113 (1998), 824–51
78 Hurnard, *Pardon*, 19.

The problem with mercy: the courts

79 J. P. Collas, *Yearbooks of Edward II: Hilary and Part of Easter Terms 1319* (London, 1953), xxv–xxxi.
80 'Rogerus de Steinton captus fuit eo quod ipse jactando quendem lapidem per infortunium occidit quondam garciam. Et testatum est quod non per feloniam. Et monstratum fuit hoc domino Regi et dominus Rex motus misericordia perdonavit ei mortem. Et ideo deliberetur.' *Select Pleas of the Crown*, vol. 1, A.D. 1200–1225, ed. F. W. Maitland (London, 1888), case 114, 67.
81 'Rogerus de Prestehop occidit Johannem de Patinton. Et Rogerus venit et profert literas J. Regis patentes in quibus continetur quod ipse perdonavit ei mortem ejusdem Johannis unde Juliana uxor ejusdem Johannis et Herebertus frater ejus eum appellaverunt, under vult quod firmam pacem inde habeat, ita quod stet recto si quis versus eum loqui. Voluerit et in hujus rei etc. Et quia nullus sequitur versus eum, eat. Inde sine die et quietus quantum ad dominum Regem pertinent. Et sciendum quod non fuit utlagatus.' *Ibid.*, case 171, 112.
82 The other possibility is of course that 'King John' is an error, and the scribe has confused the initial of the ruler with the initial of the victim in the case, and the record ought to read 'H. Regis'. Even if this is the case, the point about investment in pardon in advance of a possible case being brought at eyre still stands.
83 Turner, 'Reputation of royal judges', 313.
84 Turner, 'Richard Barre and Michael Belet', 195.
85 *Ibid.*

4

Twelfth-century models of justice and mercy

The role of judicial *exempla*

Where, then, did a twelfth-century judge turn to understand what justice looked like? How might the multiplicity of arguments addressed to those who sat in judgment be boiled down to provide some form of practical guidance? Central to the argument of this book is that one way of resolving the competing claims of justice and mercy was to emulate the most eminent historical judges. Twelfth-century judges had the history of their illustrious and distinguished predecessors to fall back on – a history of judgment and judicial biographies that stretched all the way back to the books of the Old Testament. Those judges too had made their own determinations when faced with a choice between just and merciful courses of action. If, for example, a judge confronted with the tricky job of punishing a faithless subordinate could see in his own situation a parallel with the struggle faced by Moses, he might then begin to understand how to punish both virtuously and justly. This chapter seeks to trace out those judicial *exempla*, derived from both scripture and classical texts. It outlines the most commonly invoked examples of good and bad judges – judgments to imitate and judgments to shun. It does not profess to cover all those *exempla*,[1] but to provide an account of some of the most frequently invoked, and those most fundamental to arguments about judicial conduct.

Here I assemble some of the 'building blocks' of judicial thought. Not all the writers encountered in subsequent chapters were scholastically trained (though many were); certainly not all those for whom they were writing were conversant with the finer points of scholastic arguments examined in Chapter 2. But judicial *exempla* represented one way of demonstrating how reflecting on the requirements of mercy and justice had informed the

Twelfth-century models of justice and mercy

behaviour of the virtuous and the wise in difficult cases. One does not, in any case, need to labour the point: *exempla* were a touchstone of medieval thought, a means of structuring argument, fundamental to thought and expression. As they are presented in this chapter – culled from letters, treatises and particular arguments, shorn of their context and collected together – they may seem platitudinous, even dull. But to understand these *exempla* is to understand the way in which these conflicts of justice and mercy could be thought through; a vital link between the intellectual argument between the two principles and how they were resolved in practice. In the way in which these judicial *exempla* were drawn upon and deployed, one might think of them by analogy with the idea of jazz standard in the world of music: familiar and easily recognised tunes, part of the repertoire of every player (of which there was no definitive list, but a broad understanding about what made up the core texts). While the fundamentals of the song (its tune, its meaning) might not change, its tempo, timbre and ornaments could be adapted to suit a particular setting or player.

Pre-eminent among all judges was Christ, who would ultimately sit in judgment on all. But Christ's example was not necessarily instructive: that judgment was yet to come, and belonged to an entirely different and peculiarly specific set of circumstances. It was, too, a judgment beyond understanding – beyond the conviction that it would be both just and merciful. It was the 'historical' books of scripture and works of classical history which offered more practical models for judges and those who would advise judges. It was, most particularly, the historical books of the Old Testament which provided judicial models. Looking at Old Testament judges also required an examination of the justice of the Old Law. How could Moses be considered a compelling judicial example when so many of the laws observed by the ancient Israelites had now been abrogated by the coming of Christ?

Most commentators agreed that there was a fundamental difference in the 'spirit' of the two testaments. The Old Testament, particularly in the precepts of Deuteronomy and Leviticus, appeared to take a much more severe attitude to those who transgressed the law than the gentle Christ. The contrast occupied the minds of twelfth- and thirteenth-century exegetes. On one hand, Christ had come to fulfil the Old Law, not abolish it (Matthew v.17: 'nolite putare quoniam veni solvere legem aut prophetas: non veni solvere, sed adimplere'); on the other, he had denounced the principle of *lex talionis* (Matthew v.38). Theologians went some way towards resolving the problem by examining the specific provisions of the Old Law – explaining, for example, that its various dietary prohibitions were appropriate to their time and context; that certain severe punishments for transgressors of those laws represented a necessary imposition given the moral infirmity of the Israelites of that period.[2] But even while the twelfth century explored the difference between legal provisions, it preserved the utility and value of the examples of judgment in the Old Testament.

Stephen Langton's gloss on Deuteronomy (c.1187),[3] for example, presented the case for the two laws as contrasting but complementary: though markedly different in legal practice, both were intended in the same spirit. Langton explains that where the Old Law concerns itself with things *extrinseca*, the New pertains to those *intrinseca*; the Old with behaviour *in acte*, the New *in intentio*.[4] The Old Law is consummated in the gospel and any difference between the two is therefore apparent rather than substantive. Likewise, in another late twelfth-century commentary, possibly also attributable to Stephen Langton, the Sermon on the Mount is tied to the principle of *lex talionis*.[5] Rather than argue that Christ abolished the practice of returning injury for injury, Langton explains that *lex talionis* is entirely consonant with *lex evangelica*, because both laws impose a degree of restraint on humankind. The principle of 'an eye for an eye' allows the injured party to pay back only as much punishment as they have received: it does not permit actions which are motivated by revenge, but only permits the pursuit of justice.[6]

Robert Grosseteste developed Langton's line of thought even further, by using his work on the Ten Commandments, *De decem mandatis* (composed in the late 1220s or early 1230s), to consider the pastoral relevance of Old Testament laws.[7] The utility of the commandments themselves, he argued, was enduring, and those ten principles of behaviour were entirely congruent with New Testament message of love towards God and one's neighbour. But Grosseteste also considers other less sympathetic principles of the Old Law. He observes that the exegete will have problems in expounding the principle, given at Exodus xx.5, that the sins of parents will be visited upon their children ('I, the Lord your God, am a jealous God, punishing the children for the sin of the parents to the third and fourth generation of those who hate me').[8] For Grosseteste, this is a difficult passage on a number of levels. It ostensibly contracts other Old Testament affirmations that sons will not share the guilt of their fathers (Ezekiel xviii.20). Moreover, he continues, it seems downright unmerciful. Indeed, Grosseteste notes, how can one be comfortable with a divinely given law which seems more punitive even than the laws of pagan Rome? Cicero had noted that the Roman state would never think of condemning a child for the transgressions of a father or grandfather.[9] Grosseteste accordingly posits two possible solutions for

Twelfth-century models of justice and mercy

resolving the question of inter-generational punishment: either the exegete must accept that God's punishments are inflicted righteously, and sentences imposed upon children on behalf of their parents are in some way just, according to a divine plan which cannot be comprehended. Alternatively, the exegete must interpret the passage allegorically, understanding that the term 'sons' here does not refer to natural children of the flesh, but sons who imitate their 'fathers in sin'. In the case of the latter, Grosseteste explains, such punishment can hardly be said to be unjust: indeed, it is a merciful act as it aims to turn the souls of the wicked away from sin. That last comment is worth pausing at – Grosseteste found mercy even within the apparent harshness of the Old Law.

Langton and Grosseteste serve to demonstrate that theologians thought long and hard about how the concept of justice was shaped by the relationship between the testaments. They were not prepared to write off the justice of the Old Testament as an anachronism abrogated by the coming of Christ: quite the contrary – they argued that it contained within it sound judicial principles and the kernel of the New Law. When it came to giving examples of judicial principles and judicial decision-making it was the Old Testament to which authors certainly turned. Other than, perhaps, the incident concerning Christ and the woman caught in adultery – which was regarded as an example of a refusal to pass sentence – the New Testament contained very little in the way of judicial *exempla*. Indeed, it presented its own hurdles for the exegete, such as explaining why 'judge not lest you be judged' (Matthew vii.1) was not to be interpreted as a general injunction against all forms of judgment in human courts.[10] The Old Testament, by contrast, particularly the Books of Kings, presented many instances of royal and priestly judges, and instructive lessons which could be readily adapted for a *speculum principis* or for a sermon.

The value of the Old Testament for judicial guidance is demonstrated most clearly in Ralph Niger's commentary on Kings, *Moralia in libros Regum* (composed between 1179 and 1189).[11] The work exists in only a single copy, in two volumes, today held at Lincoln Cathedral library. Ralph has gained some small measure of historiographical fame for his complaints of the avarice and ambition of contemporary civil lawyers.[12] However, the manuscript of the *Moralia* reveals a more careful reading than such a potential characterisation might suggest; in particular it provides a sophisticated demonstration of how judicial principles could be extract from scriptural histories. Ralph Niger was well placed and well qualified to perform exactly this role: in Paris he had studied law under the distinguished canonist Gerard Pucelle,[13] as well as theology, most likely under the tutelage of John of Salisbury. The marriage of Ralph's theological and legal erudition is plainly apparent. The introduction to his moralising reading of Kings explicitly pins the changes in the ruling dynasties of Israel to the judicial failings of their leaders.[14] It was for judicial failures that the priest Heli was replaced by Samuel; it was for the same mistake that David was given Saul's throne. Ralph's commentary abounds with judicial advice which he drew from these histories, and on the basis of which he expresses warnings against those judges who, like Absalom, forget the value of discipline,[15] or who allow their justice to be corrupted,[16] as well as against the danger of excessive *indulgentia* and incautious dispensations from the law.

Ralph Niger's approach to the Book of Kings serves as a useful paradigm for understanding attitudes of twelfth- and thirteenth-century exegetes, whose perceptions of contemporary judicial politics and morality were shaped by *exempla* drawn from scriptural histories. These examples were much more than stock figures which could be invoked to embellish an argument: they warned medieval readers of timeless and unchanging obstacles which imperilled righteous judgment. These scriptural *exempla* provided a familiar frame around which contemporary narratives of praiseworthy or damnable acts of judgment might be constructed. They formed historical case studies which supplied biblical precedents and typologies for the interpretation of more recent and contemporary history.[17] The invocation of such typologies of judges, of course, dates back much further than the twelfth century: such a tradition was old even by the time that the eighth-century Carolingian bishop Theodulf of Orléans composed his poetic satire *Contra iudices*, inveighing against 'unchristian' judicial corruption.[18] But the change in legal context of the twelfth century – the increasing importance of law both to rulers and those who were ruled – imbued those *exempla* with greater relevance. Scripture, as Ralph Niger noted, provided case studies of how a single instance of bad judgment might imperil the stability of an entire kingdom. Accordingly, it provided very practical advice for those judges who wanted to preserve their thrones or offices. It was a lesson not lost on contemporaries.

Biblical *exempla*

Heli and Phinehas: 1 Kings ii (1 Samuel ii) and Numbers xxv.1–9

The judgments of Heli (or Eli) and Phinehas were often treated as a complementary pair in moral treatises: Heli illustrated the dangers of excessive mercy, Phinehas the (occasional) necessity for severe judgment. Heli, the high priest of Israel, had forfeited his right, and the right of his descendants, to the hereditary priesthood when he failed in his judicial office. Instead, that priesthood was subsequently transferred to the righteous judge Samuel. Heli offended by failing adequately to rebuke his sons, who contemptuously stole the sacrifices offered to the Lord: Heli's correction was too feeble and lenient to compel a change in their behaviour.[19] Phinehas, too, had been a high priest of Israel during the exile: Numbers recounted how Phinehas had discovered that one of the Israelites had brought a Midianite woman into the camp in order to fornicate with her. On learning of this, Phinehas took immediate action, lancing the genitals of the man and the belly of the woman in order to prevent the spread of sinful and idolatrous Midianite practices among the Israelites. For this, the Lord bestowed an everlasting, hereditary priesthood on Phinehas and his descendants. The two stories represented the pairing of laxity and rigour; ineffective and praiseworthy correction.

The laudable nature of Phinehas's action had been discussed by Augustine in his vast work of commentary and reflection on the Book of Psalms, *Enarrationes in Psalmos*, an extremely widely disseminated work in twelfth-century England.[20] Here Augustine set out the argument which many later medieval interpreters faithfully followed: Phinehas's actions were praiseworthy because in striking one man, he had saved the souls of the whole people, prevented sin spreading among them and avoided much greater destruction.[21] Phinehas thus became a byword for judicial vigilance. Augustine had noted that, even if his judgment seemed severe, Phinehas's actions were not wrong because they had been motivated by the desire to avoid damnation. Nor, Augustine added, would such rectitude for justice be inappropriate even under the new dispensation. Peter the Chanter read the passage in the same way, and went on to approve of Phinehas as the model judge: his willingness to slay even a member of his own tribe demonstrated Phinehas's adherence to that most important of judicial principles – that a judge show no respect for persons.[22] When it came to judging both the poor and the wealthy, the well regarded and the suspect, impartiality was a fundamental standard of judicial conduct. This Peter found in Mosaic law, expressed in Deuteronomy i.17, 'neither shall you respect anyone's person'.[23] Robert Grosseteste gave further support to Phinehas as the model judge, explaining that his anger at the sinful Israelites was that rare example of anger motivated by love, virtuous anger: by directing punishment at the sinning individual, Phinehas had turned away the anger of the Lord from all.[24] Phinehas represented the scriptural demonstration of the judicial maxim that one should have no respect for persons but judge only according to the offence.

Twelfth-century authors wrought the history of Heli into an example to complement that of Phinehas. The moral of the biblical episode was provided in the interpretation of Rabanus Maurus in his *Commentary on Kings* (834), a text which itself drew on the *Jewish Antiquities* of Josephus. Heli had been damned because his *lenitas et mansuetudo* had prevented him from correcting sin.[25] Heli's behaviour in sparing his sons demonstrated the dangers of excessive leniency motivated by personal affection – that is, by excessive regard for persons. In turn, this touched upon questions about the role of the judge in the protection of the community. For Ralph Niger, Heli's actions were a demonstration of the failings of a judge who puts his personal reputation above the punishment of crime. Heli was motivated to avoid punishing his sons because he feared the shame it would bring him were he to acknowledge their wicked behaviour (*ac si potius vitanda esset fama quam peccatum*). As a result, Ralph explained, those who deserved to be whipped (*meruerant flagellari*) were merely lightly rebuked (*leviter castigari*).[26] The broader, practical, political dimensions of this scriptural *exemplum* became apparent when the tale was followed to its conclusion: Heli's failure to punish his sons had brought down divine punishment on Israel, causing the Israelites to be defeated in battle and to lose the Ark of the Covenant (1 Kings iv). Peter the Chanter observed that, by not punishing his sons, Heli had ensured that the *communitas* would suffer.[27] This was intended as a salutary reminder to the judge that the sentences he handed down had much wider political and social ramifications. John of Salisbury transformed this into a more unambiguously political dictum in *Policraticus*, by drawing a comparison between Heli and the Roman republican consul Brutus. John recounted that Brutus, after the expulsion of the kings from Rome, had discovered that his sons were plotting a coup to reinstitute royal government. This was an offence against the state, and, in keeping with the law, Brutus commanded that they be beaten and subsequently decapitated. John explains that Brutus, unlike Heli, realised that, in this context, paternal mercy or leniency would be deleterious to the community. John notes that, while this action may seem objectionable, Brutus's actions were in fact praiseworthy and to be approved of by Christian readers, for Brutus had chosen to put the welfare of the great mass of the people above that of his own children.[28] The cases of Heli and Phinehas underlined the links between right and proper judgment and the security of the realm itself. These *exempla* were proof of the practicality of scriptural instruction for judges. Not only do corrupt or partial judges fail: their nations fail around them too.

Samuel: 1 Kings vii (1 Samuel vii)

Even more clearly than the cases of Heli and Phinehas, the *exemplum* of the Israelite judge Samuel showed quite how closely English authors understood their systems of justice to be informed by biblical histories. Samuel presented a straightforward story of judgment done well. Indeed, Samuel's good behaviour as a judge was precisely what distinguished him from his immediate predecessor as high priest and judge of Israel, Heli. The most revealing example of this particular connection of biblical history to contemporary reality is found in John of Salisbury's *Policraticus*. John takes the description of Samuel, touring the provinces of Israel for the purposes of administering justice (1 Kings vii.15–17), and equates this judicial activity with the work of itinerant English circuit judges at the time of writing (1159). These justices-in-eyre were a relatively recent innovation in England: possibly introduced under Henry I, they had only been revived – and the institution revivified – under Henry II.[29] Samuel, like his Angevin counterparts, held an 'inquest' through which any failures of his judgment could be complained of and righted (1 Kings xii).[30] John fits Samuel into a model of Angevin judicial innovations: however, he laments that modern justices fail to emulate Samuel's lofty standards. John manipulates the biblical figure to provide both a model and a critique of contemporary legal standards. Strikingly, John's pupil (or possibly fellow student) in Paris, Ralph Niger, also praised Samuel's peregrinations as the model of good judicial practice. Samuel's dedication to doing justice by moving around provinces of Israel could be read literally, as an example of good service, as John had done. When read allegorically, however, Ralph explained that they also demonstrated Samuel's moral fitness for judicial service. Ralph's *Moralia in libros Regum* notes that Samuel's circuits of Israel as a judge prefigured his ascent to heaven.[31]

In Samuel, then, theologians found an image of excellent human judgment, a judge who avoided corruption and kept himself open to the people. Moreover, Samuel's relevance as a judicial model applied across all types of law. Thus, while John of Salisbury hoped that Angevin princes would aspire to emulation of Samuel, Robert Grosseteste saw in him a model for *episcopal* justice and conduct, explaining that, just as Samuel had toured Israel, so a bishop ought to inspect his diocese, making a circuit of it at least once a year.[32]

Susannah and the woman caught in adultery: Daniel xiii and John viii

While the *exempla* of Heli and Phinehas could be adduced to argue for strict punishment of sinners, a number of counter-examples could be deployed when medieval authors wanted to argue in favour of mercy. These included further material from the Books of Kings, such as, for example, David's choice to spare Saul (1 Kings xxiv) when he had his enemy at his mercy.[33] The most significant and popular *exempla* employed in praise of mercy, however, were Daniel's defence of Susannah and Christ's treatment of the woman caught in adultery. These two scriptural pericopes were often joined together to form a pair which emphasised the shared value of mercy, a value which transcended the apparent difference in spirit between the two testaments in which the *exempla* occurred.

Daniel xiii describes how the virtuous Susannah is falsely accused of concupiscence by two wicked elders. Susannah is to be put to death on this charge until Daniel steps forward and proves that her accusers have borne false witness. This pericope was sometimes interpreted as providing a model of a bishop's duty to assist the falsely accused. Thomas of Chobham, for example, used it to demonstrate how 'truth' (*veritas*) was an integral part of justice: it was only by speaking the truth that Daniel had challenged the unjust proceedings of a corrupt judicial process.[34] The Angevin courtier and author Walter Map, meanwhile, illustrated how such an *exemplum* had contemporary relevance by recounting the tale of how an untrue allegation of adultery at the contemporary Portuguese court had resulted in the execution of a knight and the beating to death of the pregnant queen, a second Susannah. No just man, no new Daniel, Walter Map lamented, had stepped forward to challenge the wickedness of lying counsellors.[35] More generally, however, Susannah's fate was taken to denote judicial prudence: Walter Daniel describes the Cistercian abbot Aelred of Rievaulx as a 'second Daniel' (*alterius Danielis*), on the grounds that he was able to easily disentangle the truth in cases which others found particularly hard to judge.[36]

The most common twelfth-century approach to Daniel xiii, however, was to pair the text with John viii, in order to open up a discussion of the value of mercy. John viii.1–11 presents the pericope of the woman caught in adultery, whom the Pharisees presented to Jesus, demanding that he pass sentence upon her. The law required her to be stoned to death, but Christ refused, arguing that only a sinless individual was entitled to judge the woman. The crucial line here was Christ's comment to the woman that she should 'go and sin no more (*vade, et iam amplius noli peccare*)': rather than condemning her, Christ simply instructed the adulteress to alter her behaviour. This was the interpretation of Augustine, who had explained that rather than sentencing her to death, Christ granted the woman an opportunity to correct her sins in the present life.[37] Augustine's commentary, however, did not explicitly counsel the human judge to follow the precedent of Christ: it was rather more concerned with describing how the incident revealed the perfect balance of *mansuetudo* and *misericordia* with *iustitia* and *veritas* in the person of Christ.[38] It was only later medieval commentators who worked the passage into an admonition to earthly judges. The woman caught in adultery and Susannah had long been connected in theological thought, as both passages formed the readings in the Roman rite for the third Sunday before Lent.[39] Rupert of Deutz (writing c.1112) explained the basis of the pairing: one represented a woman unjustly condemned for a crime she had not committed, the other a woman justly condemned, but both of them had been shown mercy.[40] As a result, the pericope was read by theologians and moralists as an admonition to clemency. For Thomas of Chobham in his guide for confessors and Gerald of Wales in his *speculum principis*, John viii argued the need for forgiveness, mercy allowing dispensation from the strictures of the rigid written law.[41]

John viii, however, was not solely a source of moral guidance for the judge. The passage was extensively scrutinised for the procedural guidance it could provide. Given the twelfth-century concern for stipulating the minutiae of legal procedure, it is not surprising that canon and Roman lawyers turned to scripture as a basis for legal proofs. This borrowing, however, serves once again to underscore the concrete connection between exegesis and judicial reality. Civil lawyers following Martinus Gosia (d. c.1166), one of the 'Four Doctors' of the Roman law schools at Bologna,[42] had used the pericope to illustrate the Roman principle of 'iudex secundum allegata, non secundum conscientiam iudicat' – that a judge should convict only according to the evidence presented to him by witnesses, not according to his private knowledge of the crime.[43] Rather than concentrating on Christ's injunction that the adulteress 'go and sin no more', this interpretation considered the questions which preceded Christ's 'judgment' of the woman: 'where are your accusers? Has no one condemned you? (*ubi sunt qui te accusabant? Nemo te condemnavit?*)'. Christ's words here indicated the fundamental agreement between Roman legal and scriptural precedent: without an accuser, no crime could be prosecuted.[44] Lawyers drew on John viii because it showed Christ refusing to judge without witnesses to the crime. The pericope was read as a comment on procedure: without witnesses, any judgment risked a false verdict, and this would endanger the soul of the judge.

Justice and mercy

Moses's intercession: Exodus xxxii.32

Perhaps the most frequently invoked biblical *exemplum* of judgment was Moses's intercession for the Israelites. This could – rather paradoxically – be read both as an argument for severity and as an argument for mercy. Exodus xxxii describes how the Israelites – in Moses's absence – constructed a statue of a golden calf and idolatrously begin worshipping it. Moses's response, on returning to them, was twofold. Discovering their idolatry, he commanded that 3,000 Israelites be slaughtered. It was this passage which might be read as Moses's punitive and severe judgment on sin, taking immediate action against those who transgressed.[45] But it was Moses's subsequent action which generated rather more interest, for following the slaughter he approached God, asking for forgiveness for the people – an act of intercession. Moses pleaded with the Lord, 'either forgive them this sin or delete me from the book which you have written' (*aut dimitte eis hanc noxam, aut si non facis, dele me de libro tuo quem scripsisti*). Twelfth-century commentators (in keeping with patristic and earlier medieval tradition) understood from this passage that Moses was willing to sacrifice his own salvation – his place 'in the book which you have written', namely, the 'Book of Life' – in order to secure the salvation of the Israelites.

This offer to exchange his own salvation for that of his people was frequently cited in works praising Moses as the admirable embodiment of a merciful ruler.[46] Twelfth-century preachers utilised the figure of Moses to praise the value of gentleness.[47] While the terms gentle (*mansuetus*), mild (*mitis*), merciful (*misericors*) and clement (*clemens*) had subtly different semantic connotations in scholastic *summae* on the virtues, they were very closely connected, if not interchangeable. Moses was described in the Book of Numbers as 'mitissimus', the most merciful man on the Earth: this mercy was also singled out for praise in the *Decretum*.[48] In the context of preaching, it followed that *mitis* Moses would very likely also be *misericors*. These were virtues, which, in a judicial or courtly context, led the judge to punish an offender less than was deserved, an act which demonstrated judicial virtue. An example of how these themes could be joined together is given in Thomas of Chobham's *Summa de arte praedicandi* (c.1216–22); a text compiled to assist priests in preparing sermons. Assembling a list of *exempla* which a preacher might employ when exhorting an audience to the virtue of temperance, Thomas considers one embodiment of that virtue, he who is 'mansuetus' in punishment. Moses provides the biblical precedent for this behaviour. Thomas then argues that Moses's gentleness towards the Israelites (he does not tie this quality to any specific incident) embodies the same virtue which is so highly praised in Seneca's *De clementia*, i.e. clemency. Thomas's point is a traditional one: there is no useful Roman knowledge which cannot also be found in the Bible. By presenting the example of Moses, Thomas strives to make the point that all that classical philosophy had said in praise of mercy was fundamentally in agreement with scripture.

John of Salisbury, in particular, was interested in what Exodus xxxii could reveal about the moral duties of rulership.[49] Throughout *Policraticus*, John emphasises that justice is the primary duty of a king.[50] He develops this point by arguing that justice has two essential aspects: to subject the people to law, and to subject oneself to divine law and the command of God. To demonstrate that this second command is just as vital as the first, John draws out the example of the notoriously wicked Old Testament ruler Saul. Saul was admonished by God to destroy an enemy people, the Amalekites; but he spared Agag, their king (1 Kings xv). When the prophet Samuel rebuked Saul for failing to carry out the command of God, Saul defended himself by claiming that the people had forced him to spare Agag. It is in this last action, John asserts, that Saul's sin and the instructive message of scripture is really to be found: Saul was a prince who blamed his people for his own transgression, condemning them for his own failure to carry out God's command. It is as a positive counter-example to Saul that John discusses Moses, for it was Moses who, when God's wrath was kindled against the Israelites, pleaded that they be spared. Moses was an admirable leader because he did not seek glory for himself, but put the Israelites first in everything, since 'even to his own cost he [Moses] preferred to serve the glory of God and the deliverance of the people whom he led'.[51]

Moses provided fertile ground for those who wished to discuss judges and judgment, even aside from his actions as an intercessor. He might also be invoked as a model of good judicial organisation – in this sense he could be employed in much the same way as the figure of Samuel. As leader of Israel, Moses had appointed judges under him (Exodus xxxii.20, Numbers xvi.12) to assist him with the work of judgment, allotting to them the cases which he was unable to hear. The same passages attested to the success of Moses judicial arrangements: he maintained his capacity to judge the people and settle cases (in much the same way as Samuel might be seen as the forerunner of itinerant justices).[52]

As I have discussed elsewhere,[53] Exodus xxxii was not a straightforward text: a focus on the metaphysics of the act of intercession itself could produce a much more complex and potentially subversive reading of scripture. In certain scholastic *quaestiones*, masters raised questions about the rectitude of Moses's ultimatum to God ('save them or delete me'), and discussed whether such a request was truly legitimate. This, however, represented a small subset of those handling this passage. In the context of the texts discussed here, Moses's intercessory actions are almost always invoked and quoted approvingly, evidence of a ruler's tender care towards an errant people.

Missing exempla: the prodigal son (Luke xv.11–32) and the penitent thief (Luke xxiii.43)

It is worth remarking on two biblical cases of pardon and forgiveness which (especially as they might be those most familiar to twenty-first-century readers) feature relatively *infrequently* in twelfth-century texts about judicial choices. These are two examples from the New Testament – specifically, the Gospel of Luke – the prodigal son and the penitent thief. The first (a parable) describes a younger son who wastes his inheritance and returns home as a beggar, but is received by his father and restored to his former position. When it was invoked, it stood as an admirable example of paternal *lenitas*.[54] The penitent thief of the gospel is the individual crucified alongside Christ, who confesses that he is justly condemned for his crime, but hopes that Christ will remember him once he is returned to his kingdom, whereupon Christ promises the thief that 'today you will be with me in Paradise' (*hodie mecum eris in paradiso*). The thief is occasionally, but not often, invoked in twelfth-century texts about judgment.[55]

These were two compelling examples of forgiveness – why did they not play a more central role? In the case of the penitent thief, it may simply be that Christ offering the promise of paradise was not considered a particularly suitable model for earthly judges (simply put, it was not easily translatable). More fundamentally, however, this should be considered a matter of focus. The centre of both these *exempla* is not the judge but the recipient of pardon. As such, they furnish limited scope for explaining the basis of the mercy extended to offenders. To twelfth-century authors interested in exploring the decision-making and ethical conduct of judges, the qualities of the pardon seeker were secondary. Mercy operated on a reciprocal formula, which focused the spotlight on the judge, not the people he judged: the worst consequence of a bad judgment is not the suffering of the offender, but the damage that the judge does to his own soul.

Classical *exempla*

The 'Roman' contribution to twelfth-century debates on justice was more than purely legal. While Roman law furnished a definition of *iustitia* as a matter of the precise repayment of due, classical texts also offered much material which could be harnessed to explore the nature of judgment. In this sense, the way in which classical authors defined the philosophical idea of clementia was just as influential as Roman law definitions of iustitia. The twelfth century accordingly witnessed a renewed engagement with both the legal and the philosophical strands of Roman thought. Roman texts provided models for justice and virtuous judicial behaviour. The *Topographia Hibernica* of Gerald of Wales recorded that Henry II carried a copy of the Roman moralist Seneca's *De clementia* with him when travelling around his territories (though whether Gerald inserted this detail to praise Henry or ironically to indict his inclement failings is an open question).[56] As such, the behaviour of Roman rulers was held up as a mirror to contemporary princes – and the examples of wicked or malicious Roman justice were powerful and compelling.[57] Orderic Vitalis noted that the cruelty which the malevolent Robert of Bellême inflicted on his prisoners exceeded even that of the most notorious Roman persecutors of Christians – Nero, Decius and Domitian – men lacking all humanity and mercy (*humana ratione et clementia*).[58]

Moreover, classical thought on the relative advantages of justice and mercy as judicial strategies is as ambivalent as the 'Christian' tradition, and could provide support for both approaches. Twelfth- and thirteenth-century authors were well aware of conflicting classical attitudes towards judicial punishment, and exploited them in the composition of histories and mirrors for princes. The set-piece passage which best sets out the ambiguities even in 'Roman' approaches to justice derives from Sallust. The works of Sallust experienced a renewed popularity in the eleventh and twelfth centuries, his literary style considered equal to that of Cicero.[59] The twelfth century represents the medieval high-water mark for the production and copying of Sallustian manuscripts.[60] Sallust's works formed the basis of the school curriculum in grammar and rhetoric, studied before one went on to any form of higher learning. As such, anyone who was literate (in the true Latinate sense of that term) would have known some Sallust.[61]

Judicial and moralising attention focused on parts of Sallust's *Bellum Catilinae*, the work which described the conspiracy, led by Catiline, to bring civil war to Rome. Narrating the conspiracy and its subsequent failure, Sallust had described a debate in the Roman senate in which the leaders of Rome discussed how those citizens who had been exposed as partisans of Catiline ought to be punished and the degree of punishment that would be appropriate to their crimes. In Sallust's account, the debate is dominated by two towering figures of Roman history – Julius Caesar and Marcus Porcius Cato – who, respectively, present the cases for leniency and severe treatment of the prisoners. It is Julius Caesar, Sallust's own patron, who is first to speak: he argues against imposing a penalty of death on the conspirators, urging that their goods be confiscated and their bodies imprisoned, but that their lives be spared. Caesar's argument does not turn on the worthiness of the prisoners to be pardoned, but instead makes the point that severe sentencing reflects badly on those who impose it. Although the Senate wields the authority to order executions, it is both more noble and more virtuous that it refrain from exercising that power:

> If the humble, who pass their lives in obscurity, commit any offence through anger, it is known to few; their fame and fortune are alike. But the actions of those who hold great power, and pass their lives in a lofty station, are known to all the world. So it comes to pass that in the highest position theirs is the least freedom of action. There neither partiality nor dislike is in place, and anger least of all; for what in others is called wrath, this in a ruler is term insolence and cruelty.[62]

This is a persuasive piece of deliberative oratory and makes at least implicit appeal to the conceptual foundation of *clementia* – the principle that the most powerful are most distinguished when they restrain themselves from making full use of their power.

In Sallust's account, Caesar's oration is followed and countered by the speech of Marcus Porcius Cato, also known as Cato the Younger, or Cato of Utica, the voice of senatorial Stoicism. Cato's speech presents a perspective entirely opposed to that of Caesar: he implores the Senate to put the conspirators to death. Any other course of action, Cato warns, would fatally weaken Rome: should the men be allowed to escape, they would only join the enemy forces. Indeed, in Cato's eyes, Caesar's merciful disposition and willingness to pardon the guilty – his horror of shedding blood – symbolises how decadent, effete and weak Rome has become, and he asserts that success and security is obtained only through vigilance and action.[63] Cato rejects the possibility of exiling or imprisoning the conspirators and believes that nothing other than capital punishment will secure Rome against her enemies:

> Catiline with his army is at our throats; other foes are within our walls, aye, in the very heart of Rome ... therefore the more need of haste ... [They] have confessed that they have planned murder, arson and other fearful and cruel crimes against their fellow citizens and their country, let those who have confessed be treated as though they had been caught red-handed in capital offences, and be punished after the manner of our forefathers.[64]

Twelfth-century models of justice and mercy

In Sallust's history, it is Cato who ultimately persuades the senate: having heard and weighed both arguments, the conspirators are swiftly executed in order to ensure the safety of the *res publica*. The conclusion, however, is almost irrelevant to the later medieval history of this debate: what is significant is that Sallust had 'staged' such an argument, a set-piece conflict between principles of *clementia* and *misericordia* on one hand and *iustitia* and *severitas* on the other, in which the strengths of both positions could be seen. The debate concluded with a paragraph which compared the conflicting temperaments of Julius Caesar and Cato, while making it clear that both were equal in virtue:

> In birth, then, in years and in eloquence, they were about equal; in greatness of soul they were evenly matched, and likewise in renown, although the renown of each was different. Caesar was held great because of his benefactions and lavish generosity, Cato for the uprightness of his life. The former became famous for his gentleness and compassion, the austerity of the latter had brought him prestige. Caesar gained glory by giving, helping and forgiving; Cato by never stooping to bribery. One was a refuge for the unfortunate, the other a scourge for the wicked. The good nature of the one was applauded, the steadfastness of the other. Finally, Caesar had schooled himself to work hard and sleep little, to devote himself to the welfare of his friends and neglect his own, to refuse nothing which was worth the giving. He longed for great power, an army, a new war to give scope for his brilliant merit. Cato, on the contrary, cultivated self-control, propriety, but above all austerity. He did not vie with the rich in riches nor in intrigue with the intriguer, but with the active in good works, with the self-restrained in moderation, with the blameless in integrity.[65]

Sallust had thus never explicitly concluded in favour of either Caesar or Cato, but in praising both men's approaches to justice, he further polarised the conflict between their respective positions. This passage was well known to medieval authors, being reproduced in the *Florilegium Gallicum*, a mid-twelfth-century compilation of memorable and instructive extracts from classical authors, under the heading of 'De moribus Cesaris et Catonis mixtim'.[66] The *Florilegium* also provided long extracts from both the orations of Caesar and Cato, including those discussed here.[67] Twelfth-century authors capitalised on this Sallustian text, and it informed their readings of the conflict between mercy and justice. Caesar, embodying the virtue of *clementia*, had real courtly appeal in the twelfth century, in a nascent 'chivalric' culture.[68] *Clementia* should be understood as central to the chivalric codes and mores emerging during this period, according to which a lord behaves honourably on the battlefield by allowing high-status enemies to surrender without fear of execution.[69] *Clementia* was attendant on military prowess: only he who was victorious on the battlefield then had the ability to exhibit magnanimous mercy towards a conquered enemy, a feature typified in depictions of Julius Caesar. Thus the panegyrical work which praises William the Conqueror's victory in 1066, the *Gesta Guillelmi* of William of Poitiers, the Conqueror's chaplain, makes frequent comparison between the triumphant Norman duke and Julius Caesar, for the reason that both showed extraordinary mercy towards their subject peoples.[70] The Conqueror, like Caesar, was a mighty warrior, but he was most distinguished by his refusal to use excessive force and his lenient punishment of his defeated enemies. *Clementia* was a virtue particularly associated with high office: it was exercised only by those who had the power of life or death over condemned men. Ralph Diceto reported that Caesar's goodness (*bonitas*) was so great that having defeated men by arms, he conquered them a second time with his clemency.[71]

Secondly, in *clementia* lay an element of civility and sophistication: self-restraint was a challenge which the prince or lord set for himself, and, if he could manage it, a further proof of personal virtue. For that connection between power, nobility and mercy, twelfth-century authors looked to the Roman moralist Seneca. His treatise, *De clementia*, had been intended for the edification of the emperor Nero, and explained that clemency is the virtue which distinguishes the virtuous ruler from the tyrant.[72] This had also been the argument which Sallust placed in the mouth of Caesar: the *res publica* or ruler accustomed to delighting in harsh, punitive sentences may easily slip into lawlessness and tyranny.[73] *Clementia* is the most royal of virtues, because only he who has the power to inflict punishment also possesses the power to pardon.[74] Seneca's text draws on examples from Roman history and Stoic philosophy to present the case that clemency is both the mark of good rulership and a means of securing one's rule. Manuscript copies of *De clementia*, in addition to abbreviated versions and extracts, are well attested in northern Europe from the late eleventh century onwards: by the end of the twelfth it was a familiar text not only in France, but also England and Germany.[75] The classical formulation of *clementia* presented by Seneca could also be easily assimilated to the Christian virtue of mercy, *misericordia*.[76] Counsellors who saw it as their duty to reign in the violent power of kings appealed to both Caesar and Seneca to emphasise that mercy was an integral part of justice.

Sallust's juxtaposition of Caesar and Cato provided a means of conceptualising the conflict between justice and mercy, and formed the basis of several comparisons between the principles of merciful and strict justice.⁷⁷ The chronicler Rahewin of Freising, in his continuation of the *Gesta Frederici* of Otto of Freising, c.1158–60, exploited the comparison of one 'merciful', one 'severe' man, assigning the roles of Caesar and Cato to Duke Welf VI and Henry the Lion, respectively. The two are described as *diversis moribus*, one clement, one severe, yet both are endowed with virtue, and Rahewin does not suggest whether one is to be preferred to the other. Clemency pursues fame, but severity and *constantia* are more likely to bring peace to the land.⁷⁸ Among English authors, the contrast between the two men and two virtues was readily exploited in order to explore the problems faced by judges during a century of legal revolution. It was used twice, to different effect, in the writings of Gerald of Wales. Gerald first employs the contrast in a martial setting, in which his modern-day 'Caesar' and 'Cato' debate the merits of executing a group of captured Irish prisoners during the Angevin campaigns in Ireland in the early 1170s. Gerald essentially rewrites Sallust's *Bellum Catilinae* in his *Expugnatio Hibernica*, imagining a rhetorical debate between two leaders in Ireland after the victory of Angevin and Marcher forces at the Battle of Waterford. One knight, Gerald's relative, Raymond FitzGerald (sometimes known as Raymond le Gros), reiterates the words of Caesar, arguing that as conquerors, the Angevin forces ought to exercise mercy, for it is more noble to spare a life than to take it. Invoking the familiar tropes of classical *clementia*, he argues that to kill unarmed men would represent only cruelty and savagery.

> I would not by any means insist that we should spare our enemies. However, these are not our enemies, but fellow human beings; they are not rebels, but beaten and vanquished opponents. ... They are now in such a position that in their case there is scope for showing mercy, to give them a good example, rather than for displaying cruelty to torture them. ... So let that quality of compassion which is most deserving of praise be seen in us, and enable us, who have conquered everything else, to conquer our own anger and violent passions. For self-restraint and moderation usually quieten the head-strong emotions. ... Although Julius Caesar, for whose victories the world was not wide enough, had such unbounded power, the only man he ordered to be killed was Domitius. But he had already once previously granted him his life. In any case, his mercy increased his renown and did not stand in the way of his victories. What wicked, brutish barbarity when victory is not accompanied by compassion!⁷⁹

Yet, in turn, this oration is challenged by another soldier, Hervey de Montmaurice, who counsels – following the logic of Cato's argument – that to spare the lives of the conquered Irish would be to endanger Angevin

Justice and mercy

rule in Ireland. Conquest and mercy are, in his view, irreconcilable political choices:

> While peoples are still proud and rebellious they must be subdued by all possible means, and clemency must take a back seat. But when they have been subdued, when they are ready to be obedient, then and only then are they to be treated with all possible clemency. ... But Raymond, showing truly amazing compassion, is bent on increasing the number of our enemies by adding to it these men, as if this people were already conquered and the only quality we needed to display was mercy, or as if, because our enemies are very few in number, he cannot find any field wherein virtue may distinguish itself. But in fact the whole population of Ireland has joined in plotting our destruction, not without good reason.[80]

The subsequent part of Hervey's oration makes evident the significant of this choice between two different kinds of strategy, severe and merciful, emphasising that the two are entirely incompatible.

> We must choose one of two policies. Either we must vigorously pursue that end for which we have come here, and with the aid of our armed might and our valour subdue with a strong arm this rebellious people, casting aside all pretence of clemency; or, if we consider it right to favour acts of mercy as Raymond counsels, then we should turn our ships round and leave this people which so deserves our pity to enjoy their country and ancestral lands in peace.[81]

Enemies who are not totally subjugated will only rise again and seek to destroy their conquerors. Just as Cato had argued that the Roman senate should have no time for gentleness and compassion, Gerald's interlocutor, Hervey, speaks of the dangers of pity. As in the *Bellum Catilinae*, it is the arguments against mercy and in favour of 'national security' which win the day – and the conquered Irish are executed.[82] Gerald's sympathy here seems to lie with the argument for clemency, for he notes that it was 'shameful' that the Irish were executed in such a manner – shameful, no doubt, in part because the judicious counsel of his relative had been ignored. Underlining the classical dimensions of his account, Gerald later characterised Raymond in very similar terms to those associated with Julius Caesar – 'liberalis et lenis'.[83] But Gerald also slightly alters the terms of his classical model: he does not fit Hervey to the virtuously austere model of Cato, or seek to defend Hervey's position towards the Irish. Rather, Gerald castigates him for his lack of principle and love of vice, his tendency to malice rather than courage (*plus habens malicie quam militie, plus fraudis quam laudis*).[84] All in all, Gerald implies, Hervey's case for slaughtering the captured Irish was not grounded in reasonable argument as Cato's position had been, and rather than arising from a genuine fear for the safety of the military and political position in Ireland, was the expression of vicious cruelty.

There is no evidence that such a battle, let alone such a debate, ever took place at Waterford, and it is likely that Gerald (perhaps having discussed the campaign with his relatives) imagined the argument for himself, in order to serve his own rhetorical ends. What is striking here, however, is how Gerald invokes a consciously classicising set piece (and one which would doubtless have been recognised by, and resonated with, his educated readers) to set out the possible and entirely opposed choices faced by a victorious ruler. Gerald of Wales also assigned the 'types' of Caesar and Cato to two other competing rulers, Henry II's sons, Henry the Younger and Richard respectively, directly quoting Sallust when he claims that: 'one was a refuge for the unfortunate (*miseris perfugium erat*), the other a scourge for the wicked (*malis pernicies*)'.[85] In this case, however, Gerald implies that the austerity of Cato is to be preferred in any ruler who exercises judicial functions, as Henry's clemency was akin to laxity, allowing the prince's court to become a safe haven for criminals.[86]

Multiple models

There were literary and intellectual riches on offer to twelfth-century authors looking to speak of judgment. One could combine scriptural and classical arguments (one could use both the Bible and Seneca to argue for the magnificence of mercy, both as a virtuous deed and as a demonstration of earthy power and nobility). It is important to recognise that these were not two opposed traditions, but two repositories of ideas that could be brought into agreement. While the shorthand of an 'Augustinian' view of justice informed by charity and an 'Ulpianic' view of justice predicated on due is useful, it should not be misinterpreted as disclosing respective 'Christian' and 'Roman' attitudes. This, after all, had been Augustine's point when, in a letter, he had cited Cicero's praise of merciful Caesar, and Cicero's explanation that the republic had become great because it preferred to pardon injury rather than avenge it.[87] Indeed, for Augustine, Caesar's conduct served precisely as a demonstration of the significant shared moral basis between Christian and Roman attitudes to mercy: even Roman authors endorsed the forgiveness of injuries. Yet Augustine's comment is worth dwelling upon for another reason: it was in the twelfth century, for the first time since Augustine's day, that these *exempla* once again had the relevance to create intellectual and practical judicial problems.

Justice and mercy

None of the *exempla* reviewed here were 'new', or particular to the twelfth century. Nor were they particular to English authors. But they were more important than ever from c.1100 onwards, because of the change in legal setting and because these *exempla* had the capacity to provide guidance. The difference lay in the world in which they were being read: what was different was the increased scrutiny being paid to legal authority, and the increased interesting in defining the ways in which that legal authority was constituted and used; and in the way that ministers of justice conducted themselves – not merely as individuals but as part of a professional – or at the very least, *professionalising* – group of judges.

Notes

1 For example: one less-than-straightforward example of Old Testament mercy, which appears with some frequency in discussions of mercy, is that of Joseph forgiving his brothers (Genesis xliii): see Alan of Lille, *Summa de arte praedicatoria*, PL.210.149B.
2 This is the explanation of Robert Pullen, *Sententiarum libri octo*, 3.8, PL.186.771C–772A. For further discussion see Beryl Smalley, 'William of Auvergne, John of La Rochelle and St. Thomas Aquinas on the Old Law', in A. A. Maurer (ed.), *St. Thomas Aquinas 1274–1974: Commemorative Studies* (2 vols, Toronto, 1974), 2:11–74.
3 Cf. Georges Lacombe and Beryl Smalley, *Studies on the Commentaries of Cardinal Stephen Langton* (1931), 160–6.
4 Stephen Langton, Commentary on Pentateuch, BnF, Ms. latin 14415, fo. 243v.
5 For the attribution, Lacombe and Smalley, *Studies on the Commentaries*, 148–9.
6 BnF, Ms. latin 14435, fo. 23r.
7 See Lesley Smith, 'The *De decem mandatis* of Robert Grosseteste', in M. O'Caroll (ed.), *Robert Grosseteste and the Beginning of a British Theological Tradition* (Rome, 2003), 265–88.
8 Robert Grosseteste, *De decem mandatis*, ed. Richard C. Dales and Edward B. King (Oxford, 1987), 1.24–33, 18–22; cf. *Decretum*, C.I, q.4, c.9, 1:420; Robert Pullen, *Sententiarum*, 3.5, PL.186.769B–770D.
9 Cicero, *De natura deorum*, ed. and trans. H. Rackham (London, 1979), 3.90, 376.
10 See *QEP*, Hebrews x.30, 309–10; Grosseteste, *Dictum* 24, fos 21r–22r.
11 R. M. Thomson, *Catalogue of the Manuscripts of Lincoln Cathedral Chapter Library* (Woodbridge, 1989), 19–20.
12 G. B. Flahiff, 'Ralph Niger: an introduction to his life and works', *Mediaeval Studies* 2 (1940), 104–26; H. Kantorowicz and B. Smalley, 'An English theologian's view of Roman law: Pepo, Irnerius, Ralph Niger', *Mediaeval and Renaissance Studies* 1 (1941), 244–52.
13 S. Kuttner and E. Rathbone, 'Anglo-Norman canonists of the twelfth century: an introductory study', *Traditio* 7 (1949–51), 296–300.

14 Ralph Niger, 'Moralia in libros Regum', Lincoln Cathedral Library, MS 25, fo. 5r.
15 Ibid., X.3, fo. 156v.
16 Ibid., X.4, fo. 157v.
17 For *exempla* in structuring histories see Peter von Moos, 'The use of exempla in the Policraticus of John of Salisbury', in M. Wilks (ed.), *The World of John of Salisbury* (Oxford, 1984), 207–61.
18 Theodulf, *Carmina* 28 in *Carmina*, ed. Ernst Dümmler, MGH Poetae 1 (Berlin, 1881), 493–517.
19 Luard, Ep. 11, 53; Ep. 98, 301–2.
20 R. Gameson, *The Manuscripts of Early Norman England (1066–1130)* (Oxford, 1999), finds twenty-five copies (nineteen of which are complete) of the *Enarrationes* in England in this period, making it by far the best-attested work of Augustine, and more popular than Gregory's *Moralia in Iob*, ed. M. Adriaen, CCSL 143 (3 vols, Turnhout, 1979–85), appendix 1, 42.
21 Augustine, *Enarrationes*, on Psalms cv.26, 1563.
22 VA, 1.65, 434.
23 The scriptural roots of this principle are explained by Robert Grosseteste, *Dictum* 103, fo. 85r; William of Auxerre, *Summa aurea*, 2.21, 3:671–8. Cf. Aquinas, *ST*, IIaIIae, q.67, 9:98–9, on why respect for persons is opposed to distributive justice.
24 Grosseteste, *Dictum* 75, fo. 55v.
25 Rabanus Maurus, *Commentaria in libros IV Regum*, PL.109.20–1 (quoting Josephus, *Jewish Antiquities*, 5.10–12); Rabanus Maurus and Josephus are the two authorities on this passage cited by the *Glossa ordinaria*, PL.113.544B–D.
26 Lincoln Cathedral, MS 25, I.11, fo. 15r.
27 VA, 1.72, 474.
28 *Policraticus*, 4.11, 1:535. For an alternative view see Simon of Tournai, *Disputationes*, ed. J. Warichez (Louvain, 1932), 29, 89–90: to put one's own flesh to death offends against both nature and positive law.
29 J. A. Green, *The Government of England under Henry I* (Cambridge, 1986), 107–8.
30 *Policraticus*, 4.16, 1:581.
31 Lincoln Cathedral, MS 25, II.14, fo. 29r.
32 Luard, Ep. 127, 388–9.
33 This *exemplum* is praised by Peter of Blois, *Sermo* 96, PL.207.698–700.
34 SAP, 233. Peter the Chanter had given the same example, VA, 2.12, 654.
35 DNC, 1.12, 30–4.
36 William of Rievaulx, *Vita Ailredi*, ed. and trans. F. M. Powicke (Oxford, 1978), c.14, 23.
37 *S. Aureli Augustini Hipponiensis episcopi Epistulae III*, ed. A. Goldbacher, CCSL 44 (Vienna, 1904), Ep. 153.9, 405–6.
38 Augustine, *In Johannis Evangelium tractatus*, ed. D. R. Willems, CCSL 36 (Turnhout, 1954), 33, 306–11.
39 C. Brown Tkacz, '*Susanna victrix, Christus victor*: Lenten sermons, typology and the lectionary', in C. Nederman and R. Utz (eds), *Speculum Sermonis* (Turnhout, 2004), 58–62.

40 Rupert of Deutz, *De divinis officiis*, ed. H. Haacke, CCCM 7 (Turnhout, 1967), 4.16, 130–1.
41 Thomas of Chobham, *SC*, 6.4.9a, 304; 7.2.8a, 362; Gerald of Wales, 'De principis instructione', BL, 1.7, fo. 55r; cf. *VA*, 2.55, 817; *GO*, PL.114.589–90.
42 For the Four Doctors see Brundage, *Medieval Origins*, 85–9.
43 K. W. Norr, *Zur Stellung des Richters im gelehrten Prozeß der Frühzeit: Iudex secundum allegata non secundum conscientiam iudicat* (Munich, 1968), 16–18.
44 Cf. Fraher, 'Conviction according to conscience', 24.
45 Cf. Grosseteste, Epp. 73, 98.
46 For 'positive' readings of the intercession see Bernard of Clairvaux, *Sermones super cantica canticorum*, Sermo 30.4, in *S. Bernardi opera*, vol. 1, ed. J. Leclercq, C. H. Talbot and H. M. Rochais (Rome, 1957), 212; Hugh of St Victor, *De sacramentis*, 2.13.10, PL.176.538; Richard of St Victor, *Les quatre degrés de la violente charité*, ed. Gervais Dumeige (Paris, 1955), 4.46, 175.
47 For example, *Sermo* 50 (a sermon wrongly attributed to Peter of Blois), PL.207.706–9; Grosseteste, Ep. 98, 300–1.
48 *Decretum*, C.II, q.7, c.27, 1:490.
49 *Policraticus*, 2.27, 1:463–4.
50 For example, *Policraticus*, 4.1, 1:513–4; Kate Langdon Forhan, 'Salisburian stakes: the uses of "tyranny" in John of Salisbury's *Policraticus*', *History of Political Thought* 11 (1990), 397–407.
51 *Policraticus*, 2.27, 1:464; cf. 3.9, 1:493.
52 An example easily borrowed by bishops explaining the pastoral order of their diocese or justifying their powers of visitation: see Grosseteste, Epp. 23, 73, 98, 127.
53 P. Byrne, 'Exodus 32 and the figure of Moses in twelfth-century theology', *Journal of Theological Studies* 68 (2017), 671–89.
54 Peter of Blois, *Sermo* 30, PL.207.652C; Adam Marsh, *Letters*, ed. and trans. C. H. Lawrence (2 vols, Oxford, 2006–10), Ep. 187, 456; Ep. 209, 510.
55 Adam Marsh, *Letters*, Ep. 99, 260.
56 Gerald of Wales, *Topographia Hibernica*, ed. J. F. Dimock, RS 21 (London, 1867), 3.48, 191.
57 See L. Boje Mortensen, 'The texts and contexts of Roman history in twelfth-century western scholarship', in Paul Magdalino (ed.), *The Perceptions of the Past in Twelfth-Century Europe* (London, 1992), 99–116.
58 *EH*, 8.15, 5.225–7.
59 L. D. Reynolds, 'Sallust', in L. D. Reynolds (ed.), *Texts and Transmission* (Oxford, 1983), 341–8; B. Smalley, 'Sallust in the middle ages', in R. R. Bolgar (ed.), *Classical Influences on European Culture* (Cambridge, 1971), 165–75.
60 Mortensen, 'Texts and contexts', 104.
61 Charles Homer Haskins, in *The Renaissance of the Twelfth Century* (Cambridge, MA, 1927), 226, declared that the influence of Sallust was 'slight', and that the influence was only really perceptible in Angevin *gesta*.

62 'Qui demissi in obscuro vitam habent siquid iracundia deliquere, pauci sciunt; fama atque fortuna eorum pares sunt: qui magno imperio praediti in excelso aetatem agunt, eorum facta cuncti mortales novere. Ita in maxuma fortuna minuma licentia est. Neque studere neque odisse, sed minume irasci decet. Quae apud alios iracundia dicitur, ea in imperio superbia atque crudelitas appellatur.' Sallust, *The War with Catiline*, ed. J. C. Rolfe (London, 1928), c.51, 91–3.
63 *Ibid.*, c.52, 107.
64 'Catilina cum exercitu faucibus urget; alii intra moenia atque in sinu urbis sunt hostes; neque parari neque consuli quicquam potest occulte; quo magis properandum est ... incendia aliaque se foeda atque crudelia facinora in civis patriamque paravisse, de confessis, sicuti de manufestis rerum capitalium, more maiorum supplicium sumundum.' *Ibid.*, 52, 109.
65 'Igitur eis genus, aetas, eloquentia prope aequalia fuere, magnitudo animi par, item gloria, sed alia alii. Caesar beneficiis ac munificentia magnus habebatur, integritate vitae Cato. Ille mansuetudine et misericordia clarus factus, huic severitas dignitatem addiderat. Caesar dando, sublevando, ignoscundo, Cato nihil largiundo gloriam adeptus est. In altero miseris perfugium erat, in altero malis pernicies. Illius facilitas, huius constantia laudabatur. Postremo Caesar in animum induxerat laborare, vigilare; negotiis amicorum intentus sua neglegere, nihil denegare quod dono dignum esset; sibi magnum imperium, exercitum, bellum novom exoptabat, ubi virtus enitescere posset. At Catoni studium modestiae, decoris, sed maxume severitatis erat. Non divitiis cum divite neque factione cum factioso, sed cum strenuo virtute, cum modesto pudore, cum innocente abstinentia certabat; esse quam videri bonus malebat; ita quo minus petebat gloriam, eo magis illum sequebatur.' *Ibid.*, 54, 111–13.
66 *Florilegium Gallicum: Prolegomena und Edition der Exzerpte von Petron bis Cicero, De oratore*, ed. Johannes Hamacher (Frankfurt, 1975), 190–1; R. H. Rouse, 'Florilegia and Latin classical authors in twelfth- and thirteenth-century Orleans', *Viator* 10 (1979), 135–8.
67 *Florilegium Gallicum*, 187–9.
68 John Gillingham, '1066 and the introduction of chivalry into England', in John Gillingham, *The English in the Twelfth Century: Imperialism, National Identity and Political Values* (Woodbridge, 2000), 209–31.
69 See Matthew Strickland, *War and Chivalry: The Conduct and Perception of War in England and Normandy, 1066–1217* (Cambridge, 1996), esp. 2–4.
70 William of Poitiers, *The 'Gesta Guillelmi' of William of Poitiers*, ed. and trans. R. H. C. Davis and Majorie Chibnall (Oxford, 1998), xxii, xxv.
71 Ralph Diceto, *De caesaribus*, in *Opera historica*, ed. William Stubbs, RS 67 (2 vols, London, 1876), 2:182; cf. *Abbreviationes chronicorum*, *ibid.*, 1:52.
72 Seneca, *On Mercy*, in John W. Basore (ed.), *Seneca: Moral Essays*, vol. 1 (London, 1928), 1.11, 391–5; an idea repeated by Alan of Lille, *Summa de arte praedicatoria*, PL.210.141D.
73 Sallust, *Catiline*, c.51, 95–7.

Justice and mercy

74 Seneca, *On Mercy*, 1.5, 371.
75 H. M. Hine, 'The Younger Seneca', in Reynolds, *Texts and Transmission*, 364–5.
76 For example, *VA*, 2.9, 648–50.
77 These figures, of course, might also be taken individually, e.g. Jocelin of Brakelond characterised Abbot Samson in matters of law and judgment as having 'a glance sharp and penetrating, and his brow worthy of Cato and rarely relaxed into a smile, he was said to be more inclined to severity than kindness (*magis declinare animum severitati quam benignitati*)'. *The Chronicle of Jocelin of Brakelond*, trans. H. E. Butler (London, 1949), 34.
78 Rahewin, *Gesta Frederici*, ed. G. Waitz, MGH, Scriptores rerum Germanicarum 46 (Hanover, 1912), 4.46, 285–7.
79 'Nec enim hostibus parcendum ulla ratione decreverim. Sed hi non hostes iam, sed homines; non rebelles, sed debellati ... Eo iam numero sunt constitute, ut in eis potius locum habeat pietas ad exemplum, quam crudelitas ad tormentum ... Efficiat igitur in nobis dignissima laude clementia, ut cetera qui vicimus animos vincamus et iram. Solet quippe praecipites animi motus modus et modestia mitigare ... Julius Caesar, cuius victoriis orbis angustus erat, in tanto imperio suo tantum Domitium, cui tamen et ante vitam donaverat, iussit occidi. Pietas in ipso et gloriam adauxit, et victorias non impedivity. O quam impia, quam bestialis saevitia, ubi victoriam nulla sequitur misericordia!' Gerald of Wales, *The Conquest of Ireland*, ed. and trans. A. B. Scott and F. X. Martin (Dublin, 1978), 1.14, 58–61.
80 'Dum adhuc superbi, dumque rebelles sunt populi, pietate postposita, modis sunt omnibus expungandi. Cum vero iam subditi, iam servire parati, tum demum, salvo regiminis moderamine, cum omni mansuetudine sunt tractandi ... Reimundus vero, quasi populis iam subditis sola sit opus misericordia, vel tanquam, hostibus in nimia paucitate constitutes, ubi virtus eniteat invenire non valeat, cum tamen totus Hiberniae populus in nostrum nec immerito coniuravit perniciem.' *Ibid.*, 1.15, 62–3.
81 'Duorum quippe alterutrum eligamus. Aut enim ad quod venimus, id viriliter exequamur; populumque rebellem, dissimulata prorsus clementia, armis et animositate potenti manu debellemus. Aut si pietatis operibus, iuxta Reimundi sententiam, potius indulgere dignum duxerimus, reversis velis plebe miserabili patriam et patrimonia reliquamus.' *Ibid.*, 1.15, 64–5.
82 *Ibid.*, 1.15, 65.
83 *Ibid.*, 2.8, 154–5.
84 *Ibid.*, 2.11, 158–61.
85 Cf. Sallust, *Catiline*, c.54, 113.
86 BL, 'De principis instructione', 2.9, 220; 3.8, 297; cf. *Topographia Hibernica*, 3.50, 196.
87 Augustine, *Epistulae 124–184*, ed. A. Goldbacher, CSEL 44 (Vienna, 1904), Ep. 138.9, 133–4.

5

Who should be merciful?

> We wish we were not seeking revenge but could bear it all calmly to such an extent that when we were smitten on one cheek, we would immediately turn the other, not returning evil for evil, and endeavouring not to be overcome by evil, but rather to overcome evil by good. However, we have heard this teaching of the apostle [1 Peter iii.9] quite often, but we have not had the strength to reach this absolute perfection; for we cling to an old imperfection and anyone who has robbed us we consider an enemy. We still love our friends, and hate our enemies, especially when they have plundered us incessantly and irrevocably.
>
> Gerald of Wales, *Speculum duorum*[1]

Mercy: a precept or a counsel?

Precepts and counsels

This chapter advances two arguments about the role of mercy in twelfth-century England. First, it highlights a set of discussions about whether mercy was understood to be necessary in every judgment, or whether it was understood as a virtue which, though it might be laudable, was not always essential. Secondly, it works to examine what 'mercy' meant when translated into action. One could lump many different types of behaviour under the name of *misericordia*. But even the mercy recommended by scripture could be broken down into different actions, of varying 'strengths' – mercy could be made more potent or more dilute. Moreover, if the divine promise (or divine threat) was that no one who judged without mercy would receive mercy from God, working out exactly what 'mercy' entailed in practice was vital to understanding that principle. Mercy, in a weak and watery form, might simply mean allowing an offender to avoid severe punishment. It might mean punishing slightly less than law required; it might entail abrogating punishment altogether. It might, at its strongest, mean complete forgiveness of the offender; even restoring them to the place they had previously held. It might also ('love those who persecute you', Christ instructed) mean not just legal forgiveness, but a commandment to *love* the guilty – a re-orientation of attitude and behaviour. *Misericordia* could demand a little or demand a lot. 'Be you merciful' therefore offered considerable scope for interpretation.

The second part of this chapter then deals with a problem of comparison: were royal judges (and, most particularly, kings sitting in judgment) expected to demonstrate the same 'merciful' behaviour as judges in the Church? To put it another way: was the 'standard' set for mercy the same for the lay power as the ecclesiastical power? There has long been an assumption that mercy belonged to the Church, and severe punishment was the default setting for secular judges. As this chapter argues, that complementary solution represents a neat resolution, but, ultimately it fails to capture twelfth-century thought on judicial ethics.

Asking whether mercy was considered 'necessary' in all judgments is essentially to ask whether it held the status of a precept or a counsel in the minds of twelfth- and thirteenth-century theologians and moralists. That precept–counsel distinction sought to recognise the difference between those actions which scripture commanded – without which eternal life could not be achieved – and those actions which were merely regarded as admirable and distinguished in virtue.

The model of precept and counsel is perhaps more familiar to historians in the context of a series of controversies surrounding virginity and poverty, running from c.1000 to c.1300. These controversies sprang from questions of what kinds of rules for living one constructed from the reading of scripture, both about sexual relations and about wealth. They asked whether the more 'radical' parts of the New Testament should be interpreted as commands or advice; how text and society should interact.

My argument here is that the *praeceptum–consilium* distinction was also something twelfth-century authors tried to use to analyse the concept of mercy. Indeed, recognising that twelfth-century authors struggled with the question of whether mercy was a precept or a counsel demonstrates exactly how serious an issue this was, and how much impact it could have on the practical ordering of the world. The twelfth century was actively engaged in a discussion of how much mercy (or what kinds of mercy) an individual might be expected to show.

Who should be merciful?

A brief summary of the significance of the arguments about precept and counsel in relation to arguments over poverty and virginity serves to highlight the significance of the distinction and the connection between an 'academic' argument about the classification of commands and their impact in practice. Much debate over the type and level of poverty which ought to be practised by the Church (particularly, but not exclusively, in debates within the Franciscan order) focused on how one ought to interpret the various passages in the gospels in which Christ discussed questions of wealth. The gospels had condemned those who would accrue riches (e.g. Matthew vi.19–20), yet, at certain points, that teaching appeared to have been modified: Christ had, seemingly, permitted the apostles to carry a purse (Luke xxii.36).[2] How was such an injunction to be understood? It could be argued that Christ instructed his true disciples not to covet money, not to store up their wealth on earth; alternatively, one could claim that Christ had made concessions, accepting that, at times, his followers might require the use of wealth. The issue clearly could not be generalised and expanded into a command which bound all Christians.[3] Likewise, discussions surrounding the relative merits of virginity and celibacy hinged upon a scriptural citation, in this case from Matthew xix.12: 'there are also eunuchs who made themselves eunuchs for the sake of the kingdom of heaven. He who is able to receive it, let him receive it (*qui potest capere capiat*).' Though virginity or celibacy was a demonstration of faith, a remedy against original sin and an action which would earn great reward, not everyone was capable of it. For those people mired in concupiscence, marriage was granted as a *permissio*, a concession to weakness. This was a widely accepted gloss on the passages of scripture which concerned marriage.[4] A far more problematic question then became to understand who was capable of celibacy, and indeed, who *should* be capable of adhering to this prototype. Those promoting the 'Gregorian' reforms of the eleventh and twelfth centuries, for example, had included all priests, deacons, subdeacons, canons, and monks within this category.[5] Both poverty and chastity, in sum, were essentially arguments about how broadly or narrowly the gospel message should be applied.

One way of considering these discussions was to approach them through the lens of precept (*praeceptum*) and counsel (*consilium*). The status of precept applied to all those scriptural statements without which salvation could not be achieved – the most basic of all being love of God and love of neighbour. Counsel, on the other hand, described those actions which were commended by scripture but were not incumbent upon all. Counsel typically signified an action that was more demanding or difficult to fulfil than a precept, something which only the 'perfect' attempted to observe – hence the importance of the phrase 'qui potest capere capiat', often invoked when explaining this distinction. Similarly, the injunction of Matthew xix.21, 'sell all you have and give it to the poor, and follow me' was prefaced with a clear conditional indication of its limited audience, beginning 'if you want to be perfect' (*si vis perfectus esse*).[6]

A useful and fairly typical definition of the meaning of counsel is provided by the twelfth-century Benedictine Rupert of Deutz, when he defines *consilia* as actions which are done on behalf of God, but which go beyond those tasks which he commands us to perform. Rupert glosses this with reference to Luke xvii.10: 'we are unworthy servants, we have done only our duty (*quod debuimus facere, fecimus*)'.[7] Christians follow counsels in order to earn extra merit in the eyes of God, in order to become *perfectionis amatores*. The problem highlighted by Rupert is that the individual who fulfils *only* that which is necessary to salvation, that is, who adheres only to precepts rather that attempting to follow divine counsels, cannot be judged a particularly good or worthy Christian. Rupert, writing in a monastic context, in which counsels were to be fulfilled, notes that those who follow precepts alone will never merit any great grace. Indeed, those who never attempt to implement scriptural counsels in their own lives are no more worthy of God's grace than the Israelites of the Old Testament, who simply and blindly followed the commands of Mosaic law: 'you are unworthy, who wish to add nothing in your due service on account of the love or grace of God' (*inutiles enim estis, quia nihil pro amore vel gratia Domini vestri, supra debitum servitutis pensum adicere vultis*).[8] Certainly in the cloister, where individuals aspired to serve God in all that they could, simply adhering to precepts did not by itself provide an adequate way of life for the monk, who had chosen by his vocation to follow both the counsels of poverty and celibacy as if they were precepts.

It should be noted, however, that even 'precepts' were not always hard and fast, as Abelard's *Sic et Non* made clear. There are different categories of precepts – some apparent precepts, Abelard argues, can be treated with 'indulgent remission' (*indulgentiae remissionem*), their commands modified or even let slip: some apparent precepts are not intended as commands at all, but should be read as exhortations to perfection. The only way of distinguishing between precepts which bind all and those which have a limited audience, is by identifying the context in which they were given, and the circumstances which gave rise to them.[9] Abelard thus formulates some general rules for dealing with scriptural precepts in his prologue. The exegete must first ask whether the precept is a general or particular one – does it apply to all (*communiter*), or only to some (*specialiter*)? Very often this can only be inferred through close attention to context. Further, even among precepts given *communiter*, Abelard invites the student of theology to consider whether they were given for all time, or dispensed with after a certain period.

Where, then, did *misericordia* sit within this scheme? Did it constitute an obligation for all, commanded by divine precept and without which salvation could not be achieved, or a counsel directed only to the perfect, as an additional act of virtue? On the one hand, the biblical definition of reciprocal mercy (Matthew vi.12, *dimitte nobis debita nostra*) seemed to imply that there could be no salvation for those who did not perform acts of mercy – a position which would seem to give it the status of a precept. On the other, it was possible to argue that more specific commands – such as *diligite inimicos vestros* (Matthew v.44) – demanded such a high degree of virtue that only the perfect would be able to achieve them – a position which would seem to make mercy a counsel rather than a precept.

Mercy as a precept

Most straightforwardly, there was a powerful case to be made for *misericordia* as an immutable precept, binding upon all. This argument derived ultimately from the way in which theologians conceptualised the relationship between Old and New Law. Those who wished to argue that mercy was a precept incumbent upon all judges cited Matthew v.43–44: 'You have heard that it was said, "love your neighbour and hate your enemy", but I tell you: love your enemies and pray for those who persecute you'. This passage seemed to imply that the difference between the two laws turned on the merciful treatment of one's enemies. Commentary on the passage typically noted that hatred of enemies under Mosaic law was given as a 'permissio, non praeceptum'.[10] As such, this permission had been retracted with the Incarnation, the implication being that Christians were bound now to love their enemies.

Among authors writing in an English context, a particularly detailed consideration of the status of mercy as a precept is found in Peter of Blois's *De charitate Dei et proximi*, a work paired with Peter's better-known treatise on Christian friendship, *De amicitia Christiana*.[11] The text aims to bring contemporary monastic teachings about the importance of love to the attention of a broader audience. As such, it explains why the need to love, and do good towards, one's enemies must be understood as a precept. Christ, Peter explained, had referred to the command to love one's enemies as 'praeceptum meum'. Peter further notes that Christians are

Justice and mercy

obliged to love their enemies 'ex praecepto Dei'.[12] Peter then examines the natural conflict between human will – which is to hate enemies – and the command of *caritas* to love those enemies, arguing that however strong the urge to do the former, Christians must struggle to obey the latter. If an individual truly loves God, he adds, then they must love all humans for his sake – this includes enduring enemies with patience and indulging their errors with clemency (*indulgeat clementer*).[13] It is striking that Peter singles out *misericordia* as a precept, *expressis verbis*. He observes that other virtuous actions mentioned in the gospels – virginity, alms-giving, selling one's possessions and distributing them to the poor – all fall under the category of 'counsel from God' (*consilium habemus a Domino*).[14] These actions are not necessary to ensuring salvation, and those who perform them may hope for additional divine reward. In contrast to these counsels, Peter continues: 'However, the Lord in the Gospel binds us to love our enemies as a fixed and clear statement of the law, so that he who does not love his enemy is shown to be a violator of divine law'.[15] Peter of Blois is explicit in claiming that judicial mercy is a precept, not a counsel. Moreover, Peter makes this argument in a work (*De charitate Dei et proximi*) which addresses not only a monastic audience, to whom higher standards of love and tolerance for enemies might have been applied, but also secular clerics. Peter's conclusion is explicit: only those who love their enemies and do good to their persecutors can hope to be considered as Christians, true children of God. Those who disregard the command to show mercy deviate from the central teaching of Christ and, as such, cannot be considered to be his followers (*Christi discipuli*). Peter argues that this 'dilectionis decretum' (decree of love) towards enemies is the central message of Christ. In this, he goes beyond his contemporaries, who argued simply that the message of the New Law was love – in fact, the commandment is far more taxing: the message of the New Law is love of *enemies*. Peter concludes his argument with a flourish, noting that if even under the Old Law, David and Joseph could love their persecutors, Christians living under the new dispensation are yet more deeply obliged to do so.

Turning the other cheek

At various different points in the New Testament, Christians were told (whether ordered or counselled) to love their enemies; to pray for them; to do good to their persecutors; to feed their hungry enemies; and to offer the other cheek to those who had already injured them.[16] Thus, even if an individual accepted that to love their enemy was Christ's command, what exactly did such a command imply in practice? Moreover, of these various commands, which one should be thought of as applying to the laity, and which to the perfect alone?[17] Reflecting the difficulty of resolving this latter issue, one of the questions which Abelard set out in the *Sic et Non* was whether 'love of neighbour' was considered to apply to all humans, and, if so, in what senses it applied.[18] Hugh of St Victor also considered this point when commenting on Paul's Letter to the Galatians, quoting a statement he attributes to Gregory the Great, who had set the bar for Christians in general rather low: 'it is enough (*sufficit*) not to hate our enemies, that is, to wish for their salvation'.[19] Hugh considered the generality of Christians to be obliged only to wish for their enemies' good, not bound to perform any acts of mercy towards those enemies: 'we hold as a precept that we should wish the salvation of all, but it belongs to the duties of the pious to treat enemies as they would the infirm; to the less perfect (*minos perfectos*) it is a counsel, which is to the perfect a precept'.[20]

The question of what behaviour, exactly, Christians are required to exhibit towards their enemies is addressed in detail in the works of two English authors. Robert of Melun responded to the question of 'whether we are commanded to love our enemies who do not repent the injuries they have done to us' in his *Questiones de divina pagina* (between 1145 and 1155).[21] The objection to doing so, Robert notes, would seem to be that even God does not forgive those who show no repentance: to love an unrepentant enemy would make us more merciful than God, which surely cannot be virtuous. Robert's solution still ultimately resolves the question in favour of loving even one's unrepentant enemy. Humans, he argues, should not seek to imitate God who dwells in heaven, he who pronounces 'vengeance is mine, I will repay' (Romans xii.19), but rather God 'as he walked on the earth as a man, and who prayed for his crucifiers'. Robert's formulation, then, at least implies that Christians are – as far as is possible – not only to love, but to forgive and pray for their enemies, following the example of Christ. It was Christ, not the judge of the Last Judgment, who provided an imitable and useful model for resolving human judicial problems concerning the place of mercy in judgment. Further to this, Robert – like a number of his contemporaries in the mid-twelfth century and later scholastic authors – addressed the related question of whether it was better to love one's enemies or one's friends. This question admitted a variety of solutions – for example, William of Auvergne argued that it was better for the perfect to love their enemies, but better for the imperfect to love their friends;[22] Simon of Tournai argued that it was better – for any individual – to love an enemy, because by doing that which they are less bound to do, they earn more merit with God.²³ Robert of Melun concluded that it was indeed a greater virtue to love one's enemy than a friend, although that love was less likely to be returned.²⁴

The second English theologian who provides a strikingly detailed discussion of how 'love your enemies' is to be interpreted is Thomas of Chobham in his *Summa confessorum* (c.1217). As far as Thomas was concerned, the distinction between levels of perfection was all-important and he accordingly has a far more limited view of the duties of ordinary Christians to love their neighbours than either Robert of Melun or Peter of Blois. Thomas makes a distinction between the lay person and the 'perfectus'. Those who do not aspire to perfection are not obliged to show forgiveness towards unrepentant enemies, or those who do not make satisfaction for their injuries. Nor is the ordinary Christian obliged to wish for the salvation of an enemy in the same way as they wish for the salvation of their family and friends.²⁵ Indeed, the difference between the mercy and love to be exhibited by the 'simplex' and that which is due from the perfect is quite stark. The imperfect are not obliged to remit any injuries or debts from their enemies, and may rightly seek satisfaction for those injuries in a court of law.²⁶ Thomas further considers just what level of perfection is required before a Christian is obliged to give the 'kiss of peace' as a gesture of reconciliation with his enemies. The *osculum pacis*, he notes, is useful as instrument of secular peace in the community: the most notorious recent demonstration of this in twelfth-century English politics had of course been Henry II's public refusal to grant Thomas Becket the kiss of peace at their supposed moment of reconciliation.²⁷ However, in most cases, ordinary Christians are not in any way obliged to offer the kiss of peace to their assailants, because such an action of reconciliation and peace could cause the dismissal of any suits they have against the offender. Thomas does grant the exception that, *in summa necessitate*, there may be a case for making peace. The *vir perfectus*, however, is never excused from performing the kiss of peace – he is always obliged to forgive his enemies, whether in the case of personal injury or material debts. Thomas concludes by noting that it was the perfect to whom Christ addressed himself when he commanded 'love your enemies, pray for those who persecute you'.²⁸

The sharp distinction between the mercy practised by the simple laity (*simplex*) and by the perfect is reflected in the organisation of another of Thomas's works, his *Summa de commendatione virtutum et extirpatione vitiorum* (c.1220). When addressing the virtue of *iustitia*, Thomas finds it most convenient to categorise the virtue according to the level of its practitioners, discussing *iustitia maiorum* (referring to the justice of judges and princes), *iustitia minorum* (the justice governing religious life) and *iustitia omnium* (justice among humankind in general). Patience which does not take revenge (*vindicare*), he points out, is considered a virtue which is practised exclusively by *minores*. Judicial mercy which spares lives or mitigates the worst excesses of punishment is considered with reference to the *maiores*. The section *de iustitia omnium*, by contrast, sets a relatively undemanding level of justice for the laity.[29] Indeed, *misericordia* is not mentioned in relation to their duties: the only justice that all are obliged to show is the justice of proper restitution and the undertaking always to speak the truth. The focus here, moreover, is questions of material restitution, for which Thomas runs through numerous scenarios – for example, if a criminal dies, are his wife and children obliged to make restitution to those from whom he stole? By contrast, when Thomas cites scriptural precepts such as 'dimitte nobis debita nostra', or raises the threat of 'judgment without mercy', these are invoked solely in relation to the actions of the *maiores* – princes and judges.[30] Thomas of Chobham's argument that different standards of justice apply to different groups within society (rather than different levels of perfection) is markedly unusual. In general, twelfth-century authors did not draw sharp distinctions between the levels of justice required of different groups of believers, for two reasons. First, theologians noted that preachers exhorting listeners to justice might often be speaking to a 'mixed' audience, and, in that context, drawing sharp distinctions between groups would not be appropriate or effective.[31] Secondly, theologians appreciated that to apply categories such as 'iustitia maiorum' was not a straightforward exercise. Princes and judges sometimes act in an official capacity, sometimes as private individuals. As public officials they might be obliged to uphold justice, to avenge injuries in order to preserve the stability of the political community, while as private individuals they might wish to turn the other cheek and forgive any injuries done to them.[32] Given the problems of context, few theologians tried to formulate hard and fast rules about forgiveness.

Mercy as a counsel

When we come to unpack the case for mercy as a 'non-binding' counsel, we must recognise that the term 'counsel' (*consilium*) was arguably far more complex than the term *praeceptum*. As well as deciding whether mercy was a counsel, theologians also suggested that merciful action could be the product of counsel. This understanding hinged on drawing a connection between those given the 'gift' of counsel by God, who in turn were able to develop the virtue of *misericordia*. Thus, the term *consilium* denoted an advisory statement, a recommendation (in addition to describing the body, i.e. a council, which might offer such advisory statements). But *consilium* was also a virtue in itself, falling under the cardinal virtue of prudence, and one of the gifts of the Holy Spirit described in Isaiah xi.2–3. In this sense, 'consilium' works rather like the modern English term 'judgment': one can issue a judgment, but one also exercises judgment as a demonstration of prudent decision-making.

The multiple possible points of contact between counsel and justice, counsel and mercy, are further demonstrated by Alan of Lille, who in his *Regulae theologicae* (composed at the end of the twelfth century) gave eight possible definitions of *consilium*:[33] the word could be glossed as a *suggestio*; as 'considered opinion' in a legal case – the product of consensus; as equivalent to the term *iudicium*, because judgment was only given after taking counsel; as describing the coming of Christ in humility; as a command which was binding only on the perfect – in the sense that virginity was a counsel to monks; as an alternate term for deliberation in decision-making; as a gift of the Holy Spirit; and finally, *consilium* did not merely describe counsel, but could encompass the actions which followed from acting on a counsel.[34] A number of themes emerge from Alan's definition of counsel – themes which embody many of the issues raised in subsequent discussions. From the perspective of the relationship between justice and mercy, three ideas are worth highlighting here. The first is Alan's definition of *consilium* as representing a considered judgment, from which a course of action would proceed – i.e. as an intellectual action which carried implications of implementation in practice.[35] Secondly, Alan recognised that *consilium* as an act of deliberation implies some level of difficulty in decision-making: not all *consilia* represent a straightforward choice between wicked and meritorious action – one might be required to choose between good and better actions, or two courses which seemed equally virtuous or advantageous.[36] Thirdly, *consilium* was specifically associated with the advent of Christ. This final connection could be constructed in two ways: Christ could be understood as representing a 'counsellor' in the sense that his Incarnation made the law of God known not only to the Jews, but to the Gentiles. His counsel, as provided in the gospels, was a guide to making virtuous moral choices. Alternatively, Christ's embodiment of *consilium* could be understood according to the way the Incarnation represented the mercy of God being extended towards humankind: Christ's reconciliation of man with God was a merciful act of *consilium* which challenged the previous strict precept of 'justice'.[37]

The case for identifying mercy as counsel rather than a precept ultimately derived from a particular tradition of commentary on the gospels, and,

Who should be merciful?

more specifically, Christ's words in the Sermon on the Mount. A distinctive twelfth-century development was the close attention which these commentaries paid to the language and context of the gospels.[38] The four evangelists were central to understanding the life, deeds and message of Christ, but they presented profound problems for their scholastic interpreters, not least the way in which some of their contents could or should be accommodated with twelfth-century social structures. Thus those who glossed the text of Matthew v.25 had to deal with a passage which advised Christians to avoid resorting to the law to resolve their disputes, while Matthew v.34 exhorts Christians to make no oaths, an obvious problem given the increasing importance of oath swearing in court procedure.[39] This injunction could not be interpreted simply or literally. Another potential problem was observed by William of Auxerre, who pointed to the contradiction between the message of Matthew vi.12, 'do unto others as you would be done by' and the application of this command in a judicial context. No one, William argued, who put themselves in the place of a condemned criminal would want to be hanged: therefore according to the logic of this passage, judges would be obliged not to put any criminals to death, as no one would wish such a fate for themselves. Yet if this policy were followed, he noted, and malefactors not punished, it could result in political disaster, and the *res publica* would be destroyed.[40]

The gospel passages pertaining to questions of judicial procedure and judicial action were thus subject to at least some form of moderation. In practice, Peter Comestor, for example, noted the need to consider the injunction 'love your enemies' and 'turn the other cheek' in light of the events of the crusades.[41] In order to do so, Peter first drew a distinction between those precepts which applied to those who sought to be perfect, and those which applied to the rest of society. But even the would-be perfect, he argued, fell into two classes: the perfect of the early Church and those of today. It was appropriate for the perfect of the early Church – the martyrs – to show patience and to turn the other cheek. Their demonstration of love towards their enemies had been a means of evangelising and making converts for the Church. However, this was no longer an appropriate way of acting in the twelfth century, even for the perfect. If that ban on taking vengeance were applied to the Holy Land, he points out, the heathen would abuse the patience of the Church, and Christians would be endangered. These precepts thus had to be understood as spoken 'pro tempore'.

For all these problems, the gospels – and particularly the Sermon on the Mount – became a central focus for scholastic exegesis and the subject of theological *quaestiones*. The Sermon on the Mount was so significant because it represented the moment at which Christ had set out his new law. The comparison between Moses ascending Mount Sinai to receive the Ten Commandments – the basis of the laws of the Old Testament – and Christ ascending the mountain to preach his own sermon on the law was a basic gloss on biblical history.[42] Seeking out the parallels and symmetries of scripture, scholastic commentators found in the Sermon on the Mount a complex relationship between the beatitudes, or blessings, of Christ, the petitions of the Lord's Prayer and the gifts of the Holy Spirit as set out in Isaiah. This not only provided a means of structuring the points of Christ's teaching; it also provided a link to the gifts foreseen by an Old Testament prophet. In this scheme, the beatitude of *misericordia* was usually linked to the petition 'dimitte nobis debita nostra' and the gift of *consilium*. The first modern historian to remark on this structure was Odon Lottin, who argued that it was first developed by Anselm of Laon in his commentaries.[43] Ultimately, however, the connection between the beatitudes, petitions and gifts derived from Augustine's *Commentary on the Sermon on the Mount*. Glossing *beati misericordes*, discussing the gifts and their relation to the beatitudes, Augustine had written:

> Counsel is suited to the merciful: for this is the one remedy by which great wickedness is avoided, in order that we forgive others as we wish to be forgiven, and we help others as much as we are able as much as we ourselves wish to be helped.[44]

Augustine, and Anselm of Laon following him, clearly implied that merciful action should be regarded as a response to counsel. The identification of mercy with counsel was taken up and repeated in many twelfth-century commentaries on the Sermon on the Mount. The standard work of reference on scripture – the *Glossa ordinaria* – argues that mercy cannot be achieved without counsel: 'thus mercy needs the spirit of counsel, without which no one is properly pitied'.[45] Hugh of St Victor followed the scheme of pairing mercy, counsel and the petition to forgive, but developed the symmetry even further, arguing that each beatitude, gift and petition also corresponded to one of seven sins and one of seven virtues.[46] In the early thirteenth century, the subdeacon of Salisbury, Thomas of Chobham, writing for the instruction of would-be confessors, not only repeated the scheme, connecting the fifth petition, 'dimitte', to counsel and mercy, but even included two tables in his *Summa confessorum* to make the structural relationship clear to his readers.[47]

Who should be merciful?

Table 1 Anselm of Laon's scheme of the relationship between the petitions of the Lord's Prayer, the beatitudes and the gifts of the Holy Spirit described in Isaiah. Originally identified by Lottin, 'La doctrine d'Anselme de Laon'.

Petition (Lord's Prayer)	Gift	Beatitude
Sanctificetur nomen tuum	Timor domini	Beati pauperes
Adveniat regnum tuum	Pietas	Beati mites
Fiat voluntas tua	Scientia	Beati qui lugent
Panem nostrum quotidianum	Fortitudo	Beati qui esuriunt
Dimitte nobis debita	Consilium	Beati misericordes
Et ne nos inducas	Intellectus	Beati mundo cordes
Sed libera nos a malo	Sapientia	Beati pacifici

By the later twelfth century, the connection between beatitude, gift and petition was a commonplace – it is found, for example, in the writings of Master Martinus, Alan of Lille, Stephen Langton, Geoffrey of Poitiers, William of Auxerre, Hugh of St Cher and Philip the Chancellor.[48] All these authors tied *misericordia* (which was considered both a virtue and a beatitude) to the gift of *consilium*, implying not merely that the two were complementary, but that mercy was to some extent the product of counsel and deliberation. From this connection, it was possible to infer that *misericordia* was not a precept incumbent upon all, but a special act of virtue enabled by the grace granted by the Holy Spirit to a select number. Not all theologians, however, linked *misericordia* to the petition 'dimitte'. A significant minority preferred to associate mercy with the words 'fiat voluntas tua in nobis' ('let your will be done', Matthew vi.10). This is a construction employed by the *Enarrationes in Matthaeum*, and is also found in the *Glossa ordinaria*. The justification for this alternative pairing is just as striking for what it reveals about the conceptualisation of mercy. The *Enarrationes in Matthaeum* explains, for example, that by petitioning 'fiat voluntas tua', the Christian places themself at the disposal of God, and acts according to divine wishes, not their own. This divine will is unknowable to humans, and sometimes appears without explanation, even arbitrary. The same is true of acts of mercy, which sometimes appear inconsistent – God acts with strict justice towards some, with lenient mercy towards others. Because humans cannot explain the logic of these judgments, they cannot explain acts of *misericordia*, but are simply obliged to perform them according to God's will.[49] This reasoning was clearly thought to provide an adequate explanation when referring to the mercies of the Lord, the logic of which was beyond the full

Justice and mercy

Table 2 Hugh of St Victor's fivefold model for the relationship between the petitions, gifts and beatitudes, along with the vices and virtues, from *De quinque septenis*.

Vitia	Petitio	Donum	Virtus	Beatitudo
Superbia	Sanctificetur nomen tuum	Timor domini	Paupertas spiritus – humilitas	Regnum caelorum
Invidia	Adveniat regnum tuum	Pietas	Mansuetudo sive benignitas	Possessio terrae viventium
Ira	Fiat voluntas tua	Scientia	Compunctio, sive dolor	Consolatio
Tristitia	Panem nostrum quotidianum	Fortitudo	Esuries justitiae sive desiderium bonorum	Saturitas
Avaritia	Dimitte nobis debita	Consilium	Misericordia	Misericordia
Gula	Et ne nos inducas	Intellectus	Cordis munditia	Visio Dei
Luxuria	Sed libera nos a malo	Sapientia	Pax	Appellatio Filiorum Dei

Table 3 Thomas of Chobham's construction of the relationship between the petitions of the Lord's Prayer and the gifts of Isaiah. As found in *Summa confessorum*, 3.1.

Ordo naturalis	VII petitiones in oratione dominica	Dona spiritus in Isaiah in primo ordine
Ista ad futura	Nomen patris sanctificari Adventum regni Voluntatem fieri	Spiritus timoris Spiritus pietatis Spiritus scientie
Ista ad presens	Panem dari Peccata dimitti Non induci in tentationem Liberari a malo	Spiritus fortitudinis Spiritus consilii Spiritus intellectus Spiritus sapientie

Who should be merciful?

Table 4 A second table from Thomas of Chobham's *Summa confessorum*, connecting the seven beatitudes to their corresponding rewards.

[Beatitude]	[Reward]
Paupertas spiritus	Regnum dei
Mansuetudo	Possessio terrae
Luctus	Consolatio
Esuries	Saturitas
Exhibitio misericordiae	Adeptio misericordiae
Munditia cordis	Visio dei
Pax	Appellatio filiorum dei

comprehension of humankind. That mercy should be a question of divine *voluntas* (which was of course always supremely good) was entirely acceptable. When applied to a temporal ruler, however, and to human *voluntas*, this assertion posed quite a different set of issues. In fact, linking mercy to the phrase 'fiat voluntas tua' had quite the opposite effect to associating it with the gift of *consilium*: for the gift of counsel made acts of mercy comprehensible, open to the scrutiny of the human mind.[50] To associate mercy with *consilium* was at least to imply that acts of *misericordia* were subject to deliberation, and, as such, were not binding on Christians in the same way as explicit precepts.

Beyond the beatitudes, other passages in scripture made the case for treating mercy as a counsel rather than a precept. Isaiah ix.6, foreseeing the coming of Christ, described him as King and God and had named him a 'counsellor' (*consiliarius*). When theologians sought to explain why Christ was given this latter title, they referred to his work of persuasion. Rupert of Deutz noted that 'counsellor' referred to Christ's mission to the gentiles, exhorting, encouraging and winning new souls for God. Persuasion was a term necessarily associated with counsel: Christ invited and encouraged people to follow him, but he did not command them with precepts.[51] English authors, too, drew this connection – Thomas of Chobham explained in a sermon the 'conciliatory' role of Christ by setting his work of persuasion in a scheme of salvation history.[52] The post-lapsarian pride of humankind had been so great, Thomas explained, that humans were incapable of reconciling themselves with God: 'to find redemption, however, humankind could not incline its soul to counsel' (*ad hanc autem redempcionem inveniendam, non potuit consilium hominis inclinare animum suum*).[53] It was for this reason that Christ, the height of humility, was sent to earth, embodying the spirit of

Justice and mercy

counsel, in order to advise and plead with man to relinquish his *superbia* and be reconciled to God. Framing mercy in this way – as a counsel, a course determined by advice, the product of persuasion – had the effect of situating it as an action open to discussion, even criticism. In this sense it was not a precept – mercy was a consideration to be valued in judgment, but not necessarily always to be applied, particularly when other concerns (security, propriety, necessity) might argue against it. This was as true in the application of monastic discipline as it was in the setting of penitential punishments and in the legal courts of the *saeculum*.

Dissolving the difference between precept and counsel

For all the careful attempts to categorise each utterance of Christ according to its status either as an imperative precept or as persuasive counsel, there was an important sense in which theologians dissolved much of the force of this theoretical distinction in practice. Although distinguishing between counsel and precept was valuable in terms of doctrine, in a pastoral context (in which many, if not all, of the authors cited here operated), the dividing line was deliberately blurred. One might speak, seemingly paradoxically, of a 'saving counsel'.[54] As the Victorine commentator on the Rule of Augustine had observed, even if it were possible for an individual to live their life fulfilling only those commands which would assure salvation, this was not particularly praiseworthy, and it was, in his opinion, certainly not what Christians ought to strive for. Even though a distinction between imperfect and perfect was constructed in the physical walls between secular world and cloister, the 'imperfect' should still be challenged and exhorted to follow *all* the counsels they were capable of fulfilling. As a result, sermons on mercy and justice deliberately softened the distinction between precept and counsel when it came to exhortation and practice.

One revealing demonstration of this is found in Alan of Lille's *Summa de arte praedicatoria* (1198), a text which instructs the priest how to preach – with maximum effectiveness – to a variety of groups, and on different occasions. Alan advises priests to exhort their flock (in this case, imperfect humans) to exclude anger from their minds. He suggests the preacher employ the words of Christ, exhorting the injured party not to place restrictions on their forgiveness towards an offender, but 'forgive up to seventy times seven' (Matthew xviii.22).[55] This argument for repeated forgiveness of those who have caused one injury is to be used to instruct the laity in general, even if it is considered only to be a counsel. In Alan of Lille's view, it is certainly not an exclusive value of the cloister. Alan adds that all must do their best to observe this: 'if we are not among those perfect enough to pay back good for evil, at least let us return as little evil as possible for evil'.[56] The cumulative effect of these exhortations to mercy is to blur the distinction between those actions strictly necessary for salvation (precepts) and those which are merely desirable in a good Christian (counsels). Alan of Lille drew a close connection between *misericordia, consilium* and the petition for forgiveness of sins elsewhere in his writing, most clearly in his *De virtutibus de vitiis et de donis spiritus sancti* (c.1170–80).[57] It is notable that his work on preaching, however, while it retains the link between *misericordia* and the petition 'dimitte', presents this in a much less schematic way. He instead prefers to exhort his audience to mercy through reference to exemplary figures of mercy.[58] Similarly, Alan simplifies the complex exegetical commentary surrounding the Incarnation and the traditions of *Cur Deus homo*, asking 'for what was the incarnation of Christ if not an act of *misericordia*?'.[59]

Arguments over the precise status of counsel and precept prompt the question of whether twelfth- and thirteenth-century theologians truly believed that the laity would take up the call to mercy, and that the precepts of the Sermon on the Mount could be fulfilled by all Christians in practice. A variety of responses can be observed. Rupert of Deutz, for example, criticised those individuals who foolishly considered the many precepts of God to be impossible to fulfil.[60] Rupert was explicitly thinking here of the precept 'love your enemy'. Those who averred that it was impossible to fulfil such a precept, he states, claimed that it was enough for humans simply not to hate their enemies, since to love them would be more than nature could endure. But Rupert is adamant in his rejection of this argument: it is entirely possible to love one's enemy, and this can be seen in practice on earth. Rupert here provided the example of Christ's prayers for his crucifiers, and, strikingly, seems to believe that this act of mercy could be imitated by twelfth-century Christians, clergy and laity alike. Likewise, he offers the (again, imitable) examples of the proto-martyr Stephen praying for those who stoned him and King David weeping for his persecutors. Rupert may have been writing in a monastic context, but his comments suggest that there was at least some practical consideration of how far divine precepts were achievable on earth, beyond the walls of the cloister. Even those theologians who took the opposite view and conceded that some precepts could not be fulfilled in this life, did not attribute this to any cause so simple as an irredeemably violent society which would always ignore Church teaching. Instead, they argued, it was because of the conflicted nature of post-lapsarian humankind in whom the will to obey

God's commands was often at variance with the will of the flesh, and, as such, although no amount of exhortation could actually cure man of this sinful nature, it was still valuable to dwell on those precepts. This is a compromise position, demonstrated by Hugh of St Victor, who explains that God sometimes prohibits actions which humans cannot avoid. Hugh gives the example here of the command to love God with all our heart (but he might as easily have chosen 'love your enemies'). Hugh cites Augustine, who had argued that no one could fulfil this precept in the present life, where loving God *ex toto corde, ex toto anima, ex toto mente* was impossible.[61] Hugh added to this his own comment that, although God did indeed prohibit that which no one was completely able to avoid and command that which no one was completely able to fulfil, he did this for a reason. Attempting to fulfil these precepts would humble the spirits of the proud and prepare the worthy to receive grace. Even if one could not achieve it, this was still good practice – and an exhortation worth repeating.[62]

Among English theologians, the concern over whether any divine precept might be truly fulfilled in the present life was also raised by Robert Grosseteste in his pastoral treatise on the Ten Commandments. Grosseteste noted that carnal *concupiscentia* was prohibited by the ninth commandment. However, he adds, given humankind's sinful and fleshly nature, it is not possibly to entirely prevent ourselves from committing this sin in this present life.[63] The point of its inclusion in the Decalogue, he concludes, was not to command something which was unachievable, but to encourage and exhort men to make an effort to diminish, mortify and limit their sinful urges. Grosseteste, like Hugh of St Victor, cites the same passage from Augustine on this point – there are some precepts which cannot be complete in this life, and will only be perfected in the future life. Grosseteste added his own reassurance: humans should not be considered transgressors of a precept which they could not perfect, so long as they worked towards it.[64] In a move which effectively dissolves the strictness of a hierarchical distinction between counsel and precept, he argued that simply to move towards the fulfilment of an impossible command was to be regarded, in the circumstances of the human post-lapsarian condition, as fulfilment of it.

This quotation which begins this chapter sounds a note of frustration – Gerald of Wales's frustration. To 'love' one's enemy, to love and forgive (i.e. to be merciful towards) one who had wronged you might be nearly impossible. On one hand, Gerald's statement seems to make the case for those historians who would suggest that 'mercy' was at most a castle drawn in the air by theologians – admirable in theory, all but impossible in practice given the realities of human nature. Mercy – the mercy commanded by scripture – was a high standard to achieve. Yet, on the other hand, Gerald's lament can also be read as a demonstration of exactly the quandary examined here: a desire to act virtuously in the world, to follow the admonishments of scripture and frustration when those ideas could only be realised imperfectly. Gerald does not dismiss mercy out of hand – only admits that the transition between praise of mercy in writing and merciful action is mighty difficult to achieve.

Kings and bishops

Asking 'what's the difference between a king and a bishop in a court?' sounds like the beginning of a bad joke. It is, however, a question with which medieval historians must grapple, because it forces us to examine how the judicial roles and duties of kings and bishops were constructed. Those familiar with medieval society and medieval patterns of thought might instinctively suspect that 'mercy' is constituted differently according to the group one is examining. That would follow a certain logic: for example, *sermones ad status* address different groups differently, according to a recognition of their different characteristics. The virtues that preachers expect monks to exercise are not the same as the virtues which knights have the opportunity to demonstrate; likewise, a 'good' widow showed her holy behaviour in a different way to a 'good' merchant. Different groups could do different things. But how does that rationale apply to royal ('secular') and ecclesiastical ('church') judges? Is it more useful to understand their roles as different, according to the different demands of the courts in which they gave judgment and the different types of law they administered, or fundamentally similar, based on the fact that all 'judges' represent a particular kind of category in which all members share certain kinds of characteristics? To put it more bluntly: were kings expected to be less merciful than bishops? The question about expectations of mercy matters because, ultimately, it cuts to the issue of how we conceive of the respective roles of kings and bishops, crown and Church, in judgment. The assumption, implicit in much historiography, is that as common law became more professionalised it became less 'merciful'. Royal power, as it became more assertive, became more forceful, while ecclesiastical judges understood forgiveness and mercy, and continued to understand it, as an integral part of their office.[65]

Increasing royal control over the operation of law, from the mid-twelfth century onwards, is often seen as synonymous with the increasing severity of the law. This is not just a matter of the fierce personalities of Angevin rulers,[66] for Henry II is typically depicted as the stern judge who restored the rigour and bite of his grandfather's laws, laws which had lapsed under the stewardship of Stephen.[67] Tied to the perception of a renewal of royal judicial activity under Henry is the understanding that, around 1155, the deterrent force of common law was renewed. That perception is reinforced by some of the commentary surrounding Henry II's conflict with Thomas Becket, especially concerning the punishment of 'felonious' or 'criminous' clerks.[68] Accounts of the Becket dispute have tended to treat this clash as an explicit conflict of principles of punishment, and, in that argument, the majority of historians have expressed a degree of sympathy for Henry's apparent desire to punish malefactors 'properly'.[69] From this assumption, it is but a short step to characterising ecclesiastical punishments as 'sloppy and lax'.[70] When pitted against the predestined forward march of the 'rational' common law, such negative verdicts on permissive medieval ecclesiastical courts can hardly be avoided.[71] Church courts were an 'easy option', a place of perfunctory and soft justice.

Modern historians' verdicts on the question of Church justice at Clarendon do, to some extent, reflect those of their medieval forebears. William of Newburgh, for example, characterised the entire dispute between Becket and Henry as a quarrel over the issue of punishment. His *Historia rerum Anglicarum* (c.1196–98) praises Henry for restoring the 'public discipline', which had decayed in the preceding years of civil war.[72] When the king, William recounts, turned his attention to ecclesiastical affairs, he was horrified by the laxity of Church punishments against serious felons. William deplores the 'languid' (*languida*) justice of the Church, and criticises the bishops who believe that the protection of wicked priests against royal justice is a part of their office.[73] William of Newburgh's view has largely been that of posterity. This kind of narrative about the increasing discipline of royal justice throughout the twelfth century goes some way to suggesting that kings were coming to care less for mercy and more for punitive justice.

The apparent contrast between royal stricture and ecclesiastical mildness evident in modern historiography of the common law has also been affirmed more recently in intellectual history. Philippe Buc's *L'Ambiguïté du livre* has argued for a similar contrast between punitive royal power and merciful ecclesiastical lordship. Buc studied the theological foundations for, and legitimation of, royal power according to Parisian theologians, based on his readings of numerous biblical glosses produced in the schools of the twelfth and thirteenth centuries. His comments are worth considering here because this is one point at which the intellectual history of 'power' and the legal

Who should be merciful?

and social history of English law do seem to converge in their judgments. Although Buc deals with biblical commentaries composed in Paris, his work pays particular attention to the writings of English theologians such as Stephen Langton and Ralph Niger, and also to a number of masters who had a considerable influence on English authors, such as Peter Comestor and Peter the Chanter. Buc argues that, from late antiquity onwards, theologians considered *iustitia* to be the defining attribute of royal *potestas*, whereas *misericordia* was the dominant aspect of priestly power: 'punir est essentiellement royal, épargner essentiellement sacerdotal'.[74] Excess of *misericordia* defines a martyr, endowed with 'spiritual' power but lacking in temporal authority; excess of punitive power is the hallmark of a tyrant, one who commands great *iustitia* but lacks merciful virtue. Buc asserts that only Christ was believed to be capable of 'the paradoxical and unique synthesis of the two orders and the two virtues', namely justice and mercy.[75]

For Buc, the polarisation of Church and 'state' as mercy and justice respectively provides the intellectual context for a dramatic change in the way in which twelfth-century theologians conceived of *potestas*. Certain scriptural commentators, Buc argues, began to reassess the foundations of royal power, considering whether it might not have some positive functions. If the origin of royal power did not lie in an Augustinian punishment for sin (*remedium peccati*), it might claim a basis for authority equal to, but separate from, ecclesiastical power. What prompted these discussions, Buc argues, was that the absence of mercy in royal power became increasingly apparent in the century or so following the 'feudal revolution', as European rulers became more assertive. It was only in exceptional cases (for example, that of the saintly Louis IX) that a king of outstanding virtue might be relied upon to incorporate merciful principles into the practice of secular rule.[76] There is here, then, an intellectual background for the complaints of those English chroniclers who observed the apparently excessive mercies of English ecclesiastical law.

It is worth expanding on the intellectual genealogy of the dichotomy set out by Buc, who merely notes that it had its origins in antiquity. This scheme of Church–state relations dates back to Constantine and the beginnings of Christian *imperium*. It is not the Church's office to punish; rather its members should be arguing against the excessive severity of secular justice. The role of the bishop is to rebuke the ruler who wields the sword unnecessarily, as, to borrow an image frequently invoked in *specula principum*, Ambrose of Milan had reprimanded the emperor Theodosius for permitting a massacre to take place at Thessalonica.[77] The holy man intercedes to save the life of the condemned villain; individual churches,

Justice and mercy

shrines and abbeys provide sanctuary to the accused. This *topos* of episcopal intervention in secular justice recurs frequently in medieval hagiography, including the hagiography of twelfth- and thirteenth-century England. It derives ultimately from the writings of Augustine, who argued that it is incumbent on a bishop always to sue for mercy in secular courts, always to argue against a capital sentence – the Church, and its representatives, must attempt to rehabilitate, rather than condemn.[78] Augustine's letters abound with such images of intercession: the bishop has a place within the Roman courts, mitigating their punitive excesses and reminding them of the higher laws of clemency. Augustine carved out a functional role for the bishop as intercessor, a figure as integral to the working of the secular courts as the prosecutor or defence counsel.

An example of this principle explicitly spelled out in an Angevin context can be found in the *Practica legum et decretorum* attributed to William Longchamp, Bishop of Ely and Chancellor of England under Richard I. The *Practica legum*, composed c.1183–88, is William's summary of Romano-canonical procedure, likely intended for English lawyers and judges who might be in need of an understanding of civil law principles and the procedures they might encounter in ecclesiastical courts.[79] Indeed, there was evident benefit to lawyers and judges pondering what the common law shared with other legal systems, especially when it came to problems of procedure. In that sense, for John Baker, this was as much a speculative reflection on universal ideas about law as a practical guide.[80] William's text is largely concerned with questions of how to begin an action, summons and exceptions.[81] It is, however, prefaced with several paragraphs remarking on the nature, purpose and value of law, among which are contained William's reflections on the respective role of law in the hands of the clergy and in the hands of secular rulers. William's remarks often verge on the formulaic, but it is instructive to consider the assumptions of an individual who oversaw the administration of justice in England.[82] William explains that there are two types of law, as there are two swords, and it is the secular ruler who wields the more severe power (*duritia*) in order to correct the excesses of the laity; the pope's legislative authority serves to govern the priesthood, something achieved through diligence (*diligentia*).[83] They have command in common, but their spheres are clearly delineated and (implicitly, at least), their approaches vary. Thus, William implies, the vision is bipartite: ecclesiastical law is defined against the secular, and as such, is distinguished by its more gentle approach to wrongdoers.

Further support for a 'complementary' interpretation of the judicial functions of bishop (or priest) and king (or judge) may be glimpsed in

Who should be merciful?

practice in an incident recounted in the *Chronica* of Roger of Howden.[84] In 1183, that is, around the same time that William Longchamp was composing his *Practica legum*, the Bishop of Worcester, Baldwin of Forde, was riding past a gallows when he encountered a group of royal officials about to hang a knight who had been condemned to death on the false charges of the king's justiciar, Ranulf de Glanvill. Baldwin commanded these officials that they should not put the knight to death, for it was a Sunday and the feast day of Mary Magdalene, and no execution could be carried out on such a holy day. The force of Baldwin's argument for mercy towards the knight may have been supported by the popular reputation of the Magdalene: as the greatest of sinners, but one who had nonetheless been granted forgiveness by Christ, she was frequently invoked in sermons and discussions of penance as an avatar for human sin, human repentance and divine mercy.[85] Whatever the details of Baldwin's actual argument (not provided in Howden's account), Baldwin managed to sway the royal officials, delaying the execution: ultimately the knight's innocence was proven and the sentence of death retracted. What is most striking about this incident, however, is Henry II's apparent response. According to Howden, when news reached Henry of the bishop's intervention in the execution, the king did not rage at an affront to his justice, but determined to promote Baldwin to the see of Canterbury. It seems that Baldwin performed his role precisely according to the rules of Augustinian political theory, embodying the mercy that was a necessary dictate of his office. Likewise, Henry II understood the unspoken, customary relationship between the punitive royal arm and merciful ecclesiastical intercessors: to sue for mercy was one of the primary political roles of his bishops.

These *exempla* would seem to support arguments for a contrast in contemporary understanding between the purposes of royal and ecclesiastical judgment and punishment, indeed, they lend weight to a specifically 'Augustinian' perspective on how the two should relate to one another. In a post-lapsarian world, in which harmonious political organisation is nearly impossible, royal power must aim at preserving the peace and protecting the righteous.[86] Princes exist to punish malefactors. The Church, by contrast, occupies itself with the more lofty aim of bringing humankind back into a proper relationship with God. Royal power is punitive, Church power merciful. The king puts the wicked to the sword, the Church attempts to save souls. The two institutions take different approaches but perform complementary roles in the prosecution of justice. This complementary interpretation, however, has the potential to become profoundly misleading. Buc's polarisation of Church and crown, *misericordia* and *iustitia*, may provide an orderly intellectual resolution, but is not entirely convincing when compared to the comments of twelfth-century authors on judicial duties. The first problem is that Buc's concentration on the origins and legitimacy of royal *potestas* results in a focus on *royal* justice alone. As such, he offers a detailed account of how *misericordia* might or might not fit within the prince's role, but he does not cover the same ground for sacerdotal rulers. While Buc does concede that the difference between king and priest lies in the proportion of mercy to justice found in their judgments, he fails to consider whether those proportions could pose as much of a problem in the Church as they might in secular courtrooms.[87] The difficulties which a priest might encounter in determining an appropriate penance or the many possible strategies (some mild, some more severe) which an English bishop might adopt when dealing with a group of heretics, go some way to illustrating this problem of proportions. Judges in *both* common *and* canon law were faced with a choice of possible punishments, of differing degrees of mercy and strict justice.

The second problem is to determine how well Buc's theory accords with English, rather than French, practice. His complementary model was forged in the process of compartmentalising various twelfth- and thirteenth-century theologians into three categories, representing either 'theocratic', 'monarchical' or 'egalitarian' ways of conceiving of the relationship between royal and ecclesiastical *potestas*. Buc's approach thus sets up a dynamic in which those two powers must be in competition for primacy, as theorists of royal power seek to justify its dominion. Buc begins from a point in which the relationship between *regnum* and *sacerdotium* has broken down. While this may be evident in certain biblical passages on which Buc's chosen glossators focused (not least the Book of Judges, in which kingship is instituted as punishment for the failures of the Israelite priesthood), this position does not represent the daily reality of relations between crown and Church in Anglo-Norman and Angevin England. In practice we might very well expect a royal judge to have been 'counselled' by the ecclesiastical power in some way – that is, for royal power to take on the ideas of mercy to the extent that one can no longer usefully use the terms *iustitia* and *misericordia* to describe the differences between the two powers. Such 'counsel' could take a number of forms: royal judges might be recruited from among the ranks of the Church (as Henry II famously did);[88] it might be found in the correspondence between royal justices and members of the Church, in *speculum principis* treatises, in the advice provided in a letter, or merciful principles might simply be imbibed through study, exposure to scripture and preaching. Thus, while the idea of a contrast between royal severity and

Who should be merciful?

ecclesiastical leniency should not be discarded altogether, it does at least need to be redrawn, and the contrast softened. Ecclesiastical mercy was not ordinarily expected to act as a check on over-zealous royal justices. In the same way, while it is possible to perceive in the Becket conflict certain elements of a struggle between royal and ecclesiastical jurisdictions, this should not be allowed to set the tone for the entirety of the twelfth century. It is, for example, no longer uncritically accepted that medieval conflicts over the right to sanctuary represent a clash between ecclesiastical rights and the secular power's desire to bring all of England under a single legal system, excising the ancient exceptions and anomalies within the common law, of which sanctuary was one.[89] In the same way, our understanding of the role of judicial power in twelfth-century England requires reassessment.

The case for royal and ecclesiastical mercy

Twelfth- and thirteenth-century moral theology argues that the judicial responsibilities of princes and bishops were founded on a common moral basis. Theologians sketch an image of judicial power which carefully and deliberately blurs the distinction between common and canon law courts, addressing all judges as unified by a shared commitment to mercy. It is here we should return to Thomas of Chobham. In the previous section of this chapter, Thomas of Chobham was distinguishing between the justice of the great and the justice of the laity. The great correspond to those who have 'official' roles in judgment, those who hold judicial office – a category which does not distinguish between great ones in royal or Church government.

This is also the case in the presentation of judicial power in a sermon preached by Thomas at the abbey of Saint-Germain-des-Prés in the 1220s.[90] Thomas there addresses what he describes as 'the difficult dispute between justice and mercy (*controversie inter iustitiam et misericordiam*)'.[91] The sermon considers how the contradictory passages of the Bible treating justice and mercy are to be translated into practical instructions for the judge. Thomas's conclusion is that mercy is always to be preferred to strict justice. In fact, the entire corpus of Thomas's sermons overflows with judicial guidance.[92] Elsewhere, for example, Thomas considers how the judge who presides over a doubtful case should proceed. When the motive of the accused is unclear, Thomas notes, the judge is advised always to interpret 'for the better', that is, to attribute to them the best possible motive, and to hand down the least punitive sentence.[93] Relatively little is known about the context in which these sermons were preached. Thomas had served Bishop Herbert le Poore in Salisbury as an expert on penitential discipline until the death of the bishop in 1217; sometime after this Thomas returned to Paris for a second period of study. It seems that many of these sermons, some of which are known to have been preached at the churches of Saint-Germain-des-Prés, Saint-Jacques and Saint-Victor, date from that second period in Paris, between 1222 and 1228. It is possible, however, that others were adapted from earlier sermons Thomas had given in Salisbury, and thus touch upon themes on which he had previously preached, or would subsequently preach on, in England.

One potential challenge in utilising Thomas of Chobham's sermons (which, in any case, represent an incomplete body of work and are not ordered according to any obvious organising principle) is that most seem to have been preached to educated clerics, some to 'university' audiences and others, as the rubrics suggest, to monastic *claustrales*. Unlike in Thomas's earlier work, the *Summa confessorum*, the education and edification of the laity or the ignorant priest was not a priority in these sermons. Yet although not written for a general audience, the sermon texts do still illuminate Thomas's understanding of *iustitia* and *misericordia* as the two ideas operated in the secular world. In fact, what is of interest here is not the audience for these sermons (for Thomas is not particularly concerned to exhort them to justice in judgment), but the content, which provides a sophisticated reflection on the relationship between secular and ecclesiastical processes of judgment. Strikingly, Thomas does not invoke any species of mercy particular to those in religious office. Rather he argues that the particular mercy required in judges derives from the more general mercy which *all* Christians are obliged to show when they restrain themselves from doing harm. This is the duty of all Christians called to judge, Thomas argues, and one which we are bound to through baptism. The oil with which Christian children are anointed at baptism symbolises the oil of mercy.[94] As the name 'Christiani' derives from 'Christus', meaning chrism, all Christians are known as 'anointed ones', that is to say, 'anointed with mercy'. Thomas took this etymological connection between Christianity, chrism and mercy from Augustine.[95] For the Bishop of Hippo, however, writing eight centuries earlier, this idea would have held significantly different implications. Baptism was not then a routine sacrament given to all children – as it had become by the twelfth century – but an act of dedication of one's life more usually undertaken by committed adult Christians.[96] For Thomas of Chobham, however, that all were baptised meant that all were obliged to be merciful.

Thomas of Chobham is rare – if not unique – in drawing out the relationship between mercy, unction and baptism so explicitly and to such a didactic end. Other twelfth-century authors, however, do support the connection between *oleum* (oil) and *misericordia*, the commonest explanatory gloss being that mercy is exalted above justice just as, in nature, oil floats on the surface of water.[97] The description of the 'oil of mercy' also builds on a patristic commonplace: for Gregory the Great, the exemplary case of mercy in scripture was found in the actions of the Samaritan towards the wounded man he discovered on the roadside (Luke x.34). Thus the application of oil to heal (*sanare*) the wounds of the injured man represents the application of mercy to those spiritually in need of it. Indeed, the entire incident prefigures the mercy of Christ (symbolised by the Samaritan) curing the sinful through his offer of mercy.[98] The relationship between the oil of unction and mercy is quite conventional in allegorical commentaries on scripture; it seems that Thomas of Chobham simply developed this connection a little further, turning the allegory to the moral end best fitted for his preaching. Other authors, however, do tentatively approach the same idea: Stephen Langton draws out the link between baptism and the duty to be merciful (although without directly invoking the idea of unction) in his commentary on Leviticus.[99] The association between unction, mercy and baptism is also hinted at in another (anonymous) thirteenth-century sermon, which describes the *unctio* of chrism as *oleo et balsamo*.[100] William of Auvergne provided a slightly different interpretation when discussing the virtue of clemency, but one which also stressed the role of anointing and the parallels between priestly and royal duties: 'both authorities [i.e. secular and ecclesiastical] are conferred through anointing, in order that, through sacred unction, kings and priests recognise that they preside over their subjects not as executioners, but as tender guardians and governors'.[101]

Thomas of Chobham further emphasises the duty of mercy for secular magnates in another sermon, preached in Paris at the recently founded Dominican convent of Saint-Jacques.[102] His topic is the symbolism of kingship, represented by three items: the crown, the sceptre and act of unction, and Thomas glosses the symbolic meaning of each one. The crown of gold denotes the royal duty to reward the good and distribute largesse. The other two, the sceptre and the act of unction, symbolise two complementary aspects of kingship which need to be kept in balance – mercy and justice, lenient and punitive principles.[103] Speaking of unction, Thomas repeats the admonition of his earlier sermon: *misericordia* is a duty of all Christians. When he comes to the sceptre, he glosses this item as the sword with which kings punish the wicked. Even here, however, Thomas is extremely reticent to license unchecked royal retribution against malefactors, and royal judges are counselled to use discretion (*discretio*). Christ's command to his followers 'put away your sword' (Matthew xxvi.52), applies to kings when they act as judges: it instructs them to pity, rather than condemn, the accused man. In Thomas of Chobham's view, therefore, kings must take it upon themselves to pass lenient, merciful sentences, not wait for episcopal intervention. Any 'complementary' model of punitive royal power mitigated by merciful ecclesiastical influence would, on this reckoning, fail to respect an obligation incumbent upon *all* Christian judges. Likewise, the judge in the episcopal court – who is, in any case, not permitted to pass a capital sentence – must address the same problem in weighing punishment and leniency, in judging whether to adhere to or diverge from the law. The dual duties of mercy and punishment are symbolised in the royal office by sword and unction, and in the priestly office by the *virga et baculus*, the rod and the staff. One punishes and chastises offenders, the other comforts the wretched.

In order to understand the significance of Thomas's discussion of the iconography of rulership, it is necessary to appreciate just how often this image of *virga et baculus* was employed in *pastoralia*. The pairing is drawn from scripture, where, for example, the Psalmist describes God's rod and staff as his comfort.[104] Across twelfth-century Europe the image is a commonplace used to define the pastoral role of priests. It is set out, for example, in the writings of the Benedictine Honorius of Autun, and was later explained at great length in the *Rationale divinorum officiorum* of William Durand (before 1286).[105] It is used by Adam of Eynsham in his *vita* of Hugh of Lincoln (c.1212) to demonstrate the same principle of the necessary balance in ecclesiastical judgment between chastisement and mercy.[106] Peter the Chanter, whose *Verbum abbreviatum* provides a guide to the most basic – and important – principles of pastoral theology, offers the same point in different form, advising the priest to punish with the rod of the father (*verbera patris*) and comfort with the nourishing breasts of the mother (*ubera matris*).[107] Thomas of Chobham's pronouncement is repeated to the same didactic effect in the *Liber poenitentialis* of Robert of Flamborough, his near contemporary. The *baculus pastoralis*, he writes, symbolises the rectitude of rule; the rod is the instrument through which the priest is sparing to the humble and subdues the proud (*parcere subiectis et debellare superbos*).[108] Robert also recalls a few lines of poetry attributed to Stephen Langton on this very subject of the balance of severity and mercy, a recipe for pastoral effectiveness.[109]

The *virga et baculus* constitutes a well-worn *topos*, an iconographical scheme so familiar that it has been passed over without comment by medieval historians. Indeed, it sometimes seems a rather meaningless pastoral platitude. Yet it was an image so often repeated because it was thought to be foundational to the judicial-pastoral conception of ecclesiastical office. It embodied the essential truth – a truth which was also a profound practical problem – that the ecclesiastical judge has a duty to chastise as much as pardon. This presents a rather less dramatic contrast than that of an invariably merciful priest challenging the unyielding and severe king. It is not easy, given the abundance of iconographical evidence, to preserve Buc's argument of strict division: that punishment belongs to the king, mercy to the priest. The primary problem for the Church is not to ensure its officers intervene in secular courts because of the general lack of mercy in other men – it is finding a workable pastoral compromise within its *own* courts of judgment.

Thomas of Chobham's sermons provide the most detailed explanation of the common foundation of royal and ecclesiastical judgment: kings and bishops, when sitting as judges, ought to perform the same roles in the same way. The point is also made explicit by Robert Grosseteste, in a *dictum* which compares the roles of kings and priests. Grosseteste explains that just as the office (*officium*) of a king is to use laws to reward the good and punish the wicked, so the prelates of the Church do the same. The tools of the Church are the statutes of the fathers and canonical sanctions, but like the laws of kings they are used to coerce (*cohercent*) the wicked.[110]

Naturally, there are qualifications and caveats to be made. To assert that ecclesiastical and royal judges faced the same problem is not to say that theologians equated the setting of penance to the act of giving judgment in a secular court. These were clearly different actions, with different intentions, as Nicole Bériou has demonstrated.[111] The point is rather that the moral duties for the executors of canon and common law looked rather similar, even if those laws inflicted discipline quite differently. All judges inhabited the same moral universe.

The roles of ecclesiastical and royal judges were not and should not be perceived as fundamentally different during this period. Instead of a model that polarises royal severity and ecclesiastical leniency, judicial office in both religious and secular *fora* ought to be understood as defined by choice: the choice to wield either the rod or the staff, as the particulars of the case demanded. Even if the tradition and transmission of the two laws (common and canon) look very different, the underlying principles are the same. Of course, the bishop, like Daniel in the case of Susannah, had an obligation to intervene in secular justice when he witnessed a judicial abuse, but this was the duty of every diligent minister, and, indeed, all virtuous Christians.[112] As will be seen in the next chapter, the greatest problem for Church judges in the twelfth century, however, was not the question of

Justice and mercy

how to limit the excesses of secular punishment, but how to respond to an internal, ecclesiastical, argument about how mercy and justice should be realised within the Church itself.

Notes

1 'Utinam autem vindictam omnino nullam appeteremus, sed equanimiter omnia sustinere possemus, adeo ut in una maxilla percussi et alteram incontinenti preberemus, nulli malum pro malo reddentes neque vinci a malo, sed vincere magis in bono malum per omnia satagentes! Hanc autem doctrinam apostolicam sepius quidem audivimus, sed ad eius revera perfectionem nondum pervenire prevaluimus: veterem enim imperfectonem adhuc imitantes et qui nostra tollit pro inimico reputantes, et amicos diligimus et inimicos nostros praesertim vero pertinaciter et irrevocabiliter in nos grassantes exosos habentes.' Gerald of Wales, *Speculum duorum: or, a Mirror of Two Men*, ed. Y. Lefebvre and R. B. C. Huygens, trans. B. Dawson (Cardiff, 1974), Ep. 7, 261.
2 For the outline of these debates, see Malcolm D. Lambert, *Franciscan Poverty* (revised edition, New York, 1998), 33–72, and Virpi Mäkinen, *Propery Rights in the Late Medieval Discussion on Franciscan Poverty* (Leuven, 2001). The particular relevance of precept as a category is discussed in David Burr, *Spiritual Franciscans: From Protest to Persecution in the Century after Saint Francis* (University Park, PA, 2001), 56–7 and 144–50.
3 G. Leff, 'The apostolic ideal in later medieval ecclesiology', *Journal of Theological Studies* 18 (1967), 58–82.
4 For example, *GO* on Matthew xix.12, PL.114.148C; on 1 Corinthians vii.2, 114.529C; cf. *Decretum*, C.27, q.1, c.20, 1:1055.
5 L. Melve, 'The public debate on clerical marriage in the late eleventh century', *Journal of Ecclesiastical History* 61 (2010), 688–701.
6 This preface is not included when the injunction is repeated at Mark x.21.
7 Rupert of Deutz, *De sancta trinitate et operibus eius*, ed. H. Haacke, CCCM 21–24 (4 vols, Turnhout, 1971–2), 5.16, 4:1996.
8 *Ibid.*, 5.16, 4:1996.
9 Peter Abelard, *The Sic et Non: A Critical Edition*, ed. B. B. Boyer and R. McKeon (Chicago, 1976–77), prologue, 96.
10 For example, *Enarrationes in Matthaeum*, PL.162.1302C.
11 John D. Cotts, *The Clerical Dilemma: Peter of Blois and Literature Culture in the Twelfth Century* (Washington, DC, 2009), 241–3.
12 Peter of Blois, *De charitate Dei et proximi*, 35, PL.207.935C.
13 *Ibid.*, 39, 938C.
14 *Ibid.*, 38, 936.
15 'Verumtamen de inimici dilectione certo et expresso sententiae decreto Dominus in Evangelio nos astringit, ita quod si quis inimicum non diligit, divinae legis praevaricator existit.' *Ibid.*, 38, 936.

Who should be merciful?

16 Matthew v.44; Luke vi.27; Romans xii.20; Matthew v.39.
17 The *Glossa ordinaria*, for example, notes that to love one's enemies and pray for them is the 'summit of perfection' (*cumulus perfectionis*), but does not spell out the implications of this idea – are we then to infer that only the perfect aspire to praying for their enemies (PL.114.98C)?
18 Abelard, *Sic et Non*, 36, 463–4; Abelard's discussion is primarily drawn from Augustine's *De doctrina Christiana* and Ambrosiaster's *Commentarius in epistolas Pauli ad Romanos*.
19 Hugh of St Victor, *Quaestiones in epistolas Pauli*, PL.175.567–8, discussing Luke iv, 'diligite inimicos vestros'.
20 'Praecepto tenemur omnium salutem velle; sed impendere etiam officia pietatis inimicis quantum ad infirmos, et minos perfectos, consilium est, quantum ad perfectos praeceptum.' *Ibid.*, 568.
21 Robert of Melun, *QDP*, q.90, 45–6.
22 William of Auxerre, *Summa aurea*, 15.5, 3:277.
23 Simon of Tournai, *Disputatio* 86.5, 249; cf. 89.5, 257.
24 Robert of Melun, *QEP*, q.122, 61.
25 Thomas of Chobham, *SC*, 6.5.6a, 320.
26 *Ibid.*, 6.1.3a, 245.
27 On this incident see Timothy Reuter, '*Velle sibi fieri in forma hac*: symbolic acts in the Becket dispute', in *Medieval Polities and Modern Mentalities*, ed. J. L. Nelson (Cambridge, 2006), 182–3.
28 *SC*, 6.1.3a, 245.
29 *SCV*, 4.2.2.3, 169.
30 *Ibid.*, 4.2.2.1, 150–1.
31 For example, Guerric of St Quentin, *Quaestiones de quolibet*, ed. Walter H. Principe (Toronto, 2002), appendix 1, 396–7.
32 For example, Simon of Tournai, *Disputatio* 29, 88–91; cf. *VA*, 2.9, 648–50.
33 Alan of Lille, *Regulae theologicae*, PL.210.750A–B.
34 This latter from Psalms ix.23: 'they are caught in the counsels they devise'.
35 *Consilium* could have a dual meaning as both a personal opinion and a judicial verdict. See *Enarrationes in Matthaeum*, PL.162.1294.
36 For justice as the choice between two differently advantageous counsels, see Chapter 7.
37 This idea is set out explicitly in The Four Daughters of God, discussed in Chapter 8.
38 Smalley, 'Some gospel commentaries'; Damien Van den Eynde, 'Autour des "Enarrationes in Evangelium S. Matthaei" attribuées à Geoffroi Babion', *RTAM* 26 (1959), 50–84.
39 See Brundage, *Medieval Origins*, 283–343; cf. *GO*, Matthew v.34, PL.114.95D–96B.
40 William of Auxerre, *Summa aurea*, 3.18.3, 4:378.
41 Beryl Smalley, 'Peter Comestor on the gospels and his sources', *RTAM* 46 (1979), 125.

Justice and mercy

42 For example, *GO*, Matthew v.2, PL.114.89A–B.
43 O. Lottin, 'La doctrine d'Anselme de Laon sur les dons du Saint-Esprit et son influence', *RTAM* 24 (1957), 268.
44 'Consilium congruit misericordibus. Hoc enim unum remedium est de tantis malis evadendi, ut dimittamus sicut nobis dimitti volumus, et adiuvemus in quo possumus alios, sicut nos in quo non possumus cupimus adiuvari.' Augustine, *De sermone Domini in monte*, ed. Almut Mutzenbecher, CCSL 35 (Turnhout, 1967), 1.4.11, 10.
45 *GO*, Matthew v.5–6, PL.1140.90A–B.
46 Hugh of St Victor, *De quinque septenis*, PL.175.405–14; see Table 2.
47 Thomas of Chobham, *SC*, 3.1.9a, 39; see Tables 3 and 4.
48 Lottin, 'La doctrine', and for Stephen Langton, Quinto, 'The *Conflictus vitiorum et virtutum*', 229.
49 *Enarrationes in Matthaeum*, PL.162.1287.
50 Cf. *GO*, Matthew v.48 and vi.10, PL.114.98C, 101C.
51 Rupert of Deutz, *De sancta trinitate*, 3:1509 (glossing Isaiah ii.3).
52 Thomas of Chobham, *Sermones*, ed. Franco Morenzoni, CCCM 82A (Turnhout, 1993), *Sermo* 1, 11–12.
53 *Ibid.*, *Sermo* 1, 12. This sermon also draws on the imagery of Psalms lxxxiv.11 ('mercy and truth have met each other'), the text the scriptural basis for the idea of the 'Four Daughters of God', discussed further in Chapter 7.
54 'salutis consilium', Adam Marsh, *Letters*, Ep. 146, 364.
55 Alan of Lille, *Summa de arte praedicatoria*, 9, PL.210.129D–131C.
56 *Ibid.*, 131A.
57 Alan of Lille, *De virtutibus*, 3.2, 54.
58 Alan of Lille, *Summa de arte praedicatoria*, 18, PL.210.149; cf. 15, 210.141.
59 *Ibid.*, 17, PL.210.147C–149D.
60 Rupert of Deutz, *De gloria et honore filii hominis super Mattheum*, ed. H. Haacke, CCCM 29 (Turnhout, 1979), 5.46–8, 147 (glossing Matthew v.46, 'if you love only those who love you').
61 Augustine, *De spiritu et littera*, ed. C. F. Urba and J. Zyca, CSEL 60 (Vienna, 1913), 225.
62 Hugh of St Victor, *Questiones in epistolas D. Pauli: In Epistolam ad Romanos*, q.172, PL.175.478C–D; q.173, PL.175.474D–475A.
63 Grosseteste, *De decem mandatis*, 9.9, 88.
64 *Ibid.*, 9.9, 89.
65 I have used the term 'bishop' as shorthand: this category might encompass many types of individuals within the Church, including abbots and those officials who served, and sometimes deputised for, bishops in church courts.
66 C. Warren Hollister, *Henry I* (London, 2001), 349–69; W. L. Warren, *Henry II* (London, 1973), 387–8; A. Cooper, '"The feet of those who bark shall be cut off": timorous historians and the personality of Henry I', *Anglo-Norman Studies* 23 (2001), 47–68.

67 For example, Warren, *Henry II*, 388.
68 See David Douglas and George Greenway (eds), *English Historical Documents 2, 1042–1189* (London, 1953), 766–70.
69 C. Duggan, 'The Becket dispute and the criminous clerks', *Bulletin of the Institute of Historical Research* 35:91(1962), 2; cf. L. C. Gabel, *Benefit of Clergy in England in the Later Middle Ages* (New York, 1969), 120.
70 A. K. McHardy, 'Church courts and criminous clerks in the later middle ages', in M. J. Franklin and C. Harper-Bill (eds), *Medieval Ecclesiastical Studies in Honour of Dorothy M. Owen* (Woodbridge, 1995), 166.
71 See Maitland's comment in *The History of English Law*, 1:443; John G. Bellamy, *Crime and Public Order in England in the Later Middle Ages* (London, 1973), 144; Helmholz, *The Ius Commune in England*, 89.
72 William of Newburgh, *Historia rerum Anglicarum*, ed. R. W. Howlett, *Chronicles of the Reigns of Stephen, Henry II and Richard I*, RS 82 (4 vols, London, 1884–90), 2.1, 1:101–2.
73 *Ibid.*, 2.16, 1:140–1; cf. Herbert of Bosham, *Vita Sancti Thomae*, 3.23, *MTB* 3:299–300.
74 *Ibid.*, 51.
75 *Ibid.*, 176–7.
76 *Ibid.*, 185.
77 The penance of Theodosius before Ambrose was a popular depiction of the harmonious cooperation of royal and ecclesiastical power, e.g. *Policraticus*, 4.3, 1:516.
78 For example, Augustine, Ep. 153.3, 398.
79 Brasington characterises it as an English contribution to the burgeoning literature of *ordines* in the late twelfth-century; Bruce. C. Brasington, *Order in the Court: Medieval Procedural Treatises in Translation* (Leiden, 2016), 181–2.
80 J. H. Baker, *Monuments of Endlesse Labours: English Canonists and their Work, 1300–1900* (London, 1998), 3.
81 William Longchamp, *Practica legum et decretorum*, in E. Caillemar, *Le droit civil dans les provinces anglo-normandes au XII siècle* (Caen, 1883), 50–70.
82 Longchamp, for instance, intervened with punitive force after the massacre of the Jews of York in 1190, both dismissing local officers and fining prominent citizens for their complicity. The strength of the action taken, however, is better understood as a reassertion of royal authority rather than a punishment for the anti-Jewish nature of the violence. William Longchamp, *Practica legum et decretorum*, 5, 51, 1:323–4.
83 *Ibid.*
84 Roger of Howden, *Chronica*, ed. W. Stubbs, RS 51 (4 vols, London, 1868–71), 1:314–16.
85 Cf. the tract attributed to Stephen Langton (or possibly the work of his brother, Simon), 'De poenitentia sub persona Magdalenae', Cambridge, Corpus Christi College, Parker Library, CCCC MS 226; see also N. Bériou, 'La Madeleine dans les sermons parisiens du XIIIe siècle', *Mélanges de l'École française de Rome, moyen âge* 104 (1992), 269–340.

86 For Augustine's discussion of this question see Robert Markus, *Saeculum: History and Society in the Thought of St. Augustine* (Cambridge, 1970), esp. 133–53.
87 Buc, *L'Ambiguïté*, 176–7.
88 Ralph Diceto, *Ymagines Historiarum*, in *Radulphi de Diceto decani Lundoniensis Opera Historica*, ed. W. Stubbs, RS 68 (2 vols, London, 1876), 2:434–6. Diceto notes that Henry was so at a loss for judges who would be *amatores iusticiae* that he recruited men from the Church.
89 See G. Rosser, 'Sanctuary and social negotiation', in J. Blair and B. Golding (eds), *The Cloister and the World: Essays in Medieval History in Honour of Barbara Harvey* (Oxford, 1996), 57–79; William Chester Jordan, 'A fresh look at medieval sanctuary', in Ruth Mazo Karras, Joel Kaye and E. Ann Matter (eds), *Law and the Illicit in Medieval Europe* (Philadelphia, 2008), 17–32.
90 On the sermons see Franco Morenzoni, *Des écoles aux paroisses: Thomas de Chobham et la promotion de la prédication au début du XIIIe siècle* (Paris, 1995), and G. R. Evans, 'Thomas of Chobham on preaching and exegesis', *RTAM* 52 (1985), 159–70.
91 Thomas of Chobham, *Sermo* 11, 112.
92 Morenzoni counts that in Thomas's twenty-five extant sermons, the term *iustitia* occurs thirty-two times (along with *iustus*, thirty-nine; *iudicare*, thirty-six; *iudicium*, sixty-six). Justice is by far the most frequently discussed cardinal virtue in the sermons. Likewise, *misericordia* occurs forty-four times, more often than *fortitudo*, *prudentia* or *temperantia*. Morenzoni, *Des écoles aux paroisses*, 261.
93 Thomas of Chobham, *Sermo* 2, 23.
94 Thomas of Chobham, *Sermo* 11, 117.
95 Augustine, *In Johannis Evangelium*, 15.27, 162.
96 See Peter Cramer, *Baptism and Change in the Early Middle Ages c. 200–c. 1150* (Cambridge, 1993), 117–24; 131–16.
97 *VA*, 1.64, 429; Stephen Langton on Leviticus ii.1, BnF, Ms. latin 384, fos 4v–5r, 'per oleum elemosina designatur, sicut enim oleum supernatat, ita opera misercordie semper supernatatur'.
98 Gregory the Great, *Regula pastoralis*, ed. F. Rommel (2 vols, Paris, 1992), 2.6, 1:216.
99 BnF, Ms. latin 384, fos 15r–15v, glossing Leviticus vi.2, 'in baptismo commendavit nobis omnes virtutes misericordiam et iusticiam et omnis alias et ideo misericordes esse debemus deinde estote misericordes sicut et pater vester misericors est'.
100 BnF, Ms. latin 338, fo. 58v, 'De chrismate et confirmatione dicendum est'.
101 'Unde et cum unctione utraque dignitas praestatur ut agnoscant se reges et sacerdotes per sacram unctionem non ad carnificiam subditorum se praefici, sed ad piam custodiam et gubernationem.' William of Auvergne, *De virtutibus*, 12, 1:163.
102 Thomas of Chobham, *Sermo* 20, 210–17; preached between 1222 and 1228.
103 *Ibid.*, 212–17.
104 Psalms xxiii.4; cf. Isaiah x.5.

Who should be merciful?

105 Honorius of Autun, *De gemma animae*, 1.218, PL.172.609D–610A; William Durand, *Rationale divinorum officiorum*, ed. A. Davril and T. M. Thibodeau, CCCM 140 (3 vols, Turnhout, 1995), 3.1–7, 1:214–17.
106 Adam of Eynsham, *Magna vita Sancti Hugonis*, ed. Decima L. Douie and David Hugh Farmer (2 vols, Oxford, 1985), 5.3, 2:85; cf. Gerald of Wales, *Itinerarium Kambriae*, ed. J. F. Dimock, RS 21 (London, 1868), 2.4, 121.
107 *VA*, 2.30, 715–22.
108 Robert of Flamborough, *Liber poenitentialis*, ed. J. J. F. Firth (Toronto, 1971), 3, 115.
109 *Ibid.*
110 Grosseteste, *Dictum* 51, fo. 38r.
111 N. Bériou, 'La confession dans les écrits théologiques et pastoraux du XIIIe siècle: médication de l'âme ou démarche judiciaire?', in *L'Aveu, antiquité et moyen-âge* (Rome, 1986), 278–9.
112 Thomas of Chobham, *SC*, 6.4.11a, 307.

6

Judgment in practice: the Church

Introduction

The chapter examines three case studies intended to illuminate the choice between judicial strategies of justice and mercy,[1] tracing how discussion on this topic unfolded within the English Church. It does not set out to provide a history of mercy in English ecclesiastical politics from c.1100 to c.1250: instead it sets out a particular approach – namely that a focus on justice and mercy might offer new ways of interpreting some familiar events and problems for the Church in this period. It further attempts to explain why the choice between 'strictly just' and 'merciful' strategies was so freighted (i.e. *why* the conflict between mercy and justice mattered). Typically, this was because that choice was understood to have consequences that were both personal and political, and to underline further the fact that arguments within the Church soon became arguments about secular justice too.

The evidence of this chapter is largely drawn from the correspondence of ecclesiastical writers, further emphasising the fact that this discussion of judicial decision-making was not merely a point of dry academic debate, but driven by a need to provide advice and counsel to those engaged in the business of judgment. The first case study, focusing on the treatment of a group of heretics in Worcester, examines an internal discussion (the Church's concern regarding which judicial strategy, justice or mercy, was the more prudent choice). The second, drawing on letters surrounding the Becket dispute, moves between the ecclesiastical and the secular realms, highlighting a debate about the way in which the Church should admonish and judge both internally and externally (i.e. in relation to Henry II's offences). The third – an examination of the judicial counsel to be found in the letters of Robert Grosseteste and Adam Marsh – looks at how we might observe arguments for merciful judgment turned outward, expressed as a means of persuasion. This, in turn, sets up some of the themes which will be explored in Chapter 7: at what point did petitioning for mercy cross the line into unwelcome, even malicious persuasion?

Each of these case studies, it should be noted, blurs the line between discussion of practices in judgment in a court of law (however constituted) and judgment in the 'court' of penance. None of these cases concern the setting of penance for a particular individual; but all their authors were educated in a long tradition of thinking about how judgment should be expressed. The matters of judgment discussed in this chapter (how to deal with heretics, with Henry II, with wrongdoing in secular office, are matters of *public* concern – they concern multiple parties, more than just sinner and confessor.[2] But the authors of these letters were versed in a tradition where a priest setting a penance for sin was the example of judgment *sine qua non*. And in setting penance, the priest was obliged to consider questions about the good of the community and the good of the individual offender. Discussion of penance and of punishment after judgment here draw on the same lexicon of *lenitas* and *severitas*. The writers examined here – Gilbert Foliot, Roger of Worcester, John of Salisbury, Thomas Becket, Robert Grosseteste and Adam Marsh – were thinking and writing in a world in which the setting of penance was one obvious, mundane and perhaps even the most familiar example of judgment being given.

Canon law in this period set down no firm or clear line on how a judge should go about reckoning with mercy and justice; but, following Ivo of Chartres and Alger of Liège, held that it was necessary to do so. Canonical collections, including the *Decretum*, did not give firm or foolproof guidance on this range of penalties: instead, application of punishment was left to the discretion of the ecclesiastical judge. There was space for the familiar ideal of ecclesiastical leniency; but there was room also for severity. The Church might adopt a range of attitudes towards the chastisement of offenders.[3] This was reflected in the analogy frequently employed by theologians to describe the setting of ecclesiastical punishments, the comparison of the sentencing judge to a physician (*medicus*) who determined the treatment of an illness according to the severity of a disease. For a mild sickness, that is, a minor offence, only a mild reprimand would be required. In the case of a more serious illness, the doctor might have to consider amputation of the infected parts of the body, just as the judge faced with great crimes might need to impose severe punishment for the sake of the public good. This image – the judge as surgeon – was an ancient *topos*.[4] By the eleventh century the term *medicus* had, in canonical literature, been extended to describe not only the role of priest in the confessional forum, but also the bishop sitting as judge.[5] The comparison could be used to argue for either severity or mercy: the physician cured sometimes with harsh, sometimes with gentle remedies, according to the degree of the sickness.

Twelfth-century penitential writing reflects an increasing emphasis on judicial discretion, the product of a gradual shift away from a system of penance based on prescribed tariffs for each sin, towards a system which emphasised the role of priestly judgment in determining penance. A renewed focus on the ethics of intention had complicated *all* acts of judgment, introducing the argument that the severity of a crime should be linked to the circumstances of its commission (and therefore creating increased space for mitigation).[6] Consideration of the circumstances of the offence created the possibility of mitigation of punishment. Moreover, in penitential literature, the critical role of judicial discretion was also increased by an emphasis on contrition – not entirely new, but certainly renewed in prominence in the twelfth century.[7] The purpose of setting a penance was to ensure repentance, to combat an individual's *voluntas peccandi*. Thus the priest was to judge the quality of the offender and offence, and adapt the penance accordingly. Penitential tariffs were all too blunt for this delicate work. While this development should not be oversimplified as a shift from strictly prescribed penance to a system given over entirely to the caprice of the priest,[8] twelfth-century changes did, nevertheless, concentrate attention on the priest's ability to weigh each sin and penance appropriately.[9]

The section of the *Decretum* dealing with penance – a section which draws heavily on the late eleventh-century treatise *De vera et falsa poenitentia*, a work then attributed to Augustine – enjoins the judge to consider seven factors which have a bearing on the severity of the offence: *causa*, *persona*, *locus*, *tempus*, *qualitas*, *quantitas* and *eventus*, an admission of the almost endless variety and circumstances of sin, and the intricate calculations needed to reckon a penance.[10] No less significantly, punishment was also moderated according to whether the crime was committed publicly or privately, and the ensuing possibility for scandal.[11] How then was a bishop, priest or confessor to calibrate an individual penance while still remaining within the framework established by the canons? In his guidebook for confessors, *Summa confessorum* (c.1215), Thomas of Chobham dedicates a chapter to explaining that certain penitential punishments may be moderated while others are immutable.[12] Thomas pays special attention to the contrast between 'ancient' canons and modern approaches, arguing that 'moderns' (*homo nostri temporis*) cannot be expected to endure the punishments of fasting, vigils and exile meted out in ancient times. Those canons which most severely test the body are to be mitigated according to the will and prudential discretion of the priest. Explaining this, Thomas notes that the key criterion here must be that of pastoral efficacy: the severity of the canons, if it cannot be endured, will drive sinners away from repentance.

Thomas of Chobham's advice to confessors gives voice to the need to strike a compromise between adherence to canonical ruling and appropriate pastoral practice. He serves to make the more general point that it was widely considered necessary that moral theology should sometimes 'adjust' the teachings of the canons. Indeed, some historians have gone as far as to assert that one can recognise a specifically 'English' contribution to penitential literature, characterised by a desire to adapt and modify penitential punishments to increase their pastoral efficacy. This desire, it has been claimed, derived from a characteristically English interest in practical matters.[13] Certainly, uncertainty regarding the measure of severity or mercy in penance had enormous and widespread implications. Setting penance – the ability to judge sin and impose punishment – was among the most basic of pastoral duties, and the need to instruct priests in the subtleties and practicalities of penance in turn, therefore, gave rise to the genre of *summa de poenitentia* (or *summa confessorum*) – effectively guides to confessional judgment. These were typically aimed at clerics who had attended cathedral schools or received monastic education in theology, and were expected, once their studies were completed, to take up Church positions with pastoral functions.[14] This was a task which became more demanding as the canon law tradition became increasingly complex. Thus Odo of Cheriton, writing his *summa* on penitence (after 1230), and thinking of the instruction of the 'simple' priest in penitential practice, could speak of a 'forest of laws', so deep and difficult to navigate that none could discover a path through it.[15]

An instructive example of an attempt to provide exactly such practical guidance is the *Penitential* of Bartholomew, Bishop of Exeter. A colleague of Gilbert Foliot, Roger and Becket, Bartholomew was fêted by Pope Alexander III (1159–81) as one of the most distinguished figures of the English episcopacy, praised for his probity, knowledge of the canons and his extensive service as a papal judge-delegate.[16] The penitential, composed while Bartholomew was still an archdeacon, or in the early years of his episcopate,[17] concentrates on the role of the priest as judge in a different court – the court of confession and penance. This was not a work at the cutting edge of scholarship: Bartholomew prefers to employ the *Decretum* (and also the older collections of Burchard of Worms and Ivo of Chartres) rather than newer canonical commentaries.[18] But the role of instructing the priest in confessional judgment was an exercise in providing an adequate level of guidance to clergy who had *not* studied in Paris or Bologna. As such, Bartholomew collected the best and most instructive passages from older (but still entirely respectable) traditions: Gratian's *Decretum*, the authoritative *Sentences* of Peter Lombard and the writings of the Church Fathers. The popularity of the *Penitential* suggests its utility and its success.[19]

Bartholomew's *Penitential*, 'low-tech' as it may be by later twelfth-century standards, expresses quite clearly the challenges of setting punishment. A priest must be aware of the various circumstances in which a sin has been committed: was that sin trivial (*levia*) or mortal (*mortalia*); committed publicly (*publicum*) or secretly (*occultum*); was it done deliberately (*scienter*) or accidentally (*ignoranter*); was it performed willingly (*sponte*) or unwillingly (*non sponte*)? Equally important is that the judge remains aware of his own biases in setting penance and acts to avoid them.[20] This can only be achieved through what Bartholomew describes as the will of a prudent pastor (*per prudentis pastoris arbitrium*).[21] The text of the *Penitential* is accordingly full of concern for how a penance ought to be calculated and set. Bartholomew dedicates a whole chapter (quoting from the Greek father John Chrysostom via the *Decretum*) to explaining the importance of *misericordia* in the setting of penitential punishments:

> The individual on whom you impose an oppressive burden of penance will either reject the penance, or undertaking that which they are not able to do, will fall into a greater sin. Hence, if we err in the degree of penance we impose, surely it is better to give a ruling motivated by mercy, rather than cruelty? For where a Lord is bountiful, his steward ought not to be stingy. If God is mild, will he wish his priest to appear austere?[22]

Elsewhere Bartholomew offered a similar admonition on the need to mitigate penalties, counselling that excessive austerity is to be avoided.[23] Bartholomew summarises the guidance of the canons for his reader by again invoking that familiar analogy of the priest as *sapiens medicus*.[24]

Bartholomew of Exeter was far from alone in pondering the mechanics of setting penance. While no other contemporary English bishop has left a penitential, there are indications that there was widespread concern for the practical implications of canonical principles across the dioceses of England. For example, Roger of Worcester employed an individual known as Senatus as his *archpresbiterum* in the 1170s, whose role has been described as that of 'master of penances'.[25] Like Bartholomew of Exeter, Roger is known for his reputation as a papal judge-delegate,[26] but here we find him sending questions to a theologian who specialised in resolving penitential and pastoral problems. Roger's letters to Senatus seem to have been particularly concerned with questions of absolution and indulgences and Senatus's replies set down some familiar principles: the rigour of the canons must be carefully modified, lest the penitent become arrogant through easy penances or come to despair under the burden of excessive punishment.[27] But Senatus also poses (and answers) more awkward practical questions: if the prescribed penances of the canons may be modified through softening, may they also be substituted with works – for example, by asking the rich to found hospitals, build bridges or construct churches as part of their penance?[28] Similarly, at Hereford in the last decade of the twelfth century, Bishop William de Vere also commissioned an instructional treatise on penance, in this case from Guy, prior of the Augustinian canons of Southwick, a work likely intended for the edification of the clergy of Hereford.[29] From what little we know of Guy, he seems to have studied theology at Oxford or at least interacted closely with the masters there.[30] Considered as a group, these later twelfth-century texts demonstrate, quite plainly, the evident interest of English priests in working out the relationship between penitential theory and penitential practice, and the connection between canon law (to which the subject of penitential practice strictly belonged) and theology – for the authors of these texts were trained theologians.

While the tradition of works of penitential instruction certainly burgeoned in the thirteenth century, authors continued to address much the same problems as their twelfth-century predecessors.[31] Thus Robert of Flamborough's *Liber poenitentialis* (composed c. 1208–13), commissioned by Richard Poore, Dean of Salisbury and future Bishop of Chichester, Salisbury and Durham, drew closely on the work of Bartholomew of Exeter. Robert's penitential returns to the question of how to distinguish between a 'reasonable' and an 'unreasonable' sentence.

> No one should believe that, in accordance with rigour and strictness constituted by the canons, penance always ought to be imposed without any mercy. But the rigour of the canons ought to be tempered, not according to what pleases the priest, but through canonical dispensation, in order that in setting penance the priest always be mindful of both the demand for satisfaction which sinners are held to for their fault, and also of indulgence, by which the canons truly come to the aid of the penitent through mercy.[32]

Robert's work was rapidly followed by Thomas of Chobham's *Summa confessorum*, a work begun before 1215, but subsequently adapted in light of the canons of the Fourth Lateran Council.[33] Thomas warns that there are three ways in which a pastor may set an unjust penance. *Ordines iudicii* (manuals which set down acceptable and expected standards for proof and legal process), he warns, will only guard against one of these, namely disregard for procedure.[34] The pastor must still ensure that he does not pass false sentence by ignoring the evidence or, indeed, acting 'ex animo' – through his own anger or jealousy.[35] Thomas of Chobham also advises the parish priest that, if some cases of penitence are simply too difficult to judge (for example, when they concern a particularly incorrigible offender who now wishes to be absolved), then they can be referred upwards to a superior.[36]

Robert of Flamborough's penitential writings also had a marked influence on Robert Grosseteste, who borrowed from his *Liber poenitentialis* when compiling his own schematic work on priestly pastoral responsibilities, *Templum Dei* (c.1220–30). Indeed, if Grosseteste was in Paris between 1209 and 1214, he may himself have come under the penitential jurisdiction of the abbey of Saint-Victor, and its then-penitentiary, Robert of Flamborough.[37] Grosseteste, in a second pastoral treatise focused on confession, *Deus est* (probably composed during the same period as his *Templum Dei*), once again emphasised that the greatest pastoral challenge for the priest was to adapt his stance according to the attitude of the offender.[38] Across the tradition of English penitential literature in the early thirteenth century, the theologians' focus is on alerting pastors to the variability of penance and the need to moderate their penitential punishments accordingly.[39] These later English texts were, of course, influenced by continental works of canon law, not least Raymond de Peñafort's *Summa de casibus poenitentiae* (composed 1222–29, and revised in 1235).[40] There was widespread concern across the English Church about the practical consequences of ecclesiastical judgments. This was an interest that may have intensified in the thirteenth century, but it repeated questions which had been raised over the previous century. Those questions primarily addressed how to set an appropriate penance, how to realise the directions of the canons in practice and how to formulate an effective reprimand.

Concerns about the appropriate moderation of the canons move beyond the realm of strictly 'penitential' writing and enter into works of moral instruction. Peter of Blois, for example, wrote to an abbot, identified only as 'W', berating him for excessive severity in the treatment of monks in his care.[41] Peter recognises this as the greatest pastoral challenge of the age, for 'those who exercise zeal of justice in scourging, not in leavening, in order to satisfy their anger, do not produce new growth for Christ'.[42]

Judgment in practice: the Church

In sum, the message of penitential literature was that a foolish or hasty sentence could have great ramifications, both in this world and in heavenly terms. Modulation of penance was a delicate, difficult business – like any other form of judgment.

Heretics in Worcester, 1165

In 1165, Roger of Worcester wrote urgently to his colleague, Gilbert Foliot, Bishop of London. Roger's correspondence has not survived, but the outline of his dilemma can be recreated. A group of heretics from the continent had entered his diocese (the group are described as *textores*, but this is more likely to indicate their heretical and humble status than their occupations). Roger was near the beginning of his episcopacy; Foliot had almost twenty years' experience as a bishop (and almost a decade as an abbot before that). Roger was no trained canonist, and – as was appropriate – sought the legal opinion of more experienced bishops in difficult matters.[43] There does not seem to have been any argument over diagnosis of heresy: the fact that these individuals (we do not know the size of the group) professed heretical beliefs was established. Roger did not want to know how to find heretics – he wanted to know what he should do with them, how he should treat them. Roger's heretical problem may also have been compounded further by the fact that heresy seems to have been an unusual occurrence in twelfth-century England when compared to other European lands. It was not only Roger who lacked the practical experience to deal with this problem.[44] And if English bishops lacked practical experience, the matter of how the Church should reckon with heretics (both in matters of procedure and in fundamentals) was far from settled across Christendom in the 1160s. So Roger, quite reasonably, wrote to an expert in matters of law and theology.

Before entering Cluny, c.1130, Gilbert Foliot had gained a considerable reputation as a scholar. He had studied Roman law, possibly in Bologna, and theology, possibly in Exeter under the tutelage of Robert Pullen.[45] This learning is evident in Foliot's letter collection, which provides a wealth of material on mercy and justice. It shows Foliot – whether as an archdeacon, Bishop of Hereford or Bishop of London – intervening in judicial cases and monastic affairs. He asks judges and abbots for leniency on behalf of associates and discusses the 'justice' of various canonical measures. Concerning the interdict, for example, Foliot asks whether such a punishment can be justified when it is imposed on many who have committed no crime themselves.[46]

Justice and mercy

Exactly how discussions of mercy and justice apply in cases concerning heretics was acknowledged to be a difficult question. From the late eleventh century onwards, prosecution of heretics became much more zealous and, indeed, severe.[47] In historiographical terms, the attack on heretics provides the definition of a 'persecuting society', because they form a case study for prosecution in the 'public interest', a new way for the Church to define crime.[48] Indeed, such was the public and political interest that secular powers too participated in these prosecutions.[49] The increased vehemence with which heretics were persecuted and punished is typically ascribed to the influence of Roman law, as civil law punishments for an offence of *laesa maiestas* against the emperor were applied to those guilty of an offence against the *maiestas* of God. Gratian quoted the *Codex* on this point,[50] and Innocent III's *Vergentis in senium* (1199) enjoins 'ecclesiastica districtio' on heretics.[51] Yet clear rulings on how to deal with heretics only emerged towards the end of the twelfth century, with Innocent's decretal arguably marking a watershed; a full body of legislation on the subject was established only in the thirteenth century.[52] Gilbert Foliot, addressing the question of what to do with a group of heretics in the 1160s, was in a far less certain position vis-à-vis the canons.[53] The *Decretum* itself did not resolve this ambiguity but set out a broad range of possible strategies for the punishment of heretics, including whipping, imprisonment, exile, confiscation of goods or even a death sentence.[54] Nor was the role of the bishop in punishing heretics clearly defined, particularly in reference to the involvement of the lay power, which would have been involved at least in enforcing sentences such as exile or capital punishment.[55] All these factors invite a consideration of exactly how far discussions of the treatment of heretics stood within or without the typical canonical frames of mercy and justice.

It is here that we must turn to Gilbert's own account, provided in two letters of 1165, written in response to Roger. The two letters in fact seem to represent two versions of the same letter, although they differ somewhat in their style and argument: one seems to be a letter of advice, advocating a clear course of action, while the other shows Foliot in a more reflective mood. It is not known which (if either, or both) of these drafts were ultimately sent to Roger. It would, however, be unwise to dismiss either or both of the letters as a purely literary or academic exercise, included in the collection only to teach or to impress posterity. When other letters from Foliot's collection are checked against those known to have been sent – such as those contained in the manuscripts of the Becket correspondence – the 'drafts' from Foliot's collection are markedly faithful to the final version sent to the recipient.[56] The balance of evidence argues that, in general, the collection offers faithful copies of the texts which Foliot intended to send.

Letters 157 and 158 are found only in the principal manuscript of Foliot's letters, Bodleian MS E Musaeo 249, which contains almost all of Foliot's extant letters and charters.[57] The two letters concerning the heretics do not occur together: Letter 157 is found at fo.141r, Letter 158 at 161v, and they belong to different 'sections' of the manuscript. Letter 157 is fairly straightforward, advising Roger that the heretics ought to be placed in solitary confinement and treated with 'moderate severity' until a gathering of the clergy is able to settle the question of what is to be done with them:

> But in the meantime you should hold them separately, lest together they persevere in wicked conversation. It is appropriate that good and serious men, men of proven faith, learned in divine law and letters, be appointed for their care and custody, and let them visit them with holy words of preaching, softening them with warnings, and scaring them with threats and fear of punishment, and in the meanwhile curbing with whips and lashings with moderate severity, and let them attend to calling them back to the unity of the Church, in all the ways furnished by *caritas*.[58]

The second letter (158) is altogether more expansive. It does not mention the physical discipline of the group, but simply advises Roger to place the heretics in solitary confinement, lest their continued association inspire them to defiance. Foliot repeats the idea that the heretics are to be visited by 'your most worthy and prudent' priests, who ought to call them to penance and back to unity with the Church, in the hope that preaching will rouse them. Perhaps Foliot here kept in mind the principle espoused in the *Decretum*: that when dealing which heresy, force was only of limited utility, representing a temporary, not a long-term solution, and, as such, kindness rather than severity was advocated towards those who stood in need of correction.[59] Other than these instructions, the text of Letter 158 is taken up with a disquisition on rival theories on the treatment of heretics. As a result, it appears more vacillating than the first, as Foliot enumerates the various courses of action open to a bishop in Roger's unenviable position. It may be tempting to infer, on this basis, that 157 represents the letter sent to Roger – with practical counsel – while 158 is the draft written by Foliot to be included in his collection for the instruction of posterity, with an account of the various possibilities for action against heretics. Yet even if this is the case, both letters demonstrate that Foliot was aware that his advice required some justification and that there was no sure or efficacious course for turning the heretical back to God.[60] Moreover, Foliot notes that

Justice and mercy

this is no new question – the problem of how best to minister to heretics had been a topic for debate in the early Church. He outlines the stances that could be adopted in this debate in the following way:

> It is a great question, and one considered by the holy fathers and doctors of the Church with no little concern, namely, how far the Church ought to preach gentleness and clemency, according to the expression 'the law of clemency is on her tongue' [Proverbs xxxi.26], and the words of the Lord, 'nor do I condemn you' [John viii.11], lest many are destroyed in such holy punishments by fervent and pious zeal. Some advise that those frantic sons must be kept in prison, in order to be watched over; others protest that they should be committed to irons for injuring divine religion, by which, according to the Julian laws [i.e. *Digest* 48.4], they threaten majesty by public crime; others, judging by example, sentence them to burning alive; others temper severity with the opinion of Augustine, who pleaded that the Donatists not be killed, but that they be corrected by whipping and punishment.[61]

Letter 158 goes on to suggest that concerning the treatment of heretics, the patristic judicial dilemma of choosing between justice and mercy still applies. The problem of dealing with heretics is, for the judge, the same challenge of working out the most prudent course of action for the particular case. Questions of severity *versus* mercy, and the spirit of the law *versus* its letter, must still be debated by his contemporaries. While there is mention of the Roman law offence of *laesa maiestas* as comparable to heresy, this reference is subordinate to the scriptural argument that the Church must apply all its punishments with gentleness and concern for its pastoral mission. Foliot himself offers no indication of which choice here is to be preferred. Taking these conflicting opinions as a demonstration of the difficulty of the subject, he concludes by reserving judgment of the treatment of the heretics for discussion at a future gathering.[62] The episcopal council of 1166 determined that the group were to be handed over to the secular power, to be whipped, branded and exiled.[63]

Foliot's two letters are all the more striking when consideration is given to their place within the manuscript (a context which is lost in the modern edition). The first, 157, is preceded by a letter to Matthew, Archdeacon of Gloucester, in response to a question about a woman accused of adultery.[64] Like Roger of Worcester, Matthew had written to Foliot for guidance on a question of legal practice: a woman accused of adultery by her husband, had, under threat, promised to undergo the ordeal of red-hot iron in order to determine her innocence or guilt. Matthew asked Foliot whether the woman was bound to undergo the ordeal or whether she might only be required to swear an oath as proof of her innocence. Foliot's reply to the

Judgment in practice: the Church

problem of judicial process is simple enough: he advises that in a case where adultery is only suspected, and where there are no witnesses to the crime, an oath provides sufficient determination of guilt or innocence. Moreover, he added, citing the *Decretum* on this point, the woman was not under any obligation to undergo the ordeal, for any promise extracted by force or fear cannot be binding.[65] The real interest of this preceding letter, however, is Foliot's subsequent explanation of contemporary laws relating to adultery. He explains that the Incarnation and the consequent law of grace had modified, and, indeed, mollified, the harsh punishments for adultery specified in Mosaic and Roman law. Roman law – 'the law of the emperors' – set forth numerous punishments for each moral slip; but Christ has tempered the harshness and bitterness of that law.

Foliot further explains that the 'stones' which were thrown at adulterers under the Old Law now have an allegorical meaning, representing the steps of chastisement to be administered to a sinner. Rather than physical punishment, those stones represent the many possible ways by which a sinner may be brought to confession and to making satisfaction.[66] He concludes by citing John viii.11, Christ's words to the woman caught in adultery, 'nor do I condemn you', a citation which he also provides in Letter 158, discussing the level of clemency appropriate in the treatment of heretics.

Jason Taliadoros, the leading scholar of Foliot's life and works, has argued that while Foliot may have been proficient in canon law, he was, first and foremost, a theologian.[67] The juxtaposition of these letters certainly demonstrates how theology influenced Foliot's reading of the canons. Foliot notes, in line with basic canonical tenets, that a mere suspicion of adultery is not enough to force anyone to undergo the ordeal – witnesses are required. Yet, in invoking John viii.11, the words of Christ to the woman caught in adultery, Foliot does not give a canonist's reading of the passage. Lawyers, both civil and canon, used the pericope 'nor do I condemn you' to illustrate the principle of *iudex secundum allegata, non secundum conscientiam iudicat*. Christ had instructed the judge, in other words, to convict only according to the evidence presented to him by witnesses, not according to his private knowledge of the crime. Thus the pericope was read by canonists as a procedural instruction: without witnesses, all judgments risked a false verdict which would endanger the soul of the judge. The role of John viii in canonical commentaries, in short, was not as an example of Christ's merciful behaviour, but as a case which fell down on a judicial technicality. This is, however, not the sense in which Foliot invokes the passage. He gives a 'theological' gloss on the event, implying that Christ's unwillingness to condemn the woman was due not to lack of witnesses, but due to the merciful nature of the New Law. Foliot's interpretation owes more to moral theology to than legal doctrine, which held that the incident showed a woman justly condemned, but granted mercy. In short, it was an admonition to judicial clemency. It is striking that Foliot (or his clerks, in directing the compilation of his letters) chose to place a discussion of the clemency of the law of Christ just before Foliot's first consideration of the treatment of heretics.[68] The letters are not otherwise ordered by date or addressee, although this section does seem to deal thematically with Foliot's letters on judgment and judicial procedure.[69]

Letter 158, Foliot's lengthier and more ambivalent discussion of the treatment appropriate to heretics, also occurs in the manuscript in a section of letters on judicial problems. It is preceded by a question of rights to appeal and followed by a letter on the question of the restoration of a husband who had deserted his wife.[70] Although neither of these letters provides the same depth of commentary on justice and mercy as Letter 237, they do provide a significant commentary on some further aspects of the relationship between the two concepts. The letter concerning the restoration of an errant husband is written to an unidentified bishop, exhorting him to compel the husband to return to his wife. Foliot asks the bishop to do this out of consideration for the strictures of the canons concerning marriage:

> We extend to you, our brother, affectionate prayers, beseeching and entreating you in the Lord, that, on account of your reverence for God, you censure him with the severity of the canons. In order that he make the provision due to his wife and keep this undertaking, you ought to compel him through the strict justice of the Church ... and let him understand that on all sides avengers are not lacking against transgressors of the law.[71]

The invocation of canonical severity and strict justice here may seem at odds with Foliot's previous advocacy of the lenient treatment of transgressors. However, to juxtapose the two texts in this way would be to misunderstand his approach. Foliot's ability to switch between a merciful interpretation of the canons (in the case of adulterers) and a strict invocation of unbending justice (in the case of a man who had abandoned his wife) is, in fact, an excellent demonstration of his understanding of the more general relationship between justice, mercy and canonical discretion. Twelfth-century canonical jurisprudence – and, indeed, the 'Ivonian' theory of justice and mercy subsequently adopted by Gratian and written into the *Decretum* – did not demand its practitioners consistently advocate either justice or mercy, *always* to be unbending or *always* to be lenient. Rather, it offered judges a choice, not of harmonising justice with mercy, but to select the course most appropriate to the particular case in front of them.[72]

The Becket crisis

Analysis of the Becket crisis, a topic which has gathered so much historiographical attention, has focused on the subject of conflicting laws and the relation of canon law to secular authority.[73] And yet the Becket conflict too can be explored (perhaps even reframed) with reference to the ideals of judicial severity and mercy. More recent historiography has affirmed the fact that the 'conflict', 'controversy' or 'dispute' (indeed, the choice of labels can sometimes be revealing in itself) was likewise as much a question of theology as law. The legitimacy of Becket's stance could be, and was, assessed according to principles of canon law and correct canonical process; but hagiographies, histories and letters were also places in which the 'righteousness' (*iustitia*) of Becket and Henry II's respective roles was debated.[74] Theology and law were intertwined, and the force of scripture was deployed to support legal argument. Examining the letters of some of the major figures in the controversy – Becket, Gilbert Foliot and John of Salisbury – for what they reveal about the pastoral role of the judge in the English Church in the mid-twelfth century provides a fresh perspective on the events of 1163–70.

While the dispute between the king and archbishop was a question of custom and law, as well as a matter of political theory and practical politics, Becket's stance on these issues and his responses to royal claims prompted a further debate within the English Church. The ensuing friction within the English Church, however, was not as simple as asking whether or not the ecclesiastical hierarchy should stand with Becket. Instead it turned on how the Church should reprimand a king in order to turn him towards reform. While the split between different approaches to the rebuke and punishment of a king was not the driving force behind the conflict between Becket and Henry, a close analysis of the language invoked and the framing employed in these letters reveals the gulf in understanding between two parties within the Church. This can be understood as an internal debate within the English Church about the relative political and spiritual merits of merciful and severe judicial positions. Becket presented this as a dispute between his supporters – advocates for the liberty of the Church – and the wicked, arguing that 'anyone who does not hurry to check what should be corrected is regarded as being in agreement with the wrongdoer'.[75] It was through his letters that Becket disseminated precisely such a picture.[76]

Justice and mercy

In the exchange of letters between Thomas Becket and Gilbert Foliot, the effective leader of the English Church during Becket's exile, the major cause of dissension in their correspondence is the question of *judicial* strategy. Did Becket's call for an anathema to be pronounced on Henry II, the excommunication of certain English bishops and an interdict to be placed on the English Church represent appropriate punishment or an immoderate, ill-considered response to the king's offences against the Church and its custom? Reading Foliot's letters, it seems that Becket's 'fault' is his failure to recognise that in order to rebuke a prince effectively, the would-be corrector must sometimes temper and soften his censures. Becket's response to Foliot's criticism is typically to state that a king should be censured just as any undistinguished individual would be.

The most famous letter in the conflict is perhaps Foliot's *Multiplicem nobis* (1166), in which the Bishop of London attributes the roots of the conflict to Becket's manifold failures of character, and defends his own attitude towards the king. But *Multiplicem* was itself a response to a letter which Becket had addressed to Foliot in July 1166, following the appeal of the English bishops against their excommunication.[77] Becket's address to Foliot was a justification of his severe approach to Henry and royal infractions:

> You express surprise at the threatening letter which we sent to him [i.e. Henry II].[78] What father sees his son go astray and remains silent? What father does not strike with a rod, lest his son incur the sword? A father despairs of his son if he does not reprove him by threat or the whip.[79]

Becket (alluding to both Proverbs xiii.24 and Hebrews xii.7) employs the familiar imagery of both paternal discipline and the necessity for the ecclesiastical officer to wield the rod – two figures of salutary punishment. This is an approach matched by Becket's supporters – not least John of Salisbury, whose letters on behalf of Becket to the English episcopacy follow the same line of reasoning. John exploits a series of scriptural *exempla* to explain to the bishops why Becket is unable – indeed, morally forbidden – from coming to a peaceful accommodation with Henry over the legal issues involved. The oldest and most venerable traditions of ecclesiastical office demand that Becket rebuke Henry's sins, not make allowances for them.

John dwells on those precedents in some detail. In a letter of late 1166, John tackles the counter-argument, presumably one which had been used against Becket, that scripture in fact permitted that sinners might sometimes be only *lightly* upbraided, citing the example that John the Baptist had merely criticised, not rebuked, Herod for sleeping with his brother's wife while his brother was still living (Matthew xiv.3–4). Did not this imply

Judgment in practice: the Church

that the Church might sometimes treat failing temporal rulers with gentleness, and mitigate the harshness of its criticisms? John's response is to dismiss this episode entirely as a precedent for how the Church ought to deal with Henry II. Some will say, John explains, that there is a case for gentle treatment, for:

> John [the Baptist] upbraided Herod in a gentle spirit, when he told him it was unlawful to sleep with his living brother's wife. [But] he who says as much is taking shelter behind cowardice rather than ignorance, however certain it may be that John was not on that occasion playing the role of a bishop whose function it is to correct sins, but of the Word's herald, to whom it fell to announce what was to be done and to denounce men's vices. [H]eli indeed reproved his sons, but with a father's kindly affection rather than the severe authority of a bishop. Therefore for every point in the divine law one must fight, stand up against the powers and with all one's strength strive to overthrow whatever attacks charity, which is the fulfilment of the Law.[80]

John counters the argument by invoking the counter-example of Heli and his sons, asserting that episcopal authority is at least in part defined by its ability to wield punitive authority and punish sin, a duty which must not be neglected.

Multiplicem nobis demonstrates exactly where Gilbert Foliot stood on this line of argument, suggesting that the Church's rigour might rightly and justly be occasionally softened. The final section of *Multiplicem* urges Becket to take a more conciliatory line towards Henry II, and cautions against an excessively severe attack on the king's vices (vices which Foliot does not deny Henry has shown).[81] What is most striking here is again the language in which Foliot couches this counsel to Becket: he invokes the image of the *medicus*. If Becket is to be a physician to cure the sickness in the English political community, then he must wield his scalpel with care:

> Does anyone reckon it among a doctor's skills to cure one wound by inflicting another, far greater and far more dangerous? Who calls it discretion to desert his Church in this way for what could be obtained very quickly and very easily, to rise against his prince, and, having destroyed the peace of the whole Church throughout the realm, not to trouble about the dangers to the souls and bodies of his subjects?[82]

This, of course, is Foliot's adaptation of the medical analogy so frequently used to discuss the role of the priest in setting penance for sinners. Becket's medicine for sin – the severe punishment of the king – is worse than the malady, given its deleterious effect on the peace of the English Church. Foliot invokes the same metaphor of the priest as physician when writing to

Alexander III, urging him not to approve any sentence of excommunication that Becket may pronounce; for in doing so Alexander may one day lament the consequences of his zeal, and the subversion of innumerable churches. Instead, Foliot counsels moderation, if Alexander is able (*si placet ad tempus intra fines modestie cohibeatis*), treating the English Church as if it were an injured limb of the Church's corporate body, mediating on the best course for recovery:

> For it is good for the limb to be joined to the whole, even though wounded, rather than an amputated part be cast away from the body. For wounded limbs return to a state of health, whereas, when once cut off they have great difficulty in adhering to the body. Amputation leads to desperation, [but] treatment by the surgeon frequently heals the wound.[83]

In *Multiplicem* Foliot also constructs an argument from history, presenting the precedents for the Church adopting a more 'gentle' attitude to rebuking Henry. Foliot explains that it is only ever conciliatory attitudes and moderated criticism which have succeeded in the reform of sinners. Foliot grounds his argument in English ecclesiastical history, citing the example of Augustine of Canterbury, sent by Gregory the Great to convert the English from their pagan practices. Augustine of Canterbury, Foliot explains, challenged wicked custom not with abuse and threats but with preaching, exhortation and persuasion.[84] Foliot does not deny the need to alter Henry's attitudes and position, but instead claims that Becket's excessively severe strategy will never achieve his desired end. Foliot goes as far as to argue that Becket's position – that is, his attempt to impose an anathema on Henry II – is contrary to the canons. He cites a passage from the *Decretum* (in turn, drawn from the letters of Augustine), which counsels caution before imposing a sentence and careful consideration as to whether punishment will serve the advantage of the English Church:

> In fact, sacred authority teaches thus: 'in cases of this kind, where through grave rifts and dissensions there is danger not to this or that man but confusion for the whole people, some severity must be laid aside, so that true charity may assist in curing more serious ills'.[85]

Finally, Foliot invokes the most powerful scriptural *exemplum* he can muster. The last paragraph of his letter is dedicated to reprimanding Becket's excessive severity in judgment, *severitas* which, Foliot laments, has failed to live up to the apostolic ideal of gentle fraternal correction. In his severe and unyielding condemnation of the king's vices, Foliot notes, Becket has ignored the fundamental principle of Christ's law, namely *caritas*.

Judgment in practice: the Church

> The Lord put forward a child as an example to the Apostles: he is not angered when hurt, he is not quick to remember injuries, he does not undertake anything out of malice. ...[86] He who absolved those who were crucifying him is himself the unique example of virtue, who, with all-embracing love, commands that persecutors and bearers of ill-will should be loved, and orders us to pardon the brother who sins against us, not seven times, but seventy times seven times [Mark xviii.21–22]. What cannot this humility achieve with our lord the king, what can this perfect path not obtain?[87]

There were two fundamental charges which Foliot levelled at Becket's approach to pastoral justice. The first, evident not least in the letters he wrote to Pope Alexander, was that Becket's actions were illegitimate because of the disturbance they caused to the Church. This contention held true regardless of whether Becket's severity was justified in the fight against sin and vice. Justice was never true if it threatened to overturn the peace of the Church, and hence zeal and severity had always to be moderated out of concern for the flock.[88] It is for this reason that, elsewhere in *Multiplicem*, Foliot casts Becket, not Henry, as 'disturber of the peace'.[89] The second charge brought by Foliot was to claim that Becket's zeal for justice had led him to ignore the demands of Christian love. Theological schemes of the virtues privileged *caritas* over *iustitia*, for the coming of Christ and the new dispensation symbolised the victory of forgiving love over strict justice. Actions which were not motivated by *caritas* could not truly be said to be just, regardless of their legal status. This reasoning allows Foliot to assume the moral high ground in the argument: Becket's zeal for justice may be admirable, but only *caritas* is properly and literally Christian, for to elevate *caritas* over judgment was characteristic of Christ himself.

Foliot's first charge – that Becket ought to show appropriate moderation in rebuking Henry – had already been addressed by John of Salisbury, who had considered the argument that an erring king, due to his status, deserved moderate treatment, lest harsh correction disturb the peace of the realm. This argument, however, John claims, cannot be upheld, for it is in flat contradiction of what the New Testament teaches about judicial objectivity and the condemnation of vice. John instead praises Becket for his refusal to moderate his criticism, which is consistent with the Apostle's command 'reprove, rebuke, exhort, in season, out of season' (2 Timothy iv.2).[90] Becket's response to Foliot's second charge, namely that he was obliged to act with love towards his king, could not take the form of entering into a debate on the relative merits of *iustitia* and *caritas*, as the priority of *caritas* was a basic and unchallenged theological tenet. Instead, Becket was obliged to frame Foliot's understanding of *caritas* as an example of special treatment, of judicial partiality. When Becket explains his stance, therefore, and in particular his unwillingness to moderate his condemnation of Henry despite the pleas of the English bishops, he makes a defence of judicial principle which is grounded in both law and morality. Henry, having sinned, should be punished no less than any other sinner, for the laws of the Church demand that the judge should show no respect for persons:

> For the canon excepts neither the great man nor the private citizen, but strikes those who sin equally with an equal penalty, unless you believe, perhaps, that ecclesiastical laws should be compared to civilian laws which, as Anarcarsis complains, are like spiders' webs, which catch and trap little flies, but allow the greater flying creatures to pass through, when they are torn aside. ...[91] But not thus is the law of the Lord, which initiates vengeance in his sanctuary, and inflicts a very severe judgment on those who rule, and commands that the great should be greatly punished. We read that when Israel fornicated with the Midianites, its princes were struck with penalty for the crime; for the Lord says, 'take all the princes of the people and string them up on scaffolds facing the sun' [Numbers xxv.4].[92]

Becket, accordingly, denounces any call for accommodation with Henry as special pleading. He appeals to an alternative conception of the judge – not as someone who balances severity and mercy, but as someone who weighs all cases with true impartiality. Defending his position to Alexander III in 1167, Becket urges the Church, and its vicar, not to be moved and to thus compromise an impartial sentence. He is called upon to be 'a maintainer of justice and equity; not a regarder of persons, sparing no one in judgment, fairly and faithfully dispensing equity and justice as much to the king as to the ordinary man' (*equitatis et iustitie observatorem, non acceptorem personarum, nemini parcentem in iudicio, de iuris equitate fideliter et eque dispensantem regi pariter ac privato*).[93]

The critical question of how the righteous exercise of judicial discretion was to be distinguished from arbitrary will is most sharply exemplified in the exchange of letters between Gilbert Foliot, Thomas Becket and John of Salisbury. This dilemma was not simply a polemical product of the conditions of a bitter twelfth-century ecclesiastical dispute – it lay embedded in scripture, in the principle that the judge ought to be no respecter of persons. This was an ideal that was open to a multiplicity of interpretations. Certainly the judge ought to refuse bribes, to be no respecter of wealth. Whether he ought to have sympathy for the poor, the weak or the wretched, however, was rather less clear – was this appropriate compassion or still shameful partiality? Becket's judicial strategy, Foliot lamented, was, in practice, harming the poor, the weak and the wretched, all of whom suffered with the institutional damage being caused to the English Church. Mercy towards the wretched was, moreover, the essence of justice, not in the sense of payment of due, but in an 'Augustinian' definition of justice as *subveniendo miseris*. While a judge therefore ought not to be a respecter of persons, of wealth or status, he was expected to have some regard for circumstance. This concerned both the circumstances of the crime (as is evident in the pardons of common law and the penitentials of canon law), but also the circumstances of punishment.

Robert Grosseteste and Adam Marsh: talking to judges

Robert Grosseteste and his student and confidant, the Franciscan friar Adam Marsh (d.1259), are two figures better known for their passion for pastoral reform and spiritual renovation than for their interest in law. The purpose of this discussion is not to examine how the two of them acted as judges, but to consider how they advised and spoke to those in a position to give judgment – that is to say, how they deployed their advice in letters.

Like a number of other authors discussed here, Grosseteste and Adam share the conviction that quarrelsome litigation provided a distraction from the work of spiritual perfection;[94] and that the negotiation of peace is a more fitting occupation for members of the Church. A further problem in examining what Grosseteste had to say about judges is his bitter objection to any ecclesiastical involvement in processes of secular judgment and justice.[95] As this book has already argued, however, the demand for a separation of ecclesiastical and secular judicial procedure and keeping religious men clear of 'judgments of blood' is a question of structural separation: it does not say anything about the *ethical* basis of judgment. Indeed, Grosseteste accepts that it will be necessary in certain cases to pass a capital sentence: in fact, he acknowledges that under the Old Law, individuals who fulfilled a religious function and thus prefigure bishops carried out such judgments – Moses was an 'avenger of evils' who dealt in blood punishments.[96] Yet, Grosseteste explains, since the coming of Christ, the laws dealing with the shedding of blood have been placed in the hands of secular princes and folded into the category of temporal law. Both swords are the Church's to command, but secular officers must administer these judgments. That clerics ought not, in Grosseteste's view, to involve themselves in secular judgment is symbolic only of the fact that Jesus fled temporal issues, not a denial of the fact that it is sometimes appropriate to shed blood. In short, Grosseteste's repeated objections to the involvement of officers of the Church in secular courts is not an argument about models for judicial behaviour (which, for both secular and ecclesiastical rulers derive from the same scriptural and classical sources). It is rather Grosseteste's view that the Church (usually) has more important things to do than attend to the minutiae of legal business. This distinction is significant. Lay judgment was necessarily dirtier, necessarily nastier: a *negotium* with which the Church should not concern itself, a distraction from pastoral responsibilities and/or monastic vows. But when the Church came to judge, then the same strictures about corruption and partiality, mercy and judgment, applied to all judges, even if they were observed in different court venues.

As for Adam Marsh, the difficulty is twofold: the complexity (or, less sympathetically, the overwhelming artifice) of his Latin prose,[97] and the fact that his letters are our only known extant source for Adam (aside from the suggestion that he very likely assisted Grosseteste with the compilation of the *Tabula*, or continued it). But here, too, is an advantage: though we might lament the loss of Adam's once considerable theological oeuvre,[98] his letters offer a glimpse into practical engagement with judges. This still must come with the caveat that judicial matters – or even questions of leniency and severity in their broadest construction – are not the centre of his business – and these are business letters, for the most part. Adam, at times, finds himself too busy with the work of the Franciscan order and other calls upon his time to be interested in acting as a judge: in the letters he mentions his attempts to secure exemptions from the role of papal judge-delegate.[99] While Adam and Grosseteste have little time for giving judgment themselves, their letters are full of advice for would-be judges and informed by a conviction that those who judge must be educated about the weighty matters of justice and mercy.

Grosseteste, perhaps uniquely, offers one particular way of tracing some of the sources of his ideas on judges and judgment. The *Tabula* is Grosseteste's own concordance to 440 theological and philosophical topics.[100] It offers an index to some, though not all, of the scriptural and classical references Grosseteste thought relevant to topics of particular significance, as a work of reference he must later have referred to in the composition of sermons and treatises. The sole manuscript of the *Tabula* (Lyons, Bibliothèque municipale 414) indicates that editions were also made to the concordance by Adam Marsh. A number of the topic headings touch on the matter of justice and mercy: Grosseteste's categories include De misericordia Dei;[101] De iustitia;[102] De mansuetudine;[103] as well as De consilio;[104] De misericordia;[105] and De clementia.[106] Rosemann, the modern editor of the *Tabula*, reckons the text to give a picture of Grosseteste's reading and interests up to c.1230.[107] In that sense, the *Tabula* cannot give us any picture of how Grosseteste's

Judgment in practice: the Church

later engagement with Aristotle might have supplemented (or, indeed, supplanted) some of these references. It is clear, for example, from Grosseteste's comments in a letter discussing the nature of counsel, that the *Ethics* had considerable influence in the way in which he structures his understanding of that term.[108] But while the *Tabula* cannot give us the totality of Grosseteste's mature thought (and one might ask what could, given the diversity and depth of his interests), it does serve to highlight the fact that Grosseteste's reference points when discussing divine mercy, or human justice, in the late 1220s were fundamental, the same as those used by scholastic authors in the 1120s. Though the practical context of giving judgment might have changed in the course of a century, it is still the scriptural typologies – as discussed above in Chapter 4 – which give structure to a discussion of justice. To understand *misericordia* – or, better, to begin to structure a sermon, letter or treatise on mercy – one must go to the Books of Kings, to Ruth, to Deuteronomy; as well as to Augustine (*De civitate dei*; *Confessiones*; and the pseudo-Augustinian *De conflictu vitiorum et virtutum* and the *De spiritu et anima*); to Gregory the Great's *Moralia*, *Super Ezekiel* and the *Homiliae in evangelia*; and the *Sententia* of John of Damascus.[109]

Grosseteste's most direct engagement with the particulars of secular law is found in his concern over the treatment of bastardy in the English courts. Where English law would not permit a child born out of wedlock to inherit parental goods, even where the child's parents did subsequently marry, canon law, by contrast, upheld the right of the pre-nuptial child to inherit.[110] This was a topic of particular debate in England between 1234 and 1236, with Grosseteste's refusal to answer royal mandates on the question of bastardy forcing further discussion by the barons of England at the Council of Merton in January 1236.[111] In Letter 23, Grosseteste launches into a discussion of this matter with William Raleigh, the senior royal justice. The tone is ferocious, as Grosseteste argues the common law's attitude is contrary to divine law, natural law, canon law and reason. Secular princes alone did not have the power to make such a precept law when it ran contrary to those more powerful laws; instead they subverted authority and brought the fires of hell upon themselves.[112]

While Grosseteste's ire on the subject is compelling, it is not our focus here. What is more revealing (and pertinent to the subject of this monograph) are the secondary features of this letter. He addresses this angry missive to William Raleigh, royal justice (and, from 1239, Bishop of Norwich, subsequently Bishop of Winchester), in addition to the likely author of significant parts of the legal treatise *Bracton*.[113] This was not the first time the two had come into contact: Grosseteste had previously written to William,

Justice and mercy

and one suspects their connection runs deeper than that, for Grosseteste addresses Raleigh in familial tones as 'dearly beloved'; William held several church livings, including within the diocese of Lincoln.[114] The endearments with which Grosseteste addresses Raleigh are worthy of note:

> You are more closely tied to me as a spiritual son, and by a longstanding and special affection, and by the generous bestowal of various benefits, than are the others who pass their time at court. *So to you, as I mentioned above, more than to anyone else I have an obligation to pass on the truth of the gospels, so that in you I may gain the reward of eternal salvation that I desire most of all.*[115]

What is striking here is not the fact of the communication between Grosseteste and a royal judge (the senior justice of the bench by 1233), nor the lengths to which Grosseteste goes to persuade William of his case. Rather it is the role of persuasion itself: Grosseteste explains that he feels the obligation to pass on a spiritual truth so that English judges might be educated and the law might be reshaped accordingly.

William Raleigh evidently replied testily and with some displeasure to Grosseteste's letter, possibly accusing Grosseteste of subverting the laws of the kingdom or the law-making process. According to Grosseteste, 'you imply that my goal is to try to modify the laws of the kingdom by arguments from the Old Testament'.[116] Grosseteste's response was to reply that his goal was only to *persuade*, and that he knew that William was not the only framer of law in the kingdom. 'I am not such a fool as to believe that you or anyone else can, at someone's prompting, establish or change laws without the counsel of the king and his magnates.'[117] Rather, Grosseteste insisted, he wrote only to persuade William, who might in turn use his position to persuade others: 'With that epistle I try to persuade you – along with those who have the power to frame and change laws and whom you have been able to persuade to do so.'[118] Grosseteste insisted he would gladly write to others if he believed they would be as receptive as William Raleigh.

This is not a letter which discusses mercy or justice in sentencing – although Grosseteste's underlying belief is that the common law cannot be considered just when so out of alignment with all other measurements of law and reason. The letter is focused on the principles of law rather than the moral orientation of the judge. It is considered here for the significance of the connection, and the fact that it might provide a useful way of modelling the argument of this book. This is not a case of – it is not as simple as – theologians 'telling' lawyers what to do; giving instruction and awaiting the inscription of those theological ideals in law codes. It speaks to a more complex relationship; an interaction and exchange; a

Judgment in practice: the Church

mode of persuasion. Grosseteste was reminding William of Raleigh of the complexity – moral and soteriological – of judgment and the law-making and law-giving process. There was space to manoeuvre, and space in which he could be heard. Moreover, there was a set of shared assumptions between them – a common vocabulary and a relationship open to discussion; persuadable, if not persuaded. William Raleigh wrote back with his objections.

William Raleigh is not the only secular judge or member of royal administration with whom Grosseteste was in correspondence. In 1235, the same year as the first letter to Raleigh, and the year of his election to Lincoln, Grosseteste was also writing to Michael Belet, Oxford-educated master of law, hereditary butler to Henry III. Belet first appears in royal service in 1224; in 1225 he was a justice-in-eyre for Northamptonshire; it is possible that Belet had retired from active royal service by the time that this letter – concerning the appointment of a candidate to a benefice of Lincoln – was written.[119] The letter is not, therefore, concerned with matters of judgment, but of pastoral care – and whether Grosseteste was right to rebuke this unsuitable candidate.[120] It does, however, touch on questions of moderation, Grosseteste identifying the central issue in their discussion as whether he himself had 'exceeded all measure and moderation'.[121] In 1240, an irate Grosseteste writes to Robert of Lexington and his fellow itinerant judges, reprimanding them for their mistreatment of a priest of Lincoln during their time on eyre.[122] The fracas had allegedly begun when the priest rebuked the justices for hearing capital cases on a Sunday.[123] Grosseteste does not miss the opportunity to remind them that they were endangering their own salvation by giving judgment on a Sunday, and that the priest ought to have been commended rather than reviled. One must concede that this incident does not do much to support the idea that judges listened to what theologians had to say. Indignant protestants from a chippy and inconsequential parish priest were one thing, but being reminded by the Bishop of Lincoln that your salvation was at stake if you continued to ignore judicial moral standards was quite another.

It is easy to imagine Grosseteste bending the ears of many noble parties on the subject of forgiveness and salvation whenever he came into contact with them – not least when mediating peace accords.[124] Similar points of contact can be glimpsed in Adam Marsh's correspondence: Adam writes to John of Lexington (the elder brother of Robert of Lexington, whom Grosseteste had written to), steward of the royal household, judge *coram rege* in 1246 and chief justice of the forests north of the Trent from 1252 onwards.[125] Adam shapes his epistolary address to suit John of Lexington's position, offering him in greeting 'gentle mercy in true judgment' (*in veritate iudicii misericordie mansuetudinem*).[126]

These moments of epistolary address should be seen as snatches of much longer conversations and exchanges over the lifetimes of Grosseteste and Marsh. The fact that these two prominent individuals in the Church would address men high in royal administration is unremarkable. William Raleigh and Grosseteste were both part of the political community of thirteenth-century England, with interests that overlapped, intersected and clashed: they had reason to correspond with one another. What is striking, however, is the pastoral and judicial shape of that correspondence and of the ideas exchanged.[127] Beyond revealing networks in which men who were royal justices were also linked by benefices, by roles in the Church and by familial links,[128] the letters also disclose 'practical' demonstrations of how members of the ecclesiastical hierarchy might advise judges in these letters. Grosseteste, in particular, offers two opportunities for glimpsing how a rhetorical engagement with justice and mercy could be transported into points of practical power and political import. Here the ideals distilled from Old Testament judicial *exempla* are distilled down, used directly to sue for mercy, to ask for freedom or leniency. In short, discussions of judicial ideals have tangible effect. These are Grosseteste's Letters 29 and 48, addressed, respectively, to Henry III and Simon de Montfort.

Letter 29 is a letter of 1236, addressed to Henry and suing for the release of the knight Richard Siward (or Seward).[129] Siward had a troublesome history with Henry III, having been allied with Richard Marshal against the king in 1233 and being responsible for freeing Hubert de Burgh from his Church imprisonment in Devizes. Siward's career (traced out in part by Matthew Paris[130]), had led to his being banished from England in April 1236, quite possibly for his actions in wasting the estates of Richard, Earl of Cornwall. None of this would have been Grosseteste's problem, but for the fact that – in what David Crouch has interpreted as an immediate response to limit the effect of the decision to force him from England[131] – Siward had himself marked with the cross, placing himself and his lands under the protection of the Church. This undertaking did not, however, prevent his arrest. Grosseteste was not the only individual pleading for Siward – Edmund of Canterbury involved the negotiation, along with Alexander II of Scotland. Siward was swiftly restored to the royal household.

Grosseteste's letter on behalf of Siward, therefore, represents only one thrust in a more concerted effort to see Siward released and his banishment lifted. The primary argument of Letter 29 is that because Siward has been marked with the cross, as for crusading, he is a consecrated man and

Judgment in practice: the Church

therefore beyond the royal power to dispose of. Grosseteste – ever-ready to defend fiercely the jurisdictional remit of the Church's power – adopts the approach that Henry can assert no power over Siward. This is straightforward enough. Yet, in the final paragraph of the letter, Grosseteste markedly changes his approach, and, strictly speaking, the argument is not congruent with the position that Henry has no right to Siward. Grosseteste switches from arguing that Henry has no right to appealing to royal clemency to release Siward. This represents an implicit concession that Henry has both the right and the discretion to free the knight; it might also be considered an acceptance of hard facts. What is striking here (and bears out the argument of earlier chapters) is the connection Grosseteste goes on to draw between royal mercy and the virtue of *largitas*, generosity and greatness. But it is not a Roman emperor (i.e. one famed for power and liberality) whom Grosseteste praises and to whom he compares Henry – it is rather Solomon, who, Henry is reminded, declared that mercy and truth are a king's guards, and that clemency (*clementia*) strengthens the throne (Proverbs xx.28).

Having first asserted that Henry has no power over Siward *de iure*, Grosseteste concedes the point that *de facto*, Siward is in the royal keeping. If his jurisdictional argument fails, therefore, he will appeal to the virtue of the office-holder – the virtue of the prince. The language used here, underlining that connection between royal mercy and earthly glory, is telling: 'for it is especially magnificent and fitting for the magnanimity of a king, and consistent with the perfection taught by the Gospels, to be generous even to one's enemies (Matthew v.44, 48).'[132]

An early chapter considered the real-world working out of the gospel command to 'love thine enemy' in medieval England: whether it might ever have been considered possible, rather than a lofty aspiration. But Grosseteste believed it might at least have force as an appeal: that it was not useless to put the prospect of 'perfection' before a prince, not least it that perfection could be couched in terms of earthly and outward magnificence as well as the personal achievement of a virtuous state. It could be made into an argument for glory and generosity, could be presented in such a way as to burnish a royal reputation. Undoubtedly there were more forceful arguments made for Siward's return: but Grosseteste shows us the possibility, indeed, the viability, of mercy as glorious clemency, as a strategy.

Grosseteste's second letter suing for mercy is addressed to Simon de Montfort and discusses a matter of local, rather than national concern. While Grosseteste had reason to involve himself in the matter of Richard Siward as a question of ecclesiastical rights, that is not the case here: the motivation seems to be purely personal, out of concern for de Montfort's soul should he judge hastily and unjustly. Letter 48 probably dates to 1237 and discusses de Montfort's treatment of a burgess of Leicester, whom de Montfort is now in a position to punish.[133] The burgess is not named beyond the initial 'S', but Mantello suggests that this figure is almost certainly Simon de Curlevache, an alderman of Leicester; no reference at all is made to the offence.[134]

One infers that information had reached Grosseteste that de Montfort was set on punishing 'S' severely (possibly over a matter relating to finances). Grosseteste does not simply reprimand de Montfort, nor straightforwardly remind him of the good of mercy. Instead he sets out an explanation of the relationship between guilt, innocent and punishment. The discussion is structural, rather than simply being a commendation of mercy. Grosseteste begins from the premise that it is as wrong not to punish the guilty as it is to punish the innocent. He reminds de Montfort that punishing the guilty short of what they deserve 'is justice with mercy and an imitation of Christ, who punishes everyone in this way'.[135] These, it might be said, are some very basic building blocks, upon which Grosseteste can then establish his argument. Once one appreciates that Christ punishes everyone short of what they deserve, and this is just, one then transfers that logic to human judgments. This is an argument worth quoting in full: familiar though it is, it captures expressly the logic and interconnection of human and divine mercy:

> Punishing the guilty with attention to achieving an exact correspondence and balancing with what they deserve is justice applied inflexibly, or perhaps not justice at all, for it wants the intermingling of mercy, and only makes one deserving of being judged without mercy, since it is written that judgment will be without mercy for the one who has shown no mercy [cf. James ii.13].[136]

None of these statements, taken alone, might be considered contentious: each is scripturally sanctioned. But they build to allow Grosseteste to claim that when punishment exceeds the fault, then innocence is being punished. Punishment beyond measure of the offence ceases to be punishment for a specified offence and then becomes punishment for innocent actions. And who, Grosseteste ponders, do we most associate with the punishment of innocence, but Herod; or, indeed, those who crucified Christ? For in both of those cases, punishment was being applied without grounds. The ruthless, remorseless logic of mercy is on display in this letter.

Intertwined with this soteriological argument – that excessive punishment puts the judge in the same position of Herod or even those who executed Christ – is an argument which seems to be inflected with certain classical ideas (though Grosseteste does not refer to them specifically). This is the idea that excessive punishment means putting aside human nature and assuming the form of a beast (an argument which runs throughout Seneca's *De clementia*.[137] What, however, one comes back to here is Grosseteste's utter lack of interest in the situation of 'S'. His crime is not discussed, nor are any extenuating circumstances (to employ an anachronism) discussed. It is possible that Grosseteste was not familiar with the case; more probable, however, is that the circumstances simply did not matter. The overriding concern here is not the pain of the individual exposed to excessive punishment, but the danger such punishment would pose both to the character and the soul of the judge, namely Simon de Montfort. It would first transform him, making him vicious, and then endanger him greatly.[138] It is the judge with whom Grosseteste is concerned: 'if what I have heard is true, when I see you staggering so to speak, toward a fall of this kind, I want with the warning in this letter to catch you before you fall'.[139] Simon de Montfort's judicial powers and responsibilities set a choice before him: will he line up with Christ, punishing less than is due, or with Herod, who showed no mercy?

Considering Simon de Montfort's particular dedication to religious devotion, we may not consider him a 'typical' example of how secular lords responded to spiritual counsel.[140] We may hypothesise that Grosseteste found in him a more receptive audience than in some others. But what Letter 48 demonstrates most powerfully is how these scriptural principles could be brought together and then built up, and the persuasive appeal they might have in the hands (and pen) of someone like Grosseteste, who knew how to deploy them most effectively.

Like Grosseteste, Adam Marsh also wrote to Simon de Montfort, though not on matters of specific cases. Even in the course of ordinary correspondence, however, Adam continues to remind de Montfort of his judicial responsibilities as a baron: 'the malicious are to be strictly admonished by those who preside in judgment; the loyal are to be supported by gentleness and affection'.[141] This, Adam remarks, is an integral part of governance – this is 'how citizens may be governed with wisdom' (*cives sapienter gubernatur*). In another letter, Adam affirms to Simon that the means of salvation lie in 'exercising more forgiving mercy' and 'stricter justice'.[142] In Adam's letters, the relationship between a proper balance of justice and mercy and the tenor of good governance more generally is readily apparent. Those who govern also judge, and poor judgment means bad governance.

Adam's letters, centred, for the most part, on the business of the Franciscan order, also provide a further insight into the dynamics of justice and mercy in the thirteenth-century Church. Many of them are, effectively, letters of petition to those in ecclesiastical government, arguing for the 'merciful' treatment of friars (or others) who have broken their vows but are now seeking readmission to the order. Just as Grosseteste reminds Henry III and Simon de Montfort of the importance of James ii.13 (reciprocal mercy), so does Adam address recipients in the Church. John of St Giles, Archdeacon of Oxford, is begged to delay a matter of distraint until Lent and accept a pledge of security, Adam reminding John that the Lord prefers mercy above all things, blesses the merciful 'and promises that if we forgive, we shall be forgiven'.[143] William of Nottingham, the provincial minister, being petitioned to restore a former subject (i.e. Franciscan brother) to the order is advised: 'where there is need, after the example of the Supreme Judge, let the sentence not be so harsh as to exclude mercy; let mercy not be so gentle as to make the sentence soft'.[144] In another letter he intercedes with William for another 'apostate' from the order who is keen to make restitution.[145]

Adam's letters, however, also set up a problem which we will encounter in the next chapter. Though Adam presents himself as a petitioner for repentant and wayward brothers, he is acutely conscious of the potential dangers of using persuasive techniques to sue for mercy. Whereas a well-intentioned brother might set out good arguments for encouraging a judge to mercy, a malicious advocate might try to sway the judge for their own reasons. Even in his petitions for mercy for individuals whom he considers worthy candidates for restoration, Adam is careful to hedge: he asks William of Nottingham to follow his advice only 'as far as you consider it expedient'.[146] Adam, perhaps because he sets himself up as a petitioner, rather than an impartial adviser to those with judicial power, is careful in these circumstances. He goes no further than asking his correspondents to consider pardon:

> In these cases one must, I think, act with careful deliberation and prayer, lest an easy pardon should provide encouragement to sin or the severity of man should drive away one whom divine forgiveness brings back.[147]

Adam's difficulty lies in the fact that persuasion might cut two ways, might dissuade the correct course of action as well as lend support to a just judgment. More so than any of the other authors surveyed here (John of Salisbury, Thomas Becket, Gilbert Foliot, Robert Grosseteste), Adam is nervous about the role of persuasion in the pardoning process. We might also see this reflected in Adam's choice of judicial *exempla* – for among his letters, Adam adduces one rather strange and quite particular model of a judge. This Ahasuerus (i.e. the historical king Xerxes) from the Book of Esther. This features in a letter which is not, ostensibly, a discussion of judicial behaviour. This is Letter 74, Addressed to Fulk Basset, Bishop of London, and Adam writes on behalf of the Friars Minor of London.[148] Some short time before this letter was written, the friars had recommended that an individual named Geoffrey Gross be presented to a church living in Essex, thinking him a suitable candidate for the position. This letter, however, acts to rescind that recommendation and revoke the endorsement: the London friars now believed they had been taken in by Geoffrey Gross's persuasions, when he was in fact not fitted for the ministry. Adam writes to Fulk to withdraw the endorsement, and, in the course of doing so, to explain (and, implicitly, apologise for) this change of heart.

It is in this context that Adam invokes Ahasuerus, alluding to the portion of the biblical story in which Ahasuerus has been persuaded by his wicked counsellor Haman to have all the Jews of his empire put to death. It was only when the queen, Esther, interceded with Ahasuerus (Esther vii–viii) that he rescinded this decision and agreed to write down a decree annulling his previous order. Ahasuerus is the figure whom Adam uses to explain this change of view: from a false opinion to a correct one. This is an example of a judge who changes his mind – and of how that course might be justified. Adam describes the king as 'a powerful prefigure of our blessed saviour'.[149] The decision to change his stance was praiseworthy once understood in context, both because Ahasuerus was usually constant, and because on this occasion he realised that his previous command had been given 'under cruel persuasion to the ruin of his people'.[150]

It is, to say the least, an unusual choice, and the way in which Adam introduces and positions this judicial *exemplum* perhaps suggests his awareness that it was not a perfect fit. Esther, the heroine who pleaded for justice even when maligned, not Ahasuerus, the easily manipulated ruler, was typically the lesson of this book.[151] Ahasuerus is invoked as a figure to excuse Adam and his fellow friars from embarrassing charges of inconstancy and being easily deceived. As will be seen in the next chapter, his example also serves to highlight the uneasy relationship between judgment and persuasion.

Notes

1 'Strategies of justice and mercy' should not be read as implying that these judges were choosing between two possible actions, severe punishment or complete abrogation of punishment. It rather denotes distinct punitive and merciful

Justice and mercy

principles, the rationale behind the judge's decision. 'Justice' and 'mercy' respectively encompassed a range of actions.

2 But while confession was private, penance could be staged as a public ceremony: see Mary C. Mansfield, *The Humiliation of Sinners: Public Penance in Thirteenth-Century France* (New York, 1995).
3 See T. Shogimen, 'From disobedience to toleration: William of Ockham and the medieval discourse on fraternal correction', *Journal of Ecclesiastical History* 52 (2001), 599–622.
4 J. T. McNeill, 'Medicine for sin as prescribed in the penitentials', *Church History* 1 (1932), 14–26.
5 For example, Ivo of Chartres, *Prologue*, 117. The nineteenth book of Burchard's *Decretum* was entitled 'corrector, seu medicus': *Das Dekret des Bischofs Burchard von Worms*, ed. Hartmut Hoffmann (Munich, 1991); cf. *Policraticus*, 4.8, 1:529.
6 See P. Michaud-Quantin, 'À propos de premières *Summae confessorum*: théologie et droit canonique', *RTAM* 26 (1959), 264–306; Joseph Goering, 'The internal forum and the literature of penance', in Wilfried Hartmann and Kenneth Pennington (eds), *The History of Medieval Canon Law in the Classical Period, 1140–1234: From Gratian to the Decretals of Pope Gregory IX*, (Washington, DC, 2008), 379–428.
7 On the growth of 'contritionism' see the important qualifications made by K. T. Wagner, *'De vera et falsa pentitentia*: An Edition and Study' (unpublished PhD thesis, University of Toronto, 1995), 111–29.
8 *Ibid.*, 156–8.
9 *SC*, xv; cf. Wagner, *'De vera et falsa penitentia'*, 175, 189, for the possible significance of the choice between 'iudex' and 'medicus' to describe the confessor.
10 *Decretum, De poenitentia*, D.III, c.19, 1:1161–2, circumstances drawn from Cicero, *De inventione*, 2.151, 318–21.
11 On the public–private distinction and its reception in canon law, see R. M. Fraher, 'The theoretical justification for the new criminal law of the high middle ages: "rei publicae interest, ne crimina remaneant impunita"', *University of Illinois Law Review* (1984), 577–95.
12 *SC*, 7.1.1a, 325.
13 *Ibid.*, xx; cf. R. W. Southern, 'The place of England in the twelfth-century renaissance', in his *Medieval Humanism and Other Studies* (Oxford, 1970), 158–80; M. G. Cheney, *Roger, Bishop of Worcester, 1164–1179* (Oxford, 1980), 193–212.
14 See the discussion in the editors' introduction to Robert Grosseteste, *Templum Dei*, ed. Joseph Goering and F. A. C. Mantello (Toronto, 1984), 6–7.
15 A. C. Friend, 'The Life and Unprinted Works of Master Odo of Cheriton' (unpublished DPhil thesis, University of Oxford, 1925), 150.
16 Gerald of Wales, *Vita sancti Remigii*, in *Opera omnia*, 7:28, 57–60; see A. Morey, *Bartholomew of Exeter, Bishop and Canonist* (Cambridge, 1937), 44–78.
17 Between 1155 and 1165; Morey, *Bartholomew of Exeter*, 108.
18 *Ibid.*, 173–4.

Judgment in practice: the Church

19 Ibid., 163, records eighteen extant copies of the *Penitential*, a testament to its widespread popularity.
20 *Penitential* (published in Morey, *Bartholomew of Exeter*), 26, 195.
21 *Penitential*, 37, 203; cf. 26, 195, also referring to the measuring of canons 'in arbitrio sacerdotis intelligentis' (quoting *Decretum, De poenitentia*, q.3, c.86, 1:1183).
22 'et homo, cui grave onus penitentie imponis, aut penitentiam reiciet, aut suscipiens dum ferre non potest, scandalizatus amplius peccat. Deinde, et si erramus modicum penitentiam imponentes, nonne melius erit propter misericordiam rationem dare, quam propter crudelitatem? Ubi enim paterfamilias largus est, dispensator non debet esse tenax. Si Deus benignus, ut quid sacerdos eius austerus vult apparere?' *Penitential*, 34, 201; from *Decretum*, C.XXVI, c.12, q.7, 1:1044.
23 Morey, *Bartholomew of Exeter*, 173. Cf. *Penitential*, 11, 182.
24 *Penitential*, 36, 202; cf. 26, 195.
25 P. Delhaye, 'Deux textes de Senatus de Worcester sur la pénitence', *RTAM* 19 (1952), 203–24; for Senatus see Cheney, *Roger of Worcester*, 58–67, and N. Karn, 'Monastic Letter-Writers in Twelfth-Century England' (unpublished DPhil thesis, University of Oxford, 2002), appendix 2.
26 Gerald of Wales, *Vita sancti Remigii*, 28, 57–60; Sayers, *Papal Judges-Delegate*, 10.
27 Delhaye, 'Deux textes', 206.
28 Ibid., 207.
29 D. A. Wilmart, 'Un opuscule sur la confession composé par Guy de Southwick vers la fin du XIIe siècle', *RTAM* 7 (1935), 337–52.
30 Ibid., 339.
31 L. E. Boyle, 'A Study of the Works attributed to William of Pagula with Special Reference to the *Oculum sacerdotus* and *Summa summarum*' (unpublished DPhil thesis, University of Oxford, 1956), 188–281.
32 'Nemo sic intelligat ut semper secundum rigorem et districtionem canonibus constitutam absque omni misericordia poenitentia imponi debeat, sed quod canonum rigor non pro sacerdotum libito, sed per canonum dispensationem, sit temperandus, ita ut in poenitentiis dandis semper memor sit sacerdos et districtae satisfactionis, ad quam peccatores tenentur ex culpa, et indulgentiae, per quam canones vere poenitentibus subveniunt ex misericordia.' Robert of Flamborough, *Liber poenitentialis*, 5.12, 273–4. Robert adds further: 'et in altero necesse sit excedere, minus malum credimus misericordiae lenitatem absque dissolutione servare quam rigorem iustitiae semper ubique tenere'.
33 *SC*, xv.
34 On 'procedure' in the twelfth century, see K. Pennington, 'Due process, community, and the prince in the evolution of the *Ordo iudicarius*', *Revista internazionale di diritto comune* 9 (1998), 9–47.
35 *SC*, 5.1.3a, 201.
36 Ibid., 5.1.12a, 217.
37 J. Goering and F. A. C. Mantello, 'The early penitential writings of Robert Grosseteste', *RTAM* 54 (1987), 56–7.

38 Siegfried Wenzel (ed.), 'Robert Grosseteste's treatise on confession "Deus Est"', *Franciscan Studies* 30 (1970), 218–93.
39 For further English contributions to this genre see A. Teetaert, 'Quelques *Summae de Poenitentia* anonymes de la Bibliothèque Nationale', in A. M. Albareda (ed.), *Miscellanea Giovanni Mercati II* (Rome, 1946), 326–9; J. Goering, 'The "Summa de penitentia" of John of Kent', *Bulletin of Medieval Canon Law* 18 (1988), 13–31; J. Goering, 'The *summa* "Qui bene presunt" and its author', in R. G. Newhauser and J. A. Alford (eds), *Literature and Religion in the Later Middle Ages: Philological Studies in Honor of Siegfried Wenzel* (Binghamton, NY, 1995), 143–59.
40 Robert of Flamborough also made (unacknowledged) use of Huguccio's *Summa in Decretum*; Francis Firth, 'The "Poenitentiale" of Robert of Flamborough', *Traditio* 16 (1960), 550.
41 Peter of Blois, *De poenitentia vel satisfactione*, PL.207.1091–8.
42 'Isti exercent zelum iustitiae in fermento, et non in azymo, ut iracundiae satisfaciant, non ut Christo fructificent'. *Ibid.*, 1094A.
43 Cheney, *Roger of Worcester*, 187; 247–9.
44 See the comments of R. I. Moore, 'Literacy and the making of heresy, c.1100–c.1150', in Peter Biller and Anne Hudson (eds), *Heresy and Literacy, 1000–1530* (Cambridge, 1994), 34; Ian Forrest, *The Detection of Heresy in Late Medieval England* (Oxford, 2005), 19–23. Cheney, *Roger of Worcester*, 68–9, argues that heresy was almost unheard of in England at this time, but the extent of heretical activity in medieval England is difficult to quantify. This may be a matter of absence of evidence versus evidence of absence; one must be wary of uncritically accepting a narrative of English exceptionalism or isolation.
45 Adrien Morey and C. N. L. Brooke, *Gilbert Foliot and His Letters* (Cambridge, 1965), 52–72.
46 *GFL*, Ep. 22, 56–7, to Henry of Blois, asking him to temper the severity of the interdict on Hereford; see also P. D. Clarke, *The Interdict in the Thirteenth Century: A Question of Collective Guilt* (Oxford, 2007), 12–23.
47 R. I. Moore, *The Formation of a Persecuting Society: Power and Deviance in Western Europe, 950–1250* (Oxford, 1987), esp. 4–5.
48 Edward M. Peters, 'The prosecution of heresy and theories of criminal justice in the twelfth and thirteenth centuries', in Heinz Mohnhaupt and Dieter Simon (eds), *Vorträge zur Justizforschung: Geschichte und Theorie*, vol. 2 (Frankfurt, 1993), 25–42, esp. 34–5.
49 Cf. Peter Diehl, 'Ad abolendam (X 5.7.9) and imperial legislation against heresy', *Bulletin of Medieval Canon Law* 19 (1989), 1–11.
50 *Decretum*, C.VI, q.1 c.22, 1:560, quoting *Codex* 9.8.5, 2:373–4; cf. *Digest*, 48.4, 1:844–5.
51 Innocent III, *Vergentis in senium*, X.5.7.10 (*Corpus Iuris Canonici*, 2:782–3). Cf. W. Ullmann, 'The significance of Innocent III's decretal "Vergentis"', in *Études d'histoire du droit canonique dédiées à Gabriel Le Bras* (2 vols, Paris, 1965), 1:729–41.
52 Cf. R. M. Fraher, 'IV Lateran's revolution in criminal procedure: the birth of the inquisitio, the end of ordeals, and Innocent III's vision of ecclesiastical politics',

in Rosalio Josepho (ed.), *Studia in honorem Eminentissimi Cardinalis Alfonsi M. Stickler* (Rome, 1992), 97–111.
53 This letter (c.1164–65) falls before the stipulations of c.27 of the Third Lateran Council. See Anne J. Duggan, 'Conciliar law 1123–1215: the legislation of the four Lateran Councils', in Hartmann and Pennington, *Canon Law in the Classical Period*, 337.
54 *Decretum*, C.XXIII, 1:889.
55 R. I. Moore, *The Origins of European Dissent* (London, 1977), 252.
56 Morey and Brooke, *Gilbert Foliot*, 10.
57 Ibid., 29.
58 'Illis vero interim seorsum constitutis ne mutuis se possint in malum obfirmare colloquiis, bonos viros et graves, viros probatae fidei, divinae legis et litterarum peritos eorum curae convenit et custodiae deputari, qui eos visitent in verbo predicationis sancta, monitis emollient, minis et metu penarum exterreant, flagris interdum et flagellis cum moderata severitate coherceant, et ad ecclesie unitatem omnimodis prout caritas suggeret revocare procurent.' *GFL*, Ep. 157, 207–8.
59 *Decretum*, D.XLV, c.6, 1:162, 'benivolentia plus quam seueritas erga corrigendos agat'.
60 Jason Taliadoros, 'Law and theology in Gilbert of Foliot's (c.1105/10–1187/88) correspondence', *Haskins Society Journal* 16 (2005), 93, notes that Foliot seems unaware of – or at least does not follow – the provisions made for treatment of heretics from the Council of Tours in 1163.
61 'Grandis enim hec questio est, et a sanctis patribus et ecclesie doctoribus non mediocriter agitate, quibus ecclesie mansuetudinem et clementiam predicantibus – iuxta quod dictum est "lex clementie in lingua eius"; et illud Domini: "nec ego condempnabo" – aliis ne multi pereant in talium penam sancti proculdubio zeli pietate ferventibus. Hii filium freneticum vinculis arctandum sicque custodiendum commemorant; alii quod in religionem divinam committitur in omnium ferri iniuriam protestantes, in crimen hoc publicum legem Iuliam maiestatis intentant; alii exemplis iudicantes huiusmodi cremandos iudicant; alii severitatem hanc beati Augustini sententia temperant, qui Donatistas non interfici sed flagellis et suppliciis exorat emendari.' *GFL*, Ep. 158, 209–10; cf. Augustine, *Epistulae 185–270*, ed. A. Goldbacher, CSEL 57 (Vienna, 1911), Ep. 185, 1–44.
62 'communi fratrum nostrorum conventui reservari consulimus', *GFL*, Ep. 158, 210.
63 For the narrative: Diceto, *Abbreviationes chronicorum*, 1:318; William of Newburgh, *Historia*, 2.13, 1:131; *DNC*, 1.30, 120–3.
64 *GFL*, Ep. 237, 309–10.
65 Cf. *Decretum*, C.XV, q.6, c.1, 1:754–5.
66 *GFL*, Ep. 237, 310.
67 Taliadoros, 'Law and theology', 77–94.
68 Cheney, *Letters and Charters*, 4, for the level of Foliot's involvement in assembling the collection.

69 For example, it is followed by Ep. 294, 357, a settlement on the division of the revenues of a church.
70 *GFL*, Ep. 110, 151–2; Ep. 268, 332.
71 'fraternitate vestre preces affectuose porrigimus, supplicantes et obsecrantes in Domino quatinus illum ob reverentiam in Dei canonica severitate corripiatis, et ut uxori debitum provideat et prestet subsidium, ecclesiastice districtione iustitie compellatis ... et sentiat utrimque prevaricatores eius non deesse ultores'. *Ibid.*, Ep. 268, 332.
72 As for the Worcester heretics, it seems they are to be identified with those condemned by Henry II at Oxford in 1165/6. If we accept the report of William of Newburgh, writing more than three decades later, they were driven out of the city and died from exposure – a punishment in keeping with Henry's proclamation against heretics in c.21 of the Assizes of Clarendon.
73 In addition to C. Duggan, 'Criminous clerks', see also his 'The reception of canon law in England in the later twelfth century', in S. Kuttner and J. Ryan (eds), *Proceedings of the Second International Congress of Medieval Canon Law* (Rome, 1965), 359–90; M. Cheney, 'The Compromise of Avranches of 1172 and the spread of canon law in England', *English Historical Review* 56 (1941), 177–97.
74 See Michael Staunton, *Thomas Becket and his Biographers* (Woodbridge, 2006), 182.
75 *Becket Correspondence*, Ep. 78, 1:309, quoting *Decretum*, D.LXXXIII, c.5, 1:294.
76 See D. J. A. Matthew, 'The letter-writing of Archbishop Becket', in Richard Gameson and Henrietta Leyser (eds), *Belief and Culture in the Middle Ages: Essays Presented to Henry Mayr-Harting* (Oxford, 2001), 287–303.
77 For *Multiplicem*, Morey and Brooke, *Gilbert Foliot*, 166–73. Frank Barlow, *Thomas Becket* (London, 1986), 147–8; for the appeal see *Becket Correspondence*, Ep. 93, 1:373–83.
78 This was the letter *Desiderio desideravi* (1166), the second of Becket's three appeals to Henry, *Becket Correspondence*, Ep. 74, 1:292–9.
79 'De comminatorio miraris quod nos in eum emisimus. Quis pater videt filium aberrare et tacet? Quis virga non percutit ne gladium incurrat? Desperat pater de filio quem comminatione non corripit vel flagellat.' *Becket Correspondence*, Ep. 96, 1:430–1.
80 'Sed praetendit quia Iohannes arguebat Herodem in spiritu lenitatis, illicitum esse denuncians ut fratris viventis abuteretur uxore. Quod utique dicens non tam imperitiae quam ingaviae solacium quaerit, cum certum Iohannem ibi non gessisse personam pontifices cui incumberet correctio delictorum, sed praeconis verbi penes quem erat dumtaxat gerendorum denuntiatio et increpatio vitiorum. Heli quidem corripuit filios, sed affectu potius et mansuetudine patris quam severitate et auctoritate pontificis. Pro omni ergo diviniae legis articulo contendendum est et potestatibus ascendendum ex adverso et quicquid caritatem impugnat, quae legis est plenitudo, totis viribus subvertendum.' John of Salisbury, *Letters*, ed. and trans. J. W. Miller and H. E. Butler, revised by C. N. L. Brooke (2 vols, Oxford, 1979–86), Ep. 187, 2:234.

Judgment in practice: the Church

81 Cf. the bishops' appeal, drafted by Foliot (*Becket Correspondence*, Ep. 93, 1:379): 'we are not saying, in fact, that the lord king has never sinned; but we confidently declare and proclaim that he is always ready to make amends to the Lord'.
82 'Medico namque quis ascribat industrie, ut vulnus unum sanet, aliud longe maius, longe periculosius, infligat? Discretioni quis attribuit, ob quedam que poterunt et levius et expeditious obtineri, ecclesiam sic deserere, in principem exsurgere, et ecclesie tocius regni concussa pace animarum in subditis corporumque pericula non curare.' *Becket Correspondence*, Ep. 109, 1:532–3 [= *GFL*, Ep. 170].
83 'Bonum est membrum capiti coherere vel saucium quam a corpore sequestrari iam precisum. Redeunt ad sanitatem saucia sed corpori vix coalescunt iam precisa. Adducit desperationem precisio; restituit sanitatem vulneri sepe medicantis operatio.' *GFL*, Ep. 155, 205.
84 *Becket Correspondence*, Ep. 109, 1:528–9.
85 'In hoc vero sacra sic docet auctoritas, "In eiusmodi causis ubi per graves dissensionum scissuras non huius aut illius est hominis periculum, sed populorum strages iacent, detrahendum est aliquid severitati, ut maioribus malis sanandis caritas sincera subveniat".' *Becket Correspondence*, Ep. 109, 1:530–1, *Decretum*, D.L, c.25, 1:187, quoting Augustine, Ep. 185.10.45, 39–40.
86 Cf. Luke ix.47–8, Proverbs iii.29.
87 'Puerum apostolis proposuit exemplo Dominus, qui Iesus non irascitur, iniurie cito non meminit, nec quicquam maliciose moliens. ... Singulare itaque virtutis exemplar ipse est, qui se crucifigentes absolvit, qui lata caritate persequentes et odientes amari precipit, et si peccet frater in nos, veniam non solum septies, sed et septuagies septies imperat impertiri. Ista quid non posset humilitas apud dominum nostrum regem, quid non optineret viarum ista perfectio?' *Becket Correspondence*, Ep. 109, 1:536–7.
88 *Becket Correspondence*, Ep. 93, 1:380–1 [= *GFL*, Ep. 166]: 'do not continue by too hasty a judgment to ruin and destroy, but let your paternal kindness endeavour to make provision that the sheep committed to your charge may have life, peace and security'.
89 *Becket Correspondence*, Ep. 109, 1:512–3.
90 John of Salisbury, *Letters*, Ep. 101, 1:479.
91 For the reference see Plutarch, *Lives*, vol. 1, trans. Bernadotte Perrin (London, 1914), [Solon], 414–15.
92 'Canon enim nec potestatem excipit nec privatum, sed pariliter peccantes pari condempnationis pena percellit; nisi forte leges ecclesiasticas civilibus comparandas censeatis et vos, que sicut Anarcasis conqueritur, aranearum assimilantur telis, que muscas impediunt et retinent, sed dirupte volatilia grandiora transmittunt. ... Sed non ita lex Domini, que ultionem inchoat a sanctuario suo, et in eos qui presunt durissimum exercet iudicium, et potentes dictat potenter puniendos. Cum Madianitibus fornicatus legitur Israel, et principes pena criminis percelluntur; ait enim Dominus "Tolle cunctos principes populi, et suspede eos contra solem in patibulis".' *Becket Correspondence*, Ep. 117, 1:566–7.

93 *Ibid.*, Ep. 124, 1:594–5.
94 Cf. Adam Marsh, *Letters*, Ep. 41, 116, which is in fact attempting to discourage Grosseteste himself from persisting in a lawsuit.
95 Grosseteste, Ep. 27, Luard, 105–8; Mantello, 132–5: writing to Edmund of Canterbury in 1236, asking the archbishop to persuade Henry III to rescind the appointment of the Abbot of Ramsey as an itinerant justice, on the grounds that while it is illicit for a mere clerk to spill blood, it is worse still for a Benedictine abbot to do so. Ep. 28, repeats this plea to Edmund: Luard, 108–13; Mantello, 135–40.
96 For example, Grosseteste, Ep. 23, citing Exodus xvii.19 and xxxii.27, Luard, 92; Mantello, 121.
97 For a discussion of the collection, see Lawrence's introduction, Adam Marsh, *Letters*, xliii–xlvii.
98 A brief description is provided *ibid.*, xvii–xviii.
99 *Ibid.*, Ep. 188, 456–61.
100 Grosseteste, *Tabula*, ed. P. W. Rosemann and J. McEvoy, CCCM 130 (Turnhout, 1995), 233–320.
101 *Ibid.*, Distinctio 1, 270–1.
102 *Ibid.*, 3, 280.
103 *Ibid.*, 3, 283.
104 *Ibid.*, 3, 284.
105 *Ibid.*
106 *Ibid.*, 3, 290.
107 Grosseteste, *Tabula*, introduction, 239; See also P. Rosemann, 'Robert Grosseteste's *Tabula*', in J. McEvoy (ed.), *Robert Grosseteste: New Perspectives on his Thought and Scholarship* (Turnhout, 1995), 321–55.
108 Grosseteste, Ep. 99, Luard, 302–4; Mantello, 321–2.
109 The limitation in mining the *Tabula* as a map of Grosseteste's thought is the imprecision of these references. Grosseteste notes (at most) a book and chapter of scripture without specifying the verse. In certain circumstances one can make an educated guess: the reference to James ii under the heading 'De misericordia' is almost certain to refer to James ii.13: 'for judgment without mercy is to one who has shown no mercy'.
110 The law on bastardy is complex: see R. H. Helmholz, 'Bastardy litigation in medieval England', *American Journal of Legal History* 13:4 (1969), 360–83, discussing Grosseteste at 365–6. Grosseteste is here following the claims laid down by Alexander III: the principle of legitimation by subsequent marriage, and the competency of Church courts – rather than secular courts – to adjudicate on the matter. See further M. Sheehan, 'Illegitimacy in late medieval England: laws, dispensation and practice', in B. Wiggenhauser (ed.), *Illegitimität im Spätmittelalter* (Munich, 1994), 115–21.
111 A point discussed further by Paul Brand, 'The English medieval common law (to c.1307) as a system of national institutions and legal rules: creation and

Judgment in practice: the Church

functioning', in Paul Dresch and Hannah Skoda (eds), *Legalism: Anthropology and History* (Oxford, 2012), 173–96, at 193–4.

112 Grosseteste, Ep. 23, Luard, 91; Mantello, 119.

113 For William's rise, see C. A. F. Meekings, 'Martin Pateshull and William Raleigh', *Bulletin of the Institute of Historical Research* 26:74 (1953), 157–80. On William's role in *Bracton*, see Paul Brand, 'The age of *Bracton*', in John Hudson (ed.), *The History of English Law: Centenary Essays on 'Pollock and Maitland'* (London, 1995), 65–89.

114 Grosseteste, Ep. 17, on the appointment of a candidate to a benefice: Luard 33–5.

115 'copularis insuper mihi arctius caeteris in curia degentibus filiatione spirituali, dilectione diuturna et speciali, et multiplicis beneficii collatione liberali; tibi igitur, ut supra dixi, prae caeteris debitor sum evangelicae veritatis, ut consequar in te desideratissimum fructum aeternae salutis'. Grosseteste, Ep. 23, Luard, 76–7; Mantello, 108, emphasis mine.

116 'Postea autem me insinuas ad hoc conari ut immutem leges per rationes Veteris Testamenti.' Grosseteste, Ep. 24, Luard, 95; Mantello, 123.

117 'Nec tam idiota sum quod credam ad alicujus suggestionem te vel alium sine principis et magnatum consilio posse leges condere vel commutare.' Luard, 96; Mantello, 124.

118 'Nec te solum alicubi in transmissa epistola conditorem legum insinuari, quod in curia possis quicquid volueris.' Luard, 96; Mantello, 124.

119 For Belet, S. D. Church, 'Belet, Michael (d. in or before 1247)', *Oxford Dictionary of National Biography* (Oxford, 2004), www.oxforddnb.com/view/article/56845, accessed 23 July 2017. See also Ralph Turner's discussion of his father, Michael Belet senior, whom Turner takes as a paradigm for twelfth-century professionalisation in English government: 'Richard Barre and Michael Belet'.

120 Grosseteste, Ep. 11, Luard, 50–4; Mantello, 82–6.

121 'Modum et moderamen excessit.' *Ibid.*, Luard, 50; Mantello, 83.

122 Grosseteste, Ep. 84, Luard, 266–8; Mantello, 285–7.

123 Note the parallel with the actions of Baldwin of Forde, discussed in Chapter 5.

124 Cf. Adam Marsh, *Letters*, Ep. 57, 154.

125 *Ibid.*, Ep. 147, 364–7. The letter concerns a request for a favour for Adam's relative Thomas Marsh.

126 *Ibid.*, 364–5.

127 We are, of course, at a disadvantage in that we have only one side of the correspondence, and rely on Grosseteste and Marsh to disclose the responses.

128 One might make particular note of the Lexington family in this regard: John and Robert's brother Henry would succeed Grosseteste as bishop of Lincoln, 1253–58; another brother, Stephen, became abbot of Clairvaux (1243–55).

129 Grosseteste, Ep. 29, Luard, 114–15; Mantello, 140–2. For Siward's career in full, see David Crouch, 'The last adventure of Richard Siward', *Morgannwg: Transactions of the Glamorgan Local History Society* 35 (1991), 7–30.

130 See *CM*, 3:363–9.

131 Crouch, 'The last adventure', 21.
132 'cum maxime sit magnificum et regiae magnanimitati congruum et Evangelicae perfectioni consonum etiam inimicis benefacere'. Grosseteste, Ep. 29, Luard, 115; Mantello, 142.
133 Grosseteste, Ep. 48, Luard, 141–3; Mantello, 169–72.
134 Cf. *CM*, 3:479.
135 'misericors justitia est et imitatio Christi qui omnes punit citra meritum'. Luard, 141; Mantello, 170.
136 'Punire autem nocentes ad meriti correspondentiam et aequalitatem severa justitia est, vel potius forte justitia non est, cum careat admixtione misericordiae, nec aliud est quam promereri judicium sine misericordia, cum scriptum sit: *Judicium sine misericordia erit ei qui non fecerit misericordiam.*' Luard, 141; Mantello, 170.
137 For example, i.25: taking pleasure in cruelty is a vice which transforms a human into a wild beast.
138 'Do not let savagery vent its rage against this burgess; do not let your conduct be stern and inflexible. Instead let your goodness and mercy triumph over judgment [cf. James ii.13], that you may be a model of clemency and gentleness and not a master of cruelty (*In praedictum itaque burgensem non saeviat atrocitas; non rigida sit severitas; sed superexaltet judicium vestrae misericordiae pietas; ut sitis exemplum clementiae et mansuetudinis et non magister crudelitatis*)'. Grosseteste, Ep. 48, Luard 143; Mantello, 172 (the closing lines of the letter).
139 'Videntes igitur vos, si vera sunt quae audivimus, quasi titubantes ad hujusmodi lapsum, praesantis paginate commonitione volumus labentem a lapsu eripere.' Luard, 143; Mantello, 171.
140 J. R. Maddicott, *Simon de Montfort* (Cambridge, 1994), 77–105, esp. 90.
141 'ab his qui presunt in iudicio per censuram districtionis plectantur discoli, in misericordia per affectum mansuetudinis subleventur devoti.' Adam Marsh, *Letters*, Ep. 138, 334–6.
142 *Ibid.*, Ep. 139, 338–9. 'tanto misericordia indulgentiori ... et directiori iustitia'.
143 'quique si dimiserimus spondet nobis dimitti'. *Ibid.*, Ep. 77, 198–201, here at 198; cf. Ep. 236, 554–5, reminding his Franciscan correspondent of the precept 'be merciful just as your Father is merciful'.
144 'Ubi necesse est ad exemplum summi iudicis, sic censura seviat ut non excludat clementiam; sic clementia leniat ut non emolliat censuram.' *Ibid.*, Ep. 187, 456–7.
145 *Ibid.*, Ep. 199, 488–9.
146 'prout expedire censueritis'. *Ibid.*, Ep. 187, 456–7.
147 'Agendum in his puto cum devota sedule deliberationis oratione, ne vel facilitas venie prebeat incentivum delinquendi, vel hominis severitas abigat quem adigit divina propitiatio.' *Ibid.*, Ep. 209, 510–11.
148 *Ibid.*, Ep. 74, 174–82.
149 'benedictum Salvatorem potissime figurantis'. *Ibid.*, Ep. 74, 182.

150 'ad suggestum crudelitatis mandata prius protulerat in populi perditionem'. *Ibid.*, Ep. 74, 182.
151 See Lois L. Huneycutt, 'Intercession and the high-medieval queen: the Esther topos', in Jennifer Carpenter and Sally-Beth MacLean (eds), *Power of the Weak: Studies on Medieval Women* (Urbana, IL, 1995), 126–46. Rabanus Maurus's commentary focuses on the figure of Esther, who is interpreted as prefiguring the Church, pleading with God for mercy and grace for sinners: *Expositio in librum Esther*, c.11, PL.109.660D–662D.

7

Histories of justice: the crown, persuasion and lordship

Incident at Bury St Edmunds

In the final years of the twelfth century, in the final days of the year, groups of men were accustomed to gather together in a graveyard in Bury St Edmunds for a kind of sport.[1] Some were servants who worked for the abbey of Bury St Edmunds, others men from the town. It was a tradition to assemble in the cemetery on the days following Christmas for 'colluctationes et concertationes' (wrestling matches) between the two groups – men of the town and men of the abbey. People came to watch the show, considering it a *spectaculum* worth seeing, one which began with an exchange of words and insults before culminating in fighting.

One year, however – 1197 – these matches were reported to the Abbot of Bury St Edmunds, Samson. Disturbed by the matter, Samson ordered the names of the suspected participants to be written down and their activities investigated. Once it was established that fighting had taken place in the graveyard, it was clear what had to be done. Shedding blood on holy ground was an act of sacrilege, and as such, a matter *lata sententia* – an offence for which the punishment of excommunication should follow automatically, for which there was no excuse or judicial wiggle-room.[2] Samson decided he wanted the punishment administered as publicly as possible, in order to shame the offenders, and to put a permanent end to the local Christmas tradition of brawling in graveyards. He announced that the public excommunication would be done by name, and that he would begin with his own household and servants before coming on to the townsmen who had participated in the offence. Preparations were made, as *The Chronicle of Bury St Edmunds* records: candles were lit for the ceremony; the monks and abbot robed themselves in white stoles. Before the formal pronunciation of the sentence began, and doubtless borrowing from familiar scripts of public penance,³ the offenders stripped and prostrated themselves before the doors of the abbey church, begging that the sentence not be passed. All in all, more than a hundred nearly naked men were crying out for pardon, while monks looked on. The sight must have been a dramatic one in the depths of winter in Suffolk.

What is really of interest, however, is not the show, but the hidden judicial calculations behind it. Samson's biographer, Jocelin of Brakelond, explains what happened next, after this naked demonstration of repentance. Samson, he relates, decided to absolve the penitents – moved to pity by this show of sorrow. Moreover, Samson knew well enough that mercy was exalted over judgment and that gospel principles demanded the Church receive those who were truly repentant. However, Samson did not announce this immediately, but instead made a decision to conceal (*dissimulare*) his pity, because 'he desired to be compelled by his counsellors to absolve the penitents' (*a consiliariis suis voluit cogi, ut penitentes absolverentur*). Those counsellors – a term which encompasses both monks and clerks in this context – did exactly that, arguing that the abbot should adopt a merciful course. Samson did as they advised (and as he himself had intended): the men were not excommunicated, but given penance; meanwhile a prohibition on such gatherings in the cemetery was publicly pronounced. Peace between the abbot and his subjects (both in town and cloister) was restored.

How should we read Samson's actions? Was the abbot attempting to maximise the deterrent effect of ecclesiastical sanctions, calculating that having the offenders live for a while with the real possibility of excommunication would prove a salutary memory for anyone hanging around the cemeteries of Bury St Edmunds in the future? The hundred or so men (and spectators) would go away both relieved and grateful to the Church for showing mercy. Or was this done as a matter of internal good order, for the sake of Samson's own authority? An abbot was obliged to take counsel, and appearing to be swayed by the pleas of his subjects made him appear a fairer and better judge, without actually requiring him to give any ground or depart from his own opinion (it cost him nothing). Samson may well have had all of these considerations in mind – they are not mutually exclusive.

It is that last point on which this chapter focuses: how rulers responded to counsel, how they were seen to listen to or ignore the advice of others (typically their inferiors) about how to do justice. At Bury St Edmunds in 1197, Samson must have looked as if he was persuaded by his counsellors, when in fact he had already arrived at his decision. What would Samson have done if he had been of a different opinion to his monks – if either party had believed that the sentence had to be carried out, regardless of cries for mercy? Both his authority and his judgment would have been under threat.

The examples discussed here examine contemporary concerns about following the wrong kinds of judicial counsel. These were ramifications which went beyond the individual judge's probity and virtue, and into concerns about how judicial persuasion and the inappropriate application of pardon or punishment could damage the political community. In this chapter, the earthly stakes are high.

Mercy: politic, political and rhetorical choices

As seen in the previous chapter, in the letters of Gilbert Foliot and Adam Marsh, mercy was a thing to be asked for, to be considered by the judge, but not always a thing to be given. Argument and persuasion could be used to advance justice and to assist in plotting a just course. Indeed, it was precisely because the truly 'just' course of action was often uncertain, and dependent on the weighing of particular set of circumstances, that the problem was so great. But because justice was a specific, not general, remedy, advice should be sought. But seeking or offering advice – opening up judicial choice to counsel – meant that *iustitia* as a practical objective became a topic for *rhetorical* argument.

This is evident in practice: persuasion and counsel were accepted as playing a central role in the determination and realisation of justice, and argument was as significant in determining judicial behaviour as procedural rules established by law. Moralists, theologians, interested parties and petitioners attempted to sway the judge, each offering a different opinion on what 'just' punishment might look like. But this went beyond a matter of different writers expressing different opinions: it was given particular force by the connection between legal and rhetorical traditions. What made the 'choice' between mercy and justice considerably more complex was the fact that twelfth-century writers had a classical rhetorical tradition at their fingertips. This tradition furnished them with the rhetorical and conceptual tools both to defend and to pick apart specific judicial decisions. In order to understand how justice should be applied in practice, therefore, twelfth-century authors recognised that it was essential to grasp the relationship between the virtue of justice as an ideal objective and the role of rhetoric in attaining it. In the second instance, however, this relationship presented problems all of its own.

The complexities and political dilemmas which arose from this close connection become abundantly clear from the narratives of justice that appear in contemporary histories and chronicles. Lords who are invited to make a decision between mercy and justice all too often are persuaded by sweet words and plump for the wrong option. Counsel can both support a judge in coming to the right decision and lead a king into disastrous judicial missteps.

The ambivalent relationship, and sometimes uneasy accommodation, between medieval thought and classical rhetoric has been extensively discussed in modern historiography. With some reservations, Christian thought licensed the use of classical techniques in order to endow their works with persuasive and didactic power and literary ornament.[4] For the theologians and preachers of the high middle ages, classical rhetorical techniques (and the renewed engagement with classical texts which characterised the twelfth-century renaissance) could be readily and usefully adapted when serving the laity.[5] As Thomas of Chobham explained, although one could not require every preacher to display *eloquentia*, skill in the manipulation of rhetoric would enable them to impress their case more powerfully on their audience.[6] The main mode of transmission of rhetorical ideas was through the study of Cicero: the two key texts were *De inventione* and the pseudo-Ciceronian *Rhetorica ad Herennium*, both of which were studied in the schools, while other Ciceronian works were also examined by students at earlier levels of their education. The study of rhetoric was, of course, itself part of the *trivium* of the schools, alongside the arts of *grammatica* and *dialectica*.[7] No other classical texts were quite as influential as *De inventione* and the *Ad Herennium*: while Cicero's *De oratore* and Quintilian's *Institutio oratoria* were known during this period, they were rarely employed as teaching texts, and, as such, there is no extant commentary tradition upon them which might reveal how they were read and utilised.[8] By contrast, at least fifteen commentaries on the *De inventione* and *Ad Herennium* were composed in the twelfth century.[9]

Cicero's *De inventione* and *Ad Herennium*, and the medieval commentaries upon them, explained to readers that rhetorical argumentation could be divided into three genres: epideictic (or demonstrative), judicial (or forensic) and political (or deliberative). Epideictic was that rhetoric which spoke in praise of virtue or condemnation of vice; judicial the type which was found in the law courts, governing the way in which accusations and defence were presented; political rhetoric was an argument over the righteousness and advantageousness of a certain course of action.[10] In twelfth- and thirteenth-century arguments over the relationship between justice and mercy, it is the category of *political* rhetoric which emerged as central to the discussion. The issue of whether questions of justice and mercy belong to the category of judicial rather than political rhetoric was an argument which engaged medieval commentators. Revealing in this regard is a late eleventh-century gloss on the *Rhetorica ad Herennium*, today extant only in English manuscript copies, including a twelfth-century copy from the Augustinian abbey at Leicester. This gloss, known as *In primis* (and possibly attributable to the Parisian master William of Champeaux[11]), notes a disagreement between two medieval commentators as to whether each type of rhetoric (epideictic, judicial, political) was confined to a particular place. For example, was judicial rhetoric only ever to be used in the courtroom, epideictic rhetoric only on formal occasions such as ceremonies or funerals? *In primis* notes that, while this was the answer of Manegold of Lautenbach – that each type of rhetoric always held its proper place – this was not the answer of Anselm of Laon, who argued that any of the three types of rhetoric might be used anywhere (*indiscrete ubique aguntur*).[12] This latter argument, attributed to Anselm, demonstrated agreement with the arguments of Boethius concerning the types of rhetoric. Boethius had stated that the type (epideictic, judicial or political) was determined according to the purpose at which the orator aimed. Thus, rhetoric which aimed at justice was judicial, that which set forth an advantageous course of action was political and that which discussed virtue was epideictic.[13] Boethius's principle that subject matter, rather than venue, determined the type of rhetoric was endorsed by Petrus Helias (c.1100–66) in his important commentary on *De inventione*.[14]

Not all medieval authors, however, agreed with the idea that the virtue of *iustitia* should be the subject of rhetorical argument at all. The *Formula vitae honestae* of the sixth-century bishop Martin of Braga, a text often attributed to Seneca during this period, argued that the principles of persuasion so often used to inform rhetorical argument, had no place when discussing *iustitia*, for in justice, 'there is no room for us to reckon what is expedient (*in hac non est quod aestimemus quid expediat*)'.[15] In this question, the explicitly political, pragmatic reasoning which is the basis for rhetorical persuasion should have no bearing on virtue: justice represents the fixed ideas of *divina lex* and *vinculum societatis humanae*. This position, however, was challenged in a number of twelfth- and thirteenth-century texts. Thomas of Chobham explicitly recommended the use of rhetorical techniques in exhorting men to virtue and in condemning vice. In sermons, he argued, the preacher seeks not to prove, but to persuade – and so, as a result, the preacher must resort to rhetorical techniques.[16] If the priest wishes to see the growth of justice in the community, he must be able to persuade the sinful to a course of action which runs contrary to their usual habits.[17]

The principle that Christian rhetoric and virtue were compatible was espoused by the Benedictine theologian Rupert of Deutz in his *De operibus spiritus sancti* (before 1117), which included a section on the operation of rhetoric.[18] For Rupert, the best demonstration of the virtuous power of rhetoric was to be found in the Bible. Rupert explains an argument over the forgiveness of a sinner between Christ and his disciples according to rhetorical principles. This is the scene described in Luke vii.39–50, in which the disciple Simon objects to Christ's feet being washed and anointed by a sinful woman. Christ replies that the woman's act, her tears and her care for his body are demonstrations of her repentance. He then explains that because of the 'greatness' of the woman's love, her many sins have been forgiven – and, in turn, iterates the principle that whoever demonstrates only a little love will receive only little forgiveness for their sins (Luke vii.47). For Rupert of Deutz, this passage provides one example of *controversia* – a point in debate between Simon and Christ. It demonstrates the opposition of Christ's *mansuetudo* or *temperantia* on the one hand and, on the other, the *invidia* of those who resented the repentant woman's position and who wished to deny her forgiveness. The expression 'whoever loves greatly, will be greatly forgiven; whoever loves little, will have little of their sins forgiven' is, for Rupert, a powerful piece of persuasive rhetoric as much as it is a judicial statement.[19] The significance of Rupert's rhetorical exegesis lies here in the implication that even in decisions concerning the forgiveness of sins, argument was to be expected. Even Christ, in other words, was not above resorting to rhetorical techniques to defend the righteousness of his actions as a judge of the good and the wicked.

Twelfth- and thirteenth-century authors recognised the rhetoric which concerned the preservation of justice as a type of political rhetoric. *De inventione* had determined the two ends of political rhetoric as *honestum* and *utile* (the honourable and the expedient).[20] Arguments over judicial decision-making and sentencing are concerned with these two qualities above all else. Will the punishment be 'good' for the criminal and for the soul of the judge? Will it be expedient, both in achieving the correction of the wicked and in ensuring peace for the community? Even the supposedly 'severe' Roman law could provide contradictory messages on the purpose of punishment. On the one hand, Roman law established the purpose of punishment as securing the tranquillity of the state, checking crime through fear of retribution: *Digest* 1.1.1 gives the purpose of the law as the restraint of wrongdoers (*bonus metu poenarium efficere*).[21] On the other hand, jurists such as Paulus suggested that reform of the criminal should also be an object of punishment, and thus bestowed on the judge the ability to temper the laws with gentleness (*benignitas*).²²

Because justice was not simply a personal virtue but also a public duty for rulers, it was, in the eyes of twelfth-century authors, an appropriate subject for deliberative oratory. The idea that rhetoric can serve justice is explicitly endorsed by an early twelfth-century legal text, the *Leges Henrici Primi*, which begins with a classification of the three kinds of rhetorical argument (epideictic, demonstrative and deliberative) and cautions that, in court, rhetoric must be used to serve truth and justice, not private advantage.²³ The early sections of the *Leges* draw heavily upon book 2 of Isidore's *Etymologies*, the parts of that text which discuss the role of the orator and how he is to argue causes, how to plead and how to proceed in the arrangement of arguments.²⁴ When Isidore explains that an *oratio* has four parts, exordium, narrative, argumentation and conclusion, this is knowledge which the author of the *Leges* thinks will prove useful in a twelfth-century court; as the *Etymologies* observes that there are five kinds of cases or causes, so too does the *Leges*.²⁵ This is not to suggest that early twelfth-century English pleaders saw themselves as Roman orators in miniature, as little senators in the manorial courts; but it does suggest a recognition that Roman rhetorical ideas could assist in explaining how the law functioned and what the courts were *for*.

When the judge (whether royal or ecclesiastical) is in a position of public authority, any exercise of judicial virtue (be that *misericordia* or *iustitia*) has clear implications for public welfare, for 'the rigour of the chastiser is peace for the people' (*rigor punientis pax est popularis*).²⁶ This relationship had been made explicit in the definition of justice provided by Cicero, in which the act of *suum cuique tribuens* was established for the purpose of serving the good, the 'utility' (*utilitas*) of the community.²⁷ Roman law made the same point about the centrality of the public good to the offices of law-maker and judge.²⁸ But it was not necessary to possess an education in civil law to be able to draw this connection between justice and public good: it was equally evident from classical literature, and can be found repeated in twelfth-century works of moral theology and *florilegia*.²⁹ Alan of Lille, for example, emphasises that *severitas* in particular, among all other judicial strategies, preserves the *communis utilitas*, by refusing to relinquish the due penalties of law.³⁰

Of course, discussing the idea of medieval 'public good' is a fraught endeavour. The idea of action that was justified *ratione utilitatis publicae* is, unfortunately, inextricably linked with historiographical ideas about the origins of the 'State' (with a capital 's') in the twelfth and thirteenth centuries.[31] Yet twelfth-century writers and commentators did not require an elaborate, forward-looking notion of the 'state' to appreciate the idea that justice should serve the good of the people or the kingdom. This is a patristic commonplace, and an idea so common as to be almost axiomatic. According to Augustine, the very least that individuals should expect from a ruler is that he ensure peace and protect his people from wrongdoers.[32] Moreover, the role of classical rhetorical structures was profoundly important for the way in which the debate about the nature and purpose of justice was conceptualised. Roman rhetoric demonstrated how questions about the judicial action which best served the community could be debated. Yet twelfth- and thirteenth-century authors were applying classical rhetorical terms to problems which existed in practice in order to highlight real political dilemmas for Anglo-Norman and Angevin rulers. They borrowed a Ciceronian intellectual framework to cast new light on a pre-existing debate; they did not dream up that debate by overindulging in classical texts.

A 'rhetorical' approach to justice (and the public good that was to be achieved through justice) could be used both to vindicate and to problematise judicial choices. Admittedly, there were numerous ways in which authors envisioned a hierarchy of mercy and justice, and not all twelfth-century writers chose to appeal to Ciceronian ideas.[33] The most important of all discussions concerning judicial deliberation over punishment, however, was drawn from the tradition of deliberative (i.e. political) rhetoric. Classical rhetorical theory explained how a certain course of action could be defended according to its righteousness (for example, the punitive sentence which served to discourage other offenders). Yet the toolkit of deliberative rhetoric also provided the means by which to challenge such a verdict. Particularly important in this context was the discussion of deliberative rhetoric found in the *Rhetorica ad Herennium*. The idea introduced in the *Ad Herennium* (which differed slightly from the terminology used in *De inventione*) was that deliberative rhetoric aimed at persuading listeners to follow the course which was *utile*, useful. *Utilitas*, however, contained within it two principles: *tutum* (safety) and *honestum* (the honourable or morally worthy course of action).[34] This idea was taken up in twelfth-century discussions of the virtue of justice: for example, the *Moralium dogma philosophorum* explains that *negligentia* is a vice opposed to justice precisely because it represents a failure to defend this objective of safety.[35] John of Salisbury observes that it is possible for the prince to make a dispensation from the law, so long as the principles of both *morality* and *utility* were preserved.[36] Usually the two principles of safety and worthy action will be united in a single judicial decision, but, the *Ad Herennium* allows, on occasion the two will not be in agreement. If this is the case, when deliberating one must choose between two courses, one of which secures what is honourable or worthy, the other ensures security. This rhetorical choice between the 'morally worthy' and the 'safe' course of action was repeated in *De inventione*.[37] Access to that rhetorical terminology provided twelfth-century authors with a further way of conceptualising the conflict between justice and mercy, depicting it as a battle of rhetorical persuasion. In turn, however, this could serve to make the conflict between the two principles more intractable.

This polarisation of *tutum* and *honestum* was, occasionally and revealingly, used by twelfth- and thirteenth-century authors to describe the dichotomy between *misericordia* and *iustitia*. It is found, for example, in the *Verbum abbreviatum* of Peter the Chanter, when discussing the setting of punishments.[38] Peter argues that mercy or leniency is in fact the 'safer' option: *tutius est tamen in remissione peccati quam in rigore*. Considering how the term *tutius* is being used here, it seems that safety must in this case refer not to the political community but to the safety of the individual. The Chanter may either be suggesting that it is 'safer' to be merciful, for the penitent faced with too heavy a sentence may refuse to make satisfaction altogether; or he may otherwise be thinking of 'safety' for the judge, who will be treated more severely by the divine judge for being excessively punitive than he will for being excessively merciful. In this sense, Peter argues, it is always safer for the good man, conscious of his ultimate fate, to err on the side of leniency. This statement is followed by a précis of the reasons why mercy is to be preferred to stricter punishments. Mercy lies in adherence to the mean course (between excessive severity and excessive laxity), an action praised by classical writers such as Horace, Ovid and Terence; mercy is safer for the soul and merciful action also secures worldly glory, for 'glorious is the king who punishes less than is deserved'.[39]

The same oratorical terminology of *tutum* versus *honestum* is employed by Robert of Flamborough in his *Liber poenitentialis*. That Robert was a pupil of Peter the Chanter may be significant in this regard.[40] The *Liber poenitentialis* uses the language of *tutus* and *honestus* most explicitly when discussing how and when penitential punishment can be modified. Robert uses the principle of following a 'safer' course of action as a justification for lessening heavy penances, despite the fact that such punishments are advocated in ancient canons:

> These punishments are so excessively oppressive and severe that there is scarcely anyone who is willing to undertake them or presumes to impose

them. Besides which, although you do not find this expressed clearly in a single one of the penitential books (though you find many punishments for sins), it is safer and more worthy that, having the ancient authorities before our eyes, and in this way and with consideration, we lighten them and perhaps roughen them.[41]

In this case, Robert notes, the safer course also agrees with the more worthy action, i.e. it is both *tutior* and *honestior* to consider the mitigation of penance. In context, it can be inferred that the idea of *tutius* carries the connotation that penitents may refuse an excessively harsh punishment. In this sense it is safer for the soul of the sinner that the confessor apply a softer form of correction, as the lighter form of penitential discipline is more likely to be followed.

The relationship between *tutum* and *honestum* is a theme which runs throughout the *Liber poenitentialis*, and Robert pays particular attention to the course of action which is *tutius* (although he does not always advocate such a course).[42] In the works of other authors it is possible to glimpse appeals to these classical rhetorical ideals, and they are consistently invoked in explicitly judicial contexts. John of Salisbury's *Policraticus*, for example, remarks that mercy is the 'safer' (*tutius*) course in sentencing.[43] Given Peter the Chanter seems to have raised the idea in his teaching, the choice between 'worthy' and 'safe' judicial decisions would have been in the minds of the English students who studied under him, and indeed, those who had access to his great *Verbum abbreviatum*. This is in addition to those who could consider the question of *tutum–honestus* as a judicial principle through their direct reading of the classics.

What is most striking of all, however, is that only thirty years after Peter the Chanter had influentially discussed *tutum* and *honestum* as principles of penitential punishment, at least one English author was considering how the same considerations might apply in common law. *Bracton* discusses the principles for 'safe' action when advising a judge on whether he may depart from the law in passing sentence.

> Yet although it is safer (*tutius*) to render a final account from mercy rather than judgment, it is safest (*tutissimum*) that [a judge's] eyes precede his steps, that judgment not become uncertain through lack of prudence nor mercy debased by indiscriminate application, for mercy is indeed unjust when it is extended to the incorrigible.[44]

The contrast of *tutum* with *honestum* is, of course, only implicit, but given the judicial scenario which the author of *Bracton* is envisioning, the possibility of a classical rhetorical influence should at least be considered.

In *Bracton*, *misericordia* is not necessarily the 'safest' option for the judge, because such a decision may cause the judge to depart from law and reason. While the term *tutum* is used in Roman law, and *Bracton*'s author may have drawn his terminology exclusively from this source, his use of the term to describe a choice in judicial sentencing in fact carries a meaning far closer to the contexts of deliberative rhetoric, namely by explaining the 'safe' course of judgment with reference to both its moral worth and political utility. By contrast, the invocation of the term *tutum* in Roman law usually implies a more general sense of legal protection.[45]

The frequent recourse to the principle of *tutum* in explaining more contentious judicial decisions suggests that the language and terminology of deliberative rhetoric directly impinged upon judicial decision and perceptions of the act of judgment. It opened practical justice up to alternatives and to question. The crucial point here is that, in the twelfth century, it was acknowledged in theory and in practice that in the act of doing justice there was space for *argument*. Procedural guides provided only instruction for avoiding the worst excesses of bad judgment, but when a judicial decision had 'political' implications (as the sentencing of criminals did), the best, most useful, most honourable or safest course of action was not always clear. In other words, it was not always apparent which of these principles – mercy or justice, mitigation of punishment or severity – was most closely aligned with rightful judgment. For those positions to be justified, they had first to be debated.[46]

To appreciate the ambiguity of some judicial decision making, and the role of rhetoric in both problematising and resolving judicial dilemmas, an instructive text to consider is the *Speculum universale* of Raoul Ardens, written in the last decade of the twelfth century.[47] Raoul was trained in Paris, in the circle of Peter the Chanter, and served as a chaplain to Richard I: while not 'English' *per se*, Raoul at least had a significant link to England and to the master who influenced so many English theologians.[48] The *Speculum universale* is a work of ethics, and its tenth book is dedicated to a discussion of justice. In this book, Raoul identifies *clementia* as an accessory (*collateralis*) virtue of *iustitia*, and explains that the role of *clementia* is to temper justice.[49] This prompts Raoul to consider different species of *clementia*, which he identifies as *clementia temperata*, *clementia remissa* and *clementia laxa*.[50] He then goes on to explain and rank these species. The first, *clementia temperata*, which might best be understood as 'controlled clemency', is, in Raoul's opinion, the most praiseworthy – it is *rationabilis*, in the sense that its role within justice is the rational calculation of which particular offenders ought to be spared. The third type, meanwhile, *clementia laxa*, is in fact not a virtue at all, but a vice (*vicium*) – it is thoroughly irrational (*penitus irrationabilis*), for it indifferently spares both those guilty of great offences and those who commit lesser crimes. It is a vice because it excuses both *excusabilia* and *inexcusabilia*. It is Raoul's middle category of *clementia remissa* which is by far the most interesting. This type of clemency is 'less temperate' (*minus temperata*) than 'controlled clemency', Raoul notes, but it is not altogether lacking in control: it is also *minus rationabilis*, but not entirely lacking in reason either. This type of clemency sometimes spares great crimes, finding reason to pardon the offender. The verb Raoul uses here – *invenitur* – is significant: it can bear the neutral translation of 'finding' or 'discovering' the reasons for pardon; on the other hand, the connotation is also that of 'contriving' reasons for pardon. What Raoul seems to recognise in this category is a grey area between the virtuous type of forgiveness and the lax pardon which is most assuredly vice. The borders of this category – the point at which clemency slides from being somewhat lacking in reason to being completely unreasonable and vicious – are, clearly, not easily delineated.

Raoul employs the same structure to explain the virtue of judicial justice.[51] There is, he explained, *iustitia clemens*, merciful justice, which is rational and the most temperate virtue; there is also *iustitia crudelis*, cruel justice, which is clearly a vice and spares no one. Between the vice and the virtue, however, lies a middle category, *iustitia severa* – strict justice – which is less tempered and less rational than merciful justice and which occasionally fails to spare those whom it ought to pardon. It is this middle category of justice which is the most revealing, because it contains some reason and some measure of virtue, but its righteousness is debatable. Moreover, the model presented by Raoul – a sliding scale between perfect justice and damnable excess – would not be possible had he adhered to an 'Aristotelian' model of virtue as a golden mean, with justice lying between excessive laxity and excessive clemency. Instead, justice and clemency are discussed on two separate scales. There is no suggestion that justice is the midpoint between excessive severity and excessive laxity. Instead the *Speculum universale* presents a hierarchy – merciful justice sits at the top, with actions becoming less just and less rational as they descend towards the bottom of the scale, towards cruelty.

Raoul extends his tripartite classification one step further elsewhere in his *Speculum*, when he considers the concepts of *iustum*, *honestum* and *expediens*.[52] Raoul tackles each one of these terms in turn. Beginning with the state of being just, Raoul again explains that there are three levels to this.[53] The first is simply *iustum*: this is the state in which one returns good for good. The second, higher, level is *iustius*: this is a person who (or the act which) returns good for good, but who, in addition, refuses to return evil for evil. The final level or state of justice is *iusti summum*: this is an individual who returns good for evil – an act of perfect justice. The implication is obvious here: some humans are more just than others. Raoul follows this with a discussion of the different degrees of *honestum*, or morally worthy behaviour.[54] The discussion begins by explaining that *honestum* is 'a good which is never mixed with shameful behaviour (*bonum nichil turpitudinis admixtum*)', a definition which broadly corresponds to the notions of *honestum* in classical texts. *Honestum* (and here Raoul is thinking about the idea in a spiritual context) may be divided into three categories, on a sliding scale: *magnum*, the least of the three, which is displayed by the infirm; *maius*, which is displayed by the 'proficient', and finally *maximum*, which only the accomplished (*profectum*) have mastered. The *Speculum* then goes on to define the quality of expediency (*expediens*), a concept which Raoul discusses in much less detail than *honestum*, but which follows a near-identical structure.[55] *Expediens*, as it is used here, has broadly similar connotations to the Ciceronian idea of *utilitas*. Raoul, however, goes on to explain that expediency is the quality which, when considered in a spiritual sense, pertains to the shortest (*compendiose*) path to salvation. The lowest level is that which is simply expedient (*expediens*), the second, higher level, that which is more expedient (*expedientius*) and the third and highest level (*expendientius summum*), that which is most expedient to salvation.

That all three of these concepts – justness, moral worth, and expediency – can be measured on a sliding scale is reflected in the diagrams which with Raoul illustrates his *Speculum*. With regard to the latter two categories – *honestum* and *expediens* – Raoul's arguments serve to provide a further nuance to the language of medieval deliberative rhetoric, over and above what it derived from the classical tradition. In Raoul's view, a course of action cannot merely be described as expedient without clarifying the degree of that expediency. Raoul raises the possibility that, in an ethical context, a choice may need to be made between two courses which, according to the measure of their *utilitas*, are both morally admissible, yet one will be more expedient, more profitable or advantageous, than the other. Finally, Raoul explains that these three concepts – the just, the honourable and the expedient – are ultimately in agreement (*congruenciam*).[56] That is, a just act is also honourable and expedient. This approach echoes the presupposition of the third book of Cicero's *De officiis* – that which is honourable is also that which is *utile*.

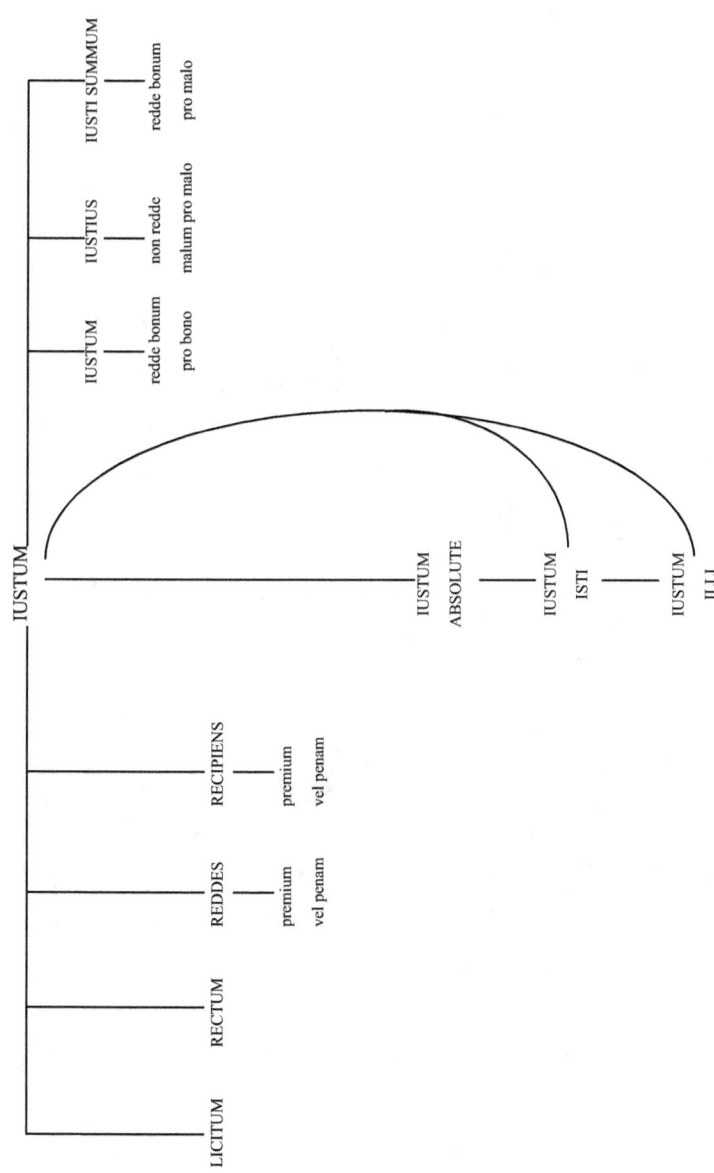

Figure 1 Diagram explaining the many parts and degrees of 'iustum'.

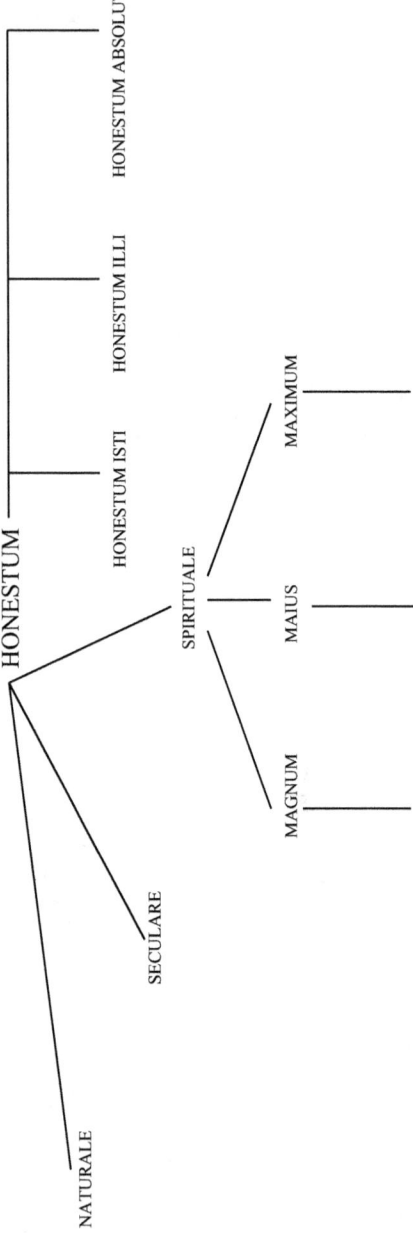

Figure 2 Diagram depicting the different parts and degrees of 'honestum'.

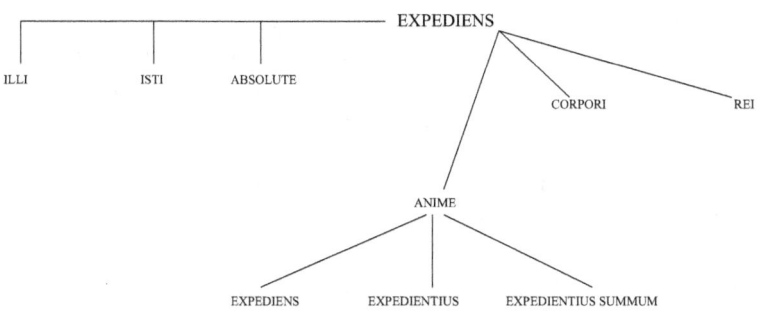

Figure 3 Diagram depicting the different types and levels of the term 'expediens'.

Raoul Ardens – with his categories of 'middlingly' or 'partially' just acts – demonstrates that twelfth- and thirteenth-century theologians considered the 'rationality' of some types of justice (and, indeed, some acts of mercy) to be debatable. It is this consideration which underlies the treatment of justice in English histories and chronicles of the twelfth and thirteenth centuries, namely the assumption that this was a subject of *debate*, not of clear-cut categories, and a debate which involved all sorts of consideration of circumstances. Kings, lords and judges argued over what the truly 'just' course of action was, invoking terms and ideas borrowed from the world of classical deliberative rhetoric and applying them directly to the events they had to deal with in court. And yet, making justice subject to rhetorical debate, a question of persuasion, invited further problems. As Raoul Ardens makes clear, it is not always apparent how the distinction between admirable clemency and vicious laxity should be drawn. Much depends on the intention and attitude of the judge. Above all, in the political context set out in twelfth- and thirteenth-century histories and chronicles, a judge could never be entirely sure whether his counsellors were presenting the case for justice or mercy because they were motivated by prudence, virtue and concern for the political community, or because of the machinations of their own *voluntas*. This was, after all, the criticism frequently levelled against the exercise of pardon: that it was a product of partiality and favouritism, not the rational weighing of the merits of judicial arguments. This issue of intention touched on a long-running point of concern for medieval rhetorical theorists – whether rhetorical skill should be utilised to argue against virtue. According to classical definitions, the accomplished and persuasive orator was also to be a morally good individual (Quintilian had described the orator as *vir bonus, dicendi peritus*).[57] This point is neatly demonstrated in commentaries on Sallust's *Bellum Catilinae*. One commentator (possibly to be identified as Alan of Lille) noted that, although Catiline had skill in speech, he could never be described as an orator, because he lacked virtue: he possessed *eloquentia* without *sapientia*.[58] If justice is achieved through persuasion, then injustice may quite as easily be achieved through manipulation. It is precisely such a dilemma that is presented in English histories.

Writing the history of justice

English chroniclers were particularly interested in the place of justice within royal office. Justice is a key theme for many historical narratives, for it is a critical variable (if not *the* critical variable) by which the success of a reign is measured. The English coronation oath, both as it had been set down in Old English in the tenth and eleventh centuries and in a twelfth-century Latin version, bound kings to show both justice and mercy (*in omnibus iudiciis equitatem et misericordiam praecipiam*).[59]

Narrative histories report on both issues of law and questions of justice, suggesting that no sharp distinction should be drawn between legal and historical endeavours, but that, in terms of content and purpose, they could serve complementary purposes. With any examination of these histories, however, the relationship between historical writing and legal record must be considered. How can one ascertain the *historicity* of legal judgments portrayed in narrative sources? When chroniclers move away from simply recording the text of assizes and instead recount acts of judgment or incidents of injustice, how can the historian be sure of the veracity of their testimony?

It is worth considering some recent case studies which have examined how medieval chroniclers recorded legal 'events'. Michael Clanchy studied Matthew Paris's *Chronica maiora* as it described a robbery and trial at Alton, Hampshire in 1244, which is also documented in the eyre roll and in select crown pleas.[60] He demonstrated that the legal record largely corroborates Matthew Paris's representation of the incident, although conceding that the *Chronica* 'probably simplified and over-dramatised' the events.[61] Clanchy argues, on the basis of this extended comparison and careful scrutiny, that Matthew Paris ought to be considered a more reliable and accurate source than he is sometimes thought to be. In fact, not only does Matthew Paris provide a largely accurate report of the legal process, but the *Chronica maiora* also serves to set that legal process in its political context. In this incident, for instance, the *Chronica* describes how Henry III personally intervened in the case – a notorious robbery – a detail which is lost if one relies solely on the legal records. Clanchy concluded that Matthew's reporting was so accurate and detailed on the legal mechanics of the case that it is possible he had access to copies of the crown rolls themselves.

Naturally, care must still be taken over historical accounts of judgment. There are limitations to the generalisations which can be drawn: Matthew Paris's accounts of other historical events may well be less reliable. However, a number of English chroniclers of the twelfth and early thirteenth centuries certainly did have good access to legal and royal records, in addition to experience as witnesses of judicial judgments. These historians and chroniclers should, by and large, be assumed to be well-informed men who recounted incidents of justice from informed and often privileged positions. Roger of Howden, for example, had served Henry II as a clerk and later as a justice of the forest, and thus his interest in royal legislative activity is far from surprising.[62] Moreover, Roger's *Chronica*, a history of England from the time of Bede to the year 1201, is found in its earliest manuscript copy (possibly with the author's own annotations) bound with a number of legal texts, including the laws of William I, *Glanvill* and the assizes of Henry II, suggesting that contemporaries envisioned a close connection between historical writing and legal records.[63]

There are also 'histories', however, which do not record *actual* political debates or historical events. The focus in those texts is the *moral* and *rhetorical* arguments surrounding questions of judgment. Some of these 'histories' may contain *argumenta*, stories which were considered to be historically plausible, rather than *historiae*, relating events whose veracity was beyond doubt.[64] By explaining how a prudent king could be persuaded into an unjust judgment, authors were performing the same function as *speculum principis* literature. Yet the value of their portrayals in historical sources was that they contained an element of truth – they are not pure invention, and they cannot be dismissed as entirely unrealistic accounts, belonging to the category of *fabulae*. Indeed, if the portrayal of legal arguments in chronicles was intended to serve a morally instructive purpose, to make a didactic point about judicial duties, then the effectiveness of their inclusion depended on an author presenting a plausible verisimilitude of the reality of legal argument and courtroom behaviour. Person, setting and narrative detail might be adjusted to sharpen the instructive value of the tale – but these texts were intimately connected to the 'real world'. They revealed the problems of doing justice to their readers, and the moral dangers which assailed the judge. In particular they highlight the moral and political problems attendant on the granting of judicial (royal) pardon, and the reconciliation of conflicting arguments in the administration of justice.

Orderic Vitalis and the judicial failings of Norman kings

The *Historia ecclesiastica* of the Anglo-Norman monk Orderic Vitalis (1075–c.1142) is a monumental work in thirteen books which spans the period from the creation of the earth to the year 1141. Within this frame, Orderic presents a multitude of *exempla* of justice and injustice, and an extensive commentary on the proper place of *misericordia* in the earthly world. Indeed, Orderic never doubts the importance of *misericordia* and repentance, for his own Benedictine abbey at Saint-Evroult was founded by a penitent thief, and the first monks comprised the repentant outlaws of the forest whom the saint had drawn away from a life of criminality.[65] But perhaps the most persistent – certainly the most striking – theme in the *Historia ecclesiastica* concerns the nature of intercession and the role of persuasion in pardoning. Orderic's exploration of the idea in the case of his explicitly historical narrative reveals how twelfth-century authors understood just how important it was to unpick and analyse not just mercy and justice but judgment and counsel. Orderic raises doubts in particular about the motives of those who seek pardon on behalf of another, and implies that pardon often poses a danger to peace in the realm.

The problem begins with William I, who, on his deathbed in 1087, makes a speech recalling the judgments he had given as a duke and king. The dying ruler recounts how he has done justice in ruling England and thus preserved peace in the land he conquered:

> I have condemned many to captivity deservedly for their own disloyalty, and many others for fear of future treachery. Right custom requires, and the divine law given through Moses commands earthly rulers to restrain evil doers so that they cannot injure the innocent. ... But now that I am at the point of death, as I myself hope to be saved and by the mercy of God pardoned for my sins, I command all prisons to be opened immediately, and all prisoners released, except my brother the bishop of Bayeux. I set them free for love of God, so that God may have mercy on me. But before they leave prison they shall first enter into an obligation by taking an oath to the officials of the realm to preserve the peace in England and Normandy.[66]

What is so revealing about Orderic's account is the emphasis he gives to the latent tension between William's Christian duty of forgiveness and his obligations as a king. William needs divine mercy, given the blood he spilt to achieve and secure the crown. Yet the only way to achieve that divine mercy is by showing it to others, a politically dangerous action. As a lawgiver, William had been bound to ensure peace by threatening and punishing the men who threaten the poor, the weak and the Church; as a sinful man he must, according to the gospel formula, show kindness towards those disturbers of the peace. Mindful, perhaps, of the undertaking in his coronation oath to observe both justice and mercy, here William is presented as attempting to plot a seemingly moderate course: he will free all captives but one from their prisons, but they must first undertake to observe the royal peace. Yet William's mercy has its limits: he is not prepared to pardon his brother, Odo, Bishop of Bayeux.

Orderic follows the account of the king's speech with an equally arresting comment: this pronouncement did not satisfy the counsellors surrounding the dying king. Robert, Count of Mortain, begs William to release Odo of Bayeux as well. But William justifies his decision, and explaining that he speaks 'not through hatred as an enemy, but as the father of my country, providing for the welfare of my Christian subjects' (*non ex odio ut hostis profero sed ut pater patriae plebi christianae provideo*),[67] he rebukes those who would seek pardon for Odo:

> I am amazed that you do not appreciate what kind of a man this is for whom you plead. Are you not interceding for a man who has long been an enemy of the Church and a cunning instigator of treacherous rebellion? Have I not kept under restraint for four years this bishop who, when he should have been a most just viceroy in England, became the worst oppressor the people and destroyer of monasteries? You are ill-advised to free this traitor and you are asking for serious trouble for yourselves.[68]

The insistence of the magnates, however, ultimately wears down the king, and Odo is granted his freedom. But William's prediction that the barons of England only store up trouble for themselves in seeking Odo's release is eventually proven true and Orderic deliberately draws attention to the lesson. In the following book of Orderic's history, the Conqueror is dead and William II now rules England, but it is once again Odo of Bayeux who threatens the peace of the country. Orderic devises a very similar scene in which William II is now granted the opportunity to exercise strict royal 'justice' against the malevolent Odo, at the siege of Rochester in 1088. Once again, the barons of England counsel the king to pardon Odo's offences and let him go free. Once again, a Norman king is initially set against leniency, as William, like his father, declares:

> He who spares traitors and robbers, oppressors and accused men destroys the peace and security of the innocent and sows the seeds of endless massacres and troubles for good, defenceless people.[69]

What ensues in this second debate is a more detailed argument over biblical precedents and typologies of justice. In defence of his decision to condemn Odo, William cites the example of David hanging Baanah and Rehab for the crime of murder (2 Kings iv.9–12), arguing that this is the kingly precedent he should follow. His opponents respond by bringing forth the example of King David sparing Shimei, the man who had cursed him (2 Kings xix.15–23). Ultimately, William Rufus is persuaded to release Odo, who, as Orderic recounts, goes on to plot against the realm and cause much destruction. While this debate over punishment and pardon could stand alone in Orderic's history, the fact that it is paralleled in a third debate, this time involving William II's successor, Henry I, strongly implies that Orderic intended to demonstrate to his readers that pardon was a recurring problem for Anglo-Norman rulers.[70]

The third and final episode in this series concerns Henry I at the siege of Bridgnorth in 1102. This time the traitor is not Odo of Bayeux (by then dead), but Robert of Bellême, a man whom Orderic considered an even more malevolent influence on Normandy than the Bishop of Bayeux.[71] The fundamental structure of the scene, however, remains the same. Once again, Orderic makes sure that the special pleading and persuasion of self-interested nobles is presented as endangering the performance of implacable royal justice. On this occasion, Orderic shows the nobles conspiring together, before the siege, to ensure that Robert of Bellême is not punished. Their reasoning is presented as follows:

> If the king defeats a mighty earl by force and carries his enmity to the point of destroying him, as he is now striving to do, he will from that moment trample on us like helpless slavegirls.[72]

Thus, when Henry is victorious at the siege, the noble lords attempt to assuage his anger and encourage him to make peace with Robert of Bellême. What they do not count on, however, and what makes this scene different from Orderic's previous examples of intercession in Norman history, is the presence of a group of knights (*milites*).[73] The knights, having overheard the barons arguing for leniency for Robert, make their own appeal to the king, shouting out:

> Henry, Lord King, don't trust these traitors. They are out to deceive you and undermine the rigour of your royal justice. Why do you listen to men

who urge you to spare a traitor and let a conspiracy against your life go unpunished? See now, we all stand loyally by you and are ready to obey the least command. Storm the fortress, press the traitor relentlessly from all sides and make no peace with him until you have him in your hands, alive or dead.[74]

On hearing these words, Orderic recounts, Henry stands firm in his original course of action and refuses to make peace with Robert. The schemes of his 'seditious lords' are confounded. Orderic's sequence of episodes presents a consistent pattern of royal justice and mercy. It is only with Henry – and with the warning of the knights who are mindful of the duties of royal justice – that the cycle of the wicked escaping their deserved punishments is broken. It is the counsel of his knights that strengthens Henry's resolve to exact appropriate punishment. Orderic's *Historia ecclesiastica* does not argue against all forms of judicial mercy, but clearly demonstrates the dangers of pardon when it is motivated purely by self-interest. It is necessary for the safety of the political community that the wicked receive appropriate punishment. The recurring dilemma in each of the episodes involving the first three Norman rulers of England is presented by Orderic as a problem about the way in which mercy is obtained. Intercession, in Orderic's account, turns on a number of motives, not all of them admirable. The saint who intercedes with God for the redemption of a sinner is to be trusted; the magnates who beg the king to overlook the crimes of an associate, much less so.

Orderic's history here sets out exactly why counsel was such a pressing problem for Anglo-Norman kings. This was the case even before the emergence of truly systematic law in England, during the 1130s, as Orderic was composing his history, and it was a problem which would only intensify with later Angevin legal reforms. However, even in the early part of this period, a ruler was bound (both pragmatically and 'constitutionally') to listen to the advice of the leading men of the realm. As the *Leges Henrici Primi* averred, the king was crowned 'communi consilio et assensu baronum regni Anglie'.[75] Orderic's history addresses a series of scenarios in which the *consilium* of the barons supports a course of action contrary to justice and peace. Ruling between different counsels – or ascertaining what is sage political advice and what is simply an argument from self-interest – was a far more difficult prospect than a royal promise to heed baronial counsel might imply. As the traditions of deliberative rhetoric made clear, the advantageous course of action could easily be divorced from that which was morally righteous. Worse still, an accomplished or deceitful orator could attempt to disguise the truly moral course of political action. It is just this warning that is found in John of Salisbury's *Policraticus*, which, composed several decades after Orderic's *Historia*, discusses some of the same themes in much greater detail. John was deeply concerned with justice and right order in the court and realm. In order, however, to achieve justice, John explains, one must overcome the problem of flattery and dishonest counsel. While 'it is impossible to rule profitably, if the prince does not follow the counsels of the wise',[76] John admonishes the ruler to distinguish between worthy and wicked counsel, for there are those at court who, in order to pursue their own ends, are willing to call good deeds wicked and wicked actions good.[77] The flatterer is really, in essence, a courtier who seeks to further his own ends by obscuring the distinction between just and unjust actions. This self-serving behaviour is demonstrated in the flatterer's refusal to rebuke the failures of the great, for fear of losing favour. Thus, John warns, quoting the words of Solomon, that it is preferable to receive rebuke from a friend than the deceitful kiss and praise of a flatterer.[78] True and wise advice is not always palatable: 'the truth is bitter and brings with it trouble, for it refuses to flatter anyone. But the bitterness of truth is more useful and more welcome to sound sense than the honey dripping from the lips of a harlot.'[79] Flatterers at the Angevin court are often disguised as counsellors; the danger is so powerful because the flatterer suggests an easy solution when really, justice is a most difficult and trying art. This is why John gives guidance as to exactly the sort of counsellors the king ought to select, criteria of wisdom and prudence being foremost in his mind.[80]

Orderic Vitalis and John of Salisbury both sound a note of warning. Twelfth-century commentators on scripture had established that the role of counsellors was to guide in setting justice and mercy in their proper order. This was typified in the scriptural *topoi* of Esther and Daniel, who argued against excessive punishment and through their skill in argument, saved the innocent and prevented judicial cruelty. Their intercession in the process of judgment had prevented the perversion of justice through the arbitrary exercise of judicial will. Yet as is evident from Orderic's three case studies, counsellors might also become an extension of the 'arbitrary will' problem: they did not simply lend support to a just verdict, but could also challenge justice through the power of their appeals to deliberative rhetoric. The false counsellor, through a well-spoken appeal to unworthy ideas of utility or political honour, was able to confuse the debate over mercy and justice, obscuring the judge's perception of which judicial strategy was most appropriate to the case before him.

Histories of justice

The justice of Stephen's reign

Orderic Vitalis had employed the early history of the Norman rulers of England as a means of demonstrating the vulnerability of even powerful rulers to misleading counsel and the deceptions of political rhetoric. The arguments made by Orderic in his history, however, were sharpened and debated in much greater detail by subsequent histories, prompted by events in England between 1135 and 1154 – the period of the 'Anarchy'.[81] The reign of Stephen, and a number of events in his struggle with Matilda for the English crown, provided historians and chroniclers with opportunities to address the questions of the relative merits of just and merciful rulership. Stephen's reign broadened the debate about royal justice and mercy, because the techniques of deliberative rhetoric could be utilised both by the king's partisans and his detractors, either to praise his commitment to morally worthy justice or to attack his neglect of the safety and utility of the people of England.

The most important and impassioned debates in contemporary and near-contemporary histories of the Anarchy concern the righteousness of Stephen's merciful behaviour towards his enemies.[82] On one hand, those historians who were hostile to Stephen employed the techniques of political rhetoric to cast this behaviour as utterly remiss *lenitas*, damaging to the political community. On the other, those histories more favourable to Stephen describe his treatment of his enemies as a demonstration of virtuous *pietas*, through which the king attempted to bring peace to the realm. The case against Stephen is best summarised by the chronicler John of Worcester, passing a contemporaneous verdict on Stephen's reign in 1141:[83]

> Stephen is the king of peace. If only he were the king of firm justice, crushing his enemies under foot, assessing all things with the balanced lance of judgment, protecting and strengthening with his mighty power the friends of peace.[84]

John's point here is clear: the king who seeks to establish peace in the realm cannot himself be a peaceful man – he must be prepared to wield the sword against the enemies of peace.[85] As such, virtue does not exist in a vacuum, but is measured according to political circumstance. Strikingly, John makes this observation before describing how, in 1139, Stephen's forces had surrounded Matilda, the rival claimant to the throne, only to permit her to escape from his clutches, by granting her safe passage from Arundel to Bristol. Matilda was able to join her supporters and continue her campaign against Stephen.[86]

Justice and mercy

In the same vein, William of Malmesbury considers the relationship between Stephen's judicial virtues and his rulership in his *Historia novella* (a work composed between late 1140 and early 1143).[87] William writes as supporter of Matilda, the history having been 'commissioned' by her half-brother and chief ally, Robert of Gloucester.[88] William describes Stephen as a man lacking in judgment (*imprudens*), one 'lenient to his enemies and easily appeased, courteous to all' (*lenis et exorabilis hostibus, affabilis omnibus*).[89] In many ways, this is an odd mixture of both positive and negative qualities, but it, in fact, amounts to a condemnation. William concedes that Stephen is 'courteous' only to demonstrate just how inappropriate this quality is in a ruler in his particular position. In the political context of the 1130s and 1140s, *lenitas* is not propitious for the realm or the people. William demonstrates the political flaw in Stephen's apparent virtue when he considers why the powerful men of the realm lent their support to his bid for the crown. Those who supported Stephen, William explains, were those who, under the strict rule of Henry I, had been prevented from plundering churches and attacking the innocent: 'all these had gladly given their support to a prince whom with little trouble they could influence to their own advantage, pushing their own fortunes at the expense of the people of the country'.[90]

William of Malmesbury's account does not condemn Stephen's character outright. It describes him as 'a very kindly man' (*mansuetissimi hominis*), and, perhaps surprisingly, agrees that the virtue of *mansuetudo* is an adornment of royal character (*regiae personae decorum*).[91] The *Historia novella* is not a work of character assassination: the problem is simply that, in the particular political circumstances of the Anarchy, Stephen cannot be a good ruler, for he lacks the judgment, and, indeed, the strength of character, to rule over the wicked and to bring them to heel.[92] Stephen is incapable of acting as a strict judge, unable to curb the rapacious barons as his uncle, Henry I, had done. Most telling of all, however, is how similar William of Malmesbury's account of Stephen's character is to that given in the history known as the *Gesta Stephani*. The work is anonymous, although sometimes attributed to the Bishop of Bath, Robert of Lewes. The piece, written in two parts (the first in 1148, the second after 1153),[93] is largely supportive of the king, although it ultimately understands Stephen's defeat as a judgment of God for his sins.[94] The *Gesta*, in fact, delivers much the same verdict as William of Malmesbury on Stephen's character – the difference being that the *Gesta* praises Stephen's merciful behaviour, which demonstrated his discretion (*discretio*):

> He made himself affable and amenable to all of whatever age. He was even of such a kindly and gentle disposition that he commonly forgot a king's exalted rank and in many affairs saw himself not superior to his men, but in every way their equal, sometimes actually their inferior.[95]

Once again, the term *mansuetudo* is applied to Stephen's character. But to the author of the *Gesta*, this virtue is a guarantee of peace and tranquillity (*pacem, quietam*), for, thanks to Stephen's virtue, England can be brought under control without violence. Indeed, Stephen's willingness to treat with his enemies is presented as a strategic masterstroke:

> The king, preferring to employ kindly patience towards them and to make every effort of affection before resorting to war, sent some of his counsellors on whom he especially relied to bring them to a cordial understanding.[96]

Stephen and his counsellors resort to persuasion and promises rather than military action, 'coaxing them [Stephen's enemies] with cajoling words and intimidating them with threats'. Even the most difficult aspect of Stephen's political judgment to explain – his willingness to let Matilda flee in 1139, when he was on the verge of capturing his challenger to the throne – is accounted for by the *Gesta Stephani* as an action motivated by concern for the good of the country and a decision made with the counsel of the Bishop of Winchester (his brother, Henry of Blois). Stephen sought to spare the people another bloody and indecisive battle:

> For if he were preparing to besiege the Countess of Anjou in one part of England, her brother would immediately rise up to disturb the kingdom in another; and so it was wiser for the king himself and more beneficial to the kingdom to let her go to her brother unharmed, that when both their forces had been brought into one place he might more easily devote himself to shattering their enterprise.[97]

Clearly visible in this passage of the *Gesta Stephani* is a defence of the righteousness of Stephen's actions, founded on the principles of deliberative rhetoric. The text emphasises that Stephen's decision to let Matilda go free was *consultius* – a term bearing the connotations of prudent deliberation and counsel – a considered decision, made after debate. Moreover, in defence of Stephen, the king's behaviour is described as seeking the *salus*, or health, of the kingdom. This too marks an appeal to deliberative rhetoric, as *salus* serves as a synonym for *tutus*, safety.[98] Stephen determines that it is 'safer' for the kingdom that Matilda be defeated decisively in a single battle, rather than spreading the conflict across the land.

Justice and mercy

The *Gesta Stephani* uses all the techniques of classical rhetorical argumentation not only to vindicate Stephan's use of *mansuetudo* as a tool of government, but to attack Matilda's rule over London as excessively strict, even inhumane.

> [She] was going beyond the bounds of moderation and sorely oppressing them [the Londoners], nor did they hope that in time to come she would have bowels of mercy or compassion for them, seeing that at the very beginning of her reign she had no pity on her subjects and demanded what they could not bear.[99]

Ultimately, then, what these historical battles to describe the soul of King Stephen (and define his place in history) amount to is an argument over the proper place and exercise of *mansuetudo* in royal government. Classical rhetorical theory provided twelfth-century authors with two ways of measuring the success of a royal reign – moral worth and political success – and those two categories helped frame contemporary historical arguments over whether Stephen was either virtuously merciful or entirely lacking in justice.

The praise afforded to Stephen's *mansuetudo* and *affabilitas* in these mid-twelfth-century texts, however, also prompts a discussion of the historical development of these ideals in courtly society. These discussions of Stephen's leniency towards those who ought to have been his enemies can be understood as evidence for the development of a kind of chivalry *avant la lettre*. John Gillingham, for example, has suggested that the Norman Conquest had brought a new set of attitudes into England: culturally 'French' values which privileged ideals of clemency and courtesy.[100] If these ideals had been imported into England c.1066, it seems they were beginning to exert an influence at Stephen's court in the 1140s. Those values included a reluctance to wield the sword against defeated men (or indeed women) of noble birth. The connection between Stephen's *mansuetudo* and a nascent sense of chivalric clemency and courtesy is evident in a passage of the *Gesta Stephani* which describes Stephen's lenient behaviour towards captured prisoners:

> They told the king that he had won a complete victory over his enemies ... and therefore it was more consonant with his lofty position and more befitting royal clemency to grant life to the suppliant prisoners than by inflicting the death penalty ruthlessly to deprive them of the little life they had left.[101]

What the conflicting attitudes to Stephen's gentle treatment of noble enemies found in the histories of the Anarchy suggests, however, is that this 'affable' ethos still seemed problematic to a generation of monastic authors who thought in terms of traditional expectations of kingly behaviour. Strikingly, these conflicting attitudes towards royal *mansuetudo* (a virtue or a vice?) do not seem to have been entirely resolved almost fifty years later. Gerald of Wales, writing his account of the Angevin dynasty, denounced similar behaviour in the Young King Henry. Henry presided over a court full of virtue and affability, but, Gerald complained, such affability made it a refuge for evildoers. At stake in such debates, then, was the question of whether justice or mercy best served the good of the *regnum*.

Rhetorical redescriptions: Walter Map and William of Newburgh

The histories of Stephen's reign provide a demonstration of how the political conflicts of the 1130s and 1140s further polarised the debate over whether mercy was really a quality which befitted a royal ruler and a royal judge. This was not a discussion, however, which ended with the death of Stephen and the accession of Henry II.

At the Angevin court, Walter Map had lived through, and observed, significant changes in the common law and the introduction of more rigorous and routine justice. He had, moreover, practical experience of judgment, serving twice as a justice-in-eyre, in 1172–3 and 1184–5. It is hardly surprising, then, that extensive discussion of the ramifications of royal leniency is found in Walter Map's *De nugis curialium* ('Courtiers' Trifles'). Map's fullest discussion of royal mercy is to be found in his description of contemporary France. Like the historians of Stephen's reign, Map's *De nugis curialium* considers the potential dangers to the safety and security of the realm posed by an excessively lenient king. What is most striking about Map's account is his appreciation of a key idea drawn from deliberative rhetoric – that while mercy may appear a virtue, it is, in many circumstances, a political menace. In the fifth book of *De nugis*, Map presents a seemingly positive portrayal of the merciful acts (*pietates*) of Louis VII, a king who seemed, in his virtue, to be worthy of the title of *rex christianissimus*.[102] Piety was a virtue closely aligned with, and, indeed, sometimes a synonym for *misericordia*. At first sight, Walter Map seems to approve of the virtuous Capetian monarchy, having Louis VII describe his own kingdom as remarkable for its peace and happiness:

> As the wealth of kings is diverse, so it is marked out by many differences. ... Your lord, the king of England, who wants for nothing, has men, horses, gold, silk, jewels, fruits, game and everything else. We in France have nothing but bread and wine and gaiety.[103]

Justice and mercy

This statement, alongside a sketch of Louis who is so well loved that he has nothing to fear from his subjects and may sleep, unguarded, in the open air, has become something of a *locus classicus* for describing the serenity of Capetian government (particularly when compared with the dynastic rebellions which shook Angevin territories during the 1170s and 1180s).[104] Gerald of Wales, who himself had experience of Capetian kingship, borrowed the same description of 'bread and wine and gaiety' to characterise the idyllic nature of Capetian rule.[105]

Yet Walter Map has some significant reservations about Capetian justice, and he complicates the picture of Capetian rulership when he relates the story of a knight named Waleran. Waleran had publicly accused the chamberlain and provost of Louis VII of stealing from royal revenues, and had sung *obscena carmina*, slandering both a noble woman and the king. In both cases the accusations were true, but the powerful men of the court demanded Waleran's exile and that Louis seize his lands and possessions.[106] Waleran, however, devised a way of winning the royal mercy. Having fled to England, he contrived (with the assistance of Henry II) to appear before Louis having assumed a guise of poverty, riding a broken horse, ragged and unshaven. When Louis saw the pathetic spectacle, he did not realise that it was feigned, and 'conceived disgust at his over-severity (*suum excessum*)'. The king then remarked that:

> For a word he [Waleran] should have been chastened by words, not cudgelled and proscribed. Alas! How merciless did I perceive myself just now, when I saw how miserable I have made him.[107]

The *exemplum* concludes with Louis's previous sentence being undone, as Waleran is restored to his former position. Crucial to understanding Walter Map's intention in including this story in *De nugis* is recognising which of the two parties – Louis VII or Waleran – has acted unjustly. Is Louis to be understood as a confused judge, or had Waleran done wrong by using deception to win his restoration to favour? While neither of the two men is presented in a particularly favourable light, Walter Map's primary focus is on Louis, and the king's judicial fickleness in particular. Indeed, Map may have intended his readers to be surprised not by the mercy Louis shows in forgiving Waleran, but by the harshness of his original sentence of expulsion.

An important passage in discussions of clemency and royal patience was the Roman law stipulation pertaining to 'flagrant insolence and wicked speech (*improbo petulantique maledicto*)'. That law specified that no penalty was to be enforced for slander, whether spoken out of drunkenness, insanity or malice.[108] Gerald of Wales, for example, cites this Roman law in his own *speculum principis*, linking it to biblical exhortations praising royal patience.[109] Moreover, good humour in enduring insults was considered a praiseworthy characteristic in a ruler.[110] Map would certainly have expected learned readers to infer that Louis's original judgment, in giving way to the cries of the powerful who had wished Waleran to be exiled, had therefore contradicted Roman law, as well as scriptural and kingly precedent. Map blames the incident on the quality of Louis's *simplicitas*, which had allowed the king to be manipulated, both by Waleran's accusers and, ultimately, by Waleran himself. Indeed, the tale of Waleran is accompanied by two other stories in which Louis is dissuaded from inflicting due punishment by appeals to his mercy.[111] Map remarks: 'he was a man of such kindliness and simple mildness ... that he might have been thought an imbecile (*cum esset homo tante benignitatis et tam simplices mansuetudinem ... ut posset ydiota videri*)'.[112] Indeed, William of Newburgh makes a similar remark on Louis VII's character, linking the king's leniency to a lack of political guile: the king was 'exceptional in his mildness towards his subjects ... however, he was a little too simple than befits a prince (*eximiae lenitatis in subditos ... paulo autem simplicior quam deceret principem*)'.[113]

By employing the term *simplicitas*, Map uses a classical rhetorical technique of redescription (*paradiastole*), disguising a vice in virtuous terms.[114] The same approach was practised by William of Malmesbury, who described Edward the Confessor as 'the Simple' (*simplex*), and cited his 'simplicity' as the reason why Edward was content with the kingdom of England, never attempting also to rule Norway.[115] The docility of *simplicitas*, being suggestible and attending to poor counsel, is the other side of the coin to praiseworthy *mansuetudo*. While Walter Map does advocate leniency, it is Henry II, rather than Louis, who strikes the correct balance as a king proficient in governance but also capable of demonstrating mercy (*pietas*). In the chapter which immediately follows his account of Louis's mercy, Map focuses on the justice of the Angevin court. Map's verdict on the Angevin administration of justice is ambivalent, to say the least – the court is flawed, full of avaricious officials – yet it does seem to have some redeeming features.[116] He recounts how a man who had stolen and forged the royal seal was brought before Henry and condemned to be hanged; yet, when Henry saw the virtuous brother of the forger weeping for the criminal, he spared the thief's life,[117] although he has the forger tonsured, 'lest his pity should appear more indulgent than was right (*ne remissa nimium videretur pietas*)'. Given the gravity of the offence of forging the royal seal – an offence tantamount to *laesa maiestas* – Henry appears extremely lenient in his punishment, but, according to Map, the king did not overstep the bounds of acceptable mercy.[118]

In these two paired chapters Walter Map provides an insight into the more general problem presented by the rhetorical redescription of the virtues of judgment. Louis VII's *misericordia* and *simplicitas*, when considered according to their effects on the political community, cannot be defined as true justice. Those virtues begin to resemble royal failings, if not vices. Personal acts of mercy in Louis, while perhaps testament to his piety, reveal his apparent inability to govern: he first passes an inappropriate sentence; he is subsequently 'fooled' into recanting a just judgment. Henry II, on the other hand, was, in Walter Map's judgment, distinguished by the ability to set appropriate punishments, and to apply royal discretion prudently and justly.

Map figures simplicity as stupidity, and softness as gullibility. He was not alone in attempting this sort of rhetorical redescription of justice, as is evident from another text from the final years of the twelfth century: William of Newburgh's *Historia rerum Anglicarum*. This is not a text particularly concerned with the workings of justice, but in the fifth book of the *Historia*, William describes the uprising led by William FitzOsbert in London in 1196 during a crisis in the city's civic governance and taxation; and the crown's subsequent attempts at arrest and punishment. FitzOsbert (also known as Longbeard) gathered a force of the poor and won a following; London teetered on the precipice of rebellion.[119] The story of FitzOsbert's rise to prominence and subsequent end is also recorded by Ralph Diceto, Gervase of Canterbury and Roger of Howden, but it is in William of Newburgh's description of this incident that the political connection between justice and the rhetoric of punishment is most evident. 'Popular' opinion is not necessarily always the correct course; opening justice up to discussion also means opening it up to distortion.

FitzOsbert, William notes, was persuasive and eloquent and so capable at winning popular support that when he was summoned by Richard to answer charges against him, the crowds were so great and the situation so dangerous that the king had to set aside any attempt to give judgment against FitzOsbert and instead proceed 'softly' (*mollius*).[120] When Hubert Walter finally smoked FitzOsbert out of the church at Mary-Le-Bow where he had taken sanctuary, he was put to death by being torn apart by horses. But still there were those who objected to, and misrepresented, this rightful exercise of public discipline (*publicae disciplinae*). Though Richard had acted rightfully in putting down a criminal figure, it was the king who was the subject of criticism.[121] Individuals in London – both the wicked and the easily misled – took justice for injustice, and criminal for a saint – so much so that they began to venerate the place where FitzOsbert he had been put to death, taking away the gibbet on which he had been hanged as a relic.[122] Ultimately, once the priest who stirred up the mob and encouraged them to believe FitzOsbert was a martyr was arrested and imprisoned, the clamour died down.[123] From these two relatively brief chapters in the *Historia*, one can make two inferences about judgment and punishment: first, that it was a more 'public' matter than we might sometimes imagine; it had an audience – both in chronicles and in the streets. Secondly, that at the same time as commentators offered their own verdicts on justice, they expressed a note of concern over its potential for rhetorical redescription: over just how easily the rightful exercise of discipline might be reconfigured as cruelty, excess, even murder.

Richard of Devizes and Matthew Paris: due process and rhetoric

Twelfth-century historians seized on the possibility of making *iustitia* the subject of deliberative rhetoric and the possibilities for argument which this strategy created. Not all chroniclers, however, thought the opportunity to debate the nature of true justice was, necessarily, a beneficial innovation. This is a problem evident in two later histories – the *Cronicon de rebus gestis Ricardi Primi* of Richard of Devizes (1192) and the *Chronica maiora* of Matthew Paris. These histories, which both consider the doings of English kings and English judges beyond England, strongly imply that justice should be understood as an inflexible and unchanging ideal. *Iustitia* is not open to the sort of debate suggested by the traditions of classical deliberative rhetoric – justice is identified as a refusal to deviate from the stipulations of the law. It is striking that these two histories – composed after Henry II's 'revolution' in law had taken effect – emphasise that rhetorical argument over justice can be a disguise for the disruption of proper legal procedure. Matthew Paris's *Chronica maiora* (covering the years 1236–59), in particular, includes detailed entries describing the punishments inflicted on those who were found to have transgressed the laws of the realm.[124] Moreover, like Walter Map had done in the 1180s, these two works identify a concern for proper legal process, and adherence to the principles of law, as characteristically 'English' concerns. It is not surprising that these historians display a sense of 'patriotism' and of national loyalty – Matthew Paris's belief in the superiority of the English is well documented.[125] What is more striking, and potentially suggestive, however, is that by the late twelfth century, historians were trying to link admirable English behaviour to English adherence to strict legal process.

This is the principle praised by Richard of Devizes in his *Cronicon*, a history of events in England and the Holy Land during the crusade of Richard I.[126] Richard of Devizes argues that it is King Richard's consistent and unwavering application of judicial standards which makes him a more virtuous ruler than his French counterpart, Philip II. He recounts an incident which took place in Messina, where both English and French soldiers were camped, and where men from both armies committed crimes:

> The king of England, immediately on the next day, had gallows built outside the camp, on which to hang thieves and plunderers. The judges he designated spared neither sex nor age, and the law and the punishment were the same for the guilty, whether they were foreigners or natives. The king of France concealed whatever his men did or suffered, or kept silent about it. The king of England, giving no heed to the nationality of anyone involved in a crime, considered every man his subject and left no offence unpunished.[127]

What is revealing about this paragraph is not the rhetorical features of Richard's vocabulary – although he was well versed in classical literature, he does not draw on any of the ideas of classical deliberative rhetoric – but their absence.[128] Richard I is unwilling to engage in debate as to whether there are mitigating circumstances to the offence, or even whether the offenders are technically his subjects. Impartial justice is the criterion for righteous rulership in this case. Justice is a universal value, binding upon all nationalities, applicable in all times and places. Those 'circumstances' of crime (in this instance the age, sex and nationality of the offender) so important in the determination of sentence according to classical philosophy, canon law and, indeed, parts of the common law tradition, do not excuse crime and have no effect on sentencing.

Likewise, it is again the context of a crusade which provides Matthew Paris with the opportunity of discussing the vital importance of impartial judgment. Matthew's account suggests that arguments which attempt to mitigate a sentence by considering the political impact of a judgment are often attempts to subvert justice entirely. While Matthew Paris's discussion clearly serves to demonstrate a more general problem for those writing about judgment – that the vocabulary of deliberative rhetoric can be used to subvert justice – his writing must also be understood in light of events in England during the personal rule of Henry III, and charges that the king had tried to establish his rule through royal will, exercising *potentia absoluta*, rather than being bound by the established processes of the common law.[129] The *Chronica maiora* reveals a clear anxiety about Henry's ability to subvert, even abuse, the tools of royal *gratia* and royal pardon.[130] The most revealing discussion of the relationship between rhetoric and justice, however, is found in the *Chronica*'s description of the experiences of an English knight, William Longespee.[131] In 1250, Matthew recounts, Longespee was serving with the French in the East. There the crusader witnessed a series of violent robberies committed by Robert I, Count of Artois, and immediately reported these offences to the French king, Louis IX, demanding that justice be done. Louis, however, refused, replying that although he was aware of the crimes, he would not discipline the count (his brother), as such punishment might damage the wavering morale of the crusaders and, in turn, endanger the success of the crusade. Louis justifies his decision with an appeal to a familiar theme of political rhetoric – that a specific injustice may be overlooked if to prosecute it would damage the good of the community, namely, the crusading army:

> Now, my friend, you can understand. A division can so easily arise in the army – God forbid! At a time of crisis it is necessary to tolerate such things and even worse with equanimity.[132]

Matthew observes that Louis presented this argument with the appearance of piety (*vultu piissimus*). Such apparently pious reasoning, however, does not convince Longespee, who replies:

> Therefore you are no king, since you are incapable of doing justice towards your men, or punishing offenders ... I will not serve such a king, I will not serve such a lord.[133]

Longespee immediately departs the French camp, and, Matthew relates, the crusaders soon felt the loss of such a fine fighter. Of course, there is a degree of irony in this outcome: Louis IX has refused to punish his brother, for fear that doing so would damage the morale and success of his army (in the terms of classical rhetoric, privileging the *utile* over the *honestum*). Yet in failing to show strict and impartial justice, Louis not only sacrifices his moral virtue, but also weakens his army anyway, because his injustice prompts the resignation of his leading knight. Matthew clearly focuses his readers' attention on the question of whether there really are circumstances in which criminal behaviour should be allowed to go unpunished, out of a concern for the good of the political community. In raising the question of what behaviour might be 'tolerated' (*tolerare*) for the sake of political advantage, Matthew Paris was invoking a series of questions which would have been familiar to learned readers. Augustine's discussion of tolerating social evils which could not be tackled without worsening them had been repeated in the *Decretum* and formed the typical basis for medieval discussion on this issue.[134] But while Augustine had offered a more tempered view – that sometimes the (ecclesiastical) ruler was obliged to suffer delinquency to avoid greater evils – Matthew suggests that, in this context, *tolerantia* is simply a cloak for *iniustitia*.

Matthew, however, clearly did not intend this incident concerning the French king to be read as an argument for summary justice. Rather it is an exhortation to regular and routine judicial procedure, even when on crusade. This is demonstrated in the incident which soon follows this account, which provides a counterpoint to Louis IX's unwillingness to punish his men adequately. Matthew turns to describe events in the enemy camp. The Sultan of Babylon, whom Matthew characterises as a proud and merciless man (*superbus nimis et immisericors*), is organising the defence of Cairo against the crusaders. A prince who had been unable to defend the port of Damietta against the Christian attack is brought before the Sultan and summarily executed. This would not be a remarkable incident, but for the comment which Matthew makes:

> Although in the judgment of others the aforementioned prince could have adequately exculpated himself, however, the Sultan, very cruelly rising up against him, ordered him to be hanged on the gallows as a traitor and blasphemer.[135]

In other words, Matthew now presents the other 'extreme' of partial justice – the refusal to listen to a legitimate defence. Just as the Sultan's arbitrary will finds reason to condemn those who have committed no crime, so the French ruler has devised reasons to exculpate the guilty and excuse them of all punishment. The parallel between the two is made more explicit when Matthew spells out the consequences of the execution. The dead prince's brother determines to defect to the side of the French, taking with him a cohort of troops. In part, this decision is coupled with a narrative of surrender to Christian forces and the possibility of religious conversion; but at the core of the story, Matthew places the idea that it is impossible to prosper in serving a ruler who lacks justice. As the prince explains to his Christian audience: once his brother had been put to death on the basis of an entirely false criminal accusation (*criminosam accusationem falsissimam*), the prince began to worry that he would meet the same end.[136] Here the parallel with the French example is unmistakable – judicial partiality caused Louis IX to lose one of his finest fighters, just as judicial partiality caused the Sultan of Babylon to be abandoned by his troops. Both rulers, in seeking that which was politically advantageous rather than that which was morally right and legally correct, have ultimately damaged their own causes. Like Richard of Devizes, Matthew Paris draws the moral – and the salutary warning to the thirteenth-century judge – that it is dangerous to allow rhetorical arguments over the impact of a judgment to remove the obligation to do justice altogether.

Classical rhetorical tools allowed English authors both to explore the complexities of doing justice and to condemn lords who judged badly. The weight of the problem is neatly summarised by Raoul Ardens, who, turning to consider what type of man a judge ought to be, wrote that so great was the responsibility of judgment (particularly when the penalty may run to the life of the accused) that the duty of the judge is 'agonizare pro iusticia', to struggle for justice.[137] Justice is a task which demands very great things of a judge, demands which extend beyond the procedural stipulations of legal textbooks and *ordines*, to the operational criteria of prudence and wisdom. As such, it would be a misreading to understand the histories of Orderic Vitalis, the chroniclers of the reign of Stephen, Walter Map, Richard of Devizes or Matthew Paris as constructing arguments against mercy. In all these works, only one passage really constitutes an attack on *misericordia* or *mansuetudo per se*, the criticism of Stephen's hazardous *lenitas*. And even this position (the assumption that a merciful ruler is necessarily an injudicious judge) is challenged by the *Gesta Stephani*.

When chroniclers of the reigns of English kings – from William the Conqueror to Henry III – discussed judgment, they were most interested in describing how the moral virtues of an individual judge were exercised in relation to the circumstances of the specific case before him. This is, however, a debate which advances in sophistication and complexity in the course of approximately 150 years. For Orderic Vitalis, writing before the emergence of truly systematic law or 'routine' justice in England, the choice between justice and mercy is determined by the royal counsellors with whom the king surrounds himself. When William I, William II or Henry I make a wrongful decision about the punishment of a magnate, the problem stems (as it had done in the biblical case of Susannah and Daniel) from bad advice, from deceitful counsellors. The events of the Anarchy, however, clearly complicated this debate in two ways. First, histories of the period explicitly state that the major political conflict was in fact an argument about whether justice or mercy was the best way to rule England. The argument between *iustitia* and *misericordia* was widely acknowledged as one way of understanding the political struggles of contemporary English history and as a means of measuring royal fitness to rule. Secondly, those histories demonstrate a marked increase in the level of sophistication with which they discuss political action founded on classical rhetorical principles. Quite how sophisticated that discussion had become by the end of the twelfth century is visible in the tripartite schema of Raoul Ardens. Similarly, the histories critical of Stephen do argue that he chose the course of action inappropriate to the political circumstances. That is, these histories point out that morally worthy mercy and politically advantageous justice might, sometimes, be entirely opposed choices. They demonstrate how this apparently theoretical argument between *honestum* and *utile* could be seen in the real political and military conflicts of the Anarchy. By the late twelfth century, moreover, it is apparent that parts of this rhetorical debate are coming into conflict with the emergence of more rigorous systematic principles of law. Walter Map's *De nugis* recognises – with some admiration – the speed and reach of Angevin administrative reforms, where no action escapes the ever-watchful eyes of the king or his officials. Louis VII, by contrast, may inhabit a world of bread, wine and gaiety – but it is also a world of persuasion and arbitrary will. A *simplex* king cannot prosper in a world of such judicial complexity. Richard of Devizes and Matthew Paris, finally, raise concerns that classical deliberative rhetoric can become a cover for legal abuses, rather than a means of debating the most appropriate course of judicial conduct. There is room for pleading and argument, but that must be part of, not an alternative to, standardised legal process.

The histories remind their readers that royal judicial decisions are political choices, with serious ramifications for the good of the realm.[138] This, in turn, demonstrates the absolute centrality of counsel to twelfth- and thirteenth-century arguments about justice and mercy. Merciful counsel was understood to be a virtue which had the endorsement of Christian teaching, but, as thrown into sharp definition by classical rhetoric, it was also understood that counsel is not always virtuous and counsellors could not always be trusted. Opening the practice of justice to discussion allowed kings to hear the advice of the virtuous, yet equally it allowed the judge to be persuaded away from virtue. The deliberative rhetoric which made the implications of different judicial strategies more stark – the appeal to the concepts of moral worth and advantage – in fact made the choice between *iustitia* and *misericordia* more fraught. In theory, justice was a subject for debate. In practice, in twelfth- and early thirteenth-century England, it was the source of bitter, often irresolvable, conflicts.

Histories of justice

Notes

1 For what follows: Jocelin of Brakelond, *Chronicle*, 92–4.
2 For a discussion of this form of the justification for this automatic punishment in the twelfth century, see P. Huizing, 'The earliest development of excommunication *latae sententiae* by Gratian and the earliest decretists', *Studia Gratiana* 3 (1955), 79–309.
3 For which see Mansfield, *The Humiliation of Sinners*, esp. 170–1; 197–8.
4 See James J. Murphy, 'Saint Augustine and the debate about a Christian rhetoric', *Quarterly Journal of Speech* 46 (1960), 1–10; and James J. Murphy, 'Saint Augustine and Rabanus Maurus: the genesis of medieval rhetoric', *Western Speech* 31 (1967), 97–110.
5 See H. Caplan, 'Classical rhetoric and the mediaeval theory of preaching', *Classical Philology* 28 (1933), 76–96.
6 Cf. Morenzoni, *Des écoles aux paroisses*, 43–4.
7 See P. O. Lewry, 'Grammar, logic and rhetoric', in J. I. Catto (ed.), *The Early Oxford Schools* (Oxford, 1984), 401–33.
8 Mary Dickey, 'Some commentaries on the *De inventione* and *Ad Herennium* of the eleventh and early twelfth centuries', *Mediaeval and Renaissance Studies* 6 (1968), 1.
9 K. M. Fredborg, 'Ciceronian rhetoric and the schools', in John van Engen (ed.), *Learning Institutionalised: Teaching in the Medieval University* (Notre Dame, IN, 2000), 21–2; B. Munk Olsen, 'La popularité des textes classiques entre la IXe et la XIIe siècle', *Revue d'histoire des textes* 14–15 (1984–5), 177.
10 Cicero, *Ad C. Herennium: De ratione dicendi (Rhetorica ad Herennium)*, ed. and trans. H. Caplan (London, 1954), 2.1, 58–9.
11 Constant Mews, '*Logica* in the service of philosophy: William of Champeaux and his influence', in Rainer Berndt (ed.), *Schrift, Schreiber, Schenker: Studien zur Abtei Sankt Viktor in Paris und den Viktorinern* (Berlin, 2005), 89–96, attributes the commentary to William of Champeaux and argues that it cannot have been written before the 1090s.
12 Dickey, 'Some commentaries', 40.
13 Boethius, *De differentiis topicis*, 4, PL.64.1207C.
14 K. M. Fredborg, 'Petrus Helias's *Summa* on Cicero's *De inventione*', *Traditio* 64 (2009), 175.
15 Martin of Braga, *Formula vitae honestae*, in *Opera omnia*, ed. Claude W. Barlow (New Haven, CT, 1950), 5, 246; Stephan Kuttner, 'A forgotten definition of justice', *Studia Gratiana* 20 (1976), 100.
16 *SAP*, 3, 123.
17 *Ibid.*, 7.2.1, 269.
18 Rupert of Deutz, *De sancta trinitate*, 40.8, CCCM 24, 2051–60.
19 *Ibid.*, 40.8, 2054.
20 For example, *De inventione*, 2.55, 216; 2.168–9, 332–6.
21 *Digest*, 1.1.1, 1:29.

22 *Ibid.*, 48.19.20, 1:867; cf. 48.19.11, 1:866.
23 *LHP*, 4.1–5, 83.
24 See Downer's commentary, *LHP*, 306–7.
25 *LHP*, 4.3, 82.
26 Gervase of Tilbury, *Otia imperialia*, preface, 2–3.
27 Cicero, *De inventione*, 2.160, 328 ('iustitia est habitus animi communi utilitate conservata suam cuique tribuens dignitatem'); *De officiis*, 1.31, 32 ('fundamenta iustitiae, primum ut ne cui noceatur deinde ut communi utilitati serviatur').
28 For example, *Digest*, 9.2.51.2, 1:162 (*communis utilitas* sometimes outweighs the arguments of reason); 43.1.2.1, 1:728; 47.10.5.11, 1:831 (*publica utilitas*).
29 For example, *Florilegium Gallicum*, 257, 271.
30 Alan of Lille, *De virtutibus*,1.2, 31.
31 For example, Gaines Post, *Studies in Medieval Legal Thought: Public Law and the State, 1100–1322* (Princeton, NJ, 1964), 309.
32 Augustine, *De civitate Dei*, ed. B. Dombart and A. Kalb, CCSL 47–8 (2 vols, Turnhout, 1955), 1.21, 23.
33 For example, Augustine, *De sermone Domini in monte*, 2.18, 154, provides 'in meliorem partem interpretemus' as an alternative judical principle; cf. GO on Romans xiv.4, PL.114.514D–515A, repeated in Peter Lombard's commentary on Romans, PL.191.1513; Robert of Melun, *QEP*, on Romans xiv.4, 162.
34 Cf. Cicero, *Ad Herennium*, 3.2.3, 160–1; it might equally be phrased as *utile–honestum*.
35 *Moralium dogma philosophorum*, ed. John Holmberg, *Das Moralium dogma philosophorum des Guillaume de Conches, lateinisch, altfranzösisch und mittelniederfränkisch, herausgegeben* (Uppsala, 1929), 28.
36 *Policraticus*, 4.7, 1:527. For another discussion of twelfth-century scholars borrowing *honestum–utile* as organising principles, see S. O. Sønnesyn, *William of Malmesbury and the Ethics of History* (Woodbridge, 2012), 65.
37 Cicero, *De inventione*, 2.174, 340.
38 *VA*, 1.66, 437.
39 'gloriosum est regi citra meritum punire'. *Ibid.*, 1.66, 438.
40 Baldwin, *Masters, Princes and Merchants*, 1:32–4.
41 'Quae licet graves sint admodum et asperae ut vix sit aliquis qui vel eas suscipere velit vel imponere praesumat, praetera licet in libris poenitentialibus non singulas singulorum invenias expressas (licet peccatorum invenias poenitentias) tutius tamen est honestius prae oculis habita antiquorum auctoritate, modo et *consideratione*, mitigabimus eas et forte exasperabimus.' Robert of Flamborough, *Liber poenitentialis*, 5, prologue, 203.
42 *Ibid.*, 3.3, 118; see also 3.3, 141–3.
43 *Policraticus*, 4.8, 1:530, 'quia tutius est cordas remitti intensius quam protendi'.
44 'Et licet tutius sit reddere rationem pro misericordia quam pro iudicio. Tutissimum tamen est ut ita palpebrae eius praecedant gressus suos quod iudicium non vacillet per imprudentiam, nec misericordia desipiat per

incircumspectionem. Misericordia siquidem iniusta est cum incorrigibili.' *Bracton*, 2:306.

45 For example, *Digest*, 4.2.14, 1:81, 'item si, cum exceptione adversus te perpetua tutus essem, coegero te acceptum mihi facere, cessare hoc edictum, quia nihil tibi abest'; cf. *Digest*, 4.2.14.11, 1:81–2. *Bracton* does elsewhere invoke the idea of *tutus* in a more general sense of 'safety': see *Bracton*, 2:104; 3:58; 3:73; 4:86; 4:138; 4:190; 4:191.

46 Historians of rhetoric have traditionally argued that classical rhetorical theory had very little influence on the reality of political discussion. See J. O. Ward, 'The commentator's rhetoric: from antiquity to the renaissance, glosses and commentaries on Cicero's *Rhetorica*', in J. J. Murphy (ed.), *Medieval Eloquence: Studies in the Theory and Practice of Medieval Rhetoric* (Berkeley, CA, 1978), 126–73; Dickey, 'Some commentaries'.

47 The first five books of the *Speculum* have now been edited: Radulfus Ardens, *Speculum universale I–V*, ed. C. Heimann and S. Ernst, CCCM 241 (Leiden, 2011).

48 Stephen C. Ferruolo, *The Origins of the University: The Schools of Paris and Their Critics, 1100–1215* (Stanford, 1985), 193; see also J. Gründel, 'L'oeuvre encyclopédique de Raoul Ardent, le *Speculum universale*', *Cahiers d'histoire mondiale* 9 (1966), 553–70.

49 'Speculum universale', BnF, Ms. latin 3240, X.57, fo. 41r.

50 *Ibid.*, X.59, fo. 42r.

51 *Ibid.*, X.60, fo. 42r.

52 'Speculum universale', BnF, Ms. latin 3229.

53 *Ibid.*, I.15, f.3v.

54 *Ibid.*, I.16, fo. 4v.

55 *Ibid.*, I.17, fo. 4v.

56 *Ibid.*, I.18, fo. 5v.

57 Quintilian, *Institutio oratoria*, ed. and trans. D. A. Russell (5 vols, London, 2001), 12.1.1, 5:196; a definition repeated by Isidore of Seville, *Etymologies*, 2.3, 69. See Richard McKeon, 'Rhetoric in the middle ages', *Speculum* 17 (1942), 15.

58 H. Caplan, 'A medieval commentary on the *Rhetorica ad Herennium*', in A. King and H. North (eds), *Of Eloquence: Studies in Ancient and Mediaeval Rhetoric* (Ithaca, NY, 1970), 247–70.

59 L. G. Wickham Legg, *English Coronation Records* (London, 1901), 30–1; Mary Clayton, 'The Old English *promissio regis*', *Anglo-Saxon England* 37 (2008), 91–150.

60 *CM*, 5:56–60.

61 M. T. Clanchy, 'Highway robbery and trial by battle in the Hampshire Eyre of 1249', in R. F. Hunnisett and J. B. Post (eds), *Medieval Legal Records: Edited in Memory of C. A. F. Meekings* (London, 1978), 37. See the similar conclusions in D. A. Carpenter, 'Matthew Paris and Henry III's speech at the exchequer in October 1256', in *The Reign of Henry III*, 137–50.

62 For Howden's involvement in royal affairs see David Corner, 'The *Gesta regis Henrici secundi* and *Chronica* of Roger, parson of Howden', *Bulletin of the Institute of Historical Research* 56:134(1983), 126–44.

Justice and mercy

63 The manuscript is BL, Royal MS 14 C II; see Howden, *Chronica*, 2:215–52; David Corner, 'The earliest surviving manuscripts of Roger of Howden's "Chronica"', *English Historical Review* 98 (1983), 297–310.
64 For the distinction, Isidore of Seville, *Etymologies*, 1.44, 67.
65 *EH*, 6.9, 3:273–5.
66 'Sic multos vinculis inieri ex merito propriae perversitatis aliosque plures pro metu futurae sedititonis. Hoc enim censura rectitudinis exigit, et divina lex per Moisen rectoribus orbis precipit ut comprimant nocentes ne perimant innocentes. Nunc autem in articulo mortis positus sicut opto salvari, et per misericordiam Dei a reatibus meis absolvi sic omnes mox iubeo carceres aperiri, omnesque vinctos preter fratrem meum Baiocensem episcopum relaxari liberosque pro amore Dei ut ipse michi misereatur dimitti. Nexi tamen tali tenore de carcere procedant ut antea iureiurando securitatem rei publicae ministris faciant quod pacem in Anglia et Normannia omnibus modis teneant et pacis adversariis pro posse suo viriliter resistant.' *EH*, 7.16, 4:96–9.
67 *Ibid.*, 7.16, 4:100–1.
68 'Miror quod prudenter non indagatis quis vel qualis est vir pro quo supplicatis. Nonne pro tali viro petitis, qui tamdiu contemptor exstitit religionis, et argutus incentor letiferae seditionis? Nonne hunc iam cohercui quattuor annis episcopum, qui dum debuerat esse iustissimus rector Anglorum, factus est pessimus oppressor popularum et monachilium destructor cenobiorum? Seditiosum liberando male facitis et vobismet ipsis ingens detrimentum queritis.' *Ibid.*, 7.16, 4:98–9.
69 'Quisquis parcit periuris et latronibus, plagiariis et execratis proditoribus aufert pacem et quietam innocentibus, unnumerasque cedes et damna serit bonis et inermibus.' *Ibid.*, 8.2, 4:130–1.
70 This incident is discussed in Paul Hyams, *Rancor and Reconciliation in Medieval England* (Ithaca, NY, 2003), 129–30; Hyams reads this as one demonstration of the conflict between the need to maintain political relations versus a desire to act on personal enmity – an analysis which broadly maps onto the discussion of the 'purpose' of punishment I set out here. The point I wish to underscore, however, is that with this scene Orderic is not just offering a judgment on William's character, but a view of the problems of persuasion for a (royal) judge.
71 See K. Thompson, 'Orderic and Robert of Bellême', *Journal of Medieval History* 20 (1994), 133–41.
72 'Si rex magnificum comitem violenter subegerit, nimaque pertinacia ut conatur eum exhaereditaverit omnes nos ut imbelles ancillas amodo conculcabit.' *EH*, 11.3, 6:26–7.
73 On this group see Chibnall's comment, *EH*, 6:26–7.
74 'Domine rex Henrice, noli proditoribus istis credere. Summopere moliuntur decipere te et regalis iusticiae rigorem tibi tollere. Cur audis illos qui suadent tibi traditori parcere, tuaeque mortis coniurationem impune dimittere? Ecce nos omnes tibi fideliter assistimus, tibique in omnibus obsecundare parati sumus. Oppidum acriter expugna, traditorem ex omni parte coarcta nec pacem

cum illo facias, donec ipsum aut vivum aut mortuum in manibus tuis teneas.' *EH*, 11.3, 6:26–7.
75 *LHP*, 1.1, 80.
76 'Impossibile enim est ut salubriter disponat principatum qui non agitur consilio sapientum.' *Policraticus*, 5.6, 1:550.
77 *Ibid.*, 3.6, 1:486.
78 *Ibid.* (quoting Proverbs xxvii.6).
79 'Veritas aspera est et plerumque molestiam parit, dum aliquem palpare dedignatur. Verum amaritudo eius utilior est et integris sensibus gratior quam meretricantis linguae distillans favus.' *Ibid.*
80 *Ibid.*, 5.9, 1:560–2.
81 Cf. G. White, 'The myth of the Anarchy', *Anglo-Norman Studies* 12 (2000), 323–37.
82 Later authors such as Gervase of Tilbury took Stephen as a case study in the failures of royal justice: *Otia imperialia*, 481–2; cf. B. Weiler, 'Kingship, usurpation and propaganda in twelfth-century Europe: the case of Stephen', *Anglo-Norman Studies* 23 (2001), 299–326.
83 For John, Martin Brett, 'John of Worcester and his contemporaries', in R. H. C. Davis and J. M. Wallace Hadrill (eds), *The Writing of History in the Middle Ages: Essays Presented to R. W. Southern* (Oxford, 1981), 101–26.
84 'Rex est pacis, et o utinam rex rigoris iustitie conterens sub pedibus inimicos, et equa lance iudicii decernens omnia in robore fortitudinis conservans et corroborans pacis amicos.' *The Chronicle of John of Worcester*, trans. J. Bray and P. McGurk (3 vols, Oxford, 1995), 3:268–9.
85 For discussion of medieval fears of the 'false peace', see Jehangir Yezdi Malgeam, *The Sleep of Behemoth: Disputing Peace and Violence in Medieval Europe, 1000–1200* (Ithaca, NY, 2013), esp. 1–7.
86 See Edmund King's introduction in E. King (ed.), *The Anarchy of King Stephen's Reign* (Oxford, 1994), 17–19.
87 William of Malmesbury, *Historia novella*, ed. and trans. Edmund King and K. R. Potter (Oxford, 1998), introduction, xxxiii.
88 *Ibid.*, xxix.
89 *Ibid.*, 1.15, 28–9.
90 *Ibid.*, 1.17, 32–3.
91 *Ibid.*, 1.19, 36–7.
92 Cf. *ibid.*, 2.30, 58–9, describing Stephen as a man of worthy promises but no action.
93 *Gesta Stephani*, ed. and trans. K. R. Potter and R. H. C. Davis (Oxford, 1976), introduction, xxi.
94 *Ibid.*, xxxiii.
95 'Omnibus cuiuslibet aetatis habilem se et flexibilem reddere. Tam benigni etiam tamque mansueti erat animi, ut regiae fere dignitatis oblitus in multis negotiis non se suis praelatum, sed omnimodis parem, quandoque etiam inferiorem videret.' *Ibid.*, 22–3.

96 'Sed rex malens circa eos benigna uti patientia, et omnia prius amore experiri quam armis, quosdam de assistentibus sibi, super quos praecipue innitebatur, ad eos in amoris concordiam reducendos transmisit.' *Ibid.*, 24–5.

97 'Si enim ex una Angliae regione Andegavensem comitissam obsidere disponeret, germanus illius ad regnum perturbandum ex alia quamfestinus parte insurgeret; ideoque consultius sibi esse et regno salubrius, ut ipsam ad fratrem damni immunem progredi permitteret, quatinus ambobus cum viribus suis in locum unum redactis, et facilius ad eorum cassandum conatum intenderet.' *Ibid.*, 89.

98 For this connection see also *Policraticus*, 4.9, 1:562.

99 'discretionis metas transcendens immoderate se contra eos erigebat, nec futurae eam mansuetudinis vel pietatis habituram erga se viscera sperabant, cum in primo iam regnandi capite suorum nequaquam miserta intolerabilila eos postularet'. *Gesta Stephani*, 61, 122–5. On this incident see J. A. Truax, 'Winning over the Londoners: King Stephen, the Empress Matilda and the politics of personality', *Haskins Society Journal* 8 (1996), 43–62.

100 J. Gillingham, 'Conquering the barbarians: war and chivalry in twelfth-century Britain and Ireland', in J. Gillingham, *The English in the Twelfth Century* (Woodbridge, 2000), 41–58.

101 'Dicebant nameque regi plenum se de hostibus conquisisse triumphum ... ideoque dignitati suae esse aptius, regiaeque pietati competentius, captivis supplicibus vitam donare, quam usque ad mortem punitis, quod parum vitae supererat immisericorditer auferre.' *Gesta Stephani*, 42–3; on the connection between 'mansuetudo' and noble behaviour see Bjorn Weiler, 'William of Malmesbury on kingship', *History* 90 (2005), 10.

102 *DNC*, 5.5, 443–55.

103 'Sicut diverse sunt regum opes, ita multis distincte sunt varietatibus ... Dominus autem tuus, rex Anglie, cui nichil deest, homines, equos, aurum et sericum, gemmas, fructus, feras et omnia possidet. Nos in Francia nichil habemus nisi panem et vinum et gaudium.' *Ibid.*, 5.5, 450–1.

104 G. Koziol, 'England, France and the problem of sacrality in twelfth-century ritual', in T. N. Bisson (ed.), *Cultures of Power: Lordship, Status, and Process in Twelfth-Century Europe* (Philadelphia, 1995), 124–48.

105 Gerald of Wales, *De principis*, 3.30, 318.

106 *DNC*, 5.5, 447–9.

107 'Corrigendus erat verbo pro verbis, non fustigandus ac proscribendus. Heu! Quam inmisericordem me comperi modo, cum viderem quam miserabilem eum per te fecerim.' *Ibid.*, 5.5, 448–51.

108 *Codex*, 9.7.1, 2:373; e.g. *Policraticus*, 3.14, 1:511.

109 Gerald of Wales, *De principis* , 1.5, 15–18.

110 For example, Geoffrey Gaimar, *Estoire des Engleis*, ed. and trans. Ian Short (Oxford, 2009), lines 5943–4, 322.

111 *DNC*, 5.5, 443–7; 455.

Histories of justice

112 Ibid., 5.5, 442–3. Map seems to underline the correctness of his opinion by emphasising the basis for the judgment: 'I speak of what I have seen or know.' Yet here, as elsewhere in *De nugis*, Map's comments are rather difficult to interpret: these two *exempla* of excessive leniency are followed by the comment that Louis was also the strictest of judges (*districtissimus erat iudex*), stiff to the proud and 'not unfair' to the meek. One is tempted to read this as Map juxtaposing *exempla* with an idealised model of royal judicial behaviour with the story of Waleran revealing that Louis had not achieved the correct balance – which required not merely good intentions, but careful sifting and weighing. One might compare this to another story recounted by Map, that of Raso, who also suffers for his 'innocencia', *DNC*, 3.5, 271.
113 William of Newburgh, *Historia*, 2.4, 1:223.
114 Cf. Quintilian, *Institutio oratoria*, 9.3.65, 138. See also Gregory the Great, *Moralia in Iob*, 3.33.65, 1:155.
115 William of Malmesbury, *Gesta regum Anglorum*, ed. and trans. R. A. B. Mynors, R. M. Thomson and M. Winterbottom (2 vols, Oxford, 1998), 3.259, 1:479.
116 For example, *DNC*, 1.1, 5; cf. 2.1, 133.
117 Ibid., 5.6, 494–5.
118 *Glanvill*, 14.7, 176–7 (on *crimen falsi*); cf. H. Summerson, 'Counterfeiters, forgers and felons in English courts 1200–1400', in A. Musson (ed.), *Expectations of Law in the Middle Ages* (Woodbridge, 2001), 105–16.
119 For FitzOsbert, see John McEwan, 'William FitzOsbert and the crisis of 1196 in London', *Florilegium* 21 (2004), 18–42.
120 William of Newburgh, *Historia*, 5.20, 2:469–70.
121 Ibid., 5.20, 2:471.
122 Ibid., 5.21, 2:472.
123 Ibid., 5.21, 2:473.
124 For example, *CM*, 5:34–5; 5:49; 5:95.
125 See R. Vaughan, *Matthew Paris* (Cambridge, 1958), 142; cf. *CM*, 5:131.
126 For Richard, see A. Gransden, *Historical Writing in England* (2 vols, London, 1974–82), 1:248–52.
127 'Rex Anglie mox die crastino erigi fecit patibula extra castra, ad suspendendos in eis latruculos et praedones. Non parcebant iudices delegati sexui vel aetati parque (fuit) ad venae et indigenae rei lex et supplicium. Rex Francie quicquid sui peccarent vel peccaretur in suos dissimulavit et tacuit. Rex Anglie, pro indifferenti habens cuiates crimen involueret, omnem hominem suum reputans, nichil iniuriarum reliquid inultum. Unde et unus dictus est agnus a Griffonibus, alter leonis nomen accepit.' Richard of Devizes, *Cronicon*, ed. J. T. Appleby (London, 1963), 16–17.
128 For Richard's reading of the classics see H. Blurton, 'Richard of Devizes's *Cronicon*, Menippean satire, and the Jews of Winchester', *Exemplaria* 22 (2010), 265–84.
129 See M. T. Clanchy, 'Did Henry III have a policy?', *History* 53 (1968), 203–16; D. A. Carpenter, 'King, magnates, and society: the personal rule of Henry III, 1234–58', *Speculum* 60 (1985), 39–70.

130 *CM*, 4:57.
131 See S. Lloyd and T. Hunt, 'William Longespee', *Nottingham Medieval Studies* 35 (1991), 41–69; (1992), 79–125.
132 'Nunc potes audire, amice. Sic cito posset oriri scisma, quod absit, in exercitu. Aequanimiter talia, et etiam his majora, necesse est in tali temporis discrimine tolerare.' *CM*, 5:133. A similar assertion about the danger of internal disputes within a crusading army is made in the *Itinerarium peregrinorum et gesta Regis Ricardi*, trans. H. Nicholson (Aldershot, 1997), 151.
133 'Ergo non es rex, cum non possis tuo justificare et punire delinquentes ... Tali regi de caetero non servio, tali domini non adhaerebo.' *CM*, 5:133–4.
134 For example, *Decretum*, C.XXIII, q.4, c.37, 1:916–17; cf. I. P. Bejczy, '*Tolerantia*: a medieval concept', *Journal of the History of Ideas* 58 (1997), 365–84.
135 'et [licet] judicio aliquorum se sufficienter princeps memoratus expurgasset, tamen insurgente ipso in eum Soldano crudelius, ipsum tanquam proditorem et blasphemum suspendi jussit in patibulo'. *CM*, 5:140.
136 Ibid., 5:141.
137 *Speculum universale*, X.64, BnF, Ms. latin 3240, fo. 44r; an allusion to Ecclesiastes iv.33, 'pro iustitia agonizare pro anima tua, et usque ad mortem certa pro iustitia'. *Agonizare* (or *agoniare*) also carries with it the association contesting or contending – whether in sport or in a law court.
138 Cf. S. D. White, 'The ambiguity of treason in Anglo-Norman-French law, c.1150–c.1250', in Karras *et al.*, *Law and the Illicit*, 89–102, esp. 91.

8

Love your enemies? Popular mercy in a vengeance culture

Popular mercy: The Four Daughters of God

Between about 1100 and 1250, a series of contending claims about the nature of mercy and justice were being argued in England by those in administration and by those with influence. These ideas had long been present in medieval thought, but they were thrown into sharper relief by the increasing importance of 'justice' to royal self-definition and royal revenue, and by the fact that processes of law touched more lives than ever before. These arguments were primarily voiced in relation to discussions of judicial office, but they spilled over and soaked out into all corners of political life and into situations which were not strictly legal, but quasi-judicial: the way a king decided to treat his conquered enemies or unsuccessful rebels; the way in which those in any kind of authority exercised jurisdiction over their inferiors. An individual with the power to exercise *iudicium* was under pressure to find the right balance, model themselves on idealised judges and was obliged to at least consider the persuasive arguments for tempering their judgments with mercy. Indeed, in many ways, the central argument of this book is that in this, the 'legal century', the concept of mercy was just as important (and exalted) as that of justice. This was a culture suffused with the idea of mercy – with images of mercy, exhortations to mercy and models of merciful behaviour – and where mercy was expected to be shown its due.

This final and briefest chapter – perhaps the most unlike the others in terms of the materials it draws upon – reflects on how broadly we can make these claims about mercy. It asks how discussions of mercy could be made popular and popularly seen and discussed. Here, I do not mean 'popular' in the sense of 'fashionable' or a desirable quality, although clearly

Justice and mercy

it was possible for mercy to be presented as such: this book has already argued that, especially when gilded with Roman comparisons and dressed as imperial *clementia*, mercy could be presented as a glorious, magnificent (and even glamorous) act.[1] By 'popular', I mean that ideas about the praiseworthy nature of mercy could be accessed by a wide audience, and that a case for mercy could be moulded into a compelling and persuasive argument, suited to an audience beyond the first rank of leaders of secular or Church hierarchies.

This chapter is more suggestive, more exploratory than the others (though it shies away from the term 'speculative'); it is not intended to be conclusive. There were ways in which fairly complex ideas about the nature and role of mercy might be conveyed to a broader public. One such source, already discussed here, was sermons. But there are others: historians have begun to draw our eyes (quite literally) to the significance of depictions of the process of justice as portrayed in sculpture and art – both sacred and secular.[2] The aim is to show that ideas which we have hitherto encountered in Latin – of the connection between counsel and mercy, the problems of judicial choice – can be found beyond an 'exclusive' Latinate realm, translated into an Anglo-Norman register. In many ways, this may seem obvious: sermons *ad populum* may be preserved in Latin, but they were not preached in it. This chapter ventures into romance-like prose, even *chanson de geste*, to see how mercy (and anxiety around the use of mercy) might make its way out into the world.

The chief example I wish to examine is known under the heading of 'The Four Daughters of God'. As such, it represents a fairly complex textual tradition and a more fiercely complex manuscript tradition. At its heart is an allegory which derives ultimately from the text of Psalms lxxxv.10, 'mercy and truth have met each other, justice and peace have kissed (*misericordia et veritas obviaverunt sibi; iustitia et pax osculatae sunt*)'.[3] Both in early medieval Christian homilies and the Hebrew Midrash, this sentence was significantly expanded: the psalmist's line was worked into an allegory in which mercy, truth, justice and peace became capitalised as Mercy, Truth, Justice and Peace, the names of the four daughters of God.[4] These four daughters came before God, in the period after the Fall, but before the Incarnation, to debate whether the human race deserved salvation. Mercy and Peace, following their names and according to their nature, asked for divine forgiveness for human sin and reconciliation with God. Their sisters, Justice and Truth, objected to any such pardon, demanding the condemnation of humankind according to its sins.[5] The only way that the fundamental differences between them could be resolved – that Mercy and Truth could 'meet' – was in the figure of the incarnate Christ.[6] In this sense, the allegory served as a means both of expounding the idea of *Deus iustus et misericors* and of explaining Christ's historical and salvific role: the damage of the Fall could not be undone without him. Above all, one might observe, this tradition was a demonstration of the flexibility and ingenuity of medieval exegetes, in terms of quite how much they could wring from their scriptural sources. The tradition was significantly adapted and expanded in the twelfth century.

Why examine this tradition – how useful can such a work expounding the basics of Christian doctrine be to a discussion of earthly judges and their role? The Four Daughters of God concerns a divine, not human, act of mercy. Humankind, as much as it features at all, is a subject to be judged – no humans are giving judgment. As such, the different variations upon the tradition have been considered according to the doctrinal instruction they impart – and particularly as an engagement with the idea of the 'Devil's rights' over a sinful human race and the concept of Christ 'ransoming' back humanity. The tradition is rightly understood as addressing the same impetus which lies – at the other end of the scale – behind Anselm's *Cur Deus homo*: the desire to explicate the theological workings behind the historical fact of the Incarnation.[7] But one can also examine this tradition for what it might reveal about popular understandings of judgment, and, in particular, the nature of persuasion in court and judicial decision-making. As an allegory, The Four Daughters of God 'works' – that is to say, serves to make a complex theological question comprehensible – because it reduces abstract ideas to a familiar setting; it renders them in 'human' terms. An allegory, after all, is no good if the representation is as complex as the idea it serves to represent.[8] The discussion of human salvation is put in an earthly court and God is a judge faced with the choice of punishing or forgiving a criminal subject. The framing itself is rather ambiguous: this is an argument being presented in a 'court' in the sense of a household where a king or lord is receiving advice from his *familiares*; but it also has the aspect of a court of law – given the language of advocacy and sentencing attached to the twelfth- and thirteenth-century versions of the story. What is fundamental to the success of the allegory, however, is the principle of opposition: until Christ's intervention, it is impossible for the two sides to come to any agreement. The allegory is predicated on the basis that justice and mercy are inherently difficult to reconcile, because they are based on two different modes of reckoning. A twelfth-century listener (or reader) could not easily have missed that point. Nor would they have been likely to miss the considerable emphasis that The Four Daughters places on persuasion. The variants of the tradition discussed here give the argument for each 'side' (punishment or pardon of humankind) at length; in some cases, the daughters have a second bite of the cherry, responding to the responses to their own arguments. In essence – sometimes implicitly, sometimes as explicitly indicated – this is a matter of counsel: both in terms of which argument is more persuasive and in terms of which argument is founded on the correct set of principles.

Read in this way, the tradition of The Four Daughters of God can reveal rather a lot about how processes of judgment might have been perceived and understood. This is the most difficult and important judgment of all (salvation versus damnation), but it shares the same problem as many of the cases discussed elsewhere in this book: where two entirely opposed courses of judicial action are both compelling and both could be considered the rightful course of action.[9] As in the examples of earthly judges and earthly judgment discussed here, the focus is on the qualities of the judge, rather than the qualities of the offender. Humankind does not plead its case – what matters is judicial advice and judicial choice.

It goes without saying that this is still an allegory which must be treated with caution. Most obviously, the fact that the dilemma of The Four Daughters is resolved through the intervention of Christ means that is hardly a 'guide' to twelfth-century judicial reckoning. The reconciliation of the two opposing points offered here is historically unique. Simply because the language of a human court is used as a means of expressing an aspect of a theological argument is not to be taken as meaning that medieval authors saw human courts as miniature replicas of the divine one – flattening out any differences.[10] With those caveats in mind, and with a healthy sense of caution, The Four Daughters of God can be taken as one means of accessing a 'popular' view of judgment and judicial dilemmas.

The Four Daughters tradition, though far from a new idea, grew considerably in popularity and profile in the twelfth century. It was adapted by both Hugh of St Victor and Bernard of Clairvaux. In Hugh's allegory, found in his homilies on the Psalms (c.1121), Justice lives in heaven with God, while Mercy is exiled to earth with humanity. The two are only balanced when the places are exchanged: Misericordia ascends to heaven to persuade God to forgive man, and Veritas descends to earth in order to compel man to repentance, ultimately permitting a reconciliation with God.[11] In Bernard's version, part of a sermon on the Annunciation, the reconciliation between divine mercy and divine justice is achieved through the Incarnation of Christ, in whom those merciful and punitive principles are combined and reconciled.[12] A third influential treatment, which drew on Bernard's sermon, is the Latin *Rex et Famulus* text.[13]

Love your enemies?

The Four Daughters tradition drew on a 'popular' understanding of the Incarnation as a divine act of mercy towards sinful mankind, who, without divine mercy, did not merit salvation. The topic was also linked to a more general understanding of divine justice as it featured in the scheme of salvation history: the Old Law had been a time of strict divine justice; the Incarnation had ushered in a new dispensation in which God acted mercifully towards humanity.[14] Yet at some point in the near future, it was argued, this merciful period would come to an end, and justice – expressed in the Last Judgment – would return again. The theme of The Four Daughters of God must be understood against this historical and temporal background – a chronological shift between periods of strict justice and periods of abundant mercy.[15] What this tradition also does, moreover, is make explicit some of the dimensions of scholastic debates about the nature of divine justice. It gives them form and shape and presents them in such a way that they can easily be comprehended. Most importantly, and a point I will return to, both sides can argue that their case (punishment or pardon) has merit.

Through the writings of Hugh of St Victor and Bernard of Clairvaux, the idea of the 'Four Daughters' was widely, and rapidly, popularised.[16] Tracking the textual history of the multiple different versions – both in Latin and Anglo-Norman – is a monumental, and sometimes confusing, labour. The story of the four daughters was transformed into Latin verse: for example, it is found alongside various works of pastoral and moral instruction by Walter Map, pseudo-Cyprian, Augustine and Alcuin, including a versified description of the Ten Commandments and seven sacraments, in an early thirteenth-century manuscript from Corpus Christi College Cambridge.[17] But it is the Anglo-Norman tradition which this chapter concentrates on.

The label 'Four Daughters' describes at least seven different thirteenth- and fourteenth-century versions of the story, French and English manuscripts which seem in turn to have drawn on the *Rex et Famulus*.[18] As Hunt set out, in the best and clearest recent work on the tradition, the earliest extant version seems to be c.1200, a work entitled 'De salvatione hominis dialogus'.[19] A slightly modified version of the *Dialogus* is found at the start of the Anglo-Norman poem *Vie de Tobie* (Life of Tobias), a lengthy retelling of the Book of Tobit, composed by Guillaume le clerc, before 1227.[20]

The *Dialogus* itself is worth briefly dwelling on: not least for a suggestion implicit in its title. 'Dialogus' conveys (more obviously than the title 'The Four Daughters') a sense of the content of the work, in that it is centred on discussion and an exchange of opinions about what a just judge should do with humankind. The Anglo-Norman text of the *Dialogus* is discussed below, in relation to Robert Grosseteste's adaptation of The Four Daughters tradition; but the text of the *Dialogus* was also copied with a Latin sermon on the same theme.[21] Examining this sermon also gives us a sense of how (and, crucially, when) these sorts of ideas about judicial mercy and counsel might have been transmitted to the laity, for this is a sermon for Christmas, preached at Christmas on the basis that *misericordia, pax, veritas* and *iustitia* all feature in the liturgy for that time of year.

One slight difference between this sermon and the other interpretations of The Four Daughters considered here is that rather than one judge, the argument over the punishment of humankind is heard before a panel of three judges ('coram divinis personis'), that is, God the Father, the Holy Spirit and Christ. The sermon also adopts an explicitly judicial framing: the daughters are also introduced as 'advocati'; the matter being heard is a 'causa' of *laese maiestatis*; and set out in terms of *allegationes*, for example as Truth attempts to persuade God of the magnitude of the crimes committed by humankind.

What is most striking about this sermon, however, is the way in which each of the daughters attempts to persuade God to follow their counsel: they appeal to scripture. In itself, this results in the rather entertaining spectacle of Truth quoting back the Ten Commandments to their author, reminding God the Father of his Old Testament undertaking to punish the children for the sins of their parents (Exodus xx.5).[22] Scripture is used as a means of reminding or informing God of what his judicial nature should be: that is, God himself must abide by the principle that the Lord does not change his mind (Numbers xxiii.19), and this means that humankind cannot be forgiven. Both sides pile up their arguments, rooted in scripture, before the judge, attempting to convince him to impose or abrogate punishment.[23] Indeed, Justice appeals to the judges to give a punishment in line with what they have previously commanded.[24] In effect, we can see Justice articulating a problem which would be familiar to earthly judges (and to those who observed earthly judges): the worry about mercy is that it is asking judges to break the established rules. But in addition to being a little like watching students quote a professor's own book back at them, the way in which the four daughters of the sermon offer choice scriptural citations to God resembles the way in which earthly judges were exhorted to look to scripture for guidance and example.

Once Peace has spoken, the sermon then goes on to describe the deliberative part of the judicial process. The ultimate resolution follows the formula of The Four Daughters story: God the Son, the third part of the Trinity, assumes human form and descends to earth, his birth and subsequent death bridging the gap between the two principles and the four sisters. But the sermon spends some time addressing the period of judicial uncertainty and the judicial impasse before Christ's intervention. This is emphasised by the fact that the author of the sermon has set up three judges (explicitly labelled Pater, Verbum, Spiritus Sanctus), rather than a single figure of a lordly judge. The judges, having heard the testimony of all four speakers, consider the 'consilium pietatis' and 'cogitabant cogitaciones'. What becomes apparent is that the bench is split. It is the Father who finds the argument of Veritas and Justice most convincing – that anything other than punishment would show misjudgment/partiality (he would be *suspectus*); and considering Truth and Justice to be familiar and close companions to him. The Holy Spirit, on the other side, tends to favour the argument of Mercy and Peace. The Holy Spirit reasons that, as it is a spirit of wisdom, and therefore its part is to be 'dulcis et benignus', it must therefore adopt the course advocated by Mercy.[25] The identity of each judge is bound up in the decision – a decision over what judicial course one follows is also a decision about the kind of judge one is. With the two – Father and Holy Spirit – in this position, the matter cannot be resolved and only the entry of the Son into the proceedings is able to realise 'equitas'.[26]

While there seem to have been multiple vernacular versions of the legend circulating in England in the early thirteenth century,[27] one particularly important adaptation of the legend (and perhaps the most influential in subsequent centuries) was Robert Grosseteste's *Le Château d'amour*. *Le Château d'amour* is not only concerned with The Four Daughters: it presents much more Christian history. It describes, in largely allegorical terms, the creation and fall of man, the Incarnation, the redemption of mankind and the Last Judgment.[28] The text is notoriously difficult to date and interpret, and various possible audiences have been suggested, ranging from the sons of Simon de Montfort to the first Franciscans in Oxford.[29] Positing a Franciscan audience would put it in the 1230s; it might also blur the boundaries of 'lay' and 'theological' usage. It might be read as a work in Anglo-Norman intended for new 'aristocratic' members of the order; alternatively, or perhaps in addition, it might have served as a preaching tool, a piece of *praedicabilia*, which could be used by Franciscans to convey some complex ideas about justice, mercy and divine judgment to audiences.[30] The composition in Anglo-Norman suggests a particular (and relatively elevated) social group and, one might infer, a group likely to wield power, among them those most likely to be in a position to give judgment. Moreover, it also serves to recreate the language of pleading (and, to some extent, even the sound) of the English royal courts.[31]

The chief advantage of examining Grosseteste's text, moreover, is that (unlike the anonymous *Dialogus*), we can read a text which we know to be the work of someone who engaged with arguments about judicial behaviour, mercy and justice, at both an 'academic-scholastic' and a pastoral level. Grosseteste, following the tradition, begins from the basics of Psalms lxxxv: setting his scene in the household of king whose servant has transgressed and who is thus condemned to severe punishment. More striking still, however, is the extent to which Grosseteste employs the techniques of deliberative rhetoric to reveal the conflict between pleaders and principles. For many years, he writes, the arguments of Justice and Truth have found favour with the king, and the servant has been condemned to punishment. The situation changes only when the king's son (that is, Christ), hears the pleas of Mercy and is moved by her oratory:

> Mercy has so moved me by the case she has presented that I have great pity for the servant. Mercy cries for mercy, and she will be heard first. I will do all she desires, and will reconcile her to Truth.[32]

This is an argument about whose counsel is more persuasive. Peace urges her Father to listen to her counsel above that of her sisters, Truth and Justice.[33] Similarly, the heated nature of the argument – the rhetorical battle for the upper hand – is found in Grosseteste's source material, the Latin text *Rex et Famulus*. There Iustitia is described as 'inflammata', and Misericordia speaks 'ejulans et clamans' (wailing and crying out), groaning and supplicating before the Father while making her appeal. Both Iustitia and Misericordia demand to know whom the Father will side with; implying that if He forsakes their particular counsel, the effect will be to disown her as a daughter.[34] The parties are left 'in gravi dissensione', apparently irreconcilable.[35]

In the *Château*, it is Peace who persuades Christ to take human form and redeem the sinful servant. It is due which is emphasised when Justice is introduced: 'to each she gives in wisdom to each whatever lawfully he ought to have (*A chescun done par saveir/Kant ke il deit part dreit aveir*)', and in her speech.[36] Christ, however, is moved more by persuasive rhetoric than any concept of due. The oration made by Peace cannot challenge the arguments in favour of continued punishment by appealing to the idea of mercy as owed to sinful humanity, and so instead her argument turns on a question of hierarchy, and that Truth and Justice must rightly be subordinate to the demands of Peace and Mercy:

> But why were Truth and Justice established if not to keep the peace? Justice has no other calling than to preserve peace. Should I then be denied when all things were made for me and set down for my existence? Yet I am not preserved at all if Mercy is not heard.[37]

Love your enemies?

Grosseteste's formulation here goes some way towards encapsulating a familiar theme in scholastic writings: why should it be that mercy is 'exalted' above justice? Through allegory, Grosseteste's virtuous interlocutors answer the question simply: because the purpose of justice is to keep the peace. If justice attempts to preserve that peace through violent or excessively severe actions, then it endangers the thing it strives to preserve. Here *pax* is synonymous with *misericordia*. Grosseteste offers his audience an extensive and careful look at divine justice: a demonstration of quite how much of the complicated relationship between mercy and justice could be made accessible to 'lay' audiences. And, as with other texts in this tradition, even the great 'lord' himself must have difficulty ruling between the equally persuasive counsels of justice and mercy.

From all these variations on The Four Daughters theme, we might assemble the case for mercy on 'popular' display. In terms of reach and audience, that case is clearest for Grosseteste's *Le Château*: enormously popular for a century or so following its composition, its appeal was broad (manuscripts in the possession of both monastic houses and lay individuals).[38] In the later fourteenth century, it inspired English translations, including texts which do not adapt the entirety of the poem, but focus exclusively on the story of The Four Daughters.[39] These texts have been well studied. But the transmission of the *De salvatione hominis dialogus*, too, reveals something about the 'popularity' of mercy and how readers might have understood or categorised the *Dialogus*, in terms of the texts it is transmitted with. There are apparent limitations here: we have only three thirteenth-century manuscripts, and, of course, the fact that a text was copied with other texts is hardly probative of anything. But it does at least contribute to a picture where judicial choices could be encountered in many contexts; where 'mercy' was a broad and commonplace topic of conversation.

In British Library, Arundel MS 292 (a late thirteenth-century manuscript), the *Dialogus* is bound with texts that span the boundaries of devotional, secular and moral literature, in English, Latin and French,[40] along with a rhymed sermon in Anglo-Norman attributed to Stephen Langton. This is Langton's 'Bele Aaliz', his adaptation of a French carol about the 'beautiful Alice' for use in a sermon. Langton's rhymed sermon explains that the 'Alice' of the song is an allegory for the Virgin Mary, and goes on to enumerate her virtuous qualities.[41] In Cambridge, Corpus Christi College MS 50, another late thirteenth-century manuscript, the *Dialogus* was copied with a number of Anglo-Norman romances; including *Amis et Amiloun* and *Gui de Warewic*. Finally, British Library, Add. MS 45103 (probably written at

Christ Church, Canterbury), includes a number of Anglo-Norman works such as *La Petite Philosophie* (a vernacular translation of the encylopaedic *Imago mundi* attributed to Honorius of Autun)[42] and part of *La Seinte Resureccion* (a play charting the story of Christ's resurrection).[43] One can imagine how a compiler at Canterbury in the late thirteenth century might have understood these texts as fitting together – works translating (both literally and metaphorically) specialised knowledge to a lay audience.[44] The intersection between romance, secular verse and theology is evident across these manuscripts, where ethical instruction adapted to fill a variety of forms, and formed according to its audiences.

A vengeance culture?

The case for 'popular' discussion of mercy set out here may seem at odds with some recent verdicts on twelfth-century England. Paul Hyams, for example, has made the case for understanding that world as a 'vengeance' culture (or better still, a culture of enmity), in which matters of self-help and personal sleights were still of paramount importance, and where enmity still remained commonplace and accepted as a feature of the social landscape.[45] Hyams's point was that we misunderstand the social world of Anglo-Norman and Angevin England if we assume the transformation of law in the twelfth century meant a switch to a bloodless world of legal fine-tuning and sophistry. In fact, the experience of being wronged and seeking 'justice' remained potent and passionate. It was also part of popular culture, as 'men and women listened attentively in their leisure hours to tales of laudable vengeance taken on villains on behalf of the wronged of all descriptions'.[46]

Vengeance and enmity and their legitimacy and status in the twelfth century have generated a great deal of recent work: it is not the topic of this book.[47] My point is that arguments for mercy could be potent and passionate, too. Scholastic definitions, with which this book began, inevitably give the sense of being rarefied and remote. But when the case for mercy was urgent (whether in pleading for salvation or pleading for royal pardon), *misericordia* could be just as rough and ready as revenge. There was space for both mercy and vengeance in public life.[48] Indeed, I would go as far as to suggest that if we are to envisage a 'popular' culture of vengeance, then this also requires us to recognise its connection to mercy. We must recognise that as Hyams unpacks the multiple possible meanings of 'vengeance', in a certain light vengeance might appear to have the same shape and outline as certain definitions of justice. Vengeance as the return of wrong for wrong, an injury done to satisfy an injury sustained, has much in common with a basic notion of justice-as-due.[49] Indeed, 'vindicta' could be folded up as one of the subordinate parts of *iustitia*. And insistence on the return of injury for injury is only so insistent because of a fear that the punishment meted out will be less sharp than the original injury warranted.

This chapter has wandered far (perhaps unforgivably far) beyond the world of Anglo-Norman and Angevin judges. But it has done so in the hopes of demonstrating how questions of judicial judgment were connected to the 'real world'. Just as (as has long been noted) speculative theological thought made space for legitimate vengeance, violence and punishment when ordered towards an appropriate end, so too did a less speculative, more 'popular' tradition recognise that mercy and intercession had a role to play in helping determine when punishment was justified and when it was not. This is a point one could expand with reference to many more texts (and *chansons de geste*) beyond The Four Daughters of God.[50] It may be too much of a stretch to characterise Anglo-Norman and Angevin England as a 'mercy culture' (for the role of mercy was hardly settled), but it was a 'counsel culture', which left space for mercy to make itself heard.

Notes

1 For example, William of Poitiers's praise for William I's *clementia* in the *Gesta Guillelmi*; and Gillingham, '1066'.
2 For example, Anthony Musson, 'Controlling human behaviour? The last judgment in late medieval art and architecture', in A. D. Boboc (ed.), *Theorizing Legal Personhood in Late Medieval England* (Leiden, 2015), 166–91; see also the approach of Paul Hyams, 'What did Henry III think in bed and in French about kingship and anger?', in B. H. Rosenwein (ed.), *Anger's Past: The Social Uses of an Emotion in the Middle Ages* (London, 1998), 92–125.
3 Hope Traver, 'The Four Daughters of God: A Study of the Versions of this Allegory with Especial Reference to those in Latin, French, and English' (unpublished PhD dissertation, Bryn Mawr College, 1907).
4 This personification of the virtues and the debate between them owes much to the *conflictus* genre developed in the earlier middle ages, in which vices and virtues exchanged arguments according to the rhetorical device of *prosopopoeia*. See Gregory the Great, *Moralia in Iob*, 31.90, 3:1611–12.
5 Pseudo-Bede, *Homiliae*, 3, PL.94.505–7; for the Midrashic influence, see Rebecca Moore, 'Jewish influence on Christian biblical interpretation: Hugh of St Victor and "The Four Daughters of God"', in Craig Evans (ed.), *Of Scribes and Sages: Early Jewish Interpretation and Transmission of Scripture* (Edinburgh, 2004), 148–58.

6 The Incarnation was not the only instance in salvation history at which medieval theologians detected, and drew attention to, conflict within divine judgment. The tradition of 'four wills in Christ' describes the struggle between 'merciful' and 'just' urges in the incarnate Christ (not to be confused with later scholastic discussions of the possible contrariety of Christ's 'two wills', i.e. human and divine). This focused on two moments in scriptural history: Christ's reaction to the foreseen destruction of Jerusalem and Christ's anticipation of his own suffering and death. At these two moments Christ had struggled to choose between what was strictly just and what was merciful. The most comprehensive treatment is found in a short treatise by Hugh of St Victor, *De quatuor voluntatibus Christi*, PL.176.841–5. Robert Pullen enquires in his *Sentences* whether there was any conflict between Christ's future role as judge of the living and the dead and the charity he felt towards his persecutors during his lifetime; *Sententiarum*, 4.10, PL.186.817–18; it is also discussed by Alan of Lille: Nikolaus Häring, 'A Commentary on the Our Father by Alan of Lille', *Analecta Cisterciensia* 30 (1975), 166, and in several sermons by William of Auvergne, *Sermones de Tempore*, ed. F. Morenzoni, CCCM 230 (2 vols, Turnhout, 2010–11), 2:270, 485–95; 270(A), 496–8; 271, 499–501; 272, 502–5.

7 See J. Leclercq, 'Nouveau temoin du conflit des filles de Dieu', *Revue bénédictine* 58 (1948), 110–24, and, more recently, C. William Marx, *The Devil's Rights and the Redemption in the Literature of Medieval England* (Cambridge, 1995), 65–79.

8 Cf. the preface to the version of *Rex et Famulus* in BL, Harley MS 309, which introduces the story as 'fabulous, but not false' (*fabulose non tamen mendose*), and repeats that it is 'non fabulum sed rem gestam'. T. Hunt, '"The Four Daughters of God": a textual contribution', *Archives d'histoire doctrinale et littéraire du moyen âge* 48 (1981), 311.

9 Moreover, this is not a matter of determining guilt: humankind has already been found guilty. The entire space of the poem is thus given over not to procedure or determination, but to an argument over due punishment.

10 This is the difficulty with the kind of argument which (for example) explains Anselm's use of the terms 'debitum' and 'satisfactio' in the *Proslogion* purely as a product of Anselm's 'feudal' context, modelling God as (simply) a great landowner. That correspondence is far too neat and misses the theological starting point. See G. R. Evans, *Anselm* (London, 1989), 79; and Richard Campbell, 'The conceptual roots of Anselm's soteriology', in D. E. Luscombe and G. R. Evans (eds), *Anselm: Aosta, Bec and Canterbury* (Sheffield, 1996), 256–63.

11 Hugh of St Victor, *Homiliae*, PL.177.621–5; cf. Traver, 'The Four Daughters', 12.

12 Bernard of Clairvaux, *In annuntiatione dominica, Sermo* 1, in *S. Bernardi opera*, vol. 5, *Sermones II*, ed. J. Leclercq and H. Rochais (Rome, 1968), 13.

13 A work attributed to the Victorine Peter of Poitiers, and influential in subsequent centuries. Sister Mary Immaculate [Creek], 'The Four Daughters of God in the *Gesta Romanorum* and the *Court of Sapience*', *Proceedings of the Modern Language Association* 57:4 (1942), 951–65.

14 Traver, 'The Four Daughters', 26, 63, 87, emphasises the importance of Anselm's *Cur Deus homo* in giving philosophical shape to this temporal scheme.
15 For this scheme see B. E. Whalen, *Dominion of God: Christendom and Apocalypse in the Middle Ages* (Cambridge, 2009), esp. 1–8 and 72–124.
16 For example, Peter Comestor's sermon, *De adventu domini*, PL.198.1736-7; a similar anonymous twelfth-century sermon is found in BL, Royal MS 6 A XIII, fos 173r–174r. For the later history of the legend in English, K. Sajavaara, *The Middle English Translations of Robert Grosseteste's Chateau d'Amour* (Helsinki, 1967).
17 Cambridge, Corpus Christi College, Parker Library, CCCC MS 481, fos 566–70; see M. R. James, *A Descriptive Catalogue of the Manuscripts in the Library of Corpus Christi College Cambridge* (2 vols, Cambridge, 1912), 2:424–32. I also note another possible variant on the tradition, found in the sermons of Peter of Blois, which takes a broadly similar theme: a king who must decide what pardon to show to sinners and how to reward the just. Here, Peter introduces *three* daughters to advise the king in his judgment – in the forms of Faith, Hope and Charity. The focus here, however, is on explaining to the audience for the sermon what they ought to do to make themselves worthy of receiving mercy – concluding with advice to read the books of Moses and the prophets, the apostles and the gospels, the Church Fathers, and ending with the Augustinian advice 'habe charitatem et fac quidquid vis'. Peter of Blois, *Sermo* LXV, PL.207.767B. Just as in The Four Daughters tradition, the 'Three Daughters' sermon also emphasises the role of counsel in persuading the king/judge to mercy.
18 For the seven different versions, as identified by A. Långfors, 'Le theme des quatre filles de Dieu', in 'Notice sur le numéro 14886 des manuscrits latins de la Bibliothèque Nationale et autres bibliothèques', *Notices et extraits* 31:2 (1886), 293–313. The text of *Rex et Famulus* is printed in Hunt, 'Four Daughters', appendix I, 308–12.
19 Printed in Francis Michel, *Libri psalmorum versio antiqua gallica* (Oxford, 1860), 364–8; Jean Rivière, *Le dogme de la rédemption au début du moyen âge* (Paris, 1934), 339. Michel attributes this text to Stephen Langton, but this seems to have been a misreading of the rubric: see Hunt, 'Four Daughters', 288–9.
20 Hunt, 'Four Daughters', 292. For the *Vie de Tobie* as an 'Old Testament vernacularisation', a piece of literature which blends biblical history with romance conventions, see Jocelyn Wogan-Browne, 'How to marry your wife with chastity, honour and fin' amor in thirteenth-century England', *Thirteenth Century England* 9 (2001), 147–50. Three late thirteenth-century manuscripts of the *Vie de Tobie* written in England have been preserved.
21 This is Cambridge, University Library, Kk.4.20.
22 Hunt, 'Four Daughters', 295.
23 For example, Misericordia quotes Psalms lxxxviii.48–49; Jeremiah xviii.7–8; Psalms xii.1; Veritas, Numbers xxiii.1; Genesis xxii.18.
24 Hunt, 'Four Daughters', 297, appealing to Psalms cxviii.4.
25 *Ibid.*, 298.

26 Ibid., 299–300.
27 See the example from British Library, Stowe MS 240, printed in Ferdinand Holthausen (ed.), *Vices and Virtues, Being a Soul's Confession of Its Sins, with Reason's Description of the Virtues: A Middle English Dialogue of about 1200 A.D.* (London, 1967), 112–16.
28 See E. A. Mackie, 'Robert Grosseteste's Anglo-Norman treatise on the loss and restoration of creation, commonly known as *Le Château d'amour*: an English prose translation', in Maura O'Caroll (ed.), *Robert Grosseteste and the Beginnings of a British Theological Tradition* (Rome, 2003), 151–79.
29 E. A. Mackie, 'Scribal intervention and the question of audience: editing *Le Château d'amour*', in E. A. Mackie and J. Goering (eds), *Editing Robert Grosseteste: Papers Given at the Thirty-Sixth Annual Conference on Editorial Problems* (Toronto, 2003), 61–77.
30 J. McEvoy, *Robert Grosseteste* (Oxford, 2000), 153, suggests Grosseteste intended it to be sung. The point about use as a preaching tool may be reinforced by the fact that The Four Daughters part of *Le Château* could also stand alone, removed from the context of the longer poem – as it does in Oxford, Bodleian Library Digby 86. See M. Corrie, 'The compilation of Oxford, Bodleian Library, MS Digby 86', *Medium Aevum* 66:2 (1997), 236–49.
31 Paul Brand, 'The language of the English legal profession: the emergence of a distinctive legal lexicon in insular French', in R. Ingham (ed.), *The Anglo-Norman Language and its Contexts* (Woodbridge, 2010), 94–101.
32 'Tant m'ad meü Misericorde/Par reson ke ele a mustré/Kar de le serf ai grand pité./Misericorde merci crie,/Primerement serra oïe./Trestut sun voleir ferai,/A Verité l'acorderai.' *Le Château*, trans. Mackie, 'Robert Grosseteste's Anglo-Norman treatise', 165.
33 *Le Château*, lines139–42: 'Bel Pere, fete le, ore oi merveilie,/Ke ma sor vus cunseilie/A deffere vostre feature/E dampner vostre creature'; cf. lines 212–14.
34 Hunt, 'Four Daughters', appendix I, 309.
35 Ibid., 209.
36 *Le Château*, lines 335–6, trans. Mackie, 'Robert Grosseteste's Anglo-Norman treatise', 164.
37 *Le Château*, lines 387–96: 'Mes purquei serreit assise/Ne Verité ne Justise/Si pur la Pès non garder?/Justise ne ad autre mestier/Mes ke la Pès seit sauvee./Serrai jo donkes refusee/Kant tuz biens sunt pur me fet/E pur mei aveir retret./Mes sauvee ne su jeo mie/Se Misericorde n'est oïe.' Trans. Mackie, 'Robert Grosseteste's Anglo-Norman treatise', 164.
38 For a discussion of some of these, Marx, *Devil's Rights*, 74–5. Mackie, 'Robert Grosseteste's Anglo-Norman treatise', 151–4, addresses how the arrangement of the text changes from early to later manuscripts.
39 Four Middle English verse translations are printed in Sajavaara, *Middle English Translations*; see also the discussion in G. Shuffleton (ed.), *Codex Ashmole 61: A Compilation of Popular Middle English Verse* (Kalamazoo, MI, 2008), no. 26, 'The King and His Four Daughters'.

40 Including the Credo, Pater Noster and Ave Maria (in English); Apollonius of Tyre and the Fables of Odo of Cheriton (in Latin); Disticha of Cato (in French).
41 For further discussion of this point, Karl Reichel, 'Plotting the map of medieval oral literature', in Karl Reichel (ed.), *Medieval Oral Literature* (Berlin, 2012), 43–4.
42 For which, see *La petite philosophie: An Anglo-Norman Poem of the Thirteenth Century*, ed. W. H. Thethewey, Anglo-Norman Text Society 1 (Oxford, 1939). For its significance, see P. Damien-Grint, *The New Historians of the Twelfth-Century Renaissance: Inventing Vernacular Authority* (Woodbridge, 1999), ch. 1, esp. 7–8.
43 For the text: *La Seinte Resureccion*, ed. T. A. Jenkins, J. M. Manly, M. K. Pope and Jean Wright, Anglo-Norman Text Society 4 (Oxford, 1943).
44 In the two other manuscripts identified by Hunt, Cambridge, University Library, Kk.4.20, and British Library, MS Harley 1801, the *Dialogus* is bound with penitential, theological and didactic works. For a list of the manuscripts of Grosseteste's *Le Château*, see Mackie, 'Robert Grosseteste's Anglo-Norman treatise', 159–60.
45 Hyams, *Rancor*, esp. 265–6.
46 *Ibid.*, 265, see also 59–68.
47 As a starting point see W. Miller, 'In defense of revenge', in B. A. Hanawalt and D. Wallace (eds), *Medieval Crime and Social Control* (Minneapolis, MN, 1999), 70–89, and R. W. Kaeuper, 'Vengeance and mercy in chivalric mentalité', in T. B. Lambert and David Rollason (eds), *Peace and Protection in the Middle Ages* (Durham, 2009), 168–80.
48 Hyams, *Rancor*, 111–12.
49 *Ibid.*, 45–6.
50 For example, the tradition of *La Venjance Nostre-Seigneur*, dating from at least the twelfth century, a story about vengeance taken against the inhabitants of Jerusalem by Roman emperors but which (in all of its versions) has moments at which mercy is counselled, sought and occasionally granted. *The Oldest Version of the Twelfth-Century Poem La Venjance Nostre-Seigneur*, ed. L. A. T. Gryrting (Baltimore, MD, 1952).

9

Conclusion

Justice, mercy and the ordering of things

Sometime in the 1220s or 1230s, Robert Grosseteste offered the observation that 'there is no true mercy except ordered mercy' (*non est vera misericordia nisi sit ordinata*).[1] It is not hard to appreciate the concerns that led Grosseteste to make such a comment. *Misericordia* was a valid and vital principle for the judge, but the challenge lay in its realisation. Mercy needed its place defined before it could be implemented appropriately. Unbounded mercy was a recipe for disaster – for the offender, the judge and the polity. Yet a concept of 'ordered mercy' might also appear something of a contradiction in terms, not least when set next to the Augustinian injunction to 'love and do what you will'. How then, could mercy be kept in order? Through providing those who judged with models to follow, and correction when they erred. For Grosseteste – as for many others – it was the duty of those who understood the nature and role of mercy to advise those whose job it was to sit in judgment. And in each judgment, the judge was obliged to make the singular choice between justice and mercy anew, to weigh, once again, a conflicting body of precedents, circumstances and counsels. At the most basic level, this book has sought to demonstrate the considerable level of interest in and engagement with judicial choices and judicial ethics in the years 1100 to 1250. This went far beyond concerns about rapacious judges and administrative corruption. Long before the codification of rules of conduct for common law judges, judicial conduct was under scrutiny in terms of its moral choices. This moral choice was expressed primarily as a matter of determining between two different courses: between severity and mercy for offenders. Of course, judicial virtue had mattered prior to 1100, but the prominence of judgment and justice in daily life meant that after the legal

Conclusion

reforms of the twelfth century, measuring and modifying judicial choice mattered more than ever before.

This book began by talking about a 'renaissance' and a 'crisis'. Those are two loaded – and perhaps also unhelpful – terms: they are all allusion, little precision. But, to my mind at least, there is no doubt that the arguments in England over justice and mercy between c.1100 and c.1250 can be described under those headings. There was a 'renaissance' in the sense that new intellectual techniques of analysis and argument were used to understand and attempt to reshape the order of human society: all the authors discussed here were concerned with the particular question of how to make judgment 'better'.[2] 'Theological' arguments were transformed into practical counsels; classical and scriptural texts were analysed to see what insight they might bring to profound and pressingly earthly problems. And while the discussions highlighted here took place in England, were applied to English judges (in common law courts, in Church courts, in all fora and places of judgment), they were discussions which tied England into the rest of Europe – and, in particular, the schools of Europe. England was a stage on which particular developments of arguments were played out under a particular set of conditions. The developing common law made the conditions distinct (see, for example, Walter Map's characterisation of English regulation versus a French laissez-faire attitude to justice), but the language used to describe judges and the analytical approach was rooted in a common language, traceable to a scholastic tradition.

There was also a 'crisis', in the sense that there was considerable uncertainty, both personal and political, about how judgment was rightly and virtuously to be exercised. Judgment – and the choice of how to treat an offender – had implications both for the judge's own soul and for the political community. Mercy cut both ways. The stakes were high. This sense of anxiety is evident in the doomful examples that authors put before their readers: Heli, Phinehas, even Daniel, were cases showing how, when judgment was wrong, its consequences could be catastrophic. This, in turn, is why one of the arguments of this book is that medieval historians need to treat references to 'iustitia et misericordia' seriously. As a pair, they are more substantial than they might otherwise seem when they pop up in the course of reading a *speculum principis*, a chronicle report or an exegetical aside. Invocations of justice and mercy are easily dismissed as platitudes, meaningless injunctions to virtue, side dishes set next to the meat of real argument. If we pass over these references, however, dismissing them as mere repetitions of an old and familiar idea that mercy and justice belong together, we miss their significance in relation to their legal context. The twelfth century overflows with advice for judges, advice for those setting about the most difficult of earthly tasks – because of both its heavenly and earthly ramifications. That advice was more urgent and necessary than ever before when the role of the judge became increasingly prominent in secular business, and as churchmen started having official judicial roles forced upon them (whether as royal servants, as papal judges-delegate or as the 'judge' in a penitential model). It was a personally dangerous role.

Chronological considerations

This has not, primarily, been a study of change. Indeed, I have argued that for over a century, discussion of judgment continued to revolve around the same pole: the conflict between the same two principles, *iustitia* and *misericordia* (expressed through their many cognate terms, constructed in multiple different ways). But focusing on this argument necessarily risks flattening out certain aspects of change and alteration over time. On the surface, there may appear to be relatively little difference between the letters urging lords to mercy written by Anselm at the turn of the twelfth century and those of Robert Grosseteste a century and a half later. Just as Anselm in the mid-1090s exhorted Count Robert II of Flanders to rule with justice and mercy, so too could Grosseteste do the same when writing to Simon de Montfort, almost a century and a half later.[3] As Anselm writes to abbots, counselling them to receive back the now-penitent servants and monks who once wronged them, and reminds his correspondents that mercy should surpass judgment,[4] so Grosseteste could do the same. And, indeed, we should expect to see these similarities: not least because both authors were constructing their arguments from the same scriptural and patristic building blocks. But the legal structures in which they operated, the conditions, times and places in which Anselm engaged with the law were significantly different from those in which Grosseteste operated. Procedure was becoming better defined; as arguments about the judge's right to dispense and the circumstances in which he might do so were elaborated on, assumptions about the legal literacy of those in the Church (and the legal capacity of those assisting bishops and abbots) changed. The same is fundamentally true in the case of 'secular' judges, as procedure became more codified, more explicitly worked out. This did not limit the royal ability to dispense mercy: nor did it quell royal desires to abrogate the law where desirable or convenient. But it did place those desires under greater scrutiny: after 1215, in particular, the arbitrary exercise of royal will in connection with the exercise of justice operated in changed

Conclusion

terrain.⁵ Henry II harnessed the power of justice as an engine of rule; for his successors (as we saw in Chapter 7), this was a double-edged sword. The power that came from royal control over the mechanisms of justice meant that justice became a standard against which kingship could be measured. Fundamentally, there was still considerable scope for mercy to be exercised – both by kings and by royal judges. The development of procedure and proliferation of legal texts did not make mercy 'easier' to do, or justice easier to hand down. Indeed, memories (even confected memories) of good 'old' law were used to critique new examples of bad judgment and bad judicial behaviour.⁶ One might think, for example, of Andrew Horn's early fourteenth-century *Mirror of Justices* approvingly citing Alfred the Great's decision to hang forty-four judges in a single year for giving false judgments.⁷

Surveying some of the material covered here – particularly laments about judicial partiality – it is worth dwelling on where this book fits into a longue-durée argument about the development of accountability. As a topic, the growth of accountability in medieval governance stretches across the twelfth and thirteenth centuries, and indeed outruns the period covered by this book. Its study was re-energised by Bisson, and more recently discussed (especially in relation to England) by John Sabapathy. Sabapathy has sketched out a developing (and sometimes tense) relationship between attempts to cultivate the character of those in government to make them fit to hold office and the hammering out of statutes to restrain them, biting laws to curb bad conduct, recognising that relying on the goodness of administrators' own hearts would not be enough to curb corruption.⁸ Where do these merciful or unmerciful twelfth-century judges fit into that model? I would position anxieties about judicial mercy as adjacent to concerns about accountability of officers, but not of a piece. There are some obvious synergies. Debates about the place of mercy in judgment were inspired by some of the same concerns, most obviously how personal virtue was brought to bear on 'public' matters. Certainly, authors worrying about judicial decision-making were also concerned about how best to inculcate virtuous behaviour (that, after all, was the ultimate aim of Gerald's *De principis*, the text from which I began – how can one teach little princes to grow up to be good judges?). But discussions of how 'merciful' a judge should be did not ultimately stem from concerns about judicial wickedness and the prevalence of vice. Bad judges, judges who lacked virtue, of course, would tend to corruption. But a well-intentioned judge might also give the 'wrong' judgment, and this might be the more worrying scenario for those concerned with pastoral care and the ordering of society. Judicial corruption could warp punishment: for example, where 'partiality' took the form of a judge accepting money in return for a pardon; where the powerful could pay to have their crimes overlooked or wiped away (Walter Map had seen plenty of such cases). But, for the most part, the problem in this book can be described more simply: when good judges make bad decisions. Good men might 'forget' to be merciful; the failure to pass an appropriate sentence was – in the eyes of the authors considered here – rarely deliberate or vicious, and often held no particular advantage for the judge himself. The biblical figure of Heli, for example, was not characterised as corrupt, but foolish, ill-advised, hasty. These authors worried less about corrupt judges than corruption through bad counsel: especially where persuasion was brought to bear, when dangerous leniency could be reconfigured as praiseworthy justice. The right course of behaviour, and the right way for a judge to be, was in itself in dispute.

In one important sense, nothing changed between 1100 and 1250, for there was no 'answer' about how to satisfactorily combine mercy and justice; nor was there consensus about the circumstances in which mercy was to be preferred over justice (or vice versa). But no one was looking for such a broad or general solution; the only answer given was to consider the particular circumstances of every offence. It would have been a foolish counsellor who advised a prince, bishop, earl or abbot that one judicial solution fitted all judicial dilemmas.

What did change – and the reason why c.1250 marks a finishing point for this study – was the intellectual background and the intellectual organisation of justice and mercy. With the reception of Aristotle's *Ethics* in the schools of Europe, new, Aristotelian ideas of equity (*epikeia*) meant the act of judgment was fundamentally reconfigured. The individual moral choice of the judge – between justice and mercy – became less significant. One is naturally wary of overreaching arguments that suggest that Aristotle changed 'everything' about medieval thought; not least when sometimes an Aristotelian change may rather denote the adoption of new terminology than a wholescale intellectual revolution. Nonetheless, Odon Lottin's position that the reception of Aristotle did fundamentally change medieval ways of thinking about justice has a basic truth to it, and 1250 marks a decisive shift in the way in which the relationship between *iustitia* and *misericordia* was conceptualised. What follows is necessarily only a brief sketch.

Firsthand knowledge of Aristotle's works had been increasing in western Europe since the mid-twelfth century.[9] The *Ethica vetus*, a translation of the second and third books of the *Nicomachean Ethics*, had been in circulation

Conclusion

since the late twelfth century, and the *Ethica nova*, a translation of the first book, from the early thirteenth century.[10] These two texts, however, did not cover what Aristotle had to say about justice, or about its moderation. In order to explore the core of Aristotle's teachings on justice, the fifth book of the *Ethics* was required, a text which only became accessible to most European readers with Robert Grosseteste's complete translation, c.1246/7. It was this translation (and, indeed, Grosseteste's accompanying commentary and his distillation of Greek commentaries on the text) which provided 'a flying start to the whole study of the *Ethics* in the schools'.[11] Aristotle's discussion of justice provided thirteenth-century theologians with a radically new structure for the understanding of justice. The *Nicomachean Ethics* did not employ the term 'cardinal' virtues, nor describe a group of four virtues privileged above all others.[12] Aristotle presented his own solution to the broad implications of 'justice' by dividing the concept into two – general and the particular (*iustitia generalis, iustitia particularis* in Latin terminology).[13] General justice describes the just, or virtuous life; particular justice refers to the rightful distribution of goods – be that rewards or punishment, honour or money. It is into this second category that the justice of the courts (*iustitia legalis*) falls. Particular justice is then divided into three further categories, distributive, rectificatory and reciprocal.[14] What is most important here is to recognise that Aristotle's distributive justice – that justice which 'when distributing goods, treats equals equally and unequals proportionately unequally according to merit'[15] – is fundamentally in accordance with a definition of justice as a return of proportionate due.[16] Aquinas, for example, considering Aristotle's discussion of justice, recognised its agreement with a 'Ciceronian' definition of justice as *suum cuique tribuens*.[17]

Yet, for all this acknowledged continuity, Lottin was right to say that the reception of Aristotle did fundamentally alter the way in which medieval authors dealt with justice, and, further, with the relationship between justice and mercy. This was the result of two distinctive innovations brought about by Aristotelian thought.[18] The first is general, and stems from the orientation of Aristotle's political philosophy: it is ordered primarily towards the good of the community. This is a fact noted by Albertus Magnus in his *Commentary on the Sentences*, when discussing the distinctiveness of Aristotelian justice:

> Justice, however, because it is not predicated absolutely, is of another order: it falls under the order of the civil law, namely, statutes and votes, and its cases vary accordingly. And therefore it concerns the order of the civic

community, and it seems that Aristotle follows this order in his *Ethics*, as is clearly apparent in the new translation.[19]

Aristotle's legal justice has no particular regard for the soul of the person who is involved in passing judgment. Justice is ordered according to the 'public community'.[20] Certainly *communis utilitas* was a crucial aspect of justice in the period before the reception of Aristotle, particularly emphasised in the definitions provided by Cicero; twelfth-century authors had not ignored the social and civil consequences of justice. But they had begun from a discussion of the judge's salvation. Aristotle's perspective, however, cuts out the measurement of 'justice' according to its impact on the judge's own soul. It effectively excludes the relevance of reciprocal mercy – the principle that every sentence the judge passes on earth must be accounted for on the Day of Judgment. This principle had set up the possibility for conflict when choosing between strict justice, beneficial for the realm (for example, in the capital punishment of an offender), and the mercy – the pardon or reprieve – which was an act of personal virtue for the judge. Public good, however, is always the motivation of the Aristotelian judge: thus Albertus Magnus recognises him as acting 'propter bonum civile'.[21] The separation of 'general' justice, i.e. justice as a virtue, and 'particular' justice, the business of giving legal judgment, to some extent excluded any consideration of how calculations about personal virtue and salvation might work their way into sentencing.

The second Aristotelian innovation which fundamentally altered the way in which justice was discussed was the introduction of *epikeia*, defined by Aristotle in book 5.10 of the *Ethics*. This term, latinised from the Greek, *epikeia* (ἐπιείκεια), is typically translated as 'moderation'. Aristotle explains that *epikeia* is the part of justice which 'corrects' the occasional inadequacies of legal justice. The term *epikeia* had not been available to authors in western Europe until the translations of the mid-thirteenth century, and, strikingly, one of the first attested uses of the term *epikeia* was made by Robert Grosseteste. Grosseteste used the term at the papal curia at Lyons in 1250, when challenging the idea of a papal exaction which was legal, but unreasonable, that is, opposed to the spirit of the law, in conflict with the principle of *epikeia*.[22] The introduction of *epikeia* represented much more than an additional synonym for *misericordia*, because of the way in which it was defined and deployed, and due to its relationship to particular justice (*iustitia particularis*). *Epikeia* fundamentally restructured the way in which scholastic texts dealt with questions of mercy and judgment. The process is not dissimilar to the developments described earlier in canon law: from the final decades of the twelfth century onwards, the general

Conclusion

terms *misericordia* and *caritas*, principles which had licensed dispensation from the canons, were replaced with the more rigid, juridical terminology of *aequitas*.[23] That term, borrowed from civil law, bore a more precise and more limited meaning. The emergence of *epikeia* hints at much the same process taking place in scholasticism after the reception of the *Ethics*. The reasons for this change are beyond the purview of this study. However, given what has been argued here about the flexibility and adaptability of *misericordia* as a conceptual tool, this transition cannot be explained with the straightforward assertion that *epikeia* replaced *misericordia* because it represents a superior conceptual principle for the ordering of justice. The success of *epikeia*, it seems, is equally bound up with the more general uptake of Aristotelian ethical terminology in the thirteenth century.[24] The significance of the reception of *epikeia* is well demonstrated in the *Summa theologica* of Aquinas, who, following *Ethics* 5.10, explains that *epikeia* is part of the virtue of justice and aims at producing equity (*aequitas*) as its outcome. *Epikeia* is the virtue which allows a judge to set aside the letter of the law and follow the dictates of justice and the common good.[25] Scholasticism in the twelfth century and in the first part of the thirteenth century already had a notion of moderation of judgment – and keenly discussed precisely this question. What *epikeia* brought, however, was a more limited sense of how that moderation should apply: it spoke specifically to *legal* judgment – whereas the great advantage (and the great conceptual challenge) of *misericordia* (and its cognates such as *clementia* or *caritas*) was that it impinged on almost *any* action of judgment, whether personal or political, not only legal. Any action which fell short of being truly just was open to correction; indeed, this intersection of general and the particular was what gave rise to substantial intellectual problems such as Moses's intercession for the Israelites.

The year 1250 does not mark the end of intellectual or political arguments about justice, therefore, nor the use of judicial discretion or pardon. It does not, of course, signal an end to the use of the terms 'misericordia' and 'iustitia'. But it does mark a change in the way the question was debated. The intellectual landscape was thus remade. The same fundamental questions were raised in later centuries, concerning the rightful exercise of pardon; the status of mercy as a particularly royal virtue; and the need to protect the courts from the arbitrary whim of the judge.[26] However, the separation of justice into general and particular, and the adoption of the principle of *epikeia*, put an end to the conceptual diversity of twelfth- and early thirteenth-century approaches to justice.[27] As such, it forms an appropriate closing point for this study.

Justice and mercy

Theology and the common law in the twelfth-century renaissance

Where do the arguments set out here fit into the broader landscape of medieval historiography? First, I would suggest, they argue for an adjustment of the way in which we conceptualise the relationship between law and theology in an English tradition. While studies of the particular influence (or lack of influence) of Roman and canon law on the common law reveal much about the genesis of the laws themselves, considering the common background of thought and piety that judges could draw on might help us understand the administrators of those laws. The relationship I am suggesting here is not one of theologians dictating to English judges, or attempting to smuggle great blocks of foreign theological thinking into common law. Such a model lacks nuance; it also misunderstands the shape of relations between judges and counsellors. Instead, we need to situate judges in a particular intellectual climate, where models, *exempla* and ideas mattered. Those models were scriptural, based on the figures of the Old Testament and the injunctions of the gospels. And, in a Christian *communitas*, for their own good, as well as the good of the polity, they expected judges to listen – and to act.

In turn, this has also led me to argue for the fundamental similarity between Church and secular judges. Contemporaries would, of course, have recognised the difference between a judge who worked for the king and a judge who worked for the Church. One might think (rather mangling the subtleties of the medieval analogy) of two different kinds of doctor, with two different kinds of specialism, operating in two different theatres. But both aimed at restoring their patient to health, at curing a dangerous sickness. The overarching category here is that of 'judge' – it could be divided into subspecies, royal and ecclesiastical. Employment by the king (and numbering among the king's servants) did not change this. Royal judges were still counselled about the danger of divine sanction; only rarely did their royal service preclude an aspiration to virtue. I argue for these 'internal' checks on judges to be taken seriously, not least the promise of divine payback for the judgments they dispensed. Here, I recognise evaluations may differ: I am minded to believe that twelfth-century judges gave real weight to the threat of the Last Judgment and their duty to the polity to give an appropriate and carefully weighed judgment. Others may be less convinced by the case for the internal agonies of twelfth-century judges. But even setting aside the fact that we cannot measure how much, or how often, judges thought about the posthumous consequences of their office, it is the case that judges of all kinds (secular, ecclesiastical and those who moved between the two roles) inhabited a moral world suffused with examples of judicial conduct, of texts, ideas and images admonishing them to weigh carefully the judgments they pronounced. It is true that we do not have a note from an English judge telling us he had decided to model himself on Samuel. What we do have is a considerable weight of evidence for a culture which encouraged its judges to see themselves as following Samuel and Moses. For the influence of 'theology' on law does not have to be conceived of as acting in the most 'elite' spaces – not every common law judge could boast the education of Richard Barre (for example). However, the moderately successful justice-on-eyre might receive an uncomfortable reminder from his own priest about the perils of judgment without mercy; he might be treated to a sermon reminding him of the fates of sinful judges. He might even have found it irritating to be so often reminded of the long history of good and bad judgments to which he was heir.

Some of the most significant conflicts of the eleventh, twelfth and thirteenth centuries concerned the question of how certain fundamental ideals – celibacy and poverty, for example – should be transferred from text to practice. In the cases of clerical celibacy and Franciscan poverty, moreover, attempts to put scriptural ideals into practice had profound practical ramifications which altered the face of medieval society. The same was true of mercy. The conflict over its meaning and interpretation was real and it was debated at every level: this is as evident in the arguments over the cost of purchasing pardon at the Angevin court as it is in discussion over when and how penance might be softened. The argument over the relationship between justice and mercy did not necessarily produce consensus, but it did create the conceptual structures which allowed medieval authors to understand the shape of the world and the shape of history: the twin opposed and polarising pillars of *iustitia* and *misericordia* stretched from the work of Creation to the day of the Last Judgment.

All who judged, or who studied judgment, were bound to ask themselves: where did virtue fit within the law? The answer was never a simple one for the judge, for it required him to weigh up considerations that were as personal as the fate of his own soul and as broad and far-reaching as the stability of the polity he was set over. There was no single 'correct' answer, but competing solutions which could call on classical, Christian, pastoral, philosophical and theological justifications. Between 1100 and 1250, much changed in the way in which *iustitia* was defined and discussed. Systematic law became a social reality; an assertive crown and ambitious royal servants could rightfully claim that justice had become a 'routine' matter. It is in this basic sense that grand narratives of English legal development do

Justice and mercy

hold true. Likewise, in the schools, *iustitia* was the subject of increasingly sophisticated intellectual labours which moved from a recapitulation of Ciceronian and Macrobian definitions to an analysis of whether true justice was ever embodied in a legal system. What commentators in 1250 recognised explicitly, however, was an idea implicit in the legal practice of a century earlier: personal virtue and discretion were integral to the exercise of justice. The English judge in 1250 inhabited a more ordered world – legally and intellectually – than any of his predecessors. Rather than resolving the vagaries of the relationship between justice and mercy, however, legal and intellectual order served only to highlight the moral complexity inherent in the act of judgment.

Notes

1 *Dictum* 2, fo. 3r.
2 This, of course, should not be taken in teleological or objective terms (after all, better never means better for everyone). It aimed at improvement in the sense of measuring judicial ethics against a twelfth-century vision of Christian community. The experience of judgment and of being judged (especially for the most marginal groups) may not have felt like much of an improvement.
3 *S. Anselmi Cantuariensis Archiepiscopi Opera omnia*, ed. F. S. Schmitt (Edinburgh, 1946); Ep. 180, 4:64–5.
4 *Ibid.*, Ep. 58, 3:172–3; Ep. 105, 3:238.
5 M. Clanchy, 'Magna Carta and the common pleas', in Henry Mayr-Harting and R. I. Moore (eds), *Studies in Medieval History Presented to R. H. C. Davis* (London, 1985), 219–32.
6 Cf. M. Clanchy, 'Remebering the past and the good old law', *History* 55 (1970), 165–76.
7 Andrew Horn, *The Mirror of Justices*, ed. W. J. Whittaker and F. W. Maitland (London, 1893), c.108, 166–71.
8 See Sabapathy, *Officers and Accountability*, esp. 23, for the tension between individual virtue and regulation of a group.
9 See C. J. Nederman, 'Nature, ethics, and the doctrine of *Habitus*: Aristotelian moral pyschology in the twelfth century', *Traditio* 45 (1989–90), 87–110, and Marcia L. Colish, '*Habitus* revisited: a reply to Cary Nederman', *Traditio* 48 (1993), 77–92.
10 For these texts, C. Marchesi, *L'Etica nicomachea nella tradizione latina medievale* (Messina, 1904), appendix, i–xxvi (*Ethica vetus*), xxvii–xl (*Ethica nova*).
11 Jean Dunbabin, 'Robert Grosseteste as translator, transmitter and commentator: the *Nichomachean Ethics*', *Traditio* 28 (1972), 472.
12 See Bejczy, 'Medieval commentaries on the *Nicomachean Ethics*'.
13 For example, *ST*, IIaIIae, q.58, 9:9–20.

14 Aristotle's 'reciprocal' justice here does not encompass the concept I have characterised above as the 'reciprocal mercy': that is to say, it does not describe a divine and post-mortem paying back for judgments given during the individual judge's life. Aristotle's notion of 'reciprocity' is also hedged by an insistence on proportion.

15 See Howard J. Curzer, *Aristotle and the Virtues* (Oxford, 2012), 223–46, quotation at 238.

16 A definition repeated in the *Rhetoric*, i.9, ed. and trans. R. C. Jebb and John Edwin Sandys (Cambridge, 1909), 37.

17 Cf. Matthias Perkhams, 'Aquinas's interpretation of the Aristotelian virtue of justice and his doctrine of natural law', in Bejczy, *Virtue Ethics in the Middle Ages*, 136.

18 There is some sense of transition here, however: for example, William of Auxerre's *Summa aurea* (c. 1215–20) employs the terminology of *generalis–specialis*, but bases its discussion of justice on scripture, Augustine and Cicero, not Aristotle. 3.28.1–2, 4:547–60.

19 'Iustita autem quoniam non simpliciter dicitur, alterius ordinis est: quoniam illa cadit sub ordine iuris civilis, scilicet secundum statute et plebiscite, et variantur casus in ipsa: et ideo illa respicit ordinem communis civitatis: et hunc ordinem videtur Aristoteles tenere in Ethicis, sicut plane patet in nova translatione.' Albertus Magnus, *Commentarii in librum Sententiarum*, 3.33.1 ad. 11, in *Opera omnia*, ed. Auguste Borgnet (38 vols, Paris, 1890–99), 28:608.

20 Cf. Aristotle, *Nichomachean Ethics*, trans. Roger Crisp (Port Chester, NY, 2000), 5.6, 92–3.

21 Albertus Magnus, *De bono*, ed. H. Kühle et al. (Aschendorff, 1951), 4.2, 301; *Commentarii in librum Sententarium*, 3.33.1, 608.

22 S. Gieben, 'Robert Grosseteste at the Papal Curia: edition of the documents', *Collectanea Franciscana* 41 (1971), 386.

23 G. Conklin, 'Stephen of Tournai and the development of *aequitas canonica*: the theory and practice of law after Gratian', in Chodorow, *Proceedings of the Eighth International Congress*, 369–86.

24 See Stefano Simonetta, 'Searching for an uneasy synthesis between Aristotelian political language and Christian political theology', in L. Bianchi (ed.), *Christian Readings of Aristotle from the Middle Ages to the Renaissance* (Turnhout, 2011), 273–85.

25 *ST*, IIaIIae, q.120, a.1, 9:468–9; cf. Albertus Magnus, *Super Ethica: Commentum et quaestiones: Pars 1: Libri quinque priores*, ed. Wilhelm Kübel (Aschendorff, 1972), 14.1, 378–83.

26 For later medieval examples see Helen Lacey, *The Royal Pardon: Access to Mercy in Fourteenth-Century England* (Woodbridge, 2009), and, for a French perspective, Claude Gauvard, *'De grace especial': Crime, état et société en France à la fin du moyen âge* (2 vols, Paris, 1991).

27 For *epikeia* in later Christian thought, see Lawrence J. Riley, *The History, Nature and Use of Epikeia in Moral Theology* (Washington, DC, 1948).

Bibliography

Manuscripts

Bibliothèque nationale de France

Ms. latin 338
Ms. latin 384
Ms. latin 393
Ms. latin 625
Ms. latin 3229
Ms. latin 3240
Ms. latin 14415
Ms. latin 14435
Ms. latin 141591

Bodleian Library, Oxford

MS Bodley 798
MS Digby 86
MS E Musaeo 249

British Library

Cotton Julius MS B XIII
Hartley MS 1801
Royal MS 6 A XIII
Royal MS 14 C II
Stowe MS 240

Bibliography

Cambridge, Corpus Christi College, Parker Library

CCCC MS 226
CCCC MS 320
CCCC MS 481

Cambridge, University Library

Kk.4.20

Lincoln Cathedral Library

MS 25
MS 26

Printed primary sources

Adam of Eynsham, *Magna vita Sancti Hugonis. The Life of St. Hugh of Lincoln*, ed. and trans. Decima L. Douie and David Hugh Farmer (2 vols, Oxford, 1985).
Adam Marsh, *The Letters of Adam Marsh*, ed. and trans. C. H. Lawrence (2 vols, Oxford, 2006–10).
Aelred of Rievaulx, *Opera omnia*, ed. A. Hoste and C. H. Talbot, CCCM 53 (Turnhout, 1971).
Alan of Lille, *Opera omnia*, PL 210 (Paris, 1855).
——, *De virtutibus, de vitiis et de donis spiritus sanctis*, ed. Odon Lottin, *Mediaeval Studies* 12 (1950).
——, *Liber poenitentialis*, ed. J. Longere (2 vols, Louvain, 1965).
——, 'A commentary on the Our Father by Alan of Lille', ed. Nikolaus Häring, *Analecta Cisterciensia* 30 (1975), 149–77.
Albertus Magnus, *Opera omnia*, ed. Auguste Borgnet (38 vols, Paris, 1890–99).
——, *De bono*, ed. H. Kühle, C. Feckes, B. Geyer and W. Kübel (Aschendorff, 1951).
——, *Super Ethica: Commentum et quaestiones: Pars 1: Libri quinque priores*, ed. Wilhelm Kübel (Aschendorff, 1972).
Alcuin, *Disputatio de rhetorica et de virtutibus*, ed. and trans. W. S. Howell, *The Rhetoric of Alcuin and Charlemagne* (Princeton, NJ, 1941).

Bibliography

Alexander Nequam, *Speculum speculationum*, ed. Rodney M. Thompson (Oxford, 1988).

Alexander of Ashby, 'Aux origines des *Artes praedicandi*: le *De artificioso modo predicandi* d'Alexandre d'Ashby', ed. F. Morenzoni, *Studi Medievali* 32 (1991), 887–935.

Alger of Liège, *Alger von Luttichs Traktat 'De Misericordia et Iustitia': ein Kanonistischer Konkordanzversuch aus der Zeit des Investiturstreits*, ed. J. Thorbecke (Sigmaringen, 1985).

Ambrose of Milan, *De officiis*, ed. Maurice Testard, CCSL 15 (Turnhout, 2000).

Ambrosiaster, *Quaestiones veteris testamenti*, PL 35 (Paris, 1845).

Andrew Horn, *The Mirror of Justices*, ed. W. J. Whittaker and F. W. Maitland (London, 1893).

Anselm of Canterbury, *S. Anselmi Cantuariensis archiepiscopi opera omnia*, ed. Francis S. Schmitt (6 vols, Edinburgh, 1940–51).

Aristotle, *Ethica vetus, Ethica nova*, in *L'Etica nicomachea nella tradizione latina medievale. Documenti e appunti*, ed. C. Marchese (Messina, 1904).

——, *Rhetoric*, ed. and trans. R. C. Jebb and John Edwin Sandys (Cambridge, 1909).

——, *Topica*, trans. W. A. Pickard-Cambridge (Oxford, 1928).

——, *Nichomachean Ethics*, trans. Roger Crisp (Port Chester, NY, 2000).

Augustine, *Tractatus in Epistolam Iohannis ad Parthos*, PL 35 (Paris, 1861).

——, *Epistulae*, ed. A. Goldbacher, CSEL 34, 44, 57–8 (4 vols, Vienna, 1895–1923).

——, *De spiritu et littera*, ed. C. F. Urba and J. Zyca, CSEL 60 (Vienna, 1913).

——, *In Johannis Evangelium tractatus*, ed. R. Willems, CCSL 36 (Turnhout, 1954).

——, *De civitate Dei*, ed. B. Dombart and A. Kalb, CCSL 47–8 (2 vols, Turnhout, 1955).

——, *Enarrationes in Psalmos*, ed. E. Dekkers and J. Fraipoint, CCSL 38–40 (Turnhout, 1956).

——, *Quaestionum in Heptateuchum libri VII. Locutionum in Heptateuchum libri VII. De octo quaestionibus ex veteri testamento*, ed. J. Fraipoint and D. De Bruyne, CCSL 33 (Turnhout, 1958).

——, *De doctrina christiana. De vera religione*, ed. K. D. Daur, CCSL 32 (Turnhout, 1962).

——, *De sermone Domini in monte*, ed. Almut Mutzenbacher, CCSL 35 (Turnhout, 1967).

——, *De trinitate libri XV*, ed. W. J. Mountain and F. Glorie, CCSL 50 (2 vols, Turnhout, 1968).

Bibliography

Bartholomew of Exeter, 'The Penitential of Bartholomew of Exeter', in A. Morey, *Bartholomew of Exeter, Bishop and Canonist: A Study in the Twelfth Century* (Cambridge, 1937).
(pseudo-)Bede, *Homiliae*, PL 94 (Paris, 1850).
Benedicti regula, ed. Rudolph Hanslik, CSEL 75 (Vienna, 1960).
Bernard of Clairvaux, *S. Bernardi opera*, ed. J. Leclercq, C. H. Talbot and H. M. Rochais (8 vols, Rome, 1957–77).
——, *Le précepte et la dispense; La conversion*, ed. J. Leclercq, H. Rochais and C. H. Talbot (Paris, 2000).
Biblia Latina cum Glossa Ordinaria: Facsimile Reprint of the Editio Princeps (Adolph Rusch of Strassburg), introduction by K. Froehlich and M. T. Gibson (4 vols, Turnhout, 1992).
Boethius, *De differentiis topicis*, PL 64 (Paris, 1847).
Bracton, *De legibus et consuetudinibus Angliae*, ed. G. E. Woodbine (4 vols, New Haven, CT and London, 1915–42).
Burchard of Worms, *Decretum*, PL 140 (Paris, 1853).
——, *Das Dekret des Bischofs Burchard von Worms: Textstufen, frühe Verbreitung, Vorlagen*, ed. Hartmut Hoffmann (Munich, 1991).
The Chronicle of Battle Abbey, ed. E. Searle (Oxford, 1980).
Cicero, *De officiis*, ed. and trans. Walter Miller (London, 1938).
——, *De inventione*, ed. and trans. H. M. Hubbell (London, 1949).
——, *The Speeches*, ed. and trans. N. H. Watts (London, 1953).
——, *De natura deorum*, ed. and trans. H. Rackham (London, 1979).
(pseudo-)Cicero, *Ad C. Herennium: De ratione dicendi (Rhetorica ad Herennium)*, ed. and trans. H. Caplan (London, 1954).
Collectio decretalium, PL 130 (Paris, 1880).
Conrad of Hirsau, *De fructibus carnis et spiritus*, PL 176 (Paris, 1854).
Corpus iuris canonici, ed. E. Friedberg (2 vols, Leipzig, 1879–81).
Corpus iuris civilis, ed. P. Krueger et al. (3 vols, Berlin, 1906–59).
Councils and Synods, with Other Documents Relating to the English Church, ed. F. M. Powicke and C. R. Cheney (2 vols, Oxford, 1964).
Curia Regis Rolls of the Reign of Richard I and John, vol. 1, ed. C. T. Flower (London, 1922).
The Earliest Lincolnshire Assize Rolls: A.D. 1202–1209, ed. Doris M. Stenton (Lincoln, 1926).
Enarrationes in Matthaeum, PL 162 (Paris, 1854).
English Coronation Records, ed. L. G. Wickham Legg (London, 1901).
English Episcopal Acta I: Lincoln 1065–1185, ed. D. M. Smith (Oxford, 1980).
English Episcopal Acta II: Canterbury, 1162–1190, ed. C. R. Cheney and Bridgett E. A. Jones (Oxford, 1986).

English Episcopal Acta IV: Lincoln, 1186–1206, ed. David M. Smith (Oxford, 1986).
English Episcopal Acta IX: Winchester, 1205–1238, ed. N. Vincent (Oxford, 1994).
English Episcopal Acta XI: Exeter, 1046–1184, ed. Frank Barlow (Oxford, 1996).
English Episcopal Acta XII: Exeter, 1186–1256, ed. Frank Barlow (Oxford, 1996).
English Episcopal Acta XVIII: Salisbury, 1078–1217, ed. B. R. Kemp (Oxford, 1999).
English Episcopal Acta XXVI: London, 1189–1228, ed. David P. Johnson (Oxford, 2003).
English Episcopal Acta XXXIII: Worcester, 1062–1185, ed. M. G. Cheney, D. M. Smith, C. N. L. Brooke and P. M. Hoskin (Oxford, 2007).
English Episcopal Acta XXXIV: Worcester, 1186–1218, ed. M. G. Cheney, D. M. Smith, C. N. L. Brooke and P. M. Hoskin (Oxford, 2008).
English Historical Documents 3, 1179–1327, ed. H. Rothwell (London, 1975).
Expositio in Regulam S. Augustini, PL 176 (Paris, 1854).
Florilegium Gallicum, ed. Johannes Hamacher, *Florilegium Gallicum: Prolegomena und Edition der Exzerpte von Petron bis Cicero, De oratore* (Frankfurt, 1975).
Florilegium morale oxoniense, ed. C. H. Talbot and P. Delhaye, *Florilegium morale oxoniense: MS. Bodl. 633* (2 vols, Namur, 1955–56).
Geoffrey Gaimar, *Estoire des Engleis*, ed. and trans. Ian Short (Oxford, 2009).
Gerald of Wales, *Opera omnia*, ed. J. S. Brewer, J. F. Dimock and G. F. Warner, RS 21 (8 vols, London, 1861–91).
——, *Speculum duorum: or, a Mirror of Two Men*, ed. Y. Lefebvre and R. B. C. Huygens, trans. B. Dawson (Cardiff, 1974).
——, *The Conquest of Ireland: A Translation of Expugnatio Hibernica*, ed. and trans. A. B. Scott and F. X. Martin (Dublin, 1978).
Gervase of Canterbury, *Historical Works*, ed. W. Stubbs, RS 73 (2 vols, London, 1879–80).
Gervase of Tilbury, *Otia imperialia. Recreation for an Emperor*, ed. and trans. S. E. Banks and J. W. Binns (Oxford, 2002).
Gesta Stephani, ed. and trans. K. R. Potter, introduction and notes by R. H. C. Davis (Oxford, 1976).
Gilbert Foliot, *The Letters and Charters of Gilbert Foliot, Abbot of Gloucester (1139–48), Bishop of Hereford (1148–63), and London (1163–87)*, ed. Z. N. Brooke, A. Morey and C. N. L. Brooke (London, 1967).
——, 'The commentary on the Lord's Prayer of Gilbert Foliot', ed. David N. Bell, *RTAM* 56 (1989), 80–101.
'Glanvill', *The Treatise on the Laws and Customs of England, Commonly Called Glanvill*, ed. and trans. G. D. G. Hall and M. T. Clanchy (Oxford, 1993).

Bibliography

Glossa ordinaria, PL 113–14 (Paris, 1852).
Gregory the Great, *Dialogi*, ed. Umberto Monicca (Rome, 1924).
——, *Moralia in Iob*, ed. M. Adriaen, CCSL 143 (3 vols, Turnhout, 1979–85).
——, *Regula pastoralis*, ed. F. Rommel (2 vols, Paris, 1992).
——, *Homiliae in evangelia*, ed. R. Étaix, CCSL 141 (Turnhout, 1999).
Guerric of St Quentin, *Quaestiones de quolibet*, ed. Walter H. Principe (Toronto, 2002).
Henry of Huntingdon, *Historia Anglorum. The History of the English People*, ed. and trans. Diana Greenway (Oxford, 1996).
Hincmar of Rheims, *De regis persona et regio ministerio*, PL 125 (Paris, 1852).
——, *De divortio Lotharii regis et Theutbergae reginae*, ed. L. Böhringer, MGH: Concilia 4/1 (Hanover, 1992).
Honorius of Autun, *Opera omnia*, PL 172 (Paris, 1854).
Hugh of St Victor, *Opera omnia*, PL 175–7 (Paris, 1854).
——, 'Questions inédites de Hugues de Saint-Victor', ed. Odon Lottin, *RTAM* 27 (1960), 42–66.
——, *Opera propaedeutica: Practica geometriae, De grammatica, Epitome Dindimi in philosophicum*, ed. R. Baron (Notre Dame, IN, 1966)
Incipits of Latin Works on the Virtues and Vices, 1100–1500 A.D.: Including a Section of Incipits of Works on the Pater Noster, ed. Morton W. Bloomfield, B.-G. Guyot, D. R. Howard and T. B. Kabealo (Cambridge, 1979).
Innocent III, *Opera omnia*, PL 214–17 ((Paris, 1855).
Isidore of Seville, *Opera omnia*, PL 80–4 (Paris, 1850–62).
——, *Etymologiarum*, ed. W. M. Lindsay (2 vols, Oxford, 1911).
——, *De differentiis*, ed. and trans. C. Codoñer (Paris, 1992).
——, *The Etymologies of Isidore of Seville*, ed. and trans. Stephen A. Barney, W. J. Lewis, J. A. Beach and Oliver Berghof (Cambridge, 2006).
Itinerarium peregrinorum et gesta Regis Ricardi, trans. H. Nicholson (Aldershot, 1997).
Ivo of Chartres, *Prologue*, in Bruce C. Brasington, *Ways of Mercy: The Prologue of Ivo of Chartres* (Münster, 2004).
Jocelin of Brakelond, *The Chronicle of Jocelin of Brakelond*, ed. and trans. H. E. Butler (London, 1949).
John of Salisbury, *Policraticus, sive de nugis curialivm et vestigiis philosophorum*, ed. C. C. J. Webb (2 vols, Oxford, 1909).
——, *Letters*, ed. and trans. J. W. Miller and H. E. Butler, revised by C. N. L. Brooke (2 vols, Oxford, 1979–86).
——, *Metalogicon*, ed. J. B. Hall and K. S. B. Keats-Rohan, CCCM 98 (Turnhout, 1991).

Bibliography

John of Worcester, *The Chronicle of John of Worcester*, ed. and trans. J. Bray and P. McGurk (3 vols, Oxford, 1995).
Leges Henrici Primi, ed. L. J. Downer (Oxford, 1972).
Liebermann, Felix (ed.), *Die Gesetze der Angelsachsen* (Aalen, 1960).
The London Eyre of 1244, ed. Helena M. Chew and Martin Weinbaum (London, 1970).
Macrobius, *Commentary on the Dream of Scipio*, ed. and trans. W. H. Stahl (New York, 1990).
Matthew Paris, *Chronica maiora*, ed. H. R. Luard, RS 57 (7 vols, London, 1872–81).
Martin of Braga, *Formula vitae honestae*, ed. C. W. Barlow, *Martini Episcopi Bracarensis Opera omnia* (New Haven, CT, 1950).
Materials for the History of Thomas Becket, ed. J. C. Robertson and J. B. Shepherd, RS 67 (7 vols, London, 1875–85).
Moralium dogma philosophorum, ed. John Holmberg, *Das Moralium dogma philosophorum des Guillaume de Conches, lateinisch, altfranzösisch und mittelniederfränkisch, herausgegeben* (Uppsala, 1929).
Odo of Tournai, *Liber de villico iniquitatis*, PL 160 (Paris, 1854).
Orderic Vitalis, *The Ecclesiastical History*, ed. and trans. M. Chibnall (6 vols, Oxford, 1969–80).
Otto of Freising, *Ottonis episcopi Frisingensis chronica: sive, Historia de duabus civitatibus*, ed. A. Hoffmeister, MGH: Scriptores rerum Germanicarum 16 (Hanover, 1912).
Otto of Freising and Rahewin of Freising, *Gesta Frederici I imperatoris*, ed. G. Waitz, MGH: Scriptores rerum Germanicarum 46 (Hanover, 1912).
Peter Abelard, *Opera theologica*, ed. M. Buytaert, CCCM 11–13, 15, 190 (Turnhout, 1969–).
——, *Ethica*, ed. and trans. D. E. Luscombe (Oxford, 1971).
——, *The Sic et Non: A Critical Edition*, ed. Blanche B. Boyer and Richard McKeon (Chicago, 1976–77).
——, *Collationes*, ed. and trans. J. Marenbon and G. Orlandi (Oxford, 2001).
Peter Comestor, *Opera omnia*, PL 198 (Paris, 1855).
——, *Scolastica historia. Liber Genesis*, ed. Agneta Sylwan, CCCM 191 (Turnhout, 2005).
Peter Damian, *Opera omnia*, PL 144–5 (Paris, 1853).
Peter Lombard, *Opera omnia*, PL 191 (Paris, 1854).
——, *Magistri Petri Lombardi Parisiensis episcopi Sententiae Libri IV*, ed. I. Brady (2 vols, Rome, 1971–81).
Peter of Blois, *Opera omnia*, PL 207 (Paris, 1855).

Bibliography

——, *Dialogus inter Regum Henricum Secundum et abbatem Bonnevallis*, ed. R. B. C. Huygens, *Revue bénédictine* 68 (1958), 97–112.
——, *The Later Letters*, ed. E. Revell (Oxford, 1993).
Peter of Poitiers, *Sententiae*, PL 211 (Paris, 1855).
——, *Sententiae Petri Pictaviensis*, ed. P. S. Moore and M. Dulong (2 vols, Notre Dame, IN, 1943–50).
——, *Summa de confessione: Compilatio praesens*, ed. J. Longère, CCCM 51 (Turnhout, 1980).
Peter the Chanter, *Summa de sacramentis et animae consiliis*, ed. J. A. Dugauquier (5 vols, Louvain, 1954–67).
——, *Verbum adbreviatum: textus conflatus*, ed. Monique Boutry (Turnhout, 2004).
Peter the Venerable, *The Letters of Peter the Venerable*, ed. G. Constable (2 vols, Cambridge, 1967).
La petite philosophie: An Anglo-Norman Poem of the Thirteenth Century, ed. W. H. Thethewey, Anglo-Norman Text Society 1 (Oxford, 1939).
Plutarch, *Lives*, vol. 1, trans. B. Perrin (London, 1914).
Quintilian, *Institutio oratoria*, ed. and trans. D. A. Russell (London, 2001).
Rabanus Maurus, *Opera omnia*, PL 107–12 (Paris, 1851–52).
Ralph Diceto, *Radulphi de Diceto decani Lundoniensis Opera Historica*, ed. W. Stubbs, RS 68 (2 vols, London, 1876).
Ralph Niger, *Chronica*, ed. R. Anstruther (London, 1851).
Ralph of Coggeshall, *Chronicon Anglicanum*, ed. J. Stevenson, RS 66 (London, 1875).
Raoul Ardens, *Radulphus Ardens: The Questions on the Sacraments. Speculum uniuersale 8.31–92*, ed. Christopher P. Evans (Toronto, 2010).
Richard FitzNigel, *Dialogus de Scaccario*, ed. and trans. E. Amt (Oxford, 2007).
Richard of Devizes, *Cronicon*, ed. and trans. J. T. Appleby (London, 1963).
Richard of St Victor, *Mysticae Adnotationes in Psalmos*, PL 196 (Paris, 1880).
——, *Les quatre degrés de la violente charité*, ed. Gervais Dumeige (Paris, 1955).
——, *Opscules théologiques*, ed. J. Riballier (Paris, 1967).
Robert Grosseteste, *Roberti Grosseteste episcopi quondam Lincolniensis epistolae*, ed. H. R. Luard, RS 25 (London, 1861).
——, *Le Château d'amour de Robert Grosseteste, évêque de Lincoln*, ed. J. Murray (Paris, 1918).
——, 'Robert Grosseteste's treatise on confession, "Deus Est"', ed. S. Wenzel, *Franciscan Studies* 30 (1970), 218–93.
——, *De decem mandatis*, ed. Richard C. Dales and Edward B. King (Oxford, 1987).
——, *Templum Dei*, ed. Joseph Goering and F. A. C. Mantello (Toronto, 1984).

——, *De cessatione legalium*, ed. Richard C. Dales and Edward B. King (London, 1986).

——, *Expositio in epistolam sancti Pauli ad Galatas*, ed. J. McEvoy, L. Rizzerio, R. C. Dales and P. W. Rosemann CCCM 130 (Turnhout, 1995).

——, *Tabula*, ed. P. W. Rosemann and J. McEvoy, CCCM 130 (Turnhout, 1995).

——, *Le Château d'amour*, trans. E. A. Mackie, in Maura O'Caroll (eds), *Robert Grosseteste and the Beginnings of a British Theological Tradition* (Rome, 2003), 151–79.

——, *The Letters of Robert Grosseteste, Bishop of Lincoln*, trans. F. A. C. Mantello and J. Goering (Toronto, 2010).

Robert of Flamborough, *Liber poenitentialis*, ed. J. J. F. Firth (Toronto, 1971).

Robert of Melun, *Oeuvres de Robert de Melun*, ed. R. M. Martin (4 vols, Louvain, 1932–52).

Robert Pullen, *Sententiarum libri octo*, PL 186 (Paris, 1854).

Roger of Howden, *Chronica Magistri Rogeri de Houedene*, ed. W. Stubbs, RS 51 (4 vols, London 1868–71).

Roger of Wendover. *Flores historiarum*, ed. H. G. Hewlett, RS 84 (3 vols, London, 1886–89).

Roland of Cremona, *Summae Magistri Rolandi Cremonensis*, ed. A. Cortesi (Bergamo, 1962).

Rolls of the Justices in Eyre for Lincolnshire (1218–1219) and Worcestershire (1221), ed. D. M. Stenton, Selden Society 53 (London, 1934).

Rupert of Deutz, *De divinis officiis*, ed. H. Haacke, CCCM 7 (Turnhout, 1967).

——, *De sancta trinitate et operibus eius*, ed. H. Haacke, CCCM 21–4 (4 vols, Turnhout, 1971–72).

——, *De gloria et honore filii hominis super Matthaeum*, ed. H. Haacke, CCCM 29 (Turnhout, 1979).

Sallust, *Bellum Catilinae*, ed. and trans. J. C. Rolfe (London and Cambridge, MA, 1928).

La Seinte Resureccion, ed. T. A. Jenkins, J. M. Manly, M. K. Pope and Jean Wright, Anglo-Norman Text Society 4 (Oxford, 1943).

Seneca, *Ad Lucillum epistulae morales*, ed. and trans. R. C. Gummere (3 vols, London, 1917–25).

——, *Moral Essays*, ed. and trans. J. W. Basore (3 vols, London, 1928–35).

Stephen Langton, *Der Sentenzenkommentar des Kardinals Stephan Langton*, ed. A. M. Landgraff (Münster, 1952).

——, *Selected Sermons of Stephen Langton*, ed. Phyllis B. Roberts (Toronto, 1980).

——, 'A partial edition of Stephen Langton's *Summa* and *Quaestiones* with parallels from Andrew Sunesen's *Hexaemeron*', ed. Sten Ebbesen and Lars

Boje Mortensen, *Cahiers de l'Institut du moyen-âge grec et latin* 49 (1985), 25–244.

——, 'The *Conflictus vitiorum et virtutum* attributed to Stephen Langton', ed. Riccardo Quinto, in István P. Bejczy and Richard Newhauser (eds), *Virtue and Ethics in the Twelfth Century* (Leiden, 2005), 197–267.

——, 'Two questions of Stephen Langton on the cardinal virtues', ed. I. P. Bejczy, *Medioevo. Rivista di Storia della Filosofia Medievale* 31 (2006), 299–335.

Stephen of Tournai, *Epistolae*, PL 211 (Paris, 1855).

——, *Les Disputationes de Simon de Tournai*, ed. J. Warichez (Louvain, 1932).

Thomas Aquinas, *Doctoris angelici divi Thomae Aquinatis Opera omnia*, ed. Stanislas Eduard Fretté and Paul Maré (34 vols, Paris, 1871–80).

Thomas Becket, *The Correspondence of Thomas Becket, Archbishop of Canterbury, 1162–70*, ed. and trans. A. Duggan (2 vols, Oxford, 2000).

Thomas of Chobham, *Summa confessorum*, ed. F. Broomfield (Louvain, 1968).

——, *Summa de arte praedicandi*, ed. F. Morenzoni, CCCM 82 (Turnhout, 1988).

——, *Sermones*, ed. Franco Morenzoni, CCCM 82A (Turnhout, 1993).

——, *Summa de commendatione virtutum et extirpatione vitorum*, ed. F. Morenzoni, CCCM 82B (Turnhout, 1997).

La Venjance Nostre-Seigneur, ed. L. A. T. Gryrting, *The Oldest Version of the Twelfth-Century Poem La Venjance Nostre-Seigneur* (Baltimore, MD, 1952).

Vincent of Beauvais, *Speculum quadruplex, sive, Speculum maius* (4 vols, Graz, 1964–5).

Walter Map, *De nugis curialium*, trans. M. R. James, revised by C. N. L. Brooke and R. A. B. Mynors (Oxford, 1983).

William of Auvergne, *Guilielmi Alverni Opera omnia* (2 vols, Frankfurt, 1963).

——, *Sermones de Tempore*, ed. F. Morenzoni, CCCM 230 (2 vols, Turnhout, 2010–11).

William of Auxerre, *Magistri Guillelmi Altissiodorensis Summa aurea*, ed. J. Ribaillier (5 vols, Paris, 1980–87).

——, *On the Virtues: Part One of On the Virtues and Vices*, trans. R. J. Teske (Milwaukee, WI, 2009).

William Durand, *Rationale divinorum officiorum*, ed. A. Davril and T. M. Thibodeau, CCCM 140 (3 vols, Turnhout, 1995).

William Longchamp, *Practica legum et decretorum*, in E. Caillemar, *Le droit civil dans les provinces anglo-normandes au XII siècle* (Caen, 1883), 50–70.

William of Malmesbury, *Historia novella*, ed. and trans. K. R. Potter (London, 1955).

——, *Gesta regum Anglorum*, ed. and trans. R. A. B. Mynors, completed by R. M. Thomson and M. Winterbottom (2 vols, Oxford, 1998–99).

——, *Gesta pontificum Anglorum*, ed. and trans. M. Winterbottom and R. M. Thomson (2 vols, Oxford, 2007).
William of Newburgh, *Historia rerum Anglicarum*, ed. R. Howlett, *Chronicles of the Reigns of Stephen, Henry II and Richard I*, RS 82 (4 vols, London, 1884).
——, *The History of English Affairs*, ed. and trans. P. G. Walsh and M. J. Kennedy (2 vols, Warminster, 1988).
William of Poitiers, *The 'Gesta Guillelmi' of William of Poitiers*, ed. and trans. R. H. C. Davis and Marjorie Chibnall (Oxford, 1998).
William of Rievaulx, *Vita Ailredi*, ed. and trans. F. M. Powicke (Oxford, 1978).
William of St Thierry, *Opera didactica et spiritualia*, ed. S. Ceglar and P. Verdeyen, CCCM 88 (Turnhout, 2003).
Year Books of Edward II, vol. 25, *12 Edward II: Parts of Easter and Trinity 1319*, ed. J. P. Collas, Selden Society 81 (London, 1964).
Ysagoge in theologiam, ed. A. Landgraf, *Écrits théologiques de l'école d'Abelard: Textes inédits* (Louvain, 1934).

Printed secondary sources

Alexander, James W., 'The Becket conflict in recent historiography', *Journal of British Studies* 9 (1970), 1–26.
Alford, J. A., 'Literature and law in medieval England', *Proceedings of the Modern Language Association* 92 (1977), 941–51.
Althoff, G., '*Ira regis*: prolegomena to a history of royal anger', in B. H. Rosenwein (ed.), *Anger's Past: The Social Uses of an Emotion in the Middle Ages* (Ithaca, NY and London, 1998), 51–74.
Amt, E., 'The Forest Regard of 1155', *Haskins Society Journal* 2 (1990), 189–95.
——, 'The reputation of the sheriff, 1100–1216', *Haskins Society Journal* 8 (1996), 91–8.
Arnold, M. S., 'Law and fact in the medieval jury trial: out of sight, out of mind', *American Journal of Legal History* 18 (1974), 267–80.
Austin, G., *Shaping Church Law around the Year 1000: The Decretum of Burchard of Worms* (Farnham, 2009).
Bacher, John Rea, *The Prosecution of Heretics in Mediaeval England* (Philadelphia, 1942).
Bagge, S., *Kings, Politics and the Right Order of the World in German Historiography c.950–1150* (Leiden, 2002).
Baker, J. H., *Monuments of Endlesse Labours: English Canonists and their Work, 1300–1900* (London, 1998).

Baldwin, J. W., 'The intellectual preparation for the canon of 1215 against ordeals', *Speculum* 36 (1961), 613–36.

——, 'Critics of the legal profession: Peter the Chanter and his circle', in S. Kuttner and J. Ryan (eds), *Proceedings of the Second International Congress of Medieval Canon Law* (Rome, 1965), 249–59.

——, 'A debate at Paris over Thomas Becket between Master Roger and Master Peter the Chanter', *Studia Gratiana* 11 (1967), 121–32.

——, *Masters, Princes and Merchants: The Social Views of Peter the Chanter and his Circle* (2 vols, Princeton, NJ, 1970).

——, 'Master Stephen Langton, future Archbishop of Canterbury: the Paris schools and Magna Carta', *English Historical Review* 123 (2008), 811–46.

Barbour, Reid, *John Selden: Measures of the Holy Commonwealth in Seventeenth-Century England* (Toronto, 2003).

Barker, Lynn K., 'MS Bodleian Canon. Pat. Lat. 131 and a lost Lactantius of John of Salisbury: evidence in search of a French critic of Thomas Becket', *Albion* 22:1 (1990), 21–37.

——, 'Ivo of Chartres and the Anglo-Norman cultural tradition', *Anglo-Norman Studies* 13 (1991), 15–34.

Barlow, Frank, *Thomas Becket* (London, 1986).

——, 'The Constitutions of Clarendon', *Medieval History* 1 (1991), 39–52.

Baron, R., 'À propos des ramifications des vertus au XIIe siècle', *RTAM* 23 (1956), 19–39.

Barrau, Julie, 'Gilbert Foliot et l'écriture, un exégète en politique', *Anglo-Norman Studies* 27 (2004), 16–31.

——, 'La *conversio* de Jean de Salisbury: la Bible au service de Thomas Becket?', *Cahiers de civilisation médiévale, Xe–XIIe siècles* 50 (2007), 229–43.

Barrow, J., 'A twelfth-century bishop and literary patron: William de Vere', *Viator* 18 (1987), 175–89.

Bartlett, R., *Trial by Fire and Water: The Medieval Judicial Ordeal* (Oxford, 1990).

——, *Gerald of Wales: A Voice of the Middle Ages* (2nd edn, Stroud, 2006).

Barton, J. L., 'On the teaching of Roman Law in England around 1200', *Journal of Legal History* 14 (1993), 53–8.

Barton, Richard E., '"Zealous anger" and the renegotiation of aristocratic relationships in eleventh- and twelfth-century France', in B. H. Rosenwein (ed.), *Anger's Past: The Social Uses of an Emotion in the Middle Ages* (Ithaca, NY and London, 1998), 153–70.

——, 'Emotions and power in Orderic Vitalis', *Anglo-Norman Studies* 33 (2010), 41–60.

Bateson, M., 'A London municipal collection of the reign of King John', *English Historical Review* 17 (1902), 707–30.

Bibliography

Bejczy, I. P., '*Tolerantia*: a medieval concept', *Journal of the History of Ideas* 58 (1997), 365–84.

——, '*De origine virtutum et vitiorum*: an anonymous treatise of moral philosophy (c.1200–1230)', *Archives d'histoire doctrinal et littéraire du moyen âge* 72 (2005), 105–45.

——, 'Law and ethics: twelfth-century jurists on the virtue of justice', *Viator* 36 (2005), 197–216.

——,'Cardinal virtues in a Christian context: the antithesis between fortitude and humility in the twelfth century', *Medioevo* 31 (2006), 49–67.

——, 'Gerald of Wales on the cardinal virtues: a reappraisal of *De principis instructione*', *Medium Aevum* 75:2 (2006), 191–201.

——, 'The cardinal virtues in medieval commentaries on the *Nicomachean Ethics*, 1250–1350', in I. P. Bejczy (ed.), *Virtue Ethics in the Middle Ages: Commentaries on Aristotle's Nicomachean Ethics, 1200–1500* (Leiden, 2008), 199–221.

Bellamy, J. G., *The Law of Treason in England in the Later Middle Ages* (Cambridge, 1970).

——, *Crime and Public Order in England in the Later Middle Ages* (London, 1973).

——, *The Criminal Trial in Later Medieval England: Felony before the Courts from Edward I to the Sixteenth Century* (Toronto, 1998).

Bériou, N., 'La confession dans les écrits théologiques et pastoraux du XIIIe siècle: médication de l'âme ou démarche judiciaire?', in *L'Aveu, antiquité et moyen-âge* (Rome, 1986), 261–82.

——, 'La Madeleine dans les sermons parisiens du XIIIe siècle', *Mélanges de l'École française de Rome, moyen âge* 104 (1992), 269–340.

Biancalana, Joseph, 'For want of justice: legal reforms of Henry II', *Columbia Law Review* 88 (1988), 433–536.

Biller, Peter, 'William of Newburgh and the Cathar mission to England', in Diana Wood (ed.), *Life and Thought in the Northern Church, c.1100–c.1700* (Woodbridge, 1999), 10–30.

Bisson, T. N., 'Celebration and persuasion: reflections on the cultural evolution of medieval consultation', *Legislative Studies Quarterly* 7 (1982), 181–204.

——, *The Crisis of the Twelfth Century: Power, Lordship, and the Origins of European Government* (Princeton, NJ and Oxford, 2009).

Blurton, H., 'From *chanson de geste* to Magna Carta: genre and the barons in Matthew Paris' *Chronica Majora*', in R. Copeland, D. Lawton and W. Scase (eds), *New Medieval Literatures* 9 (Turnhout, 2007), 117–38.

——, 'Richard of Devizes's *Cronicon*, Menippean satire, and the Jews of Winchester', *Exemplaria* 22 (2010), 265–84.

Bond, Lawrence H., 'Another look at Abelard's commentary on Romans 3.26', in W. S. Campbell, P. S. Hawkins and B. Deen Schildgen (eds), *Medieval Readings of Romans* (London, 2007), 11–32.

Boureau, A., 'Conflicting norms: liturgical procedure and the separation of divine law from human law (England, eleventh century)', *Medieval History Journal* 3 (2000), 17–40.

———, 'How law came to the monks: the use of law in English society at the beginning of the thirteenth century', *Past and Present* 167 (2000), 29–74.

Boutemy, A., 'Giraud de Barrie et Pierre le Chantre, une source de la *Gemma ecclesiastica*,' *Revue du moyen âge latin* 2 (1946), 45–62.

Boyle, L. E., 'The beginnings of legal study at Oxford', *Viator* 14 (1983), 107–31.

———, 'The Fourth Lateran Council and manuals of popular theology', in Thomas J. Heffernan (ed.), *The Popular Literature of Medieval England* (Knoxville, TN, 1985), 30–43.

———, 'The inter-conciliar period 1179–1215 and the beginnings of pastoral manuals', in R. Tofanini (ed.), *Miscellanea Rolando Bandinelli, Papa Alessandro III* (Siena, 1986), 45–56.

Brand, P. A., 'Chief Justice and felon: the career of Thomas Weyland', in Richard Eales and David Sullivan (eds), *The Political Context of Law* (London, 1987), 26–47.

———, 'Courtroom and schoolroom', *Historical Research* 60 (1990), 147–65.

———, '*Multis vigiliis excogitatam et inventam*: Henry II and the creation of the English common law', in P. A. Brand, *The Making of the Common Law* (London, 1992), 77–102.

———, *The Origins of the English Legal Profession* (Oxford, 1992).

———, 'Legal education in England before the Inns of Court', in Jonathan A. Bush and Alain Wijffels (eds), *Learning the Law: Teaching and the Transmission of Law in England, 1150–1900* (London, 1999), 51–84.

———, 'Ethical standards for royal justices in England c.1175–1307', *University of Chicago Law School Roundtable* 239 (2001), 239–80.

———, 'The English difference: the application of bureaucratic norms within a legal system', *Law and History Review* 21 (2003), 383–7.

———, 'The date and authorship of *Bracton*: a response', *Journal of Legal History* 31 (2010), 217–44.

———, 'The language of the English legal profession: the emergence of a distinctive legal lexicon in insular French', in R. Ingham (ed.), *The Anglo-Norman Language and its Contexts* (Woodbridge, 2010), 94–101.

———, 'The English medieval common law (to c.1307) as a system of national institutions and legal rules: creation and functioning', in Paul Dresch and

Hannah Skoda (eds), *Legalism: Anthropology and History* (Oxford, 2012), 173–96.

Brasington, B. C., '*Non imitanda sed veneranda*: the dilemma of sacred precedent in twelfth-century canon law', *Viator* 23 (1992), 135–52.

——, 'Studies in the "Nachleben" of Ivo of Chartres: the influence of his Prologue on several Panormia-derivative collections', in Peter Landau and Joers Mueller (eds), *Proceedings of the Ninth International Congress of Medieval Canon Law* (Rome, 1997), 63–86.

——, 'Canon law in the *Leges Henrici Primi*', *Zeitschrift der Savigny-Stiftung für Rechtsgeschichte: Kanonistische Abteilung* 123 (2006), 288–305.

——, 'Lessons of love: Bishop Ivo of Chartres as teacher', in Sally N. Vaughn and Jay Rubenstein (eds), *Teaching and Learning in Northern Europe 1000–1200* (Turnhout, 2006), 129–47.

——, *Order in the Court: Medieval Procedural Treatises in Translation* (Leiden, 2016).

Brett, Martin, 'John of Worcester and his contemporaries', in R. H. C. Davis and J. M. Wallace-Hadrill (eds) *The Writing of History in the Middle Ages: Essays Presented to Richard William Southern* (Oxford, 1981), 101–26.

Brown Tkacz, C., '*Susanna victrix, Christus victor*: Lenten sermons, typology and the lectionary', in C. J. Nederman and R. Utz (eds), *Speculum Sermonis: Interdisciplinary Reflections on the Medieval Sermon* (Turnhout, 2004), 55–80.

Brundage, J. A., 'The hierarchy of violence in twelfth- and thirteenth-century canonists', *International History Review* 17 (1995), 670–92.

——, *The Medieval Origins of the Legal Profession: Canonists, Civilians and Courts* (London, 2008).

——, 'The managerial revolution in the English church', in J. S. Loengard (ed.), *Magna Carta and the England of King John* (Woodbridge, 2010), 83–98.

Buc, P., *L'Ambiguïté du livre: prince, pouvoir, et peuple dans les commentaires de la Bible au moyen âge* (Paris, 1994).

——, '*Principes gentium dominatur eorum*: princely power between legitimacy and illegitimacy in twelfth-century exegesis', in T. N. Bisson (ed.) *Cultures of Power: Lordship, Status and Process in Twelfth-Century Europe* (Philadelphia, 1995), 310–31.

Burr, D., *Olivi and Franciscan Poverty* (Philadelphia, 1989).

——, *Spiritual Franciscans: From Protest to Persecution in the Century after Saint Francis* (University Park, PA, 2001).

Byrne, P., 'Exodus 32 and the figure of Moses in twelfth-century theology', *Journal of Theological Studies* 68 (2017), 671–89.

Callus, Daniel A., 'The date of Grosseteste's translations and commentaries of Pseudo-Dionysius and the Nicomachean Ethics', *RTAM* 14 (1947), 186–209.
Cam, Helen M., 'The evolution of the mediaeval English franchise', *Speculum* 32 (1957), 427–42.
Campbell, James, 'The Anglo-Saxon origins of English constitutionalism', in Richard W. Kaeuper (ed.), *Law, Governance, and Justice: New Views on Medieval Constitutionalism* (Leiden, 2013), 15–25.
Campbell, Richard, 'The conceptual roots of Anselm's soteriology', in D. E. Luscombe and G. R. Evans (eds), *Anselm: Aosta, Bec and Canterbury* (Sheffield, 1996), 256–63.
Caplan, H., 'Classical rhetoric and the mediaeval theory of preaching', *Classical Philology* 28 (1933), 76–96.
——, 'A medieval commentary on the *Rhetorica ad Herennium*', in A. King and H. North (eds), *Of Eloquence: Studies in Ancient and Mediaeval Rhetoric* (Ithaca, NY, 1970) 247–70.
Caron, P. G., '"Aequitas et interpretatio" dans la doctrine canonique aux XIIIe et XIVe siècles', in Stephan Kuttner (ed.), *Proceedings of the Third International Conference of Medieval Canon Law* (Rome, 1971) 131–41.
Carpenter, C., 'Law, justice and landowners in late medieval England', *Law and History Review* 1 (1983), 205–37.
Carpenter, David A., 'The decline of the curial sheriff in England, 1194–1258', *English Historical Review* 91 (1976), 1–32.
——, 'The fall of Hubert de Burgh', *Journal of British Studies* 19 (1980), 1–17.
——, 'King, magnates and society: the personal rule of Henry III, 1234–1258', *Speculum* 60 (1985), 39–70.
——, 'Justice and jurisdiction under King John and King Henry III', in David A. Carpenter (ed.), *The Reign of Henry III* (London, 1996), 17–43.
Cheney, C. R., 'Legislation of the medieval English church', *English Historical Review* 50 (1935), 193–224, 385–417.
——, *English Bishops' Chanceries, 1100–1250* (Manchester, 1950).
——, *From Becket to Langton* (Manchester, 1956).
——, 'Aspects de la législation diocésaine en Angleterre au XIIIe siècle', in *Études d'histoire du droit canonique dédiées à Gabriel le Bras* (2 vols, Paris, 1965), vol. 1, 41–54.
——, *Hubert Walter* (London, 1967).
——, 'Hubert Walter and Bologna', *Bulletin of Medieval Canon Law* 2 (1972), 81–4.
——, 'Statute-making in the English church in the thirteenth century', in C. R. Cheney, *Medieval Texts and Studies* (Oxford, 1973), 138–57.

Cheney, M. G., 'The Compromise of Avranches and the spread of canon law in England', *English Historical Review* 56 (1941), 177–97.
——, 'Pope Alexander III and Roger, Bishop of Worcester, 1164–79: the exchange of ideas', in Stephan Kuttner (ed.), *Proceedings of the Fourth International Congress of Medieval Canon Law* (Rome, 1976), 207–28.
——, *Roger, Bishop of Worcester, 1164–1179* (Oxford, 1980).
——, 'A decree of King Henry II on defect of justice', in D. Greenway (ed.), *Tradition and Change: Essays in Honour of Majorie Chibnall* (Cambridge, 1985), 183–93.
Cheyette, Frederic L., 'Custom, case law and medieval "constitutionalism": a re-examination', *Political Science Quarterly* 78:3 (1963), 362–90.
——, 'Suum cuique tribuere', *French Historical Studies* 6 (1970), 287–99.
Chibnall, M., 'John of Salisbury as historian', *Studies in Church History* 3 (1984), 169–77.
——, '"Clio's legal cosmetics": law and custom in the work of medieval historians', *Anglo-Norman Studies* 20 (1998), 31–43.
——, 'The Latin of William of Poitiers', in M. W. Herren, C. J. McDonough and R. G. Arthur (eds), *Latin Culture in the Eleventh Century* (Turnhout, 2002), 135–43.
Church, S. D., 'Belet, Michael (d. in or before 1247)', *Oxford Dictionary of National Biography* (Oxford, 2004), www.oxforddnb.com/view/article/56845, accessed 23 July 2017.
Clanchy, M. T., 'Did Henry III have a policy?', *History* 53 (1968), 203–16.
——, 'Remembering the past and the good old law', *History* 55 (1970), 165–76.
——, 'Highway robbery and trial by battle in the Hampshire Eyre of 1249', in R. F. Hunnisett and J. B. Post (eds), *Medieval Legal Records: Edited in Memory of C. A. F. Meekings* (London, 1978), 26–61.
——, 'Law and love in the middle ages', in J. Bossy (ed.), *Disputes and Settlements: Law and Human Relations in the West* (Cambridge, 1983), 47–67.
——, 'Magna Carta and the common pleas', in Henry Mayr-Harting and R. I. Moore (eds), *Studies in Medieval History presented to R. H. C. Davis* (London, 1985), 219–32.
——, *From Memory to Written Record: England 1066–1307* (2nd edn, London, 1993).
Clayton, Mary, 'The Old English *promissio regis*', *Anglo-Saxon England* 37 (2008), 91–150.
Coing, H., 'English equity and the *Denunciatio evangelica* of the common law', *Law Quarterly Review* 71 (1955), 223–41.

Colish, Marcia L., 'Systematic theology and theological renewal in the twelfth century', *Journal of Medieval and Renaissance Studies* 18 (1988), 131–56.
——, *The Stoic Tradition from Late Antiquity to the Early Middle Ages* (2 vols, Leiden, 1990).
——, '*Habitus* revisited: a reply to Cary Nederman', *Traditio* 48 (1993), 77–92.
——, *Peter Lombard* (2 vols, Leiden, 2004).
——, *Studies in Scholasticism* (Aldershot, 2006).
——, 'Scholastic theology at Paris around 1200', in Spencer E. Young (ed.), *Crossing Boundaries at Medieval Universities* (Leiden, 2011), 29–50.
Colman, Rebecca V., 'Reason and unreason in early medieval law', *Journal of Interdisciplinary History* 4 (1974), 571–91.
Conklin, G., 'Stephen of Tournai and the development of *aequitas canonica*: the theory and practice of law after Gratian', in Stanley Chodorow (ed.), *Proceedings of the Eighth International Congress of Medieval Canon Law* (Rome, 1992), 369–86.
Constable, G., *'Love and Do What You Will': The Medieval History of an Augustinian Precept. The Morton W. Bloomfield Lectures on English Literature* (Kalamazoo, MI, 1999).
Coolman, B. T., 'Hugh of St. Victor on "Jesus Wept": compassion as ideal *humanitas*', *Theological Studies* 69 (2008), 528–56.
Cooper, A., 'The king's four highways: legal fiction meets fictional law', *Journal of Medieval History* 26 (2000), 351–70.
——, '"The feet of those who bark shall be cut off": timorous historians and the personality of Henry I', *Anglo-Norman Studies* 23 (2001), 47–68.
Corner, David, 'The texts of Henry II's assizes', in A. Harding (ed.), *Law-Making and Law-Makers in British History* (London, 1980), 7–20.
——, 'The earliest surviving manuscripts of Roger of Howden's "Chronica"', *English Historical Review* 98 (1983), 297–310.
——, 'The *Gesta Regis Henrici Secundi* and *Chronica* of Roger, Parson of Howden', *Bulletin of the Institute of Historical Research* 56:134 (1983), 126–44.
Corrie, M., 'The compilation of Oxford, Bodleian Library, MS Digby 86', *Medium Aevum* 66:2 (1997), 236–49.
Cotts, J. D., 'Peter of Blois and the problem of the "court" in the late twelfth century', *Anglo-Norman Studies* 27 (2004), 68–84.
——, *The Clerical Dilemma: Peter of Blois and Literature Culture in the Twelfth Century* (Washington, DC, 2009).
Courtney, F., *Cardinal Robert Pullen: An English Theologian of the Twelfth Century* (Rome, 1954).

Coutre, R. A., 'The use of epikeia in natural law: its early developments', Église et théologie 4 (1973), 71–93.
Cowdrey, H. E. J., 'Pope Gregory VII and the chastity of the clergy', in M. Frassetto (ed.), Medieval Purity and Piety: Essays on Medieval Clerical Celibacy and Religious Reform (New York and London, 1998), 269–304.
Cramer, Peter, 'Ernulf of Rochester and early Anglo-Norman canon law', Journal of Ecclesiastical History 40 (1989), 483–510.
——, Baptism and Change in the Early Middle Ages c. 200–c. 1150 (Cambridge, 1993).
Crook, D., 'The records of Forest Eyres in the Public Record Office, 1179 to 1670', Journal of the Society of Archivists 17:2 (1996), 183–93.
Crouch, D., 'The last adventure of Richard Siward', Morgannwg: Transactions of the Glamorgan Local History Society 35 (1991), 7–30.
Cubitt, C., 'Bishops, priests and penance in late Anglo-Saxon England', Early Medieval Europe 14 (2006), 41–63.
Dalton, Paul, 'Churchmen and the promotion of peace in King Stephen's reign', Viator 31 (2000), 79–119.
D'Alverny, M., 'L'Obit de Raoul Ardent', Archives d'histoire doctrinale et littéraire du moyen âge 15/17 (1940), 403–5.
Damien-Grint, P., The New Historians of the Twelfth-Century Renaissance: Inventing Vernacular Authority (Woodbridge, 1999).
Dammery, R., 'Editing the Anglo-Saxon laws: Felix Liebermann and beyond', in D. G. Scragg and P. E. Szarmach (eds), The Editing of Old English: Papers from the 1990 Manchester Conference (Woodbridge, 1994), 251–61.
Dannenberg, Lars-Arne, 'Charity and law. The juristic implementation of a core monastic principle', in Gert Melville (ed.), Aspects of Charity: Concern for One's Neighbour in the Medieval Vita Religiosa (Münster, 2011), 11–28.
Davies, Wendy, 'Judges and judging: truth and justice in Northern Iberia on the eve of the millennium', Journal of Medieval History 36 (2010), 193–203.
D'Avray, D., 'Magna Carta: its background in Stephen Langton's academic biblical exegesis and its episcopal reception', Studi Medievali 38 (1997), 423–38.
Delhaye, P., 'L'enseignement de la philosophie morale au XIIe siècle', Mediaeval Studies 11 (1949), 77–99.
——, 'Deux textes de Senatus de Worcester sur la pénitence', RTAM 19 (1952), 203–24.
——, 'La vertu et les vertus dans les oeuvres d'Alain de Lille', Cahiers de civilisation médiévale 6 (1963), 13–25.

Bibliography

Denholm-Young, N., 'Who wrote *Fleta*?', *English Historical Review* 58 (1943), 1–12.

Dickey, Mary, 'Some commentaries on the *De inventione* and *Ad Herennium* of the eleventh and early twelfth centuries', *Mediaeval and Renaissance Studies* 6 (1968), 1–41.

Diehl, Peter, 'Ad abolendam (X 5.7.9) and imperial legislation against heresy', *Bulletin of Medieval Canon Law* 19 (1989), 1–11.

Dodaro, R., *Christ and the Just Society in the Thought of Augustine* (Cambridge, 2004).

Donahue, Charles, Jr., 'Proof by witnesses in the church courts of medieval England: an imperfect reception of the learned law', in M. S. Arnold (ed.), *On the Laws and Customs of England: Essays in Honor of Samuel E. Thorne* (Chapel Hill, NC, 1981), 127–58.

Dowling, Melissa Barden, *Clemency and Cruelty in the Roman World* (Ann Abor, MI, 2006).

Downer, L. J., 'Legal history – is it human?', *Melbourne University Law Review* 1 (1963), 1–16.

Duggan, Anne J., 'John of Salisbury and Thomas Becket', in M. Wilks (ed.), *The World of John of Salisbury* (Oxford, 1984), 427–38.

———, 'Classical quotations and allusions in the correspondence of Thomas Becket: an investigation of their sources', *Viator* 32 (2001), 1–22.

———, '"Tempering in the wind ...": moderation and discretion in late twelfth-century papal decretals', *Studies in Church History* 43 (2007), 180–90.

———, 'Conciliar law 1123–1215: the legislation of the four Lateran Councils', in Wilfried Hartmann and Kenneth Pennington (eds), *The History of Medieval Canon Law in the Classical Period, 1140–1234: From Gratian to the Decretals of Pope Gregory IX* (Washington, DC, 2008), 318–66.

Duggan, C., 'The Becket dispute and the criminous clerks', *Bulletin of the Institute of Historical Research* 35:91 (1962), 1–28.

———, 'English canonists and the "Appendix Concilii Lateranensis" with an analysis of St. John's College, Cambridge, MS 148', *Traditio* 18 (1962), 459–68.

———, *Twelfth-Century Decretal Collections and Their Importance in English History* (London, 1963).

———, 'The reception of canon law in England in the later-twelfth century', in S. Kuttner and J. Ryan (eds), *Proceedings of the Second International Congress of Medieval Canon Law* (Rome, 1965), 359–90.

———, 'Equity and compassion in papal marriage decretals to England', in Willy van Hoecke and Andries Welkhuysen (eds), *Love and Marriage in the Twelfth Century* (Louvain, 1981), 59–87.

———, 'Papal judges delegate and the making of the 'new law' in the twelfth century', in T. N. Bisson (ed.), *Cultures of Power: Lordship, Status, and Process in Twelfth-Century Europe* (Philadelphia, 1995), 172–99.

Dunbabin, Jean, 'Robert Grosseteste as translator, transmitter and commentator: the *Nicomachean Ethics*', *Traditio* 28 (1972), 460–72.

Evans, G. R., *Anselm and a New Generation* (Oxford, 1980).

———, *Old Arts and New Theology: The Beginnings of Theology as an Academic Discipline* (Oxford, 1980).

———, *Alan of Lille: The Frontiers of Theology in the Later Twelfth Century* (Cambridge, 1983).

———, 'Thomas of Chobham on preaching and exegesis', *RTAM* 52 (1985), 159–70.

———, *Anselm* (London, 1989).

———, 'Exegesis and authority in the thirteenth century', in M. D. Jordan and K. Emery (eds), *Ad litteram: Authoritative Texts and Their Medieval Readers* (Notre Dame, IN, 1992), 93–111.

———, *Law and Theology in the Middle Ages* (London, 2001).

Ferguson, Everett, *Baptism in the Early Church: History, Theology and Liturgy in the First Five Centuries* (Cambridge, 2009).

Ferruolo, Stephen C., *The Origins of the University: The Schools of Paris and Their Critics, 1100–1215* (Stanford, 1985).

———, '"Quid dant artes nisi luctum?" Learning, ambition, and careers in the medieval university', *History of Education Quarterly* 28 (1988), 1–22.

Firey, A., '"For I was hungry and you fed me": social justice and economic thought in the Latin patristic and medieval christian traditions', in S. Lowry and B. Gordon (eds), *Ancient and Medieval Economic Ideas and Concepts of Social Justice* (Leiden, 1997), 333–70.

Firth, Francis, 'The "Poenitentiale" of Robert of Flamborough', *Traditio* 16 (1960), 541–61.

———, 'More about Robert of Flamborough's Penitential', *Traditio* 17 (1961), 531–3.

Flahiff, G. B., 'Ralph Niger: an introduction to his life and works', *Mediaeval Studies* 2 (1940), 104–26.

Flint, Valerie I. J., 'The saint and the operations of the law: reflections upon the miracles of St. Thomas Cantilupe', in Richard Gameson and Henrietta Leyser (eds), *Belief and Culture in the Middle Ages: Essays Presented to Henry Mayr-Harting* (Oxford, 2001), 342–57.

Forhan, Kate Langdon, 'Salisburian stakes: the uses of "tyranny" in John of Salisbury's *Policraticus*', *History of Political Thought* 11 (1990), 397–407.

Bibliography

Forrest, Ian, *The Detection of Heresy in Late Medieval England* (Oxford, 2005).

Fraher, R. M., 'The theoretical justification for the new criminal law of the high middle ages: "rei publicae interest, ne crimina remaneant impunita"', *University of Illinois Law Review* (1984), 577–95.

——, 'Conviction according to conscience: the medieval jurists' debate concerning judicial discretion and the law of proof', *Law and History Review* 7 (1989), 23–88.

Fredborg, Karin Margareta, 'The commentaries on Cicero's *De inventione* and *Rhetorica ad Herennium* by William of Champeaux', *Cahiers de l'Institut du moyen-âge grec et latin* 17 (1976), 1–39.

——, 'The scholastic teaching of rhetoric in the middle ages', *Cahiers de l'Institut du moyen-âge grec et latin* 55 (1987), 85–105.

——, 'Ciceronian rhetoric and the schools', in John van Engen (ed.), *Learning Institutionalised: Teaching in the Medieval University* (Notre Dame, IN, 2000), 21–41.

——, 'Petrus Helias's *Summa* on Cicero's *De inventione*', *Traditio* 64 (2009), 139–82.

Fried, Johannes, 'Gerard Pucelle und Köln', *Zeitschrift der Savigny-Stiftung für Rechtsgeschichte: Romanistische Abteilung* 99 (1982), 125–35.

Fryde, Natalie M., 'The roots of Magna Carta: opposition to the Plantagenets', in Joseph Canning and Otto Gerhard Oexele (eds), *Political Thought and the Realities of Power in the Middle Ages* (Göttingen, 1998), 53–65.

Gabel, Leona C., *Benefit of Clergy in England in the Later Middle Ages* (New York, 1969).

Gameson, Richard, *The Manuscripts of Early Norman England (1066–1130)* (Oxford, 1999).

Garnett, George, 'The third recension of the English Coronation *Ordo*: the manuscripts', *Haskins Society Journal* 11 (2003), 43–71.

——, *Conquered England: Kingship, Succession and Tenure 1066–1166* (Oxford, 2007).

Gauvard, Claude, *'De grace especial': crime, état et société en France à la fin du moyen âge* (2 vols, Paris, 1991).

Gibson, Margaret, 'Lanfranc's commentary on the Pauline epistles', *Journal of Theological Studies* 22 (1971), 86–112.

——, 'The twelfth-century glossed Bible', *Studia Patristica* 23 (1990), 232–44.

Gieben, S., 'Robert Grosseteste at the papal curia: edition of the documents', *Collectanea Franciscana* 41 (1971), 340–93.

Gildea, J., 'Extant manuscripts of the *Compendium in Job* of Peter of Blois', *Scriptorium: revue internationale des études relatives aux manuscrits* 30 (1976), 285–7.
Gillingham, John, 'Conquering the barbarians: war and chivalry in Britain and Ireland', *Haskins Society Journal* 4 (1992), 67–84.
——, 'The English invasion of Ireland', in Brendan Bradshaw, Andrew Hadfield and Willy Maley (eds), *Representing Ireland: Literature and the Origins of Conflict* (Cambridge, 1993), 24–42.
——, '1066 and the introduction of chivalry into England', in G. Garnett and J. Hudson (eds), *Law and Government in Medieval England and Normandy: Essays in Honour of Sir James Holt* (Cambridge, 1994), 31–55.
——, 'Writing the biography of Roger of Howden, king's clerk and chronicler', in David Bates, Julia Crick, Sarah Hamilton and Frank Barlow (eds), *Writing Medieval Biography, 750–1250: Essays in Honour of Professor Frank Barlow* (Woodbridge, 2006), 207–20.
Glorieux, Palémon, *Répertoire des maîtres en théologie de Paris au XIIIe siècle* (2 vols, Paris, 1933–34).
Goddu, A. A., and Rouse, R. H., 'Gerald of Wales and the *Florilegium Angelicum*', *Speculum* 52 (1977), 488–521.
Goebel, J., Jr, *Felony and Misdemeanour: A Study in the History of Criminal Law* (New York, 1937).
Goering, Joseph, 'The *Summa de penitentia* of Magister Serlo', *Mediaeval Studies* 38 (1976), 1–53.
——, 'The *Summa* of Magister Serlo and thirteenth-century penitential literature', *Mediaeval Studies* 40 (1978), 290–311.
——, 'The early penitential writings of Robert Grosseteste', *RTAM* 54 (1987), 68–111.
——, *William de Montibus: The Schools and the Literature of Pastoral Care* (Toronto, 1992).
——, 'The *summa* "Qui bene presunt" and its author', in R. G. Newhauser and J. A. Alford (eds), *Literature and Religion in the Later Middle Ages: Philological Studies in Honor of Siegfried Wenzel* (Binghamton, NY, 1995), 143–59.
——, 'The scholastic turn (1100–1500): penitential theology and law in the schools', in Abigail Firey (ed.), *A New History of Penance* (Leiden, 2007), 219–38.
——, 'The internal forum and the literature of penance', in Wilfried Hartmann and Kenneth Pennington (eds), *The History of Medieval Canon Law in the Classical Period, 1140–1234: From Gratian to the Decretals of Pope Gregory IX* (Washington, DC, 2008), 379–428.

Bibliography

Goodrich, W. E., 'The limits of friendship: a disagreement between Saint Bernard and Peter the Venerable on the role of charity in dispensation from the Rule', *Cistercian Studies* 2 (1981), 81–97.

Goodwin, Deborah L., 'Herbert of Bosham and the horizons of twelfth-century exegesis', *Traditio* 58 (2003), 133–73.

Gransden, A., *Historical Writing in England* (2 vols, London, 1974–82).

Green, Judith A., *The Government of England under Henry I* (Cambridge, 1986).

Green, T. A., 'Societal concepts of criminal liability for homicide in medieval England', *Speculum* 47 (1972), 669–94.

——, 'The criminal trial jury: origins and early development – an interpretive overview', in T. A. Green, *Verdict According to Conscience: Perspectives on the English Criminal Trial Jury, 1200–1800* (Chicago, 1985), 3–27.

Groot, Roger D., 'The jury of presentment before 1215', *American Journal of Legal History* 26 (1982), 1–24.

Gründel, Johannes, 'L'Oeuvre encyclopédique de Raoul Ardent, le *Speculum universale*', *Cahiers d'histoire mondiale* 9 (1966), 553–70.

——, *Die Lehre des Radulfus Ardens von den Berstandestugenden auf dem Hintergund seinen Seelenlehre* (Munich, 1976).

Hamilton, Sarah, '"Remedies for great transgressions": penance and excommunication in late Anglo-Saxon England', in Francesca Tinti (ed.), *Pastoral Care in Late Anglo-Saxon England* (Woodbridge, 2005), 83–105.

Harding, Alan, 'The reflection of thirteenth-century legal growth in Saint Thomas's writings', in G. Verbeke and D. Verhelst (eds), *Aquinas and the Problems of his Time* (Louvain, 1970), 18–37.

Haskins, Charles Homer, *The Renaissance of the Twelfth Century* (Cambridge, MA, 1927).

Helmholz, R. M., 'Bastardy litigation in medieval England', *American Journal of Legal History* 13:4 (1969), 360–83.

——, 'Canonists and standards of impartiality for papal judges delegate', *Traditio* 25 (1969), 386–404.

——, 'Ethical standards for advocates and proctors in theory and practice', in Stephan Kuttner (ed.), *Proceedings of the Fourth International Congress of Medieval Canon Law* (Rome, 1976), 283–99.

——, *Canon Law and the Law of England* (London, 1987).

——, 'Excommunication in twelfth century England', *Journal of Law and Religion* 11 (1994–95), 235–53.

——, 'Excommunication and the Angevin leap forward', *Haskins Society Journal* 5 (1995), 133–49.

———, 'The learned laws in Pollock and Maitland', in John Hudson (ed.), *The History of English Law: Centenary Essays on 'Pollock and Maitland'* (Oxford, 1996), 145–69.

———, *The Ius Commune in England: Four Studies* (Oxford, 2001).

Higonnet, E. C., 'Spiritual ideas in the letters of Peter of Blois', *Speculum* 50 (1975), 218–44.

Hill, Rosalind, 'The theory and practice of excommunication in medieval England', *History* 42 (1957), 1–11.

Hine, H. M., 'The younger Seneca', in L. D. Reynolds (ed.), *Texts and Transmission: A Survey of the Latin Classics in the Middle Ages* (Oxford, 1983), 376–8.

Hinton, J., 'Walter Map's *De nugis curialium*: its plan and composition', *Proceedings of the Modern Language Association* 32 (1917), 81–132.

Hollister, C. Warren, 'Royal acts of mutilation: the case against Henry I', *Albion* 10:4 (1978), 330–40.

———, *Henry I* (London, 2001).

Holt, J. C., *Magna Carta* (Cambridge, 1965).

Hudson, John, 'Administration, family and perceptions of the past in late twelfth-century England: Richard FitzNigel and the "Dialogue of the Exchequer"', in Paul Magdalino (ed.), *Perceptions of the Past in Twelfth-Century Europe* (London, 1992), 75–98.

———, *Land, Law and Lordship in Anglo-Norman England* (Oxford, 1994).

———, *The Formation of English Common Law: Law and Society in England from the Norman Conquest to Magna Carta* (London, 1996).

———, 'Maitland and Anglo-Norman Law', in John Hudson (ed.), *The History of English Law: Centenary Essays on 'Pollock and Maitland'* (Oxford, 1996), 21–46.

———, 'Court Cases and Legal Arguments in England, c.1066–1166', *Transactions of the Royal Historical Society* 10 (2000), 91–116.

———, 'Power, law, and the administration of justice in England, 900–1200', in P. Andersen, Mia Münster-Swendsen and Helle Vogt (eds), *Law and Power in the Middle Ages* (Copenhagen, 2008), 153–70.

———, 'From the *Leges* to *Glanvill*: legal expertise and legal reasoning', in Andrew Rabin, Stefan Jurasinski and Lisi Oliver (eds), *English Law before Magna Carta: Felix Liebermann and 'Die Gesetze der Angelsachsen'* (Leiden, 2010), 221–50.

———, 'Magna Carta, the *Ius Commune* and English common law', in J. S. Loengard (ed.) *Magna Carta and the England of King John* (Woodbridge, 2010), 99–119.

Huizing, P., 'The earliest development of excommunication *latae sententiae* by Gratian and the earliest decretists', *Studia Gratiana* 3 (1955), 279–309.

Huneycutt, Lois L., 'Intercession and the high-medieval queen: the Esther topos', in Jennifer Carpenter and Sally-Beth MacLean (eds), *Power of the Weak: Studies in Medieval Women* (Toronto, 1990), 126–46.

Hunt, R. W., *The Schools and the Cloister: The Life and Writings of Alexander Nequam, 1157–1217*, ed. and revised by M. Gibson (Oxford, 1984).

Hunt, T., '"The Four Daughters of God": a textual contribution', *Archives d'histoire doctrinale et littéraire du moyen âge* 48 (1981), 287–316.

Hurnard, Naomi D., 'The jury of presentment and the Assize of Clarendon', *English Historical Review* 56 (1941), 374–410.

——, 'The Anglo-Norman franchises', *English Historical Review* 64 (1949), 289–327.

——, 'The Anglo-Norman franchises (continued)', *English Historical Review* 64 (1949), 433–60.

——, *The King's Pardon for Homicide before 1307 A.D.* (Oxford, 1969).

Hyams, Paul R., 'Trial by ordeal: the key to proof in the early common law', in M. S. Arnold (ed.), *On the Laws and Customs of England: Essays in Honor of Samuel E. Thorne* (Chapel Hill, NC, 1981), 90–126.

——, 'The common law and the French connection', *Anglo-Norman Studies* 4 (1982), 77–92.

——, 'Warranty and good lordship in twelfth-century England', *Law and History Review* 5 (1987), 437–503.

——, 'What did Edwardian villagers understand by "law"?', in Z. Razi and R. M. Smith (eds), *Medieval Society and the Manor Court* (Oxford, 1996), 69–102.

——, 'What did Henry III think in bed and in French about kingship and anger?', in B. H. Rosenwein (ed.), *Anger's Past: The Social Uses of an Emotion in the Middle Ages* (Ithaca, NY and London, 1998), 92–125.

——, *Rancor and Reconciliation in Medieval England* (Ithaca, NY and London, 2003).

——, 'Thinking English law in French: the Angevins and the common law', in Belle S. Tuten and Tracey L. Billado (eds), *Feud, Violence and Practice: Essays in Medieval Studies in Honor of Stephen D. White* (Farnham, 2010), 175–96.

Iozzio, Mary Jo, 'Odon Lottin, OSB (1880–1965) and the renewal of agent-centered moral thought', *Modern Schoolman* 84 (2006), 1–16.

James, M. R., *A Descriptive Catalogue of the Manuscripts in the Library of Gonville and Gaius College* (2 vols, Cambridge, 1907–8).

Bibliography

——, *A Descriptive Catalogue of the Manuscripts in the Library of Corpus Christi College Cambridge* (2 vols, Cambridge, 1912).
——, 'Robert Grosseteste on the psalms', *Journal of Theological Studies* 23 (1922), 181–5.
Jordan, W. C., 'A fresh look at medieval sanctuary', in Ruth Mazo Karras, Joel Kaye and E. Ann Matter (eds), *Law and the Illicit in Medieval Europe* (Philadelphia, 2008), 17–32.
Kaeuper, Richard W., *Chivalry and Violence in Medieval Europe* (Oxford, 1999).
——, 'Vengeance and mercy in chivalric mentalité', in T. B. Lambert and David Rollason (eds), *Peace and Protection in the Middle Ages* (Durham, 2009), 168–80.
Kantorowicz, H., and Smalley, B., 'An English theologian's view of Roman law: Pepo, Irnerius, Ralph Niger', *Mediaeval and Renaissance Studies* 1 (1941), 237–52.
Karn, Nicholas, 'Rethinking the *Leges Henrici Primi*', in Andrew Rabin, Stefan Jurasinski and Lisi Oliver (eds), *English Law before Magna Carta: Felix Liebermann and 'Die Gesetze der Angelsachsen'* (Leiden, 2010), 199–220.
Kay, R., 'Gerald of Wales and the Fourth Lateran Council', *Viator* 29 (1998), 79–94.
Kemp, B. R., 'Exchequer and bench in the later twelfth century – separate or identical tribunals?', *English Historical Review* 88 (1973), 559–73.
King, Edmund, 'Dispute settlement in Anglo-Norman England', *Anglo-Norman Studies* 14 (1992), 115–30.
Knight, G. R., *The Correspondence between Peter the Venerable and Bernard of Clairvaux: A Semantic and Structural Analysis* (Aldershot, 2002).
Knowles, David, *The Episcopal Colleagues of Archbishop Thomas Becket* (Cambridge, 1951).
——, *Great Historical Enterprises; Problems in Monastic History* (London, 1963).
Koziol, G., *Begging Pardon and Favor: Ritual and Political Order in Early Medieval France* (London, 1992).
——, 'England, France and the problem of sacrality in twelfth-century ritual', in T. N. Bisson (ed.), *Cultures of Power: Lordship, Status, and Process in Twelfth-Century Europe* (Philadelphia, 1995), 124–48.
Kramer, S. R., 'The priest in the house of conscience: sins of thought and the twelfth-century schoolmen', *Viator* 37 (2006), 149–66.
Kuttner, Stephan, 'Pierre de Roissy and Robert of Flamborough', *Traditio* 2 (1944), 489–99.
——, *Harmony from Dissonance: An Interpretation of Medieval Canon Law* (Latrobe, PA, 1960).

——, 'Urban II and the doctrine of interpretation: a turning point?', *Studia Gratiana* 15 (1972), 55–85.

——, 'The decretal "Presbiterum" (JL 13912) – a letter of Leo IX', *Bulletin of Medieval Canon Law* 5 (1975), 133–5.

——, 'A forgotten definition of justice', *Studia Gratiana* 20 (1976), 73–110.

Kuttner, Stephan, and Rathbone, Eleanor, 'Anglo-Norman canonists of the twelfth century: an introductory study', *Traditio* 7 (1949–51), 279–348.

Lacey, Helen, *The Royal Pardon: Access to Mercy in Fourteenth-Century England* (Woodbridge, 2009).

Lachaud, Frédérique, 'Ethics and office in England in the thirteenth century', *Thirteenth-Century England* 11 (2005), 16–30.

Lacombe, George, 'The authenticity of the *Summa* of Cardinal Stephen Langton', *New Scholasticism* 4 (1930), 97–114.

Lacombe, George, and Smalley, Beryl, *Studies on the Commentaries of Cardinal Stephen Langton* (reprinted from *Archives d'histoire doctrinale et littéraire du moyen âge*, 1931).

Lambert, Malcolm D., *Franciscan Poverty: The Doctrine of Absolute Poverty of Christ and the Apostles in the Franciscan Order, 1210–1323* (New York, 1998).

Lambertini, Roberto, 'Political prudence in some medieval commentaries on the sixth book of the *Nicomachean Ethics*', in I. P. Bejczy (ed.), *Virtue Ethics in the Middle Ages: Commentaries on Aristotle's Nicomachean Ethics, 1200–1500* (Leiden, 2008), 223–46.

Landgraf, Artur M., 'Problèmes relatifs aux premières gloses des Sentences', *RTAM* 3 (1931), 140–57.

——, *Einführung in die Geschichte der theologischen Literatur der Frühscholastik, unter dem Gesichtspunkte der Schulenbildung* (Regensburg, 1948).

——, *Dogmengeschichte der Frühscholastik* (4 vols, Regensburg, 1952).

Långfors, A., 'Le theme des quatre filles de Dieu', in 'Notice sur le numéro 14886 des manuscrits latins de la Bibliothèque Nationale et autres bibliothèques', *Notices et extraits* 31:2 (1886), 293–313.

Langmuir, G. I., 'Community and legal change in Capetian France', *French Historical Studies* 6 (1970), 275–86.

Larson, Atria A., 'The evolution of Gratian's *Tractatus de Penitentia*', *Bulletin of Medieval Canon Law* 26 (2004–6), 59–123.

Lefebvre, C., '"Aequitas canonica" et "Periculum animae" dans la doctrine de l'Hostiensis', *Ephemerides Iuris Canonici* 8 (1952), 305–21.

——, 'La notion d'équité chez Pierre Lombard', *Ephemerides Iuris Canonici* 9 (1953), 291–304.

——, 'Natural equity and canonical equity', *Natural Law Forum* 8 (1963), 122–36.

Bibliography

Leff, G., 'The apostolic ideal in later medieval ecclesiology', *Journal of Theological Studies* 18 (1967), 58–82.

Leftow, B., 'Anselm's perfect being theology', in Brian Davies and Brian Leftow (eds), *The Cambridge Companion to Anselm* (Cambridge, 2004), 132–56.

Legg, L. G. Wickham, *English Coronation Records* (London, 1901).

Legge, M. Dominica, *Anglo-Norman Literature and its Background* (Oxford, 1963).

Lewis, Charles E., 'Canonists and law clerks in the household of Archbishop Hubert Walter', in Richard H. Bowers (ed.), *Seven Studies in Medieval English History and Other Historical Essays: Presented to Harold S. Snellgrove* (Jackson, MS, 1983), 57–64.

Liu, W., 'Competing for justice beyond law between Croyland and Spalding, 1189–1202', *Anglo-American Law Review* 29 (2000), 67–96.

Lloyd, S., and Hunt, T., 'William Longespee', *Nottingham Medieval Studies* 35 (1991), 41–69.

——, 'William Longespee II', *Nottingham Medieval Studies* 36 (1992), 79–125.

Lottin, O., 'Le problème de l'*ignorantia iuris* de Gratien à saint Thomas d'Aquin', *RTAM* 5 (1933), 345–68.

——, 'Le concept de justice chez les théologiens du moyen âge avant l'introduction d'Aristote', *Revue thomiste* 44 (1938), 511–21.

——, *Psychologie et morale aux XIIe et XIIIe siècles* (6 vols, Louvain: Abbaye du Mont-César, 1942–60).

——, 'La doctrine d'Anselme de Laon sur les dons du Saint-Esprit et son influence', *RTAM* 24 (1957), 267–95.

Lutz-Bachmann, M., 'The discovery of a normative theory of justice in medieval philosophy', *Medieval Philosophy and Theology* 9 (2001), 1–14.

McEvoy, J., 'Robert Grosseteste on the Ten Commandments', *RTAM* 58 (1991), 167–205.

——, *Robert Grosseteste* (Oxford, 2000).

——, 'The edition of a sermon on the Decalogue attributed to Robert Grosseteste', *Recherches de théologie et philosophie médiévales* 67 (2001), 228–44.

McGrath, Alister, *Iustitia Dei: A History of the Christian Doctrine of Justification* (Cambridge, 1986).

McHardy, A. K., 'Church courts and criminous clerks in the later middle ages', in M. J. Franklin and C. Harper-Bill (eds), *Medieval Ecclesiastical Studies in Honour of Dorothy M. Owen* (Woodbridge, 1995), 165–83.

McKeon, Richard, 'Rhetoric in the middle ages', *Speculum* 17 (1942), 1–32.

Mackie, E. A., 'Scribal intervention and the question of audience: editing *Le Château d'amour*', in E. A. Mackie and J. Goering (eds), *Editing Robert*

Bibliography

Grosseteste: Papers Given at the Thirty-Sixth Annual Conference on Editorial Problems (Toronto, 2003), 61–77.

McKitterick, R., 'Perceptions of justice in Western Europe in the ninth and tenth centuries', in *La giustizia nell'alto Medioevo (secoli IX–XI)* (2 vols, Spoleto, 1997), vol. 2, 1075–104.

McLoughlin, John, 'The language of persecution: John of Salisbury and the early phase of the Becket dispute (1163–66)', *Studies in Church History* 21 (1984), 73–87.

McNeill, J. T., 'Medicine for sin as prescribed in the penitentials', *Church History* 1 (1932), 14–26.

McSweeney, Thomas J., 'Between England and France: a cross-channel legal culture in the late thirteenth century', in Richard W. Kaeuper (ed.), *Law, Governance, and Justice: New Views on Medieval Constitutionalism* (Leiden, 2013), 73–100.

Maddicott, John, *Royal Justices as Retainers in Thirteenth- and Fourteenth-Century England* (Oxford, 1978).

——, 'Magna Carta and the local community, 1215–1259', *Past and Present* 102 (1984), 25–65.

——, *Simon de Montfort* (Cambridge, 1994).

Maitland, Frederic William, *Bracton's Note Book: A Collection of Cases Decided in the King's Courts during the Reign of Henry the Third* (3 vols, London, 1887).

——, *The Collected Papers of Frederic William Maitland, Downing Professor of the Laws of England*, ed. H. A. L. Fisher (3 vols, Cambridge, 1911).

Mäkinen, Virpi, *Property Rights in the Late Medieval Discussion on Franciscan Poverty* (Leuven, 2001).

Malegam, Jehangir Yezdi, *The Sleep of Behemoth: Disputing Peace and Violence in Medieval Europe, 1000–1200* (Ithaca, NY, 2013).

Mansfield, M., *The Humiliation of Sinners: Public Penance in Thirteenth-Century France* (Ithaca, NY, 1995).

Mantello, F. A. C., 'Robert Grosseteste and his cathedral chapter: an edition of the chapter's objections to episcopal visitations', *Mediaeval Studies* 47 (1985), 367–78.

Markus, Robert A., *Saeculum: History and Society in the Thought of St. Augustine* (Cambridge, 1970).

Martin, Janet, 'John of Salisbury as classical scholar', in M. Wilks (ed.), *The World of John of Salisbury* (Oxford, 1984), 179–201.

Martin, N., 'Die "Compilatio decretorum" des Kardinal Laborans', in Peter Linehan (ed.), *Proceedings of the Seventh International Congress of Medieval Canon Law* (Rome, 1988), 125–39.

Bibliography

Martindale, Jane, '"His special friend"? The settlement of disputes and political power in the kingdom of the French (tenth to twelfth century)', *Transactions of the Royal Historical Society* 5 (1996), 21–57.

——, 'Between law and politics: the judicial duel under the Angevin Kings (mid-twelfth century to 1204)', in Pauline Stafford, Janet L. Nelson and Jane Martindale (eds), *Law, Laity and Solidarities: Essays in Honour of Susan Reynolds* (Manchester, 2001), 116–49.

Marx, C. William, *The Devil's Rights and the Redemption in the Literature of Medieval England* (Cambridge, 1995).

——, 'The *Conflictus inter Deum et Diabolum* and the emergence of the literature of law in thirteenth-century England', *Thirteenth-Century England* 13 (2009), 57–66.

Mary Immaculate, Sr [Creek], 'The Four Daughters of God in the *Gesta Romanorum* and the *Court of Sapience*', *Proceedings of the Modern Language Association* 57:4 (1942), 951–65.

Matthew, D. J. A., 'The letter-writing of Archbishop Becket', in Richard Gameson and Henrietta Leyser (eds), *Belief and Culture in the Middle Ages: Essays Presented to Henry Mayr-Harting* (Oxford, 2001), 287–303.

Mayr-Harting, Henry, 'Henry II and the papacy, 1170–89', *Journal of Ecclesiastical History* 16 (1965), 39–53.

——, 'The role of Benedictine abbeys in the development of Oxford as a centre of legal learning', in H. Wansbrough and A. Marett-Todd (eds), *Benedictines in Oxford* (London, 1997), 11–19.

Meekings, C. A. F., 'Martin Pateshull and William Raleigh', *Bulletin of the Institute of Historical Research* 26:74 (1953), 157–80.

Melve, L., 'The public debate on clerical marriage in the late eleventh century', *Journal of Ecclesiastical History* 61 (2010), 688–701.

Mews, Constant, '*Logica* in the service of philosophy: William of Champeaux and his influence', in Rainer Berndt (ed.), *Schrift, Schreiber, Schenker: Studien zur Abtei Sankt Viktor in Paris und den Viktorinern* (Berlin, 2005), 89–96.

Michaud-Quantin P., 'Die Psychologie bei Radulphus Ardens, einem Theologen des ausgehenden XII. Jahrunderts', *Münchener theologische Zeitschrift* 9 (1958), 81–96.

——, 'A propos de premières *Summae confessorum*: théologie et droit canonique, *RTAM* 26 (1959), 264–306.

——, 'Les méthodes de la pastorale du XIIIe au XVe siècle', in Albert Zimmermann (ed.), *Methoden in Wissenschaft und Kunst des Mittelalters. Miscellanea Mediaevalia* 7 (Berlin, 1970), 76–91.

Miller, W., 'In defense of revenge', in B. A. Hanawalt and D. Wallace (eds), *Medieval Crime and Social Control* (Minneapolis, MN, 1999), 70–89

Milsom, S. F. C., *The Historical Foundations of the Common Law* (London, 1981).

Minio-Paluello, L., 'Iacobus Veneticus Grecus: Canonist and Translator of Aristotle', *Traditio* 8 (1952), 265–304.

Mooers Christelow, S., 'The royal love in Anglo-Norman England: fiscal or courtly concept?', *Haskins Society Journal* 8 (1996), 26–41.

Moore, John C., 'Papal justice in France around the time of Pope Innocent III', *Church History* 41 (1972), 295–306.

Moore, R. I., *The Origins of European Dissent* (London, 1977).

——, *The Formation of a Persecuting Society: Power and Deviance in Western Europe, 950–1250* (Oxford, 1987).

——, 'Literacy and the making of heresy, c.1000–c.1150', in Peter Biller and Anne Hudson (eds), *Heresy and Literacy, 1000–1530* (Cambridge, 1994), 19–37.

Moore, Rebecca, 'Jewish influence on Christian biblical interpretation: Hugh of St Victor and "The Four Daughters of God"', in Craig Evans (ed.), *Of Scribes and Sages: Early Jewish Interpretation and Transmission of Scripture* (Edinburgh, 2004), 148–58.

Morenzoni, Franco, *Des écoles aux paroisses: Thomas de Chobham et la promotion de la prédication au début du XIIIe siècle* (Paris, 1995).

Morey, A., *Bartholomew of Exeter, Bishop and Canonist: A Study in the Twelfth Century* (Cambridge, 1937).

Morey, A., and Brooke, C. N. L., *Gilbert Foliot and His Letters* (Cambridge, 1965).

Morris, Colin, 'William I and the church courts', *English Historical Review* 82 (1967), 449–63.

——, 'From synod to consistory: the bishops' courts in England, 1150–1250', *Journal of Ecclesiastical History* 22 (1971), 115–23.

Mortensen, Lars Boje, 'The texts and contexts of Roman history in twelfth-century western scholarship', in Paul Magdalino (ed.), *The Perceptions of the Past in Twelfth-Century Europe* (London, 1992), 99–116.

Munk-Olsen, B., 'Les classiques latines dans les florilèges médiévaux antérieurs aux XIIIe siècle', *Revue d'histoire des textes* 9 (1979), 47–121 and 10 (1980), 47–172.

——, 'La popularité des textes classiques entre la IXe et la XIIe siècle', *Revue d'histoire des textes* 14–15 (1984–85), 169–81.

——, 'La diffusion et l'étude des historiens antiques au XIIe siècle', in Andries Welkenhuysen, Herman Braet and Werner Verbeke (eds), *Medieval Antiquity* (Leuven, 1995), 21–43.

Münster-Swendsen, Mia, 'Settings things straight: law, justice and ethics in the *Orationes* of Lawrence of Durham', *Anglo-Norman Studies* 27 (2005), 151–68.

Murphy, James J., 'Saint Augustine and the debate about a Christian rhetoric', *Quarterly Journal of Speech* 46 (1960), 1–10.

——, 'Saint Augustine and Rabanus Maurus: the genesis of medieval rhetoric', *Western Speech* 31 (1967), 97–110.

Murray, A., 'Confession before 1215', *Transactions of the Royal Historical Society* 3 (1993), 51–81.

Musson, Anthony J., *Medieval Law in Context: The Growth of Legal Consciousness from Magna Carta to the Peasants' Revolt* (Manchester, 2001).

——, 'Controlling human behaviour? The last judgment in late medieval art and architecture', in A. D. Boboc (ed.), *Theorizing Legal Personhood in Late Medieval England* (Leiden, 2015), 166–91.

Nederman, C., 'The Aristotelian doctrine of the mean and John of Salisbury's concept of liberty', *Vivarium* 24 (1986), 128–42.

——, 'Nature, ethics, and the doctrine of *habitus*: Aristotelian moral psychology in the twelfth century', *Traditio* 45 (1989–90), 87–110.

——, 'Aristotelianism and the origins of "political science" in the twelfth century', *Journal of the History of Ideas* 52 (1991), 179–94.

Nederman, C., and Brückmann, J., 'Aristotelianism in John of Salisbury's *Policraticus*', *Journal of the History of Philosophy* 21 (1983), 203–29.

Nelson, J. L., 'Bad kingship in the earlier middle ages', *Haskins Society Journal* 8 (1996), 1–26.

——, 'Kings with justice, kings without justice: an early medieval paradox', in *La giustizia nell'alto Medioevo (secoli IX–XI)* (Spoleto, 1997), vol. 2, 797–823.

——, 'Liturgy or law: misconceived alternatives?', in S. Baxter, C. Karkov, J. L. Nelson and D. Pelteret (eds), *Early Medieval Studies in Memory of Patrick Wormald* (Farnham, 2009), 433–47.

Newhauser, R., 'Justice and liberality: opposition to avarice in the twelfth century', in István P. Bejczy and Richard Newhauser (eds), *Virtue and Ethics in the Twelfth Century* (Leiden, 2005), 293–316.

Norgate, K., 'The date of composition of William of Newburgh's History', *English Historical Review* 19 (1904), 288–97.

Norr, K. W., *Zur Stellung des Richters im gelehrten Prozeß der Frühzeit: Iudex secundum allegata non secundum conscientiam iudicat* (Munich, 1968).

Nothdurft, K. D., *Studien zum Einfluss Senecas auf die Philosophie und Theologie des zwölften Jahrhunderts* (Leiden, 1963).

Oakley, T. P., 'Commutation and redemption of penance in the penitentials', *Catholic Historical Review* 18 (1932), 341–51.

——, 'Alleviations of penance in the continental penitentials', *Speculum* 12 (1937), 488–502.

O'Brien, Bruce, 'The Becket conflict and the invention of the myth of *lex non scripta*', in J. A. Bush and A. Wijffels (eds), *Learning the Law* (London, 1999), 1–16.

——, *God's Peace and King's Peace: The Laws of Edward the Confessor* (Philadelphia, 1999).

——, 'The *Instituta Cnuti* and the translation of English law', *Anglo-Norman Studies* 25 (2003), 177–97.

——, 'Legal treatises as perceptions of law in Stephen's reign', in Paul Dalton and Graeme J. White (eds), *King Stephen's Reign* (Woodbridge, 2008), 182–95.

——, 'An English book of laws from the time of Glanvill', in Susanne Jenks, J. Rose and C. Whittick (eds), *Laws, Lawyers and Texts: Studies in Medieval Legal History in Honour of Paul Brand* (Leiden, 2012), 51–67.

Padoa-Schioppa, Antonio, 'Sur la conscience du juge dans le ius commune européan', in J.-M. Carbasse and L. Depambour-Tarride (eds), *La conscience du juge dans la tradition juridique européenne* (Paris, 1999), 95–129.

Palmer, Robert C., *The County Courts of Medieval England, 1150–1350* (Princeton, NJ, 1982).

Parsons, John Carmi, 'The queen's intercession in thirteenth-century England', in Jennifer Carpenter and Sally-Beth MacLean (eds) *Power of the Weak: Studies in Medieval Women* (Toronto, 1990), 147–77.

Partner, N., *Serious Entertainments: The Writing of History in Twelfth-Century England* (Chicago, 1977).

Pellens, K., 'The tracts of the Norman Anonymous: C.C.C.C. MS. 415', *Transactions of the Cambridge Bibliographic Society* 4 (1965), 155–65.

Pennington, Kenneth, '"Pro peccatis patrum puniri": a moral and legal problem of the Inquisition', *Church History* 47 (1978), 37–54.

——, *The Prince and the Law, 1200–1600: Sovereignty and Rights in the Western Legal Tradition* (Berkeley, CA, 1993).

——, 'Due process, community, and the prince in the evolution of the *Ordo iudicarius*', *Revista internazionale di diritto comune* 9 (1998), 9–47.

——, 'The practical use of Roman law in the early twelfth century', in Matthias Lutz-Bachmann and Alexander Fidora (eds), *Handlung und Wissenschaft: die Epistemologie der Praktischen Wissenschaften im 12. und 13. Jahrhundert* (Berlin, 2008), 11–31.

Perkhams, Matthias, 'Aquinas's interpretation of the Aristotelian virtue of justice and his doctrine of natural law', in I. P. Bejczy (ed.), *Virtue Ethics in the Middle Ages: Commentaries on Aristotle's Nicomachean Ethics, 1200–1500* (Leiden, 2008), 131–50.

Peters, Edward M., 'The prosecution of heresy and theories of criminal justice in the twelfth and thirteenth centuries', in Heinz Mohnhaupt and Dieter Simon (eds), *Vorträge zur Justizforschung: Geschichte und Theorie* (Frankfurt, 1993), vol. 2, 25–42.

Pétré, H., '*Misericordia*: historie du mot et de l'idée du paganisme au christianisme', *Latomus: revue des études latines* 12 (1934), 376–89.

——, *Caritas: Étude sur le vocabulaire latin de la charité chretienne* (Louvain, 1948).

Plucknett, T. F. T., *Early English Legal Literature* (Cambridge, 1958).

Pollock, Frederick, and Maitland, Frederic William, *The History of English Law before the Time of Edward I* (2 vols, Cambridge, 1895).

Post, Gaines, *Studies in Medieval Legal Thought: Public Law and the State, 1100–1322* (Princeton, NJ, 1964).

——, 'Bracton as jurist and theologian on kingship', in S. Kuttner (ed.), *Proceedings of the Third International Congress on Medieval Canon Law* (Rome, 1971), 113–30.

Post, J. B., 'Some limitations of the medieval peace rolls', *Journal of the Society of Archivists* 4:8 (1973), 633–9.

Powicke, F. M., '*Per iudicium parium vel per legem terrae*', in Henry Eliot Malden (ed.), *Magna Carta Commemoration Essays* (London, 1917), 96–121.

——, *Stephen Langton* (Oxford, 1928).

——, 'Robert Grosseteste and the *Nicomachean Ethics*', *Proceedings of the British Academy* 16 (1930), 85–104.

Pugh, R. B., 'The king's prisons before 1250', *Transactions of the Royal Historical Society* 5 (1955), 1–22.

Quinto, Riccardo, *'Doctor Nominatissimus': Stefano Langton e la tradizione delle sue opere* (Münster, 1994).

——, 'The *Conflictus vitiorum et virtutum* attributed to Stephen Langton', in István P. Bejczy and Richard Newhauser (eds), *Virtue and Ethics in the Twelfth Century* (Leiden, 2005), 197–267.

——, 'Dalla discussione in aula alla *Summa quaestionum theologiae* di Stefano Langton: testi sul timore di Dio dal ms. Paris, BnF, lat. 14526 ed Erlangen, Universitätsbibliothek-Hauptbibliothek, 260', *Rivista di storia della filosofia* 2 (2009), 363–98.

Ralston, Michael E., 'The Four Daughters of God in *The Castell of Perseverance*', *Comitatus: A Journal of Medieval and Renaissance Studies* 15 (1984), 35–44.

Rathbone, Eleanor, 'John of Cornwall: a brief biography', *RTAM* 17 (1950), 46–60.
——, 'Roman law in the Anglo-Norman realm', in J. Forchielli and A. M. Stickler (eds), *Studia Gratiana post octava decreti saecularia auctore consilio commemorationi Gratianae Instruendae edita* (Rome, 1967), 253–71.
Reader, Rebecca, 'Sweet charity and sour grapes: the historical imagination of Matthew Paris', *Medieval History* 4 (1994), 102–18.
Reedy, W. T., 'The origins of the general eyre in the reign of Henry I', *Speculum* 41 (1966), 688–724.
Reeve, M. D., and Rouse, R. H., 'Cicero: speeches', in L. D. Reynolds (ed.), *Texts and Transmission: A Survey of the Latin Classics in the Middle Ages* (Oxford, 1983), 66–7.
Reichel, Karl, 'Plotting the map of medieval oral literature', in K. Reichel (ed.), *Medieval Oral Literature* (Berlin, 2012), 3–70.
Reuter, T., '*Velle sibi fieri in forma hac*: symbolic acts in the Becket dispute', in T. Reuter, *Medieval Polities and Modern Mentalities*, ed. J. L. Nelson (Cambridge, 2006), 167–90.
Reynolds, L. D., *The Medieval Tradition of Seneca's Letters* (London, 1965).
——, 'Sallust', in L. D. Reynolds (ed.), *Texts and Transmission: A Survey of the Latin Classics in the Middle Ages* (Oxford, 1983), 341–8.
Reynolds, Susan, 'Law and communities in western Christendom, c. 900–1140', *American Journal of Legal History* 25 (1981), 205–24.
——, *Fiefs and Vassals: The Medieval Evidence Reinterpreted* (Oxford, 1994).
——, 'The emergence of professional law in the long twelfth century', *Law and History Review* 21 (2003), 347–66.
——, 'Secular power and authority in the middle ages', in Huw Pryce and John Watts (eds), *Power and Identity in the Middle Ages: Essays in Memory of Rees Davies* (Oxford, 2007), 11–22.
Richardson, H. G., 'Henry I's charter to London', *English Historical Review* 42 (1927), 80–7.
——, 'Heresy and the lay power under Richard II', *English Historical Review* 51 (1936), 1–28.
——, 'The coronation in medieval England', *Traditio* 16 (1940), 111–202.
Riley, Lawrence J., *The History, Nature and Use of Epikeia in Moral Theology* (Washington, DC, 1948).
Rivière, Jean, *Le dogme de la rédemption au début du moyen âge* (Paris, 1934).
Roberts, Phyllis B., *Stephanus de Lingua-Tonante: Studies in the Sermons of Stephen Langton* (Toronto, 1968).
Rolker, Christof, *Canon Law and the Letters of Ivo of Chartres* (Cambridge, 2010).

Bibliography

Rose, Jonathan, 'English legal history and interdisciplinary legal studies', in Anthony Musson (ed.), *Boundaries of the Law: Geography, Gender and Jurisdiction in Medieval and Early Modern Europe* (Aldershot, 2005), 169–86.

Rosemann, Philip W., 'Robert Grosseteste's *Tabula*', in J. McEvoy (ed.), *Robert Grosseteste: New Perspectives on his Thought and Scholarship* (Turnhout, 1995), 321–55.

——, *The Story of a Great Medieval Book: Peter Lombard's Sentences* (Toronto, 2007).

Rosser, A. G., 'Sanctuary and social negotiation', in J. Blair and B. Golding (eds), *The Cloister and the World: Essays in Medieval History in Honour of Barbara Harvey* (Oxford, 1996), 57–79.

Rouse, R. H., 'Florilegia and Latin classical authors in twelfth- and thirteenth-century Orleans', *Viator* 10 (1979), 131–60.

Rouse, R. H., and Rouse, M. A., 'John of Salisbury's doctrine of tyrannicide', *Speculum* 42 (1967), 697–709.

——, 'Biblical distinctions in the thirteenth century', *Archives d'histoire doctrinale et littéraire du moyen âge* 41 (1974), 27–37.

Rubin, Miri, *Charity and Community in Medieval Cambridge* (Cambridge, 1987).

Sabapathy, John, *Officers and Accountability in Medieval England 1170–1300* (Oxford, 2014).

Sadler, Gregory B., 'Mercy and justice in St. Anselm's *Proslogion*', *American Catholic Philosophical Quarterly* 80 (2006), 41–61.

Sajavaara, K., *The Middle English Translations of Robert Grosseteste's Château d'Amour* (Helsinki, 1967).

Saltman, Avrom, 'John of Salisbury and the world of the Old Testament' in M. Wilks (ed.), *The World of John of Salisbury* (Oxford, 1984), 343–63.

Sandford, Eva Matthews, 'The *Verbum abbreviatum* of Petrus Cantor', *Transactions and Proceedings of the American Philological Association* 74 (1943), 33–48.

——, 'Giraldus Cambrensis' debt to Petrus Cantor', *Medievalia et Humanistica* 3 (1945), 16–32.

Sayers, Jane E., *Papal Judges-Delegate in the Province of Canterbury, 1198–1254: A Study in Ecclesiastical Jurisdiction and Administration* (London, 1971).

Scholl, Edith, 'The mother of all virtues: *discretio*', *Cistercian Studies Quarterly* 36 (2001), 389–401.

——, 'Mercy within mercy: *Misericordia* and *miseria*', *Cistercian Studies Quarterly* 42 (2007), 63–82.

Seipp, David J., '*Bracton*, the Year Books, and the "transformation of elementary legal ideas" in the early common law', *Law and History Review* 7 (1989), 175–217.

Shaffern, R. W., 'Learned discussions of indulgences for the dead in the middle ages', *Church History* 61 (1992), 367–81.
——, 'Images, jurisdiction and the treasury of merit', *Journal of Medieval History* 22 (1996), 237–47.
——, *The Penitents' Treasury: Indulgences in Latin Christendom, 1175–1375* (London, 2007).
Sharpe, Richard, 'The prefaces of Quadripartitus', in G. Garnett and J. Hudson (eds), *Law and Government in Medieval England and Normandy: Essays in Honour of Sir James Holt* (Cambridge, 1994), 148–72.
——, 'Richard Barre's *Compendium Veteris et Novi Testamenti*', *Journal of Medieval Latin* 14 (2004), 128–46.
Sheehan, M., 'Illegitimacy in Late Medieval England: Laws, Dispensation and Practice', in B. Wiggenhauser (ed.), *Illegitimität im Spätmittelalter* (Munich, 1994), 115–21.
Shuffleton, G., *Codex Ashmole 61: A Compilation of Popular Middle English Verse* (Kalamazoo, MI, 2008).
Simonetta, Stefano, 'Searching for an uneasy synthesis between Aristotelian political language and Christian political theology', in L. Bianchi (ed.), *Christian Readings of Aristotle from the Middle Ages to the Renaissance* (Turnhout, 2011), 273–85.
Smalley, Beryl, '*Exempla* in the commentaries of Stephen Langton', *Bulletin of the John Rylands Library* 17 (1933), 121–9.
——, 'A commentary on Isaias by Guerric of Saint-Quentin', *Studi e testi* 122 (1946), 383–7.
——, 'Two biblical commentaries of Simon of Hinton', *RTAM* 13 (1946), 57–85.
——, 'The *Quaestiones* of Simon of Hinton', in R. W. Hunt, W. A. Pantin and R. W. Southern (eds), *Studies in Medieval History Presented to Frederick Maurice Powicke* (Oxford, 1948), 209–22.
——, 'Some more exegetical works of Simon of Hinton', *RTAM* 15 (1948), 97–106.
——, 'Sallust in the middle ages', in R. R. Bolgar (ed.), *Classical Influences on European Culture* (Cambridge, 1971), 165–75.
——, *The Becket Conflict and the Schools. A Study of Intellectuals in Politics* (Oxford, 1973).
——, *Historians in the Middle Ages* (London, 1974).
——, 'William of Auvergne, John of La Rochelle and St. Thomas Aquinas on the Old Law' in A. A. Maurer (ed.), *St. Thomas Aquinas 1274–1974: Commemorative Studies* (2 vols, Toronto, 1974), vol. 2, 11–74.

———, 'Some gospel commentaries of the early twelfth century', *RTAM* 45 (1978), 147–80.
———, 'Peter Comestor on the gospels and his sources', *RTAM* 46 (1979), 84–130.
———, *The Study of the Bible in the Middle Ages* (Oxford, 1983).
Smith, Lesley, 'The *De decem mandatis* of Robert Grosseteste, in M. O'Caroll (ed.), *Robert Grosseteste and the Beginning of a British Theological Tradition* (Rome, 2003), 265–88.
———, 'William of Auvergne and the law', in Thomas J. Heffernan and Thomas E. Burman (eds), *Scripture and Pluralism: Reading the Bible in the Religiously Plural Worlds of the Middle Ages and Renaissance* (Leiden, 2005), 123–42.
———, *The Glossa Ordinaria: The Making of a Medieval Bible Commentary* (Leiden, 2009).
Somerville, R., 'Mercy and justice in the early months of Urban II's pontificate', in *Chiesa, diritto e ordinamento della 'Societas Christiana' nei secoli XI e XII* (Milan, 1986), 138–58.
Sønnesyn, S. O., *William of Malmesbury and the Ethics of History* (Woodbridge, 2012).
Southern, R. W., 'Peter of Blois: a twelfth-century humanist?', in R. W. Southern, *Medieval Humanism and Other Studies* (Oxford, 1970), 105–32.
———, 'The place of England in the twelfth-century renaissance', in R. W. Southern, *Medieval Humanism and Other Studies* (Oxford, 1970), 158–80.
———, 'Master Vacarius and the beginnings of an English academic tradition', in J. J. G. Alexander and M. T. Gibson (eds), *Medieval Learning and Literature: Essays Presented to Richard William Hunt* (Oxford, 1976), 257–86.
———, *Robert Grosseteste: The Growth of an English Mind in Medieval Europe* (Oxford, 1986).
———, *Scholastic Humanism and the Unification of Europe* (2 vols, Oxford, 1995).
Spitzer, Anne L., 'The legal careers of Thomas of Weyland and Gilbert of Thorton', *Journal of Legal History* 6 (1985), 62–83.
Staunton, Michael, *Thomas Becket and his Biographers* (Woodbridge, 2006).
Stenton, D. M., 'King John and the courts of justice', *Proceedings of the British Academy* 44 (1959), 103–28.
———, *English Justice between the Norman Conquest and the Great Charter 1066–1215* (London, 1965).
Stone, M. W. F., 'Equity and moderation: the reception and uses of Aristotle's doctrine of epieikeia in thirteenth-century ethics', in R. Pasnau (ed.), *The Cambridge History of Medieval Philosophy* (2 vols, Cambridge, 2010), vol. 1, 121–56.

Strickland, Matthew, *War and Chivalry: The Conduct and Perception of War in England and Normandy, 1066–1217* (Cambridge, 1996).

Summerson, H. R. T., 'Maitland and the criminal law in the age of *Bracton*', in John Hudson (ed.), *The History of English Law: Centenary Essays on 'Pollock and Maitland'* (Oxford, 1996), 115–43.

——, 'Attitudes to capital punishment in England, 1200–1350', *Thirteenth-Century England* 8 (1999), 123–33.

——, 'Suicide and fear of the gallows', *Journal of Legal History* 21 (2000), 49–56.

Sutherland, Donald W., 'Legal reasoning in the fourteenth century: the invention of "color" in pleading', in Morris S. Arnold, Sally A. Scully and Stephen S. White (eds), *On the Laws and Customs of England: Essays in Honor of Samuel E. Thorne* (Chapel Hill, NC, 1981), 182–94.

Taliadoros, Jason, 'Law and theology in Gilbert of Foliot's (c. 1105/10–1187/88) correspondence', *Haskins Society Journal* 16 (2005), 77–94.

——, *Law and Theology in Twelfth-Century England: The Works of Master Vacarius (c. 1115/20–c.1200)* (Turnout, 2006).

Teetaert, A., 'Quelques *Summae de Poenitentia* anonymes de la Bibliothèque Nationale', in A. M. Albareda (ed.), *Miscellanea Giovanni Mercati II* (Rome, 1946), 311–43.

Thompson, K., 'Orderic and Robert of Bellême', *Journal of Medieval History* 20 (1994), 133–41.

Thomson, Rodney M., *Catalogue of the Manuscripts of Lincoln Cathedral Chapter Library* (Woodbridge, 1989).

——, 'Serlo of Wilton and the school of Oxford', *Medium Aevum* 68:1 (1999), 1–12.

Traver, Hope, 'The Four Daughters of God: a mirror of changing doctrine', *Proceedings of the Modern Language Association* 40:1 (1925), 44–92.

Truax, J. A., 'Winning over the Londoners: King Stephen, the Empress Matilda and the politics of personality', *Haskins Society Journal* 8 (1996), 43–62.

Tullis, S., 'Glanvill continued: a reassessment', in A. D. E. Lewis, P. Brand and P. Mitchell (eds), *Law in the City: Proceedings of the Seventeenth British Legal History Conference, London, 2005* (Dublin, 2007), 15–23.

——, '*Glanvill* after Glanvill: the afterlife of a medieval legal treatise', in Susanne Jenks, J. Rose and C. Whittick (eds), *Laws, Lawyers and Texts: Studies in Medieval Legal History in Honour of Paul Brand* (Leiden, 2012), 327–59.

Turner, Ralph V., 'Clerical judges in English secular courts: the ideal vs. the reality', in Ralph V. Turner, *Judges, Administrators and the Common Law in Angevin England* (London, 1994), 159–80.

——, 'Henry II's aims in reforming England's land law: feudal or royalist?', in Ralph V. Turner, *Judges, Administrators and the Common Law in Angevin England* (London, 1994), 1–16.

——, 'The reputation of royal judges under the Angevin kings', in Ralph V. Turner, *Judges, Administrators and the Common Law in Angevin England* (London, 1994), 103–18.

——, 'Richard Barre and Michael Belet: two Angevin civil servants', in Ralph V. Turner, *Judges, Administrators and the Common Law in Angevin England* (London, 1994), 181–98.

——, 'Who was the author of *Glanvill*? Reflections on the education of Henry II's common lawyers', in Ralph V. Turner, *Judges, Administrators and the Common Law in Angevin England* (London, 1994), 71–102.

Uhalde, Kevin, *Expectations of Justine in the Age of Augustine* (Philadelphia, 2007).

Ullmann, W., 'The significance of Innocent III's decretal "Vergentis", in *Études d'histoire du droit canonique dédiées à Gabriel Le Bras* (2 vols, Paris, 1965), vol. 1, 729–41.

Unger, Daniel, 'Robert Grosseteste on the reason for the Incarnation', *Franciscan Studies* 16 (1956), 1–36.

Valente, L., '*Iustus et misericors*: l'usage théologique des notions de consignificatio et connotation dans la seconde moitié du XIIe siècle', in Constantino Marmo (ed.), *Vestigia, Imagines, Verba: Semiotics and Logic in Medieval Theological Texts (XIIth–XIVth century)* (Turnhout, 1997), 207–36.

Van Caenegem, R. C., *Royal Writs in England from the Conquest to Glanvill: Studies in the Early History of the Common Law* (London, 1959).

——, 'Public prosecution of crime in twelfth-century England', in C. N. L. Brooke, D. E. Luscombe, G. H. Martin and D. M. Owen (eds), *Church and Government in the Middle Ages* (Cambridge, 1976), 41–76.

——, 'Criminal law in England and Flanders under King Henry II and Count Philip of Alsace', in R. C. Van Caenegem (ed.), *Legal History: A European Perspective* (London, 1991), 37–60.

Van den Ende, P. D., 'Précisions chronologiques sur quelques ouvrages théologiques du XIIe siècle', *Antonianum* 26 (1951), 223–46.

Van den Eynde, Damien, 'Autour des "Enarrationes in Evangelium S. Matthaei" attribuées à Geoffroi Babion', *RTAM* 26 (1959), 50–84.

Van Dijk, Conrad, 'Giving each his due: Langland, Gower and the question of equity', *Journal of English and Germanic Philology* 108 (2009), 310–35.

Van Engen, John, *Rupert of Deutz* (Berkeley and Los Angeles, 1983).

——, 'God is no respecter of persons: sacred texts and social realities', in Lesley Smith and Benedicta Ward (eds), *Intellectual Life in the Middle Ages: Essays Presented to Margaret Gibson* (London, 1992), 243–64.

Vaughan, R., *Matthew Paris* (Cambridge, 1958).

Vaughn, Sally N., 'Anselm of Canterbury's view of God's law in England: definitions, political applications and philosophical implications', in Per Andersen, Mia Münster-Swendsen and Helle Vogt (eds), *Law and Power in the Middle Ages* (Copenhagen, 2008), 235–56.

Verweij, Michiel, 'Princely virtues or virtues for princes? William Peraldus and his *De eruditione principum*', in István P. Bejczy and Cary Nederman (eds), *Princely Virtues in the Middle Ages, 1200–1500* (Turnhout, 2007), 51–71.

Vincent, Nicholas, 'Some pardoners' tales: the earliest English indulgences', *Transactions of the Royal Historical Society* 12 (2003), 23–58.

——, 'Why 1199? Bureaucracy and enrolment under John and his contemporaries', in Adrian Jobson (ed.), *English Government in the Thirteenth Century* (Woodbridge, 2004), 17–48.

de Visscher, Eva, *Reading the Rabbis: Christian Hebraism in the Works of Herbert of Bosham* (Leiden, 2014).

Visser, Sandra, and Williams, Thomas, *Anselm* (Oxford, 2009).

Von Moos, Peter, 'The use of *exempla* in the *Policraticus* of John of Salisbury', in M. Wilks (ed.), *The World of John of Salisbury* (Oxford, 1984), 207–61.

Wagner, Karen, '*Cum aliquis venerit ad sacerdotem*: penitential experience in the central middle ages', in Abigail Firey (ed.), *A New History of Penance* (Leiden, 2007), 201–18.

Walker Bynum, Caroline, 'Jesus as mother and abbot as mother: some themes in twelfth-century cistercian writing', in Caroline Walker Bynum, *Jesus as Mother: Studies in the Spirituality of the High Middle Ages* (Berkeley, CA, 1982), 110–69.

Ward, John O., 'The commentator's rhetoric: from antiquity to the renaissance, glosses and commentaries on Cicero's *Rhetorica*', in J. J. Murphy (ed.), *Medieval Eloquence: Studies in the Theory and Practice of Medieval Rhetoric* (Berkeley and Los Angeles, 1978), 126–73.

——, 'What the middle ages missed of Cicero, and why', in William H. F. Altman (ed.), *Brill's Companion to the Reception of Cicero* (Leiden, 2015), 307–26.

Ward, P. L., 'The coronation ceremony in medieval England', *Speculum* 14 (1939), 160–78.

Warren, W. L., *Henry II* (London, 1973).

Waugh, S. L., 'Reluctant knights and jurors: respites, exemptions and obligations in the reign of Henry III', *Speculum* 50 (1983), 937–86.

Weiler, Bjorn, 'Kingship, usurpation and propaganda in twelfth-century Europe: the case of Stephen', *Anglo-Norman Studies* 23 (2001), 299–326.

——, 'Royal virtue and royal justice in Walter Map's *De nugis curialium* and William of Malmesbury's *Historia novella*', in István P. Bejczy and Richard Newhauser (eds), *Virtue and Ethics in the Twelfth Century* (Leiden, 2005), 317–39.

——, 'William of Malmesbury on kingship', *History* 90 (2005), 3–22.

Wenzel, Siegfried, 'The seven deadly sins: some problems of research', *Speculum* 43 (1968), 1–22.

——, 'Vices, virtues, and popular preaching', *Medieval and Renaissance Studies* 6 (1976), 28–54.

——, 'The continuing life of William Peraldus' *Summa vitiorum*', in M. D. Jordan and K. Emery (eds), *Ad litteram: Authoritative Texts and Their Medieval Readers* (Notre Dame, IN, 1992), 135–63.

West, F., *The Justiciarship in England, 1066–1232* (Cambridge, 1966).

Westermann, Edwin J., 'A comparison of some of the sermons and the *dicta* of Robert Grosseteste', *Medievalia et Humanistica* 3 (1945), 49–68.

Whalen, B. E., *Dominion of God: Christendom and Apocalypse in the Middle Ages* (Cambridge, 2009).

White, G. J., 'The myth of the Anarchy', *Anglo-Norman Studies* 12 (2000), 323–37.

——, *Restoration and Reform, 1153–1165: Recovery from Civil War in England* (Cambridge, 2000).

White, Stephen D., '"*Pactum ... legem vincit et amor judicium*": the settlement of disputes by compromise in eleventh-century France', *American Journal of Legal History* 22 (1978), 281–308.

——, 'The politics of anger', in B. H. Rosenwein (ed.), *Anger's Past: The Social Uses of an Emotion in the Middle Ages* (Ithaca, NY and London, 1998), 127–52.

——, 'The ambiguity of treason in Anglo-Norman-French law, c.1150–c.1250', in R. M. Karras, J. Kaye and E. Matter (eds), *Law and the Illicit in Medieval Europe* (Philadelphia, 2008), 89–102.

Whitman, James Q., *The Origins of Reasonable Doubt: The Theological Roots of the Criminal Trial* (London, 2008).

Wickham, C., 'Dispute processes and social structures', in W. Davies and P. Fouracre (eds), *The Settlement of Disputes in Early Medieval Europe* (Cambridge, 1986), 228–37.

Williams, John R., 'The authorship of the *Moralium dogma philosophorum*', *Speculum* 6 (1931), 392–411.

Wilmart, D. A., 'Un opuscule sur la confession composé par Guy de Southwick vers la fin du XIIe siècle', *RTAM* 7 (1935), 337–52.
Winroth, Anders, *The Making of Gratian's Decretum* (Cambridge, 2000).
Wogan-Browne, Jocelyn, 'How to marry your wife with chastity, honour and fin' amor in thirteenth-century England', *Thirteenth Century England* 9 (2001), 131–50
Wolf, G., 'La préface perdue des sermons de Raoul Ardent, chapelain de Richard Ier', *Archives d'histoire doctrinale et littéraire du moyen âge* 42 (1979), 35–9.
Wolsterstorff, N., *Justice: Rights and Wrongs* (Princeton, NJ, 2008).
Wormald, Patrick, 'Charters, law and the settlement of disputes in Anglo-Saxon England', in W. Davies and P. Fouracre (eds), *The Settlement of Disputes in Early Medieval Europe* (Cambridge, 1986), 149–68.
——, 'Quadripartitus', in G. Garnett and J. Hudson (eds), *Law and Government in Medieval England and Normandy: Essays in Honour of Sir James Holt* (Cambridge, 1994), 111–47.
——, *The Making of English Law: King Alfred to the Twelfth Century*, vol. 1, *Legislation and its Limits* (Oxford, 1999).
——, *Lawyers and the State: The Varieties of Legal History* (London, 2006).
Wright, E. C., 'Common law in the thirteenth-century English royal forest', *Speculum* 3 (1928), 166–91.
Young, C. R., 'English royal forests under the Angevin Kings', *Journal of British Studies* 12 (1972), 1–14.
Zinn, G. A., Jr., 'The influence of Hugh of St Victor's *Chronicon* on the *Abbreviationes chronicorum* of Ralph of Diceto', *Speculum* 52 (1977), 38–61.
de Zuleta, F., and Stein, Peter, *The Teaching of Roman Law in England around 1200* (London, 1990).

Unpublished theses

Boyle, L. E., 'A Study of the Works Attributed to William of Pagula with Special Reference to the *Oculum sacerdotus* and *Summa summarum*' (DPhil thesis, University of Oxford, 1956).
Friend, A. C., 'The Life and Unprinted Works of Master Odo of Cheriton' (DPhil thesis, University of Oxford, 1925).
Hill, Christopher P., 'Gilbert Foliot and the Two Swords: Law and Political Theory in Twelfth-Century England' (PhD thesis, University of Austin, Texas, 2008).
Karn, N., 'Monastic Letter-Writers in Twelfth-Century England' (DPhil thesis, University of Oxford, 2002).

Bibliography

Lambert, Thomas Benedict, 'Protection, Feud and Royal Power: Violence and its Regulation in English Law, c.850–c.1250' (PhD thesis, University of Durham, 2009).

McCune, Patricia Helen, 'The Ideology of Mercy in English Literature and Law, 1200–1600' (2 vols, PhD thesis, University of Michigan, 1989).

MacKinnon, Hugh, 'The Life and Works of William de Montibus' (DPhil thesis, University of Oxford, 1959).

Paul, Suzanne, 'An Edition and Study of the Selected Sermons of Robert Grosseteste' (2 vols, PhD thesis, University of Leeds, 2002).

Traver, Hope, 'The Four Daughters of God: A Study of the Versions of this Allegory with Especial Reference to those in Latin, French, and English' (PhD thesis, Bryn Mawr College, 1907).

Tullis, Sarah, 'Glanvill after Glanvill' (DPhil thesis, University of Oxford, 2008).

Wagner, Karen Theresa, '*De vera et falsa pentitentia*: An Edition and Study' (PhD thesis, University of Toronto, 1995).

Index

Adam Marsh advice to judges 122, 141–51
aequitas *see* equity
Ahasuerus, biblical ruler 151
Alan of Lille
   definition of justice 28–9
   justice and persuasion 178
   mercy and counsel 96, 99, 103
Albertus Magnus 227–8
Alger of Liège 39–40, 123
Ambrose of Milan xvi, 24–5, 107
Anarchy, the 185–9
   see also Stephen, king of England
Anselm of Canterbury 224
   Cur Deus homo 103, 209
   Proslogion 218n9
   rectitude as justice 25
   see also Four Daughters of God
Anselm of Laon 98–9, 166
Aristotle
   Ethics 143, 226–7
   influence 4–5, 25–6, 143, 226–8
Augustine
   De civitate Dei 45, 143
   definition of justice 32, 81, 108
   definition of mercy 81, 108, 112, 141
   De trinitate 20
   Ennarationes in Psalmos 67–8
   influence 20, 23, 32, 46, 132, 143, 195–6

baptism 112–13
Bartholomew, bishop of Exeter 125–7
beatitudes 98–101
Bernard of Clairvaux 25
   Four Daughters of God and 210–11
Bisson, Thomas
   Crisis of the Twelfth Century 10–11, 225
Boethius 25, 166
Bracton, *De legibus et consuetudinibus Angliae* 48–9, 143, 171–2

canon law 38–41, 122–9
cardinal virtues 4–5, 20, 24, 96, 120n92, 227
   caritas and 23
   see also fortitude; prudence; temperance
caritas
   Becket dispute and 138–9
   canon law and 39–40
   cognate terms for 28, 229
   dispensation from law 31, 39–40
   love of enemies 92
   relationship to equity 228–9
   relationship to justice 18, 23–4
Cato of Utica, Cato the Younger 76–81, 221n40
chivalry 77, 188

Index

Cicero
  De inventione 18, 27, 165–70
  De officiis 35n52, 174
  influence xvi, 26–9, 152n10
  justice as a virtue 27, 64, 228, 232
  justice treated rhetorically 165, 169, 174
  mercy 28, 81
  Rhetorica ad Herrenium, pseudo-Cicero 165–6, 169–70
  suum cuique tribuens 18, 168, 227
civil law 71, 108, 130, 133, 140, 168, 229
  see also Digest, Roman law; *Institutes*, Roman law
common good 123, 130, 168, 229–30
compassio 28, 45, 49
counsel 87–91, 164–6, 198, 210
  connection to mercy 95–102
  counsellors 163, 180–4, 187, 197
  Four Daughters of God and 214, 217
  see also precept
crusades 97, 195–7

Daniel, biblical figure 70, 115, 197
debt 20, 22, 47, 94
Decretum of Gratian 40, 72, 123, 196
  mercy in setting penance 124, 126, 130–1, 133–4, 138
Deuteronomy 63, 143
  standards of judicial conduct derived from 67
  Stephen Langton's commentary on 64
Dialogue of the Exchequer 46–8
  see also Richard FitzNigel
Digest, Roman law 18, 132
discretion in judgment 16, 31, 40, 113, 192
  common law 43–4, 47–50
  ecclesiastical judges 113, 124, 137
  relationship to mercy 16
dispensation 29, 49, 66, 169, 228–9
  see also caritas; discretion in judgment
Dominican order 113

epikeia 228–9
equity 23, 40, 43, 140, 229
Esther, biblical figure 151

florilegia collections xv, 31, 36n62
Florilegium Gallicum 77
fortitude 4–5, 100
Four Daughters of God 208–16
Fourth Lateran Council 128
Franciscan order 149–50, 213
  debates on counsel and precept 89
  see also Adam Marsh advice to judges

Gerald of Wales
  De principis instructione xv–xviii, 225
  dispensation from law 71
  Expugnatio Hibernica 79–81
  mercy and forgiveness of enemies 104–5
  royal justice 75, 189–90
Gesta Stephani 186–8
Gilbert Foliot 123, 125
  advice on treatment of heretics 129–35
  Becket crisis and 135–41
  scripture and 133–4
Glanvill 7, 43, 53, 179
Glossa ordinaria 26, 98, 99
good Samaritan, parable 113
gratia 23, 27, 28, 51, 90, 195
Gratian *see Decretum* of Gratian
Guy of Southwick 127

Heli, biblical figure 66–9, 137, 223
Henry I, king of England 44
  legal reforms 69
  Orderic Vitalis and 182–3
  punishment of offenders 53
  reputation for justice 41, 186
Henry II, king of England
  dispute with Thomas Becket 94, 106, 135–41
  legal reforms 2, 41, 69, 225
  reputation for justice 47, 75, 106, 191–2

Index

sons 81
  verdict of Walter Map 189–93
Henry III, king of England 55
  Matthew Paris and 178–9
  Robert Grosseteste and 146–7, 150
Henry, the Young King 7, 189
heresy 129–34
Historia novella see William of Malmesbury
honestum 167, 175–7
  see also *utile*
Hugh of St Victor
  Four Daughters of God 210–11
  obligations to be merciful 93, 104
  petitions, gifts and beatitudes 100
humanitas
  association with *misericordia* 28, 45, 75
Hurnard, Naomi 42–3

Incarnation of Christ 96, 103, 208–10
  see also Four Daughters of God
Innocent III 44, 130
Institutes, Roman law 18
intercession 107–9, 180–1
Isidore of Seville
  Etymologies 28
  rhetorical theory 168
ius commune 38, 50
Ivo of Chartres 39–40, 59n46, 125, 134

John of Salisbury
  Becket dispute and 136–7, 139–40
  Policraticus 11–12, 68, 69, 73, 171
  Ralph Niger and 68
Julius Caesar 8, 76–9, 81

largitas 26–7, 147
  see also Julius Caesar
Leges Henrici Primi 44–6, 49, 52
  rhetoric and 168–9
lex talionis 63–4
liberalitas 23–4, 28, 147

Lord's Prayer, the 19, 32, 98–101
Lottin, Odon 4–5, 98–9
Louis VII, king of France 189–92
Louis IX, king of France 195–6

Mary Magdalene 109
Matthew Paris 146
  Chronica maiora 178–9, 198
  Henry III and 194–5
  Louis IX and 195–6
medicus analogy 123–4, 126, 137
Michael Belet, royal judge 56, 145
moderatio 25, 28–9
money
  relationship to justice 48, 53–4, 89, 227
Moralium dogma philosophorum 28, 169
mosaic law see Old Testament
Moses 63, 72–4, 98, 180, 229, 231

New Testament 88, 139
  lack of judicial *exempla* 65, 74

oil 112–13
Old Testament 65, 98
  as a source for judicial *exempla* 62–4, 146
Orderic Vitalis 180–4
osculum pacis see peace

pardon
  concept of pardon 21, 30, 46–8, 150, 229
  records of pardon 3, 52–5
  royal pardons 2, 31, 41–2, 44–5, 50, 181–3
  see also *gratia*; Hurnard, Naomi
partiality 16, 196–7, 226
  see also discretion
pastoral care 18, 102, 104
  pastoral theology or moral theology 17
  role of judgment in pastoral care 114–16, 125–9, 139, 225
paternoster see Lord's Prayer

Index

patience 92, 97, 190–1
peace 22, 56, 80, 109, 137, 139, 145,
   168–9, 181–3, 185, 187, 189
  character in *The Four Daughters of
   God* 208, 213–15
  kiss of peace 94
penance 122–9
  nature of penitential judgment 123
  penitential writing in the twelfth
   century 124–5
  see also Alger of Liège; Ivo of Chartres
Peter Abelard 4, 18
  counsel and precept 90–1
  treatment of mercy 29
Peter of Blois
  Four Daughters of God
   tradition 291n17
  loving one's enemy 91–2, 94
Peter the Chanter
  definition of justice 18
  dispensation from law 31
  Verbum abbreviatum 30–2, 114, 170–1
Peter Lombard 20
petitions *see* Lord's Prayer
Phinehas, biblical figure 66–9
piety 23, 28, 185, 191
  as a gift of the Holy Spirit 99–100
  see also simplicitas
power
  problems with the term 10–11, 106–7
precept xv, 39, 63, 87–95, 102–5, 143
  see also counsel
procedure xvii, 9, 11, 49, 71, 97, 108,
   128–9, 134, 193, 196, 224–5
professionalisation of justice 2, 6, 41–2,
   82, 105
prudence xv, 5, 96, 177, 197

Quintilian 165, 177

Ralph Niger 65–6, 68–9, 107
Raoul Ardens 172–8
rebuke 67–8, 107, 136, 139, 145, 184

reciprocal mercy 22, 46–7, 74, 91, 148,
   150, 158n109, 228, 233n14
Richard I, king of England 172, 192, 194
Richard Barre, royal judge 7, 56, 231
Richard FitzNigel 7–8
  see also Dialogue of the Exchequer
Richard of Devizes 193–4, 198
Robert of Flamborough 114, 127–8
Robert Grosseteste
  advice to royal judges 141–51
  counsel and precept 104
  definition of justice 19, 25
  judgment 69, 115, 128
  Le Château d'amour 213–16
  relationship between Old and New
   Testaments 64–5
  Tabula 142–3
Robert of Melun 93–4
rod and staff, iconography 114–15
Roger, bishop of Worcester 129–32
Rupert of Deutz
  counsel and precept 90, 103
  examples of mercy 71
  relationship between rhetoric and
   justice 167

Sabapathy, John 9, 47–8, 225
safety
  concept in classical rhetoric 169–70
  political community and 77, 183, 185,
   187, 189
Sallust xvi, 75–9, 178
salvation 31, 72, 89, 91–4, 102–3, 145,
   149, 174, 208, 210–11, 228
  De salvatione hominis dialogus 215–16
Samson, abbot of Bury St
   Edmunds 162–4
Samuel, biblical judge 68–9, 73, 231
seal, royal 191–2
Senatus of Worcester 126–7
Seneca
  De clementia 73, 78, 149
  Moralium dogma philosophorum and 28

Index

Sermon on the Mount 46, 64, 97–98, 103
　see also beatitudes
severitas 28–9, 77, 123, 138
Simon de Montfort 147–50
simplicitas 94, 191–2
speculum principis literature xvi–xviii, 5, 71, 179, 191, 223
Stephen, king of England 185–9
Stephen Langton 107, 114
　Bele Aaliz 215
　justice as a midpoint between vices 26–7
　proportional relationship between justice and mercy 21
　relationship between Old and New Testaments 64
Stephen of Tournai 7
Susannah, biblical figure 70–1, 115, 197

temperance 5, 72, 167
Ten Commandments 64, 212
Theodosius, emperor 107
Thomas Aquinas 3, 83n23, 227, 229
Thomas Becket 10, 94, 106, 135–41
Thomas of Chobham
　definition of justice 19, 70
　love for one's enemies 94
　necessity of dispensation from law 71
　petitions, gifts and beatitudes 100–1
　rhetoric of justice 166–7
　royal and ecclesiastical mercy 112–16
　sermons 72, 111–12

Summa de arte praedicandi 72
Summa confessorum 124–5, 127–8
twelfth-century renaissance 1–2, 165, 223, 230
tutum see safety

Ulpian 18, 81
unforgiving servant, parable of 22, 47
utile 167–9, 174, 198
　see also honestum

vengeance 93, 97, 216–17
veritas
　as part of justice 27, 70–1
　character in *The Four Daughters of God* 208–16
virga et baculus see rod and staff, iconography

Walter Map 70, 189–93, 197–8, 211, 226
William I, king of England 180–1
William II, king of England 181–2
William of Auvergne 26, 93, 113
William FitzOsbert 192–3
William Longchamp 7, 108–9
William of Malmesbury 186–7, 191
William of Newburgh 106, 156n72, 191–2
William Raleigh, royal judge 143–6
woman caught in adultery, parable xvi–xviii, 70–1, 132–3
wrestling 162

EU authorised representative for GPSR:
Easy Access System Europe, Mustamäe tee 50,
10621 Tallinn, Estonia
gpsr.requests@easproject.com